PHILOSOPHY OF

ART

PHILOSOPHY OF
ART

Aesthetic Theory and Practice

DAVID BOERSEMA

PACIFIC UNIVERSITY

WESTVIEW
PRESS

A Member of the Perseus Books Group

Westview Press was founded in 1975 in Boulder, Colorado, by notable publisher and intellectual Fred Praeger. Westview Press continues to publish scholarly titles and high-quality undergraduate- and graduate-level textbooks in core social science disciplines. With books developed, written, and edited with the needs of serious nonfiction readers, professors, and students in mind, Westview Press honors its long history of publishing books that matter.

Published by Westview Press,
A Member of the Perseus Books Group

Find us on the World Wide Web at www.westviewpress.com.

Every effort has been made to secure required permissions for all text, images, maps, and other art reprinted in this volume.
Westview Press books are available at special discounts for bulk purchases in the United States by corporations, institutions, and other organizations. For more information, please contact the Special Markets Department at the Perseus Books Group, 2300 Chestnut Street, Suite 200, Philadelphia, PA 19103, or call (800) 810-4145, ext. 5000, or e-mail special.markets@perseusbooks.com.

Typeset in 11 point Garamond by the Perseus Books Group

Library of Congress Cataloging-in-Publication Data

Boersema, David.
    Philosophy of art : aesthetic theory and practice / David Boersema, Pacific University.
        p.   cm
    Includes bibliographical references and index.
    ISBN 978-0-8133-4719-6 (pbk.)—ISBN 978-0-8133-4720-2 (e-book)
    1. Arts—Philosophy. 2 Aesthetics. I. Title.
  BH39.B616   2012
  111'.85—dc23
                                                    2012012171

10 9 8 7 6 5 4 3 2 1

Contents

Preface

Works that are presently available—and there are many fine ones—for instructors to teach courses in the philosophy of art tend to fall into two categories: (1) anthologies of readings and (2) self-contained, single-author books. The benefit of anthologies, of course, is that the works of many philosophers are conveniently packaged. The drawback with such books, however, is that many of the readings (frequently reprinted articles from professional journals) are written by professionals usually for other professionals. They sometimes prove to be difficult for students to read profitably, especially for nonphilosophy students who are taking a course on aesthetics (for example, a student who is majoring in one of the arts and is taking a philosophy class; not uncommonly, it is the first philosophy class for that student). I have found that over the years I usually need to walk students through these readings in fairly close detail because they are not used to or comfortable with the conceptual, theoretical approaches taken by philosophers or because they lack a background in the languages and issues with which the philosophers are dealing. The result is less time for "doing" philosophy, for analyzing and evaluating the arguments contained in the readings.

On the other hand, the virtue of single-authored books is that they present a sustained perspective and treatment of the topic at hand, in the present case, art. For the purposes of an introductory textbook, however, this virtue can be a vice, as such books do not necessarily provide students with fair treatments of alternative perspectives, and often omit relevant conceptual, philosophical issues (for example, such a work might not include the issue of the relationship between art and society or how general aesthetic concerns relate to specific arts). So works such as these single-authored books, although they offer students a coherent, consistent voice, do not provide the primary source materials that we as philosophers value (namely, the philosophical process of wrestling with the arguments of others in their own words in order to gain greater understanding).

This book is a hybrid. It will, I hope, build on the strengths of both anthologies and single-authored texts. My intent is to provide primary source material and also give context and commentary of those readings for students. Such an approach, I believe, is more accessible to students than the primary readings by themselves, yet those readings, being sandwiched inside the author's introductions and commentary, are more understandable to students. In addition, this book addresses issues in the philosophy of art through the lenses of the three broad areas of philosophy: metaphysics, epistemology, and axiology (or value theory). That is, I will deal with various issues in the philosophy of art (for example, the nature of artistic expression or representation, the nature of aesthetic experience and interpretation, or the relationship of art and society) by focusing on the metaphysical aspects of these issues, as well as on their epistemological and axiological aspects. This approach, I hope, will give greater structure to the text and to the topics at hand. As an example: within the issue of the nature of aesthetic expression, there are concerns about *what* is expressed, *how* it is expressed, and *why* it is expressed. These concerns of what/how/why are the foci of metaphysics, epistemology, and axiology.

Textbooks mean different things to different people. My intention is that this one will be a tool, a springboard for faculty and students to pursue questions about art and aesthetics. But it is only a tool. It is written with the assumption that what is contained here is only a beginning and that engagement in individual classrooms by faculty and students will go beyond what can be included here (or in any single text). For example, there is only one primary reading that focuses directly on the interpretation of art, yet an entire semester could be dedicated to this topic. Also, there is only one primary reading on aesthetics and dance, yet, again, this topic could easily warrant an entire semester's attention. This text, then, like any text, needs to be supplemented by interaction and elaboration in the classroom. In that sense, this text is incomplete, but because this is a springboard, I see this not as a failing but as, rather, an opportunity. The value of this text will be determined during and after its use with students, not before. I hope it will prove to be fruitful to that end.

Every book is a collaborative effort, and this book would not have been possible without the help, assistance, and guidance of a number of people. In particular, I want to thank Kelsey Mitchell at Westview Press for her support and patience, as well as the anonymous reviewers of the manuscript, all of whom gave thoughtful, substantive, and good-spirited suggestions and advice. Thanks also to Collin Tracy, at Westview, for helping to move the publication along smoothly and to Kathy Delfosse for gracious and careful suggestions to make the book more readable and accessible. Any flaws and faults that remain here are in spite of the fine work of all these good people. Finally, I want to thank Kari Middleton for her thoughtful commentary and assistance with this project.

CHAPTER 1

INTRODUCTION TO THE PHILOSOPHY OF ART

During the tumultuous days following 9/11/2001, a photojournalist, Tom Franklin, took a photograph of three firefighters raising a flag at Ground Zero (Figure 1.1), where the World Trade Center in New York City had been hit in a terrorist attack. The three firefighters were Dan McWilliams, George Johnson, and Billy Eisengrein; all three were white males. After seeing this photograph, Bruce Ratner, president of a New York City real estate management company, wanted to memorialize the heroism and meaning of that day by commissioning an honorific bronze statue. Ratner consulted with various fire department officials and with Ivan Schwartz, the president of StudioEIS, in Brooklyn. Collectively, they decided to pay homage to the firefighters and rescue workers of the day and chose to employ "artistic license" and have a commemorative statue created that would depict three generic firefighters, portraying what were believed to be characteristically white facial features, black facial features, and Hispanic facial features. A clay model of the statue was unveiled in December 2001 (Figure 1.2) and was met with immediate criticism. Some people claimed that choosing to portray three ethnically identified faces was an act of political correctness. The photograph was of a real event, they said, capturing the heroics of three particular individuals, and the proposed statue was a betrayal of and insult to the three individuals who were originally photographed. Those who defended the proposed statue claimed that the statue was not meant to be merely a three-dimensional version of that photograph; it was meant to be a symbolic statement honoring

1

1.1 *Ground Zero Spirit* photo by Tom Franklin. Courtesy AP Photo/Thomas E. Franklin/ The Record (Bergen County, NJ).

1.2 Clay model of proposed 9/11 statue. Courtesy AP Photo/Robert Spencer.

not only the three specific firefighters but also all those who engaged in acts of heroism that day. Yet others claimed that the statue was not even only about acts of heroism *that day* but was, rather, about heroism generally, or perhaps about the virtue of sacrifice or the vigor of the American spirit. Because of the uproar, the full statue was never made.

This simple case raises a great many questions and issues. For example, as has been at least hinted at, what was the purpose (or purposes) of creating such a statue? If the purpose of the statue was to be honorific, exactly who or what was supposed to be honored? If the purpose was to honor specific people and a specific act via a work of art, how should that (best) be done? Should the work of art be a "mirror" of the people and event? What if the specific people that day (in this case, the three firefighters pictured) were all wearing hats; would it have been inappropriate for the work of art (in this case, a statue) to omit hats? What if the flag that was being raised had been hanging in a limp and droopy way; would it have been inappropriate for the work of art to portray it more fully, say, in a more unfurled manner? So in what ways, and why, should the statue have been strictly a three-dimensional duplication of the photograph?

Obviously, those who created the clay model did not think their task was simply to make the photograph into a three-dimensional sculpture. They made decisions about what to include and exclude—in part, what to portray and depict—as well as how to do so. For that matter, the photographer also made decisions when taking the photograph. He framed the picture in a certain way. He could not include everything that was happening at that moment in that setting in the photograph. He decided, for example, to include the flag in the picture, to have the firefighters a certain size and position relative to the background (for instance, he could have focused only on the flag or included only the heads of the firefighters). He could have waited a bit longer before snapping the photograph or taken it slightly sooner than he did. He could have aimed the camera at a different angle than he did. The point is that the photograph itself was not merely a "mirror" of the situation; it, too, involved deliberation and decision making, not only at that moment of taking the picture, but certainly also later, in the process of developing the picture.

Some questions, then, are about the content of the photograph and of the clay model. *What* was actually, or intended to be, portrayed or depicted? What did the content of the photograph and of the clay model represent (if anything)? In addition, *how* did the content portray or depict whatever it was that it portrayed or depicted? That is, did it do so by accurately and precisely duplicating the situation, or were other factors involved? Also, *why* was the content portrayed or depicted, and why was it done so in the way it was? Was it, in fact, to honor specific people in a specific act? Even if that were the case for the photograph, why should it be the case for a separate work of art, the proposed statue?

Besides questions about the content of the photograph and of the clay model, there are, as already noted, questions about the relationship between the photograph and the model. With respect to art, these questions arise not only for this particular case but also for such relations generally. Some specific object or event could be the inspiration or cause for someone to create a work of art. Think of how many examples of art you are aware of that were inspired by, say, the birth of Jesus, or by the Madonna and Child.

If we focus only on the issue of something being represented in an artwork, we can ask, what is an artist doing via the creation of a work of art? For instance, what was Pablo Picasso doing in and with his painting *Guernica* (Figure 1.3), or Johannes Brahms in and with his Third Symphony? Assuming that something is represented in these works, what the artist was doing involves issues of *what* was represented, *how* it was represented, and *why* it was represented. What was Picasso doing? He was representing a particular

1.3 *Guernica* by Pablo Picasso, copyright © 2012 Estate of Pablo Picasso/Artists Rights Society (ARS), New York.

historical event, but also much more. Indeed, in representing the event, he necessarily focused on certain aspects of it and not on others. Likewise, he expressed or communicated or attempted to evoke (or provoke) by means of certain colors, textures, shapes, and so on. As with what he represented, how he represented was a matter of selectivity on his part. In addition, why he represented what he represented and why he did it in the way(s) he did (for example, why he chose black, white, and gray rather than a rainbow of colors) matter. To truly understand what these phenomena are (that is, the object *Guernica* as well as the phenomenon that is the creation of the object *Guernica*), all these questions involving representation—what, how, and why—are pertinent. Of course, those same issues are relevant to the 9/11 photograph and statue, as well as to art in general.

WHAT IS PHILOSOPHY?

This book is an introduction to the philosophy of art, including to some of the kinds of questions and issues that were just noted. As an introduction, it will raise a number of issues and touch on a number of topics, but, because it is an introduction, it will only survey these issues and topics. Any one of them—for instance, the issue of representation in art or the issue of the relationship between art and morality—could be, and has been, the subject of full-length books. In addition, many issues and topics will only be mentioned but not discussed in detail (and others will not even be mentioned at all). For example, with respect to the social dimensions of art, a lot has been written on the nature and meaning of art museums, asking, for example, how and why certain works of art receive a special status by being placed in a museum (but in this book the effect of museum placement will not be mentioned at all beyond right here). Nonetheless, in this book we will survey many important and pervasive topics connected to a philosophical understanding of art. The first topic within the philosophy of art—as opposed to, say, the history of art or the sociology of art—is the *philosophy* aspect. Before looking at philosophy of *art*, then, we first need to look at what philosophy is (or what a philosophical approach to art is).

The word *philosophy* comes from two Greek words, *philo*, meaning "love," and *sophia*, meaning "wisdom." Philosophy, then, is the love of wisdom, and a philosopher is a lover of wisdom. However, both *love* and *wisdom* themselves carry various meanings. Here *love* is taken to mean both an activity and also an attitude. To love something or someone is to act in certain ways with respect to that thing or person. It is to act for the care and well-being of that thing or person. *Wisdom* here also means both an activity and an attitude. To be wise is to know things, but it is not "merely" having knowledge. Knowing lots of information, being very good at games like Trivial Pursuit, is not the same thing as being wise. Knowledge of facts is important, but it is not enough.

One sense of wisdom, then, at least for the early Greek philosophers, was the search not merely for a lot of factual information but for what they saw as "first principles." Principles refer not to specific cases or instances but to basic, fundamental, unifying notions or conditions. For example, a moral principle, such as "Murder is wrong," is meant to apply not just to a few particular situations but, rather, universally. Likewise, a natural principle (what today we would call a scientific law), such as the law $F = ma$ (force equals mass times acceleration), is said to apply not just to a few particular situations but, rather, universally. So by seeking wisdom, philosophers were looking for underlying, unifying principles. By speaking of *first* principles, they meant the most basic, fundamental principles.

Wisdom also involves actively seeking knowledge, as well as analyzing and evaluating it. It is an openness toward asking questions, with the view that every good question has an answer, but also that every good answer generates another question. One way to characterize a philosophical attitude is to say that it treats what is common as uncommon and what is uncommon as common. That is, it asks questions about those things that seem obvious and common, and treats them as if they are strange and in need of explanation. The result is that one sees them in a new light and sees the underlying

assumptions one had about them. At the same time, a philosophical attitude treats uncommon things as common; that is, it looks for connections
and relationships between those things that seem to be strange or unfamiliar and things that one already knows or understands. This is a philosophical attitude and acting philosophically (not merely speaking one's opinions
or views).

Philosophy usually proceeds in two ways: analyzing and synthesizing.
The first notion of analyzing means asking, What is X? where X might be
knowledge, truth, beauty, goodness, personhood, freedom, and so on. These
seem to be very broad and abstract notions, but more concrete ones would
be notions such as *person* or *mind* or *rights*. For example, the question, What
is a person? has very practical and important ramifications. One is connected with the issue of abortion. It is undeniable that a human fetus is human, because being human is a biological concept. A human fetus has
human DNA. The more important social and moral issue is whether or not
(or in what important ways) a human fetus is a person. It is persons that we
claim have rights, for instance, or are part of our moral concerns. So the issue
of abortion rests in large part on whether or not a human fetus is a person.
What is a person? then, is a conceptual, philosophical question. Although it
sounds abstract at first, in fact answers to it have very practical and important consequences.

The way philosophers address questions and analyze concepts is often by
looking for necessary and sufficient conditions for something. A *necessary
condition* for something is a condition that the thing must have in order for
it to be what it is. For example, a necessary condition for something to be a
mother is that the thing must be female. To give another example: a necessary condition for someone to be elected president of the United States is
that the person must be at least thirty-five years old. A *sufficient condition* for
something is a condition that the thing could have (but would not necessarily
have) that would "be enough" for that thing to be what it is. For example, it
is not necessary to have ten dimes in order to have a dollar (you could have,
say, a hundred pennies or four quarters), but it is sufficient; as long as you
have ten dimes, you have a dollar. Another example: being a citizen of Oregon is sufficient for being a citizen of the United States; as long as you are a
citizen of Oregon, you are a citizen of the United States. Some conditions are
said to be *both necessary and sufficient*. For instance, having a certain chemical
structure (say, being H_2O) is both necessary and sufficient for something to
be water. Or there might be a set of conditions that are said to be "jointly"

necessary and sufficient. For instance, if something is a bachelor, that thing needs to be an unmarried adult human male. All of the four conditions (being unmarried, being adult, being human, and being male) are necessary, but none by itself is sufficient. Together, however, they are said to be *jointly necessary and sufficient.*

The reason philosophers care about necessary and sufficient conditions is that these are said to be important components for understanding what something is and for distinguishing what something is. Take the case of what it is to be a person. One might ask whether being a human is the same thing as being a person. This is simply a way of asking if there could be nonhumans that we would consider to be persons. Or philosophers will often ask about "borderline" cases. For instance, would we consider a human body with no brain in it to be a person, or if we could somehow keep a human brain alive and functioning without it being in a body, would that brain be a person? With respect to art, one might ask whether or not human intention is a necessary or sufficient condition for something to be art. Indeed, this is one topic that will be explored in later chapters. So questions of looking for necessary and/or sufficient conditions might appear to be abstract, but they are the thought experiments that philosophers use to try to clarify our concepts. (However, as we will see in later chapters, many philosophers claim that looking for necessary and/or sufficient conditions can itself be a mistake. Some things, they say, simply do not have necessary and/or sufficient conditions. A famous example comes from the twentieth-century philosopher Ludwig Wittgenstein. He used the example of games and claimed that there simply are no necessary and/or sufficient conditions for what makes something a game, because the term *game* is too loose and vague.)

Clarity about concepts is important and useful, but there is more to philosophy than analyzing things. There is also the second component of philosophy, namely, synthesizing. That is, we are concerned about how things make sense, broadly speaking. Being clear about things is good, but what does it all mean? Even if we could get a clear notion of what a person is, then what? One focus of philosophy is to help see how things fit together or relate to each other and to meeting our goals. Not only do we want to know the assumptions and presuppositions that we have about things, but we also want to know about the implications of believing certain things or acting in certain ways. We want to know how things cohere or hang together in meaningful ways. As the twentieth-century philosopher Wilfrid Sellars put it, we want to understand how things in the broadest possible sense of the term hang together in the broadest possible sense of the term. For example, if we were to say that a person is whatever (or whoever) has the ability to learn from its environment or to set personal goals or projects, then, if it turned out that some nonhumans do these things, would they be persons? Furthermore, if they were persons, would they, then, have rights? If so, what would this imply about how other persons would need to act or behave? These are the types of synthesizing questions that philosophers ask.

Philosophy's content (that is, the answers to these sorts of questions, rather than its activity or attitude) is usually divided into three very broad categories: metaphysics, epistemology, and axiology. Metaphysics is the study of reality. This is not the same thing as science studying nature or social science studying human cultures. Rather, metaphysics asks about basic kinds of reality. For example, we take it for granted that there are things or objects in the world, such as trees and cats and water. But what about events? Are events real? An event, such as the falling of a leaf or the buttering of toast, is not the same "thing" as the physical leaf or the toast. That is, events are not equivalent to the objects involved in them. So are events real, and how are we to understand them? Another kind of example: are abstract "things" real? For example, are numbers real? When we write the numeral 2, we are writing down a representation of the number two. But when we erase that numeral, and it no longer exists, we do not erase the number two. If the number two is real, it is abstract and cannot be erased. So are numbers real? These are metaphysical questions; they are questions about what kinds of things are real, or are part of a good description of reality. (What is a person? is also a metaphysical question.)

As we will see in later chapters, such questions abound in the context of art. For instance, what, exactly, is a musical composition? Or: what is its metaphysical nature? Is it the notes written in a score? But of course, those notes themselves are abstract things. If we tear up a particular copy of the score, we do not destroy the score itself. And we certainly do not destroy musical notes. Furthermore, what about different musical performances of the "same" composition? What makes them the "same" composition? For that matter, what constitutes a performance? Also, some musical compositions are never scored; they might be impromptu. So what, exactly, is a musical score, and what is its relation to a musical composition? To take another perspective, is the musical composition a set of sounds inside a composer's mind? Is it the set of all the performances of what is thought to be the "same" composition? These are questions about the metaphysics of music.

Another metaphysical question asks what else might be real besides or instead of things or objects. Consider two common objects: say, a piece of paper and a cat. In addition to taking these two objects as real, we speak of their *properties* or traits. For instance, the piece of paper is white, it is rectangular, it is flat, it is smooth, and, no doubt, it has some flavor to it. Are these properties real, as well as the object itself being real? In addition, let us assume the paper is smaller than the cat. That the paper is smaller than the cat is a fact of the world. Now, "is smaller than" is not an object, such as a cat or piece of paper, and it is not a property of either object, such as being rectangular. Rather, it is a relation between two objects, the paper and the cat. So although we could say "The paper is flat," we could not meaningfully say "The paper is smaller than." To speak of "smaller than" we need to relate the paper to something else. Are relations real? As just noted, we certainly say that the paper *really* is smaller than the cat. Asking about the nature and status of relations is a metaphysical question. In the next chapter, on the nature of art, we will see this issue of properties and relations come up as a major part of the discussion.

Metaphysics, then, is a major branch of philosophy. A second major branch is epistemology. Epistemology is the study of knowledge. Again, it looks not merely at questions of specific knowledge claims but at broader questions such as, What is knowledge? What is the difference between knowledge and belief or knowledge and opinion? What are the kinds of "things" that are knowable? What justifies someone's claim that she knows something (as opposed to her claim that she simply believes it)? Even the question of whether anyone can really know anything at all is an epistemological question. Logic is related to epistemology because logic focuses in large part on principles and rules of inferences and implications (that is, on standards that relate to what is known or knowable).

Philosophers speak of various kinds of knowledge. All of us claim to know lots of things; I know when I have a headache, I know that 2 + 2 = 4, I know that the earth is smaller than the sun, I know how to ride a bike, and so on. These examples illustrate different kinds of knowledge. Sometimes by "knowledge" we mean *knowledge by acquaintance*, or knowledge of something with which we are immediately connected to (or acquainted with), such as having a headache. There is also *propositional knowledge*, or knowledge that something is the case (that is, knowledge that some proposition is true), such as knowing that the earth is smaller than the sun. In addition, there is *practical knowledge*, which in the case of my knowledge just mentioned, means knowing how, that is, knowing how to ride a bike. One issue within epistemology is the examination of how these various kinds of knowledge are related to each other. For example, is all propositional knowledge based finally on knowledge by acquaintance?

In addition, we believe many things, but it does not follow that we know those things. For example, I believe that Plato spoke Greek; I believe that humans will some day walk on Mars; I believe that there is no largest prime number; I believe I can successfully repair some basic kitchen appliances if I need to. However, I might be wrong about these things, so even though I believe them—and have good reasons for believing them—it might be incorrect to say that I know them. We make a distinction between belief and knowledge.

The fact that we make this distinction points to a long-standing issue in epistemology: What is knowledge? A traditional answer to this question, at least for propositional knowledge, is that knowledge is *justified true belief*. Philosophers usually state this in this way: *S knows that p* (meaning some person S knows that some proposition p is the case) involves three necessary conditions: (1) S believes that p, (2) p is true, and (3) S is justified in believing that p.

The first condition, the *belief condition*, simply says that for us to know something, we have to at least believe it. It would be strange to claim that I know Denver is in Colorado but that I do not believe it. So, believing that p is a necessary condition for knowing that p, but it is not sufficient, because we can believe things without knowing them.

A second condition for knowledge is the *truth condition*. This states that p, the proposition we know, is true. This means we cannot know something that is false. Now, we can know that something is false. For instance, I know that it is false that my cat is a dog. I can know that a proposition is false, but I cannot know a false proposition. Another way of saying this is that, although there can be false beliefs, there cannot be false knowledge. Again, I cannot know that 2 + 2 = 3 or that the sun is smaller than the earth, no matter how strongly I believe it. In those cases, I am just wrong.

The third traditional condition for knowledge is the *justification condition*. The first two conditions by themselves, having a true belief, are not enough for knowledge. I must also have justification, some warrant or evidence, for the belief. We all have true beliefs, but that is not the same as having knowledge. Every student who has been faced with multiple-choice exams has had the experience of making a lucky guess at an answer and getting it right. In such a case, that person had a true belief, but it certainly was not a case of knowing. So knowledge cannot just be true belief, otherwise any lucky guess that turned out correct would be a case of knowledge.

For the record, many philosophers reject the view that knowledge is justified true belief, but that is not the concern here. Instead, the point now is that each of these three conditions (justification, truth, belief) is itself subject to further analysis. For instance, there are different notions of what truth is. If a belief is true, what makes it true? A commonsense view is called the *correspondence* conception of truth. This view of truth states that what makes a particular proposition or belief true is that it corresponds to facts in the world. If my belief that the earth is smaller than the sun is true, it is because in fact the earth is smaller than the sun (independent of what I believe)! It is that simple; if my belief corresponds to the facts, it is true (indeed, that is what makes it true), and if it does not correspond, it is not true. Another philosophical view of truth is called the *coherence* conception of truth. This view of truth states that what makes a particular belief true is that it coheres with other accepted beliefs. That is, no belief exists in isolation, and when we say some belief is true (or false, for that matter), what we mean is that it is consistent with other beliefs. Many, probably most, of those other beliefs concern facts about the world, so truth is not just some coherent fairy tale, according to the supporters of this view. A third view of truth is called the *pragmatist* conception of truth. This view of truth states that what makes a particular belief true is how it affects us in the future, that is, what consequences follow from taking it as true. The point of the *pragmatist* conception is that "true" is not just a descriptive property of propositions or beliefs but, rather, is also a prescriptive notion, directing our future beliefs and actions (that is, it prescribes, or directs, us). As the American pragmatist philosopher William James put it: truth happens to an idea, which is made true by events; its verity is itself an event or process. Now, the point for us with respect to philosophy of art is not to resolve the nature of truth, but to see that one epistemological concern is the nature of truth, especially as it relates to the nature of knowledge.

What makes our beliefs true (or false)? It is fairly common to hear someone state that truth is relative or that something is "true for me." There are several things to say about this. First, there is a difference between *relativity* and *subjectivism*. The claim that something is "true for me" is really a claim that truth is subjective, that there are no objective standards for assessing whether some belief is true or not. To say that truth is relative is not the same thing. We can speak of a belief being judged true or false relative to certain standards (for example, legal standards of evidence or proof versus scientific standards of evidence or mathematical standards of proof), but that is not the same as saying that that belief's truth is subjective. So one point is that the notion of truth as relative is not the same as the notion of truth as subjective.

Beyond that, saying that "p is true for me" really comes down to just saying that "I believe p" (and perhaps believe it so strongly that I will act in certain ways on that belief). But there must be some reason why something is "true for me" as opposed to being "false for me." In saying that something is "true for me," the "for me" part does not really add anything. It just says that I believe it. That does not move us toward distinguishing true beliefs and false beliefs nor toward determining what makes some beliefs true and others false. This points to the third condition of knowledge discussed above, namely, the justification condition.

Today philosophers tend to address the issue of justification of beliefs in terms of *externalism* and *internalism*. Simply put, externalism is the view that what justifies a person's beliefs must be external to the person, and internalism is the view that something internal to the believer can (at least in part) be relevant to justifying that person's beliefs.

As we will see throughout this book, there are many epistemological issues that come up in the context of art. One such issue is the question of artistic truth. Can a work of art be true (or false)? For those people who were upset about the proposed 9/11 statue, among their concerns was the sense that the photograph gave a true representation of a specific event but the proposed statue did not. But what could it mean to say that a work of art is true (or false)? Another epistemological issue that arises in the context of art is intention and meaning. We often hear people ask about some artwork, What does it mean? Issues about intention and interpretation deal directly with epistemological topics.

The third major branch of philosophy is axiology. Axiology is the study of value and values. This includes ethics, but it is broader than just that, because there are values other than ethical or moral values. For example, when we say that a particular song is a good song, we do not (usually) mean that it is morally good; rather, we (usually) mean that it is pleasing to listen to or that it makes us feel good in some way or other. So another area of axiology is aesthetics, or values that we associate with art. (That area, aesthetics, is obviously the primary concern for this book!) Aesthetics involves the examination of value(s) that might have nothing at all to do with ethics and morality.

When we say that some book or movie or song or statue is a good one, we do not mean that it was morally good (well, at least most of us do not mean that). A song might be good because it has a beat that makes it easy to dance to, not because it carries some approved moral message. Nonetheless, as we will see in Chapter 6, an important issue within the philosophy of art is the relationship between ethical value(s) and artistic value(s).

Yet another part of the larger field of axiology is the field of social and political philosophy. If we ask about the proper role and function of the state, we are asking a value question. Or to speak of a good citizen might very well be different from speaking of a good person (or what it means to be a good citizen is not the same thing as what it means to be a good person, although they might overlap).

It is very common to hear people speak of the issue of value (and values) as being a matter not of analysis or evaluation but, at best, of reporting. That is, a common view is that people's values are relative and that that is pretty much all that can be said. Our values, this view holds, are simply a matter of what we learn from our upbringing and our cultural environment. However, there are a number of things to be said about this. First, as was noted above when discussing beliefs, to say that something is relative does not mean the same thing as saying that it is subjective. Relativity implies some standard(s). But even with subjective beliefs or values, it is appropriate—and, indeed, useful—to ask why one has a particular value (or why one values A over B). There is always some reason or cause even for a subjective value.

In addition, when we ask, Why?—for example, Why do you like A? or Why do you like A over B?—we can be asking for the origin of this value, or we can be asking for the justification of this value. Although the origin and the justification of value(s) are related issues, they are not the same thing. Consider this example: Suppose we are talking, and I make some outrageous sexist or racist remark. You are astonished, and you ask me, "Why do you believe that?" I answer, "Well, that's what my father told me." Now, I have given you the origin of my belief/value, namely, it came from my family upbringing. But clearly, I have not given a justification for that belief/value. You would be quite right in thinking that not only am I reprehensible, but so is my father. The point is that answering such a question simply by providing the origin sometimes does not really answer the question. The question did not ask, How did I come to have this belief/value? Rather, it asked, What would justify having this belief/value? Although they might be related, these are not at all necessarily the same thing, and it is the latter question that philosophy asks.

Clearly, many axiological issues arise in the philosophy of art. Broadly speaking, some have to do with values within art, and others have to do with values about art. Those within art are ones that concern, say, what makes an artwork good. For instance, is balance within a painting part of what makes it a good painting? Is gracefulness of movement or dramatic athleticism more important for dance (or for a particular dance)? For that matter, what, exactly, is gracefulness of movement? Values about art concern the relation of art to society and to other values, such as moral values. For instance, when, if ever, is censorship of art legitimate? Should art be used to promote particular political agendas? What is the difference between art and propaganda? Such questions are, of course, common, and they will be considered throughout the upcoming chapters, especially in Chapter 6.

Although these three broad areas within philosophy—metaphysics, epistemology, and axiology—are distinct, they also overlap. For example, the question, Is there moral knowledge? involves both epistemology and axiology. That is, if we ask whether someone can *know* what is right or good, rather than simply believe or assert it, we are asking an epistemological question. At the same time, it is about values, so it is axiological. It is even about metaphysics, because to answer the question would involve saying something about what "right" or "good" is; that is, what kind of things they are. In addition to questions that overlap the three areas of philosophy, there are questions about the three areas themselves. For instance, we might well ask, What is the value of studying metaphysics? This is an axiological question about metaphysics. Or, as just noted, we can ask, How, if at all, can we know that some action is right or wrong? This is an epistemological question about axiology. Sometimes philosophers refer to such questions as being *metaphilosophy*, meaning questions about philosophy. Even though they are about philosophy, they are still part of the love of wisdom if they are asked with the genuine attitude of seeking wisdom.

One final word before turning directly to philosophy of art issues. We frequently hear that in philosophy (and perhaps elsewhere), there are no right answers. Who can say, after all, what knowledge is or what truth is? Philosophical questions often seem very abstract (because, sometimes at least, they are), but this is not because they are not important. The value of asking such questions can often be that they make us think about common (and uncommon) phenomena in new ways that shed light on the topic at hand and often on other topics, too. And even if there is no recognized, single "right" answer to a philosophical question, it does not follow that asking and addressing that question is not valuable. For one thing, although we might not come up with a "right" answer, we could very well identify wrong answers. For example, we might not know the "right" answer to the question, How many stars are there in the Milky Way galaxy? But we do know that "twelve" is a wrong answer. This question about stars is not a philosophical one, but the same point holds for philosophical questions: What is knowledge? What is a person? What is an artist's intention? We can identify wrong answers, even if we cannot or have not identified a "right" answer. So not having "the right answer" is not, in itself, necessarily a bad thing; we can still learn by asking the question and coming to find out that some answers are not correct. And, of course, not having "the right answer" now does not mean that we will not or cannot find it at some point. And, as the old saying goes, getting there is half the fun!

PHILOSOPHY OF ART AND AESTHETICS

What, then, is philosophy of *art*? Put very briefly, *philosophy of art is the analysis and evaluation of basic concepts and practices within art* (such as the nature of artistic expression) *and about art* (such as the role of art in society). This entire book is about this brief answer: expanding it, explaining it in more detail, and demonstrating the analysis and evaluation. However, a few preliminary words are in order. First, the term *art* will not be defined here or even given any characterization. Indeed, the question, What is art? will be the subject of Chapter 2. For now, what is meant by *art* will be taken as a given, but also as something that will be a subject for further exploration throughout this book.

Second, the phrase *philosophy of art* should probably be replaced with the phrase *philosophy of the arts*, because many different arts will be considered and discussed. Those various arts include, as one would expect, the usual suspects—painting, dance, drama and theater, literature, music, photography, and film—as well as some that might not immediately come to mind, such as architecture and landscape architecture. But what about, say, juggling or cartoons or synchronized swimming? How about fashion design or computer-generated compositions? Why should or should not these practices be considered arts? After all, some of the usual suspects just mentioned, such as photography, were not always accepted as "legitimate" arts. Among those practices that are accepted as arts, there is great variation. Some are physical, three-dimensional (such as sculpture); others are not (such as photography). Some involve words (such as literature); others do not (such as music). Some are primarily performative (such as dance); others are not (such as architecture). Nonetheless, all are treated as arts. The point here is that, as its starting point, this book will take those things and activities that are commonly accepted as forms of art as the subject matter for philosophical interest. In particular, the focus will be on metaphysical, epistemological, and axiological aspects of art, both in terms of what these philosophical lenses can reveal about the arts, and also in terms of what the arts can disclose about these philosophical topics. For example, when looking at the issue of representation, we can (and will) ask about *what* is being represented in art, *how* it is being represented, and *why* it is being represented. That is, we will be looking at metaphysical, epistemological, and axiological concerns related to artistic representation. At the same time, by looking at artistic representation, we can (and will) also reflect on what artistic representation (as opposed to, say, scientific representation) says about metaphysics, epistemology, and axiology. That is, if artistic representation is something quite different from scientific representation, then what does that say about the nature of knowledge? So philosophy of art is a two-way street; it uses the lens of philosophy to look at art, but at the same time, it uses the lens of art to look at philosophy.

Aesthetics is the branch of philosophy that is concerned with the study of beauty and matters that are related to beauty. It is closely connected with the broader topic of the philosophy of art. However, philosophy of art covers topics that extend beyond beauty, such as the social and moral aspects of art (for example, under what conditions, if any, it is appropriate to censor art in public settings) and the relationship between art and language, because both involve meaning and representation (for example, how works of art can have or convey meaning about something). Some philosophers say that there is no important difference between aesthetics and the philosophy of art; rather, they hold, the term *aesthetics* is merely an older word that has been replaced by the term *philosophy of art*. The reason, they say, for the newer term is that *philosophy of art* parallels other more recent areas in philosophy, such as philosophy of science, philosophy of religion, philosophy of education, and so on. In addition, they say, the focus of philosophy itself has shifted over the years away from making claims directly about art and instead, like philosophy of science and other areas, analyzes the concept of art and related concepts (such as expression and meaning).

The word *aesthetics* comes from the Greek term *aistheta*, meaning "things that are perceptible by the senses." This word was used to distinguish those things that could be known by the senses from those immaterial things that could be known only by reason or imagination, which were called *noeta*. So the original meaning of aesthetics was not simply about beauty or beautiful things but encompassed a broader sense of knowledge. Nonetheless, early on this type of knowledge became connected to beauty. For instance, in the writings of Plato, a distinction was made between knowledge of physical, material things and knowledge of nonphysical, immaterial things. We can know particular objects, such as dogs or trees, by encountering them with our senses (we see and hear and touch them), but that knowledge is different than our knowledge of the concept of Dog or Tree (which involve no particular dogs or trees, but the ideal concept of them). For Plato, there is a progression of knowledge from particular things to their ideal Forms. Likewise, there is a progression from knowing the beauty of material things to knowing the beauty of ideal things. Eventually, the term *aesthetics* was used not as a general sense of knowing, but only for knowing in relation to beauty. Also, although today most people think of aesthetics and beauty in relation to art, the term actually includes the notion of beauty in other things, such as nature and even in, say, mathematical patterns.

One philosophical issue connected to beauty and aesthetics is the very nature of beauty (and also the lack of or opposite of beauty, ugliness). The first distinction to note about the nature of beauty is that it is sometimes taken in a *descriptive* way and other times taken in an *evaluative* way. The descriptive way simply means that something is described as being beautiful. The evaluative way means that beauty is not merely a feature of a thing, like its size or weight, but involves some value. That is, a comparison between two things, one said to weigh ten pounds and the other said to weigh twenty pounds, is quite different from a comparison between two things, one said to be beautiful and the other said to be ugly (or plain), because the former involves merely a matter of fact, a matter of the things' features, whereas the latter involves a value judgment, that the beautiful one is better (or worse) than the ugly one.

This distinction between descriptive and evaluative ways of speaking of things points to another fundamental issue connected to the nature of beauty: the nature of aesthetic objects. What kinds of things, or objects, can properly be described or evaluated as being aesthetic at all, and why? What kinds of things are even within the realm of aesthetics? This relates to what philosophers sometimes call a category mistake. For example, the notion of "weight" is relevant to some things, but not others; dogs and trees are properly said to have some weight or other (that is, a given dog weighs a certain amount), but ideas or colors are not properly said to have any weight (that is, it simply makes no sense to ask how much red weighs and if red is heavier than yellow). The concept of weight applies to some things, but not all things. So the question is, to what things does the concept "beauty" apply?

Aesthetic properties, or features, are yet another issue related to the very nature of beauty and aesthetics. Even among those things that are properly said to be within the realm of beauty, is beauty *in* those things? That is, is beauty something that is part of those things and something we can discover in them (just as having a certain size or weight is something we can discover in them)? Or is the beauty in things not a property of the things themselves but, rather, a feature we "impose" on them? The philosophical term for this latter position is that beauty is a *relation*, not a property. In other words, nothing is beautiful in itself, but beauty is a relation between something and us. An analogy is that nothing is food in and of itself; rather, it is food only to the extent that it is related to something that eats it. An apple is just an apple, according to this view, but what makes an apple food is that something (say, some human) consumes it, and it is food only in relation to being consumed as food. There are features about apples and about humans that makes apples food for humans (and there are features about poisonous things and about humans that makes those things not food for humans), but the concept of *food* is a relational concept. Likewise, this view says, beauty is also a relation. This is not exactly the same thing as saying that beauty is in the eye of the beholder, that is, that beauty is subjective. Something being food is not "in the eye (or mouth) of the beholder." That is, there are facts about some objects and facts about humans that account for the fact that some things are food for humans and some things are poisons for humans. So being a relation is not the same thing as being subjective.

One more issue about the very nature of beauty and aesthetics is the nature of an *aesthetic experience*. What makes a certain experience one that is aesthetic rather than, say, one that is ethical or political? Two people might encounter the same thing, perhaps a work of art or some natural landscape, but have very different experiences. One might look at a painting or a sunset over the mountains and have the experience of having seen something beautiful and moving; the other might look at them and have the experience of thinking of ways those things might be made profitable, that is, be sold so that he could receive money for them. The first person has an aesthetic experience, but the second person does not. The issue, then, is, what is the nature of an aesthetic experience; what makes that experience aesthetic?

All the issues above are said to be metaphysical issues about aesthetics. That is, they are about the nature of beauty and aesthetics. There are also epistemological issues about beauty and aesthetics, about how beauty is known. One view is that beauty is known by having a certain kind of aesthetic sense. Just as people can know, say, colors by having a sense of sight or can know sounds by having a sense of hearing, so, too, people can know beauty by having a sense of aesthetics. This is sometimes referred to as *taste*, in the sense not of tasting things with one's mouth but of having "good taste," of being refined. Some philosophers claim that taste is something that is inborn (or not) and that cannot be learned. They make an analogy with blind persons, who cannot learn to see colors (even if they learn facts about colors or how to speak about them), or deaf persons, who cannot learn to actually hear sounds (even if they learn facts about sounds or how to speak about them). In the same way, they say, aesthetic taste, or an aesthetic sense, cannot be learned (even if people learn facts about beauty or how to speak about it). Other philosophers, however, claim that taste can be learned, much like a wine-tasting expert can learn to make very fine distinctions about different wines.

Another view holds that beauty can be known not by having some aesthetic sense or taste but by knowing facts that relate to beauty and aesthetics. For example, two people might hear a particular song. One of them knows nothing about musical theory or musical structure, whereas the other is very knowledgeable about those things. The first person might not think that the song is beautiful, but the second person (the expert) might understand the very complex patterns and rhythms that have been blended together in the song, and that second person might claim to see beauty in the song because of knowing these facts. For that person, the ability to see and appreciate the beauty is a matter of knowing and understanding the complex arrangements contained in the song.

This appreciation by the expert might well be the result of greater understanding and awareness. But another view holds that knowing beauty is a matter not of factual knowledge but of emotional feeling. That is, a different view of what it is to know beauty is that such knowledge is not so much a matter of cognitive awareness of facts as a matter of a type and level of feeling. Knowing beauty and having an aesthetic experience, they say, is less like knowing facts about the complexity and structure of something and more like having an intense emotional response to that thing. The knowledge, or perhaps recognition and appreciation, of the beauty of a song or a sunset, they say, is more like the unstructured joy that a young child feels at play than it is like the logical process an engineer applies to solving some problem. A child can know the beauty of a flower, they say, as much as or more than a botanist, even if the botanist knows much more about the flower.

This last view points toward the issue of what philosophers have called "the sublime." There is something, say some philosophers, that is awe inspiring or lofty about real beauty. There is sublimity relating to something that is overwhelming and has grandeur. Some philosophers have argued that an encounter with genuine beauty—perhaps a stunning landscape—makes one speechless at that moment. It makes a person feel reverential and spiritual, but not because one knows lots of facts. Few people are geologists, but many people have encountered some natural beauty and felt awe. The question for many philosophers is, What is the nature of that (feeling of) awe and how does it relate to other things that we feel and know? This feeling is not the same as pleasure. Although such a feeling can be pleasurable and can make us feel very good—perhaps because we feel connected to other things—it can also make us feel overwhelmed and even unimportant in the grand scheme of things. That feeling of awe and sublimity is dramatic and perhaps even indescribable, but nonetheless it leads to the question of the nature of that feeling: Is it the result of some feature of beauty in things or the features of things or, like food, is it the result of being a relation to other things? For example, does—or could—a wild animal have a sublime experience? Even if only humans could have such an experience, is that because the thing that is experienced is itself sublime?

PREVIEW OF UPCOMING CHAPTERS

As mentioned above, this book is an introduction to the philosophy of art, and, as an introduction, it only provides a broad survey of some of the many issues and topics within the field. At the end of the book, a short list of further readings suggests works that go into these issues and topics in greater detail. As for what is included here, Chapter 2 addresses the very broad question of the nature of art. What is art, or, perhaps more fruitfully, what is an art? What, if anything, makes fashion design or juggling (an) art, or what makes it not (an) art? Are there certain properties they have or fail to have? Are there certain relations that they have or fail to have?

Chapters 3, 4, and 5 consider art from the respective perspectives of the artwork, the artist, and the audience. That is, some issues and topics both within art and about art are primarily concerned with artworks themselves. The term *artwork* can refer both to some product or outcome, such as a sculpted statue or a painting or a musical score, and to some action or performance, such as a specific instance of a dance or dramatic reading of a poem or live rendering of a song. In addition, the term *artwork* might refer to a process of generating some specific artistic object or performance. In any case, there are aspects of artworks that bear philosophical questioning. For instance, what is meant by artistic form? How important, if at all, does the understanding or appreciation of a given artwork depend upon knowing other information "outside" the artwork itself? Sometimes we hear talk of form versus content; what, exactly, does that mean, and why, if at all, does it matter? Likewise, we often hear that an artwork can really only be understood or appreciated if one knows the context, or contexts, in which it was created. So another issue is that of form versus context. This focus on the artwork is the subject of Chapter 3.

Chapter 4 emphasizes issues that arise and are more salient with respect to the artist. For example, a traditional view of art is that it is a matter of someone (the artist) trying to represent something or other. That is, whether by form or content, an artist is trying to say something by representing something through the artwork that is created. An alternative view of art is that it is a matter of someone (the artist) expressing his or her feelings or beliefs or values through the creation of an artwork. Yet another view of art is that it is a matter of not only reflecting on things, but of making a difference, of changing things, through the creation of an artwork.

Whatever an artist might be doing by creating an artwork, how that object or performance is received by an audience raises other issues and topics. These issues and topics are the concern of Chapter 5. One such issue is the nature of aesthetic experience. When we listen to a musical performance and it moves us emotionally, what is it about that experience that makes it an aesthetic experience (as opposed to some other kind of experience)? We can be brought to tears by experiencing physical pain, and we can be brought to tears by experiencing a deeply moving artwork; what is the difference between those experiences, and what makes the one aesthetic but not the other? In addition, whatever the artist might intend his or her artwork to mean, someone who experiences that artwork (the audience) might take it to mean something altogether different. How, then, can or should an artwork be interpreted? Also, on what basis (or bases) can or should an artwork be evaluated (or critiqued)? These are issues that arise from the perspective of the audience.

Neither artworks nor artists nor audiences exist in a vacuum. Art exists in social settings. Indeed, it exists in all human cultures. Naturally, then, philosophical issues arise involving the relation between art and society. This is the focus of Chapter 6, particularly the issue of art and values. There are values within art (such as balance or harmony) and also values about art (such as its appropriate role in, say, promoting certain behaviors or attitudes). Is it ever appropriate to censor or ban art that is offensive to a given community? Should public funds support artists who create such artworks? Who, if anyone, can legitimately make such decisions?

Because the term *art* is so broad, even approaching asking what it is can be difficult. Nonetheless, many people treat it as something (whatever it is!) that is different from science. Think of the connotations that come to mind when someone is said to be an artist versus those that arise when someone is said to be a scientist. Or think of how schools make difficult and unhappy decisions about cutting programs and activities in hard financial times. Do they say that science programs, such as biology, must be cut, or do they typically say that arts programs, such as theater, must be cut? What, exactly, is the relation (if any?) between art and science, or arts and sciences? This is the focus in Chapter 7.

Finally, Chapters 8 through 10 look at the broad philosophical issues that arise in the previous chapters and apply them to specific arts. Chapter 8 looks at some performing arts, particularly dance, theater, and music. Questions about topics such as representation or intention or interpretation as they relate specifically to these forms of art are considered. Chapter 9 does the same for visual arts (in particular, painting, film, and architecture), as does Chapter 10 for literary arts (in particular, fiction, poetry, and creative nonfiction).

Because this book is about the philosophy of art, the emphasis will be to take the broad areas of philosophy—metaphysics, epistemology, and axiology—as lenses for addressing the various issues and topics that are dealt with in the different chapters. Again, the focus on philosophical investigation can be on *what* we are looking at (that is, metaphysical concerns), *how* we are looking at it (epistemological concerns), and *why* we are looking at it (axiological concerns). As has been noted several times in this chapter, one topic of concern is that of representation. For example, when looking at Picasso's *Guernica*, we could ask what he was trying to represent in his painting, as well as how he tried to do it and why he did it. Using these three philosophical lenses, then, I hope will prove fruitful as we consider the variety of concerns throughout this book.

Questions for Discussion

1. In the dispute over the proposed 9/11 statue, what would you have recommended, had you been asked?
2. Can there be artistic knowledge? Are there artistic facts? If there are, what are some examples of artistic facts? If there are none, why not?
3. Is there such a thing as art, as opposed to arts? If there is, what is it? If there is not, why not?
4. On what bases, if any, can artworks be evaluated? Is it only a matter of personal preference that one work of art is good or bad, or better or worse than another work of art?
5. Where is Ludwig van Beethoven's Fifth Symphony? Where is Leonardo da Vinci's *Mona Lisa*? Why is there a difference in the answers to these questions?

THE NATURE OF ART

At your local grocery store, there is probably a display of a cleaning product called Brillo soap pads. That display might be in the form of a stack of boxes, each containing dozens of Brillo soap pads. Whatever you might think of that display, or of Brillo soap pads, you probably do not think of the display (or the pads) as art.

At the National Gallery of Canada, in Ottawa, there is an artwork on display. That particular artwork was created by the artist Andy Warhol in the 1960s. It is entitled *Brillo Soap Pad Boxes*, and here is what the National Gallery tells its viewers about that artwork:

> Andy Warhol shocked people with his paintings of Campbell's soup cans, coupled with such provocative statements as: "The reason I'm painting this way is because I want to be a machine." By taking his imagery from advertising and the mass media, Warhol attacked the separation of art from mass culture. Unlike the corrugated cardboard originals represented in "Brillo," these sculptures are made of wood. By making the cartons non-functional and uprooting them from their ordinary context, Warhol forces us to look at them freshly. They comment on the way that commercial packaging transforms a mundane, household product into a glamorous, desirable commodity. Warhol also focuses our attention on the significance of these objects as representatives of the impersonal, commercialized consumer society in which we live.

Given this commentary—Warhol "attacked the separation of art from mass culture"; he makes us look at mundane things such as soap pads "freshly"; he "focuses our attention on the significance of these objects as representatives of the impersonal, commercialized consumer society in which we live"—this certainly is presented as an artwork.

What is the difference? Why is a stack of soap pad boxes in the grocery store not art, while, in an art museum, the same stack is art? (Yes, the "stack" in the National Gallery is not actually a stack of boxes, but it could easily, and perhaps just as well, have been.) What is at issue here, of course, is, What is art? What makes something an artwork? In some respects, this question will permeate all the chapters of this book, but it is the focal point of this particular chapter. Warning: there will not be a definitive, final answer in this chapter! However, there will be some discussion of some of the philosophical aspects of trying to answer the question, and there will be several proposed answers. And, as noted in Chapter 1, even if no final, "right" answer is forthcoming, that does not mean that the question is unimportant or not worth addressing. So let us begin.

DEFINING ART

We noted in Chapter 1 that a typical, and reasonable, approach to answering the question of what X is, is to look for features or characteristics of the thing in question. For example, if you are wondering what a chair is or what makes something a chair, you would want some defining or characteristic features that a thing would need in order for it to be a chair. Likewise, if you wanted to know what chlorine is, you would want to know some defining or characteristic features of chlorine. This approach is especially obvious if you have no idea at all what some word means. For instance, if you heard someone remark that her hair seems "tove," and you wanted to know what "tove" is, you would want to know what features or characteristics identify her hair as being tove.

One way of approaching the question of what art is, then, is to ask what features or characteristics would constitute something as being art. That is, you would want to identify some *property* or properties of art. If Brillo boxes in the store are not art, why not? Do they lack some feature or characteristic such that, if they had that feature or characteristic, they would be art? (Even if you think that Brillo boxes in the store *are* art, you would, no doubt, still answer the question of what makes them art by identifying some feature or characteristic about them that makes them examples or instances of art.) Another way of putting this is that there is some essence (or essential features) of art.

Historically, philosophers (and others) have put forward various features or characteristics as essential to art. For example, Plato claimed that art is imitation: artworks are representations of certain aspects of the world. Plays and movies represent people interacting with each other, and paintings (at least some paintings) represent things in the world. Later thinkers claimed that the essence of art is that it is an expression of the feelings or thoughts of the artist. In this view, whereas the Brillo box display in the grocery store is (we assume) merely a means of getting us to purchase a particular product, the Brillo box display in the National Gallery is (we assume) an intentional statement by the artist about, say, mass culture or consumerism or something else. These two notions—that art is fundamentally representation or expression—will be taken up again in Chapter 4; the point here is that they are examples of one way of trying to answer the question of what makes something art.

Besides looking for some essential, or defining, property or properties of art, another approach is to identify some essential *relation* that something must be part of to be art. In Chapter 1, we noted that some aspects of the world are properties (for instance, having a tail is a typical property of a cat, but not of a chair) and that some aspects are relations (for instance, "being older than" is a relation between a father and his child). The defining or characteristic aspects of some things, at least, might well be not properties but relations. For instance, what is a chair? Some chairs have four legs or feet, but not all do; a chair might have only three legs or feet or even, as in the case of a beanbag chair, no legs or feet at all. Some chairs have a back as well as a seat, but not all do; some chairs have arms, but not all do. What does seem to be essential, or at least crucial, for something to be a chair is that it functions in a certain way, namely, as something people sit on. So it might well be that the essence of chairs (if they have an essence) is not any particular physical or structural characteristics but, rather, their function, which is a relation between them and us. Likewise, because there are so many kinds of arts, and because they have such very different features (think of the differences between music and painting and architecture), if art has any sort of essence, it might well be a relation. Later in this chapter we will look more closely at this notion, in particular at the view that the essence of art is constituted by historical relations.

Whether speaking of properties or relations, a common attempt to define something is to identify its necessary conditions, its sufficient conditions, or both. We say that some things are artworks and some things are not. So is there any property or relation that is necessary for something to be art? For example, must something be a representation for it to be art? That, at least, is unlikely. Think of abstract art or music; they do not necessarily represent anything. Is representation sufficient for something to be art? Again, unlikely. Many things, in fact, represent something or other, but that does not mean they are art. For example, the symbol $ represents dollars, but that does not make the symbol an artwork. The same holds for expression or other aspects that have been suggested as being characteristic of art.

ANTIESSENTIALISM

Many people, then, including many philosophers and artists, have been critical of the view that there is any essence to art, to what makes something an artwork. Among those critics was the philosopher Morris Weitz. Following the work of the twentieth-century philosopher Ludwig Wittgenstein, Weitz claimed that there simply is no essence to art. Artworks are artworks not because of any defining property or relation but, rather, because they share a "family resemblance." The notion of family resemblance points to the similarities, and at the same time to the differences, between family members. That is, individuals share certain features with their family members, but only certain features. For example, a boy might look like his mother in the sense that they have similarly colored eyes or similarly colored hair or similarly shaped noses. On the other hand, he might look like his sister in various ways, say, having similarly colored eyes, a similar basic face shape, and so on. At the same time, he might not share other features with those family members. For instance, his hair color might be different from his sister's, or his face shape might be different from his mother's. The fact is that people look like their fellow family members in some respects, but not necessarily in all respects. They resemble their family members, but are not carbon copies of them.

Wittgenstein claimed that many concepts have no essence and, hence, have no set of necessary and sufficient conditions that they satisfy. For example, he said, consider all the things that we call "games." Some games, such as Monopoly or Scrabble, involve a game board and various game pieces, but that is not true of all games (for instance, playing tag). Some games involve scoring points, but not all games do (for instance, tag, again). Some games involve multiple, competing players, but not all games do (for instance, playing solitaire). It might be the case that all games involve some set of rules in order to play the game (although that might not be true), but many things besides games also involve sets of rules, so having rules does not necessarily characterize or specify the unique essence of games. An analogy to help illustrate this point is to consider the nature of a rope. A rope is composed of many overlapping threads, but no single strand of thread runs through the entire length of the rope. So there might be no single feature that "runs through" all cases of games; instead, there might be a collection of overlapping features. That is to say, some, but not all, games involve multiple players, while other, but not all, games involve scoring points, and so on.

Wittgenstein's point, then, is that it is philosophically a mistake to insist that concepts or things (or words) must have an essence. Rather than having an essence, many basic concepts might just have a family resemblance. Weitz argues that this view applies to art. A major part of Weitz's claim for this view is that art is an open concept, meaning that how the concept is used and understood (and, hence, what it means) changes over time. As an analogy, the word *feed* is open. Today we might say that we feed coins into a parking meter or we feed paper into a copy machine. Metaphorical uses of a word can become so common that the meaning of the word itself evolves over time. For Weitz, this sort of openness is true of art; what counts as being an artwork has changed over time and will continue to change. As a result, no attempt at identifying necessary or sufficient conditions is possible for art. Here is what Weitz says:

▌ MORRIS WEITZ, "THE ROLE OF THEORY IN AESTHETICS"*

Is aesthetic theory, in the sense of a true definition of a set of necessary and sufficient properties of art, possible? If nothing else does, the history of aesthetic itself should give one enormous pause here. For, in spite of the many theories, we seem no nearer our goal today than we were in Plato's time. Each age, each art-movement, each philosophy of art, tries over and over again to establish the stated ideal only to be succeeded by a new or revised theory, rooted, at least in

Journal of Aesthetics and Art Criticism 15 (1956): 27–35.

part, in the repudiation of preceding ones. Even today, almost everyone interested in aesthetic matters is still deeply wedded to the hope that the correct theory of art is forthcoming. We need only examine the numerous new books on art in which new definitions are proffered; or, in our own country [the United States] especially, the basic textbooks and anthologies to recognize how strong the priority of a theory of art is.

In this essay I want to plead for the rejection of this problem. I want to show that theory—in the requisite classical sense—is *never* forthcoming in aesthetics, and that we would do much better as philosophers to supplant the question, "What is the nature of art?," by other questions, the answers to which will provide us with all the understanding of the arts there can be. I want to show that the inadequacies of the theories are not primarily occasioned by any legitimate difficulty such as the vast complexity of art, which might be corrected by further probing and research. Their basic inadequacies reside instead in a fundamental misconception of art. Aesthetic theory—all of it—is wrong in principle in thinking that a correct theory is possible because it radically misconstrues the logic of the concept of art. Its main contention that "art" is amenable to real or any kind of true definition is false. Its attempt to discover the necessary and sufficient properties of art is logically misbegotten for the very simple reason that such a set and, consequently, such a formula about it, is never forthcoming. Art, as the logic of the concept shows, has no set of necessary and sufficient properties, hence a theory of it is logically impossible and not merely factually difficult. Aesthetic theory tries to define what cannot be defined in its requisite sense. But in recommending the repudiation of aesthetic theory I shall not argue from this, as too many others have done, that its logical confusions render it meaningless or worthless. On the contrary, I wish to reassess its role and its contribution primarily in order to show that it is of the greatest importance to our understanding of the arts. . . .

The problem with which we must begin is not "What is art?," but "What sort of concept is 'art'?" Indeed, the root problem of philosophy itself is to explain the relation between the employment of certain kinds of concepts and the conditions under which they can be correctly applied. If I may paraphrase Wittgenstein, we must not ask, What is the nature of any philosophical *x*?, or even, according to the semanticist, What does "*x*" mean?, a transformation that leads to the disastrous interpretation of "art" as a name for some specifiable class of objects; but rather, What is the use or employment of "*x*"? What does "*x*" do in the language? This, I take it, is the initial question, the begin-all if not the end-all of any philosophical problem and solution. Thus, in aesthetics, our first problem is the elucidation of the actual employment of the concept of art, to give a logical description of the actual functioning of the concept, including a description of the conditions under which we correctly use it or its correlates.

My model of this type of logical description or philosophy derives from Wittgenstein. It is also he who, in his refutation of philosophical theorizing in the sense of constructing definitions of philosophical entities, has furnished contemporary aesthetics with a starting point for any future progress. In his new work, *Philosophical Investigations*, Wittgenstein raises as an illustrative question, What is a game? The traditional philosophical, theoretical answer would be in terms of some exhaustive set of properties common to all games. To this Wittgenstein says, let us consider what we call "games": "I mean boardgames, card-games, ball-games, Olympic games, and so on. What is common to them all?—Don't say: 'there *must* be something common, or they would not be called "games"' but *look and see* whether there is anything common to all.— For if you look at them you will not see something that is common to *all*, but similarities, relationships, and a whole series of them at that." . . .

Card games are like board games in some respects but not in others. Not all games are amusing, nor is there always winning or losing or competition. Some games resemble others in some respects—that is all. What we find are no necessary and sufficient properties, only a "complicated network of similarities overlapping and crisscrossing," such that we can say of games that they form a family with family resemblances and no common trait. If one asks what a game is, we pick out sample games, describe these, and add, "This and *similar things* are called 'games.'" That is all we need to say and indeed all any of us knows about games. Knowing what a game is is not knowing some real definition or theory but being able to recognize and explain games and to decide which among imaginary and new examples would or would not be called "games."

The problem of the nature of art is like that of the nature of games, at least in these respects: If we actually look and see what it is that we call "art," we will also find no common properties—only strands of similarities. Knowing what art is is not apprehending some manifest or latent essence but being able to recognize, describe, and explain those things we call "art" in virtue of those similarities.

But the basic resemblance between these concepts is their open texture. In elucidating them, certain (paradigm) cases can be given, about which there can be no question as to their being correctly described as "art" or "game," but no exhaustive set of cases can be given. I can list some cases and some conditions under which I can apply correctly the concept of art but I cannot list all of them, for the all-important reason that unforeseeable or novel conditions are always forthcoming or envisageable.

A concept is open if its conditions of application are emendable and corrigible; i.e., if a situation or case can be imagined or secured which would call for some sort of *decision* on our part to extend the use of the concept to cover this, or to close the concept and invent a new one to deal with the new case and its new property. If necessary and sufficient conditions for the application of a concept can be stated, the concept is a closed one. But this can happen only in logic or mathematics where concepts are constructed and completely defined. It cannot occur with empirically-descriptive and normative concepts unless we arbitrarily close them by stipulating the ranges of their uses.

I can illustrate this open character of "art" best by examples drawn from its sub-concepts. Consider questions like "Is Dos Passos' *U.S.A.* a novel?," "Is V. Woolf's *To the Lighthouse* a novel?," "Is Joyce's *Finnegan's Wake* a novel?" On the traditional view, these are construed as factual problems to be answered yes or no in accordance with the presence or absence of defining properties. But certainly this is not how any of these questions is answered. Once it arises, as it has many times in the development of the novel from Richardson to Joyce (e.g., "Is Gide's *The School for Wives* a novel or a diary?"), what is at stake is no factual analysis concerning necessary and sufficient properties but a decision as to whether the work under examination is similar in certain respects to other works, already called "novels," and consequently warrants the extension of the concept to cover the new case. The new work is narrative, fictional, contains character delineation and dialogue but (say) it has no regular time-sequence in the plot or is interspersed with actual newspaper reports. It is like recognized novels A, B, C . . . , in some respects but not like them in others. But then neither were B and C like A in some respects when it was decided to extend the concept applied to A to B and C. Because work N + 1 (the brand new work) is like A, B, C . . . N in certain respects—has strands of similarity to them—the concept is extended and a new phase of the novel engendered. "Is N + 1 a novel?," then, is no factual, but rather a decision problem, where the verdict turns on whether or not we enlarge our set of conditions for applying the concept.

What is true of the novel is, I think, true of every sub-concept of art: "tragedy," "comedy," "painting," "opera," etc., of "art" itself. No "Is X a novel, painting, opera, work of art, etc.?" question allows of a definitive answer in the sense of a factual yes or no report. "Is this *collage* a painting or not?" does not rest on any set of necessary and sufficient properties of painting but on whether we decide—as we did!—to extend "painting" to cover this case.

"Art," itself, is an open concept. New conditions (cases) have constantly arisen and will undoubtedly constantly arise; new art forms, new movements will emerge, which will demand decisions on the part of those interested, usually professional critics, as to whether the concept should be extended or not. Aestheticians may lay down similarity conditions but never necessary and sufficient ones for the correct application of the concept. With "art" its conditions of application can never be exhaustively enumerated since new cases can always be envisaged or created by artists, or even nature, which would call for a decision on someone's part to extend or to close the old or to invent a new concept. (E.g., "It's not a sculpture, it's a mobile.")

What I am arguing, then, is that the very expansive, adventurous character of art, its ever-present changes and novel creations, makes it logically impossible to ensure any set of defining properties. We can, of course, choose to close the concept. But to do this with "art" or "tragedy" or "portraiture," etc., is ludicrous since it forecloses on the very conditions of creativity in the arts.

Of course there are legitimate and serviceable closed concepts in art. But these are always those whose boundaries of conditions have been drawn for a special purpose. Consider the difference, for example, between "tragedy" and "(extant) Greek tragedy." The first is open and must remain so to allow for the possibility of new conditions, e.g., a play in which the hero is not noble or fallen or in which there is no hero but other elements that are like those of plays we already call "tragedy." The second is closed. The plays it can be applied to, the conditions under which it can be correctly used are all in, once the boundary, "Greek," is drawn. Here the critic can work out a theory or real definition in which he lists the common properties at least of the extant Greek tragedies. Aristotle's definition, false as it is as a theory of all the plays of Aeschylus, Sophocles, and Euripides, since it does not cover some of them, properly called "tragedies," can be interpreted as a real (albeit incorrect) definition of this closed concept; although it can also be, as it unfortunately has been, conceived as a purported real definition of "tragedy," in which case it suffers from the logical mistake of trying to define what cannot be defined—of trying to squeeze what is an open concept into an honorific formula for a closed concept. . . .

The primary task of aesthetics is not to seek a theory but to elucidate the concept of art. Specifically, it is to describe the conditions under which we employ the concept correctly. Definition, reconstruction, patterns of analysis are out of place here since they distort and add nothing to our understanding of art. What, then, is the logic of "*X* is a work of art?"

As we actually use the concept, "Art" is both descriptive (like "chair") and evaluative (like "good"); i.e., we sometimes say, "This is a work of art," to describe something and we sometimes say it to evaluate something. Neither use surprises anyone.

What, first, is the logic of "*X* is a work of art," when it is a descriptive utterance? What are the conditions under which we would be making such an utterance correctly? There are no necessary and sufficient conditions but there are strands of similarity conditions, i.e., bundles of properties, none of which need be present but most of which are, when we describe things as works of art. I shall call these the "criteria of recognition" of works of art. All of these have served as the defining criteria of the individual traditional theories of art; so we are already familiar with them. Thus, mostly, when we describe something as a work of art, we do so under the conditions of there being present some sort of artifact, made by human skill, ingenuity, and imagination, which embodies in its sensuous, public medium—stone, wood, sounds, words, etc.—certain distinguishable elements and relations. . . . None of the criteria of recognition is a defining one, either necessary or sufficient, because we can sometimes assert of something that it is a work of art and go on to deny any one of these conditions, even the one which has traditionally been taken to be basic, namely, that of being an artifact: Consider, "This piece of driftwood is a lovely piece of sculpture." Thus, to say of anything that it is a work of art is to commit oneself to the presence of *some* of these conditions. . . . If none of the conditions were present, if there were no criteria present for recognizing something as a work of art, we would not describe it as one. But, even so, no one of these or any collection of them is either necessary or sufficient.

The elucidation of the descriptive use of "Art" creates little difficulty. But the elucidation of the evaluative use does. For many, especially theorists, "This is a work of art" does more than describe; it also praises. Its conditions of utterance, therefore, include certain preferred properties or characteristics of art. I shall call these "criteria of evaluation." Consider a typical example of this evaluative use, the view according to which to say of something that it is a work of art is to imply that it is a *successful* harmonization of elements. Many of the honorific definitions of art and its sub-concepts are of this form. What is at stake here is that "Art" is construed as an evaluative term which is either identified with its criterion or justified in terms of it. "Art" is defined in terms of its evaluative property, e.g., successful harmonization. On such a view, to say "*X* is a work of art" is (1) to say something which is taken *to mean* "*X* is a successful harmonization" (e.g., "Art is significant form") or (2) to say something praiseworthy *on the basis* of its successful harmonization. Theorists are never clear if it is (1) or (2) which is being put forward. Most of them, concerned as they are with this evaluative use, formulate (2), i.e., that feature of art that *makes* it art in the praise-sense, and then go on to state (1), i.e., the definition of "Art" in terms of its art-making feature. And this is clearly to confuse the conditions under which we say something evaluatively with the meaning of what we say. . . .

There is nothing wrong with the evaluative use; in fact, there is good reason for using "Art" to praise. But what cannot be maintained is that theories of the evaluative use of "Art" are true and real definitions of the necessary and sufficient properties of art. Instead they are honorific definitions, pure and simple, in which "Art" has been redefined in terms of chosen criteria.

But what makes them—these honorific definitions—so supremely valuable is not their disguised linguistic recommendations; rather it is the *debates* over the reasons for changing the criteria of the concept of art which are built into the definitions. In each of the great theories of art, whether correctly understood as honorific definitions or incorrectly accepted as real definitions, what is of the utmost importance are the reasons proffered in the arguments for the respective theory, that is, the reasons given for the chosen or preferred criterion of excellence and evaluation. It is this perennial debate over these criteria of evaluation which makes the history of aesthetic theory the important study it is. . . .

Once we, as philosophers, understand this distinction between the formula and what lies behind it, it behooves us to deal generously with the traditional theories of art; because incorporated in every one of them is a debate over and argument for emphasizing or centering upon some particular feature of art that has been neglected or perverted. . . . What is central and must be articulated in all the theories are their debates over the reasons for excellence in art—debates over emotional depth, profound truths, natural beauty, exactitude, freshness of treatment, and so on, as criteria of evaluation—the whole of which converges on the perennial problems of what makes a work of art good. To understand the role of aesthetic theory is not to conceive it as definition, logically doomed to failure, but to read it as summaries of seriously made recommendations to attend in certain ways to certain features of art. ◣

REDEFINING ART

Weitz makes a strong case for antiessentialism, that is, the position that there is simply no essence to art. Given the tremendous variation among the arts and given that new endeavors and practices come along that are taken as art, it certainly seems reasonable to say (as Weitz does) that there simply are no necessary or sufficient features for art. Nevertheless, quite a few aestheticians have rejected Weitz's view. They have tended to do this for two broad reasons: (1) Some claim that the "family resemblance" view itself does not hold up to criticism. (2) Some claim that there are, indeed, conditions that characterize (if not outright define) art.

One philosopher who directly criticized Weitz was Maurice Mandelbaum. Mandelbaum pointed out that although some concepts are open, as Weitz said, they are not wide open! There might not be any necessary or sufficient conditions for something to be a game (or a chair or art), but surely it is not the case that anything and everything is a game (or a chair or art). Cats are not games and cupcakes are not chairs! There must be reasons for why some things are games and some things are not, even if we cannot say exactly what those reasons are and even if those reasons might change over time. Or, another way of saying this, there must be some conditions for some things to be games and other things not to be games, again, even if we cannot say exactly what those conditions are and even if those conditions change over time, so that we count certain new things that come along as games (and other new things that come along as nongames). So although it might be true that "art" is an open concept, it is not a wide-open concept without any constraints at all.

And Mandelbaum made a second point: family resemblances are not random. There are underlying causes for family resemblances. In the case of literal family resemblances (that is, looking like one's parents or siblings), those underlying causes are biological. To extend the notion of family resemblance, then, to art, said Mandelbaum, does not negate some possible underlying essence. Once again, there must be some reasons (conditions) or other for why some things are art and other things are not. We might not know what those reasons or conditions are, but that does not mean that there are none or that we could not at some point be able to identify them.

This point of claiming that there are underlying causes of family resemblances speaks to the broader issue of attempting definitions, including definitions of art. One way of attempting to define something is to look for conditions (such as properties or relations) that something must have. The technical term for this type of definition is *synchronic* definition. *Synchronic* simply means "at one time," and synchronic definition, as philosophers speak of it, connotes defining something by identifying conditions that are taken (at the time of the definition) to be invariant (in a sense, those conditions are frozen in time). So we might say that for something to be, say, a human, it must have a certain biological genetic structure and that is the case now and at any other time. Things are what they are. A second way of attempting to define something is what is called a *diachronic* definition. *Diachronic* means "across, or through, time." With this sort of definition, the conditions for something to fall under the definition might change over time. For example, biologists sometimes speak of classifying organisms and groups of organisms by reference to their evolutionary origins rather than by their particular physical or behavioral traits. Even though certain organisms, or groups of organisms, might appear physically to be similar to other organisms or groups, because of their evolutionary history, they might be classified quite differently. Likewise, some organisms or groups of organisms physically appear to be quite different from others, but they are, in fact, evolutionarily similar, having descended from a common ancestor. The point here is that, like classifications, definitions might be based on origin and lineage (that is, history) rather than on specific features or characteristics of things. Just as some biologists have argued that evolutionary criteria for classifications of organisms and groups of organisms are better criteria than overt physical features, so, too, some aestheticians have argued that diachronic definitions—also based on origins and lineage—are better than synchronic definitions with respect to understanding the nature of art. One person who argues for a diachronic definitional approach is Jerrold Levinson; selections from his "Defining Art Historically" appear on page 40.

Underlying Levinson's view is a history of recent art theory that focuses on the social, collective nature of art. As we have already noted several times, the wide diversity of arts and of the features of those arts makes it difficult, perhaps impossible, to identify defining features of art. If all we did in attempting to define art was to look at examples of artworks (including performances as instances of artworks), it appears that no useful definition would be forthcoming. This fact led a number of aestheticians to focus on the historical and social nature of art as the important basis for understanding and (they hoped) defining art.

Two especially well-known aestheticians who took this focus were George Dickie and Arthur Danto. Dickie proposed what he called the "institutional theory of art." Like Mandelbaum, Dickie rejected Weitz's view that the concept of family resemblance can help illuminate our understanding (and appreciation) of art. Resemblances and similarities, Dickie said, apply to anything and everything. That is, anything can be said to resemble pretty much anything else in some respect or other. (For instance, a cat resembles a chair in the sense that both have legs, that both can be found in someone's house, that both are physical objects, and in numerous other ways.) So looking for features of artworks, even "only" family resemblances, is not fruitful. Furthermore, some things are art only because we treat them as such. For instance, a piece of pottery might have been created merely as a vessel for carrying liquids, with no thought or intention of its being an artwork. Yet it could come to be treated as such by others. What makes something art, for Dickie, is that it came to be treated as such. As he put it, in the "classificatory sense" (that is, just describing and not evaluating), something is art if it is an artifact (in other words, created by someone) and if it has some aspects that the social institutions of the artworld have determined makes it art (in other words, it is treated as art by certain people). So it is the relation of being treated in certain ways by certain people that makes something art. A stack of Brillo boxes, if treated as art, then, is (or becomes) art; a stack of Brillo boxes, if not treated as art, is not art. It is the social relation that determines art, not any features of the thing itself.

Arthur Danto extended this view and spoke of the social, relational nature of art in terms of "the artworld." Like Dickie, Danto noted that how something was treated by certain people was fundamental to that thing's being art. However, there were always reasons why something was treated as art and something else was not, so simply being treated as art was not by itself explanatory. After all, we could always ask why this particular stack of Brillo boxes was treated as art and why that particular stack was not. For Danto, artworks have the features—the relational features—of (1) being about something and (2) being subject to interpretation. A stack of Brillo boxes in the grocery store is not about anything (or, perhaps, is only "about" being purchased so that someone makes a profit), whereas a stack of Brillo boxes placed on display in a gallery is about, say, the nature of mass culture or consumerism or commercial values. What makes something art, then, is a matter of social relationships and institutional practices, where "institutional" is understood as being shaped and determined by what is already connected with responding to things aesthetically.

It is against this background of seeing art as being defined via social and historical relations that Levinson proposes his own notion. His view is that art is a relation between thought and action. One of the important aspects of art that he sees missing in the institutional and artworld views is the role of the artist. Levinson sees the relation of thought and action in terms of the intention of individuals (that is, artists), but not in isolation; rather, those thoughts and actions are carried out in an institutional setting, where the intention "makes reference" to the history of art, and not just to the present artworld.

There is an analogy here to language. The nature of language seems to involve the intentions of someone, say, speaking, as well as the nature of the language independent of that speaker and the fact that language is used to communicate about the world. For example, if I say, "Happy Jack is sleeping," one component of the meaning is what I am intending to say. I might be intending to just inform you of something, or I might be intending to get you to be quiet. However, the meaning here cannot simply be a matter of what I intend because the words I use have meaning independent of me and my intentions. For example, I might intend to refer to an elm tree when I say, "Meet me under the elm tree in the park," but because I do not know much about trees, it might turn out that what I thought was an elm tree was actually a maple tree. So I intended to refer to a maple tree, but I spoke of an elm tree. If you waited at the elm and I waited at the maple, you would be correct to point out to me that I said "elm" and that "elm" refers to elms, not to maples. So linguistic meaning involves both what I mean and what the words (independent of me) mean. Although language and linguistic meaning are certainly social, communication involves speakers and the language that speakers speak. Likewise, for Levinson, the social relational nature of art involves both the intentions of artists and the social reality of what is treated as art. Unlike Dickie and Danto, however, Levinson emphasizes what he calls "to-regard-as-a-work-of-art." That is, a crucial aspect of what gives something status as an artwork is that it is regarded as art by the artist in the sense that it is intended to be connected to a lineage and history of art. This lineage and history are social, that is, they go beyond the purely private world of the artist, so there is still a fundamental social nature of art (just as a speaker speaks a public language that goes beyond his or her purely private intentions).

Toward the end of his remarks below, Levinson notes that defining art historically does not preclude the possibility of revolutionary art. Obviously, new styles and forms and whole new arts emerge, but, as he remarks, "to get a revolutionary mode of activity to *be* art it is necessary that its creator (or the creator's subsequent proxy) should consciously nod in the direction of past artistic activity," otherwise there is no reason to think of this new or revolutionary activity as art, as opposed to something else. That said, here is Levinson:

JERROLD LEVINSON, "DEFINING ART HISTORICALLY"*

The question of what makes something art is probably the most venerable in aesthetics. What is the artness of an artwork? Wherein does it reside? We would certainly like to know. We would certainly be interested to learn what ties to-gether Dickens's *Oliver Twist*, Tallis's *Spem in alium*, Flavin's *Pink and Gold*, Balanchine's *Variations for a Door and a Sigh,* Wilson and Glass's *Einstein on the Beach*, the Parthenon, and countless other unknown and unsung objects under the common banner of art. After rejecting the many proposals made by philosophers from Plato to the present on grounds of narrowness, tendentious-ness, inflexibility, vagueness, or circularity, one would appear to be left with no answer to the question at all, and perhaps a suspicion that it is unanswerable. Nevertheless, the question has been taken up in recent years and given a new sort of answer: the institutional theory of art, adumbrated by Arthur Danto and propounded explicitly by George Dickie. In short, the theory is that artworks are artworks because they occupy a certain place, which they must be given, in a certain institution, that of Art.

I

In this essay I would like to begin to develop an alternative to the institutional theory of art, albeit one that is clearly inspired by it. What I will retain from that theory is the crucial idea that artwork is not an intrinsic exhibited property of a thing, but rather a matter of being related in the right way to human activity and thought. However, I propose to construe this relation solely in terms of the *intention* of an *independent individual* (or individuals)—as opposed to an overt *act* (that of conferring the status of a candidate for application) performed in an *institutional setting* constituted by many individuals—where the intention makes reference (either transparently or opaquely) to the *history of art* (what art has been) as opposed to that murky and somewhat exclusive institution, the *artworld*. The core of my proposal will be an account of what it is to regard-as-a-work-of-art, an account that gives this an essential historicity. It is this which will do the work in my theory which the notion of artworld is supposed to do in the institutional theory. That art is necessarily backward-looking (though in some cases not consciously so) is a fact that the definition of art must

British Journal of Aesthetics 19 (1979): 232–250.

recognize. To ignore it is to miss the only satisfying explanation of the unity of art across time and of its inherently continuous evolution—the manner in which art of a given moment must *involve*, as opposed to merely *follow*, that which preceded it. . . .

III

. . . My idea is roughly this: a work of art is a thing intended for regard-as-a-work-of-art, regard in any of the ways works of art existing prior to it have been correctly regarded. In the absence of any identifiable "aesthetic attitude," how else can "regard-as-a-work-of-art" be understood? Obviously, in adopting this proposal we are not analyzing art completely in nonart terms. Rather, what we are doing is explicating what it is for an object to be art at a given time with reference to the body of past art taken as unproblematic. But what it is for a thing to be art at any time can eventually be exhibited in this manner, by starting with the present and working backward. New art is art because of this relation to past art, art of the recent past is art because of this relation to art of the not-so-recent past, art of the not-so-recent past is art because of this relation to art of the distant past . . . until one arrives presumably at the *ur*-arts of our tradition—those to which the mantle of *art* can be initially attached, but which are art *not* in virtue of any relation to preceding objects. . . .

The concept of artwork is unlike that of other sorts of things that surround us—e.g., cars, chairs, persons. *Artwork* seems to lack antecedently defined limits in terms of intrinsic features, even flexible ones—as opposed to car, chair, person. There is no question of determining in all cases that something is art by weighing it against some archetype or other. The *only* clue one has is the particular, concrete, and multifarious population that art has acquired at any point (that is, assuming, as I do, the nebulousness and/or inessentiality of that institution, the artworld). It appears almost obvious, then, that for a prospective object to count as art must be for it to be related in some way to those objects that have already been decided or determined. For a thing to be art it must be linked by its creator to the repository of art existing at the time, as opposed to being aligned by him with some abstracted template of required characteristics. What I am saying is that currently the concept of art has no content beyond what art *has been*. It is this content that must figure in a successful definition. . . .

IV

A definition that preserves my basic idea, but adds certain qualifications, is the following:

(*I*) X is an artwork = df [that is, "by definition"] X is an object that a person or persons having the appropriate proprietary right over X, nonpassingly intends for regard-as-a-work-of-art, i.e., regard in any way (or ways) in which prior artworks are or were correctly (or standardly) regarded.

Several comments on this initial definition are in order. First, there is the phrase "intends for." This is to be understood as short for "makes, appropriates or conceives for the purpose of," so as to comprehend fashioned, found, and conceptual art. Second, there is the notion that the intent must be fairly stable ("nonpassingly"), as opposed to merely transient. In other words, it is not enough to turn an object into art that one momentarily considers it for regard-as-a-work-of-art. Third, I have construed regard-as-a-work-of-art as equivalent to ways of regarding past art only in so far as they are or were *correct* (or *standard*) ways. If one omits this qualification, or appeals instead to *common* ways of regard, or even *rewarding* ways of regard, the definition will go awry. . . .

Fourth, the definition includes a proprietary-right condition. What this amounts to is basically *ownership*—you cannot "artify" what you do not own and thus have no right to dispose of. All your intentions will not avail in such a case, because another person's intention, that of the owner, has priority over yours. . . .

V

The definition presented in the preceding section conveys in a fairly perspicuous fashion what I believe it now means for something to be an artwork. However, at the expense of some perspicuity but in the name of greater precision and flexibility, I offer a second definition that makes explicit the time-dependence of the status of "artwork," clarifies the interpretation of "prior artworks," and indicates more exactly what sort of definition of art I am giving.

(I_t) X is an artwork at t = df X is an object of which it is true at t that some person or persons having the appropriate proprietary right over X, nonpassingly intends (or intended) X for regard-as-a-work-of-art—i.e., regard in any way (or ways) in which artworks existing prior to t are or were correctly (or standardly) regarded.

An object can thus be an artwork at one time and not another. This definition recognizes that an object may not be an artwork from the moment of its physical creation, but may only become an artwork even subsequent to the death of its creator. . . .

I can almost see readers shake their heads at this point and ask: But does this definition *really tell* me what art is? Doesn't it seem that I have to *know* what is art in order to use it? In fact, isn't the definition simply *circular*, in that it defines art in terms of art? This response is perfectly understandable, but it is nonetheless mistaken. True, there is something reflexive about the definition, in that it exhibits art as essentially referring to itself. But to eliminate this reflexiveness would be to eviscerate the term "art" of the only universal constant it now retains. If artworks at one time are essentially intentionally related to artworks at an earlier time, then on the assumption that definitions attempt to give essences, how could a definition of art fail to explicate artworks—to put it bluntly—in terms of artworks? Thus the *appearance* of circularity.

But, strictly speaking, I_t is *not* circular. What it does is define the *concept: being art at a given time* by reference to the *actual body of things* that are art prior to that time. True, one cannot tell what counts as art at *t* without its being granted what things count as art prior to *t*—but this is in fact just the way art itself works. Furthermore, and this also conforms to the reality of art, to the extent that it is unclear what objects *prior to t* are artworks, it will be equally unclear which objects *at t* count as art. True, one cannot use the definition to tell, all at once, what has, does, and will count as art at all times, but this is because the applicability of "art" at any stage is always tied to its concrete, historical realization at that stage. That the definition is not circular if properly understood can be seen by reflecting that one doesn't have to know what "artwork at *t*" *means* in order for I_t to *tell* you; one only has to grant that there is a set of things which are artworks prior to *t*—*whatever* they are and *whatever* that (viz., "artwork") might mean.

The last point suggests another way of expressing the analysis of art that I offer, a way I think that removes any lingering suspicion of circularity. Basically, what I have proposed is the *meaning* of "art now" involves the extension of "art previously"—that the *meaning* of "art at *t*" is to be given in terms of the extension of "art prior to *t*." Formulating a variant of I_t to make this explicit, we have:

(I'_t) X is an artwork at *t* = df X is an object of which it is true at *t* that some person or persons, having the appropriate proprietary right over *X*, nonpassingly intends (or intended) *X* for regard-as-a-work-of-art—i.e., regard in any way (or ways) in which objects in the extension of "artwork" prior to *t* are or were correctly (or standardly) regarded.

It is clear that the *meaning* of "artwork" is not involved in the righthand side of this definition, but only its past *extension* at some point. Thus, I maintain that I'_t or I_t captures our present concept of art—and without presupposing that concept in doing so.

VI

On the view I have presented, which makes art a necessarily backward-looking affair, one may wonder how the *revolutionary* aspect of art can be accommodated. Surely, one might say, if art is continually looking to the rear, how can it change or advance? Won't it always remain the same? To begin to answer this let me first distinguish revolutionary from merely new or original art. A new artwork is simply one nonidentical to any previously existing artwork. An original artwork is a new one significantly different in structure or aesthetic properties from any previously existing artwork. The production of original art could continue indefinitely without there being any additions to the stock of ways in which artworks are regarded. But by a revolutionary artwork I mean one for which any of the past ways of approaching art seems inadequate, inappropriate, pointless, or impossible; a revolutionary artwork appears to be ultimately calling for a kind of regard which is totally *unprecedented*. It is plainly only revolutionary art that poses any difficulty for my analysis.

Art that is revolutionary because it demands or requires a new approach to yield up its fruits to spectators is not per se a problem. A problem only arises for artworks—e.g., Dadaist ones—which are *intended* as revolutionary by their artists, that is to say, intended for treatment in a manner completely distinct from what has gone before. (Whether all intentionally revolutionary art is thereby revolutionary *simpliciter* is a complicated question I will not go into here.) Two strategies suggest themselves for reconciling my proposal to this important and characteristic mode of art making. One is to maintain that although consciously revolutionary artists desire that eventually their objects will be dealt with in unprecedented ways, to make them *art* they must initially direct their audiences to take them (or try taking them) in some way that art *has* been taken—otherwise, what can we make of the claim that they have given us *art*, as opposed to something else? The art-making intention of consciously revolutionary artists may thus have to be a covertly disingenuous one, somewhat along these lines: "My object is for regarding in any way artworks have been regarded in the past (but with the expectation that this will prove frustrating or unrewarding, thus prodding the spectator to adopt some other point of view—this being my ultimate intention)." The secondary intention embodies the true *aim* of such art, but the primary intention must be present to make it *art* at all.

A second strategy for dealing with this issue perhaps does less violence to the outward stance of the consciously revolutionary artist. This requires a liberalization of what regard-as-a-work-of-art amounts to. Instead of construing it as restricted to past correct ways of regarding artworks, broaden it to include completely unheralded types of regard so long as one is directed to adopt such regards in conscious opposition to those past correct ways. The liberalized version of regard-as-a-work-of-art then reads as follows: regard in any way (or ways) in which prior artworks are or were correctly (or standardly) regarded, or *in some other way or in contrast to and against the* background of those ways. (Call this "regard-as-a-work-of-art*.") If this second strategy is adopted, one simply substitutes "regard-as-a-work-of-art*" for "regard-as-a-work-of-art" in I, I_t, and I'_t to get definitions adequate for revolutionary art. Whereas the idea of the first strategy was that self-aware revolutionary artists must on one level intend the existing correct art regards, freeing them to intend on another level some entirely new regard, the present strategy does not insist that they should directly intend the existing ways at all, but only that they should project the new way *in relation* (albeit antagonistic relation) to its predecessors. If they fail to do even that, I think there are no grounds on which one could deny that they fail to make art. Of course it is open at that point for some other member of the art community, assuming they have the proprietary right, to appropriate the would-be artist's work at a later date with the right intention, and so bring it into the sphere of art. The point is, to get a revolutionary mode of activity to *be* art it is necessary that its creator (or the creator's subsequent proxy) should consciously nod in the direction of past artistic activity. . . .

IX

The concept of art has certainly changed over time. There is no doubt of that. It is thus worth emphasizing in this final section that my analysis is aimed just at capturing what the concept of art is *at present*—that is, what it *now* means for an object created *at any time* (past, present, or future) to count as art at that time, rather than what it meant at the time of the object's creation. . . .

I have already noted that the historical definition of art provides a powerful and direct explanation of the inherent unity and continuity of the development of art. In short, for something to be an artwork at any time is for it to be intentionally related to artworks that precede it—no more and no less. And the historical definition, if accepted, helps to dispel the lingering effects of the so-called "intentional fallacy" understood as a claim about the irrelevance of artists' intentions to correct or full appreciation of their works. For if artists' intentions are recognized as central to the difference between art and nonart, they are not so likely to be offhandedly declared irrelevant to an understanding of artworks once seen as so constituted. In particular, the historical definition indicates the overwhelming importance for appreciation of those past artworks/genres/ ways of regard/modes of treatment which artists connect to their current productions through their art-making intentions.

The historical definition of art also casts a useful light on the fact that in art anything goes, but not everything works. The reason anything goes is that there are no clear limits to the sorts of things people may seriously intend us to regard-as-a-work-of-art. The reason not everything works is that regarding-something-as-a-work-of-art necessarily involves bringing the past of art to bear on what is being offered as art in the present. That the present object and past regards will mesh is not guaranteed. The interaction of the two sometimes satisfies immediately, sometimes only after an interval. Sometimes we are shocked and unsettled, but recover and are illuminated. Sometimes we are forcibly impelled to adopt new modes of regard, leaving old ones aside. But sometimes we are simply bewildered, bored, bothered—or all three—and in a manner that is never transcended. In such cases we have artworks, all right, but such works don't work.

In conclusion, let me say that I do not mean to deny that there is a common practice of art, and a group of people bound together under that umbrella, nor do I deny that artworks need to be understood in relation to their cultural situation. What I do deny is that the institutions of art in a society are essential to art, and that an analysis of arthood must therefore involve them. The making of art is primary; the social frameworks and conventions that grow up around it are not. While the sociology of art is of great interest, the essence of art does not lie there but instead in art's relation to its contingent history. The theory I offer sketches in its main outlines what this relation is. ◣

ART AND EXPERIENCE

Levinson's view of art as defined historically emphasizes artists and their intentions as being fundamental to what makes something art. This, of course, does not neglect the importance of artworks (whether they are objects, such as a painting, or performances, such as a dance), because, for Levinson, there is something that is meant to be regarded-as-a-work-of-art. However, the regarding-as-a-work-of-art does point to an important aspect of thinking about the nature of art, namely, the question of *what* it is that is being defined. As has already been noted, many philosophers have offered suggestions or candidates for the kinds of features (whether properties or relations) that best define or characterize art. But they have done so, as philosophers like to say, *simplicatur*—that is, they have tried to define "art" independent of anything and everything else. Other philosophers have said that this approach is mistaken, that the concept of art (as well as every other concept) is not independent of anything and everything else. Rather than asking, What is art? it is better to ask, What is art as opposed to X? This is a better question, they say, because what we mean by art varies depending upon what we compare or contrast it to. As an analogy, suppose we ask someone, "Have you read all the Harry Potter books?" Although this seems like a very straightforward, simple question, answering it might depend upon what is being compared or contrasted. For instance, if the person had not actually looked at the pages of the books but had listened to all of the books on audiotape or had heard someone reading them aloud, then how should he or she answer that question? The answer would be no if the question meant was, Have you read all the Harry Potter books as opposed to listening to them on tape? But the answer would be yes if the question meant was, Have you read all the Harry Potter books as opposed to having avoided or ignored them, and so you know their details firsthand? Another (actual) example is the infamous bank-robber Willie Sutton's answer to the question of why he robbed banks: "That's where the money is." Of course, the questioner meant, Why do you rob banks as opposed to doing something else (say, writing philosophy books)? But Willie took the question to mean, Why do you rob banks as opposed to robbing other places (say, professors' offices)? The point is that meaningful questions need to have points of comparison or contrast in order for answers to be informative. With respect to the current issue, the point is that asking what art is does not yield informative answers if asked simplicatur. The way philosophers put it is that we need a comparison (or contrast) class when asking about something. We need to ask, What is art as opposed to X? We might well get different answers to the questions What is art as opposed to science? and What is art as opposed to crafts?

Still, even by refining the question about the nature of art by including some comparison or contrast class, we are still asking about *what* it is to be art. This is, in effect, the metaphysical issue of the nature of art. In other words, here we are focused on what it is that is being defined. There are also, of course, epistemological and axiological issues about defining art. The epistemological issues—*how* art is to be defined or how we can know the nature of art—certainly overlap with the metaphysical ones. How are we to know the nature of art? Some philosophers have taken our knowledge of art to be intuitive. They have spoken of an immediate awareness of artistic features of things. For example, the eighteenth-century philosopher David Hume spoke of a sense of taste, meaning artistic or aesthetic taste. Just as we have the senses of vision and touch and smell, we have a sense of aesthetics. Another eighteenth-century philosopher, Immanuel Kant, spoke of humans' natural sense of the sublime. This gets at the topic of aesthetic experience, and we will delve more into this issue in Chapter 5, but for now the point is that one answer to how we know what we do (or at least why we believe what we do) about the nature of art is intuitively.

Other sorts of epistemological questions about the nature of art include whether or not there is knowledge of art in a cognitive sense. That is, are there facts that can be known empirically, cognitively, that would determine, or even be relevant to determining, whether or not something is art? Consider Figures 2.1 and 2.2. They both seem to be instances of art. However, Figure 2.1 was created by an elephant (2.2 was created by a human). Is (knowing) this fact relevant to saying whether these works are artworks?

In addition to metaphysical and epistemological issues about the nature

2.1 *Blue Winston* (by an elephant). Courtesy David Boersema.

2.2 *Splatter Paint Party* by Katherine Scrimshaw. Courtesy Katherine Scrimshaw.

of (defining) art, there are axiological, or value, issues. Perhaps the most basic axiological question about defining art is, Why define it? That is, why does it matter to have a definition of art? There are concerns that immediately arise when asking this question. For instance, as was noted above, this question really needs to be phrased as, Why define art as opposed to X? This can mean either asking why we should define art as opposed to defining something else (say, science) or as asking why we should define art as opposed to doing something else with art.

So why define art as opposed to defining something else (again, say, science)? Why does it matter to have a definition of art in order to distinguish it from science? In Chapter 7 we will look at relations between art and science, so here let's change this question and ask instead, Why does it matter to have a definition of art in order to distinguish it from crafts? In what contexts and for what reasons is it important to distinguish art from crafts? Why is such as distinction important? Who decides what the distinction is and why it is important?

Of course, there are many answers to these questions. It might be important to distinguish art (or fine art) from, say, crafts because of structural features of artworks. A symphonic piece composed by Beethoven, for instance, is structurally much more complex than a folk tune composed by Billy Bob, the local balladeer. A choreographed ballet requires much greater training (just at a physical level) than a break-dance. So it might be that having a definitional distinction reflects different aspects and features of (fine) art and crafts.

As for the second meaning of the question (that is, why we should define art as opposed to doing something else with art, such as simply appreciating it), there, too, many answers can and have been offered. One answer is that defining art leads to understanding. If the term *art* has any meaning, we should be able to say what it is, and that includes being able to identify (define) what it is. Related to this, but conceptually separate, is the answer that defining art has social value. At a very mundane level, for instance, we might want to provide funding for art teachers. Without a definition, or at least some sense of what art is (and what it is not), how would we know what sorts of projects or activities to fund?

The point here is not to actually provide answers to these questions or to resolve the issues that have been raised. Rather, the point has been to indicate some of the sorts of metaphysical, epistemological, and axiological questions and issues that arise in the context of considering the nature of art and what is involved in attempting to define art.

Against the background of these various concerns that have been raised (such as needing a comparison or contrast class and asking about the value and purpose of defining art), the twentieth-century philosopher John Dewey remarked that most attempts by philosophers to define art were attempts that focused on art as though it were abstracted from the rest of human life and experience. Most attempts at defining art, he claimed, presumed and perpetuated the notion of "fine art," artworks that are encountered in museums or concert halls. Although Levinson wrote after Dewey died, his essay would be an example of what Dewey thought was mistaken about the usual attempts to define art. For Dewey, art is a process; it is an interaction between an organism (he spoke only of humans here) and its environments, that is, as we will see, art is experience.

Underlying this claim that art is experience is Dewey's overall view that organisms exist in various environments. Among them, we live in physical environments (for example, in certain geographical or climate conditions), cultural environments (for example, in a given political or religious context), historical environments (for example, in a time whose communication technology makes our lives different from those of people living a hundred years ago), and so on. People must respond and interact with those environments in order to survive and flourish. We respond in many ways, but fundamental among those ways is to develop habits of action and beliefs and values. We learn that certain behaviors lead to certain consequences. But our interactions are not merely passive; humans in particular create and change their environments via their actions and interactions. For Dewey, to understand human action we need to see that it arises in the context of "bumping into the world" and interacting. In a word, it is experience. Experience is a natural process and, so the various sorts of human endeavors and institutions must be understood as responses to our engaging in our environments. The origin of language, for instance, is, for Dewey, a natural response to the need for communication and the ability to conceptualize beyond what is immediately present. (We can talk about things that happened in the past, for example, or things that are abstract or fictional.) Likewise, the origin of political systems and institutions is, for Dewey, a natural response to the need for security and well-being.

The origin of art, for Dewey, is likewise a natural response to our conditions in our various environments. Art is very much like other aspects of human life. Not only are there features of art that are like features of other human interactions—for instance, patterns and rhythms and forms—but also art is a basic way of creating meaning and shaping those very environments in which we live. That art is a natural human action and interaction is evident from the fact that it is universal across time and culture. No culture that we know of lacks arts or notions of aesthetics. We all know of cave paintings from prehistoric times; artistic rituals are found in cultures and societies across the world.

Although art, for Dewey, is one sort of experience among many, it is a particular sort. As he puts it, art is "an experience." All experiences, he said, are immediate, but they also go beyond what is immediate. All experiences involve both a principle of continuity and a principle of interaction. That is, no experience happens in isolation. The experiences I have today are related to (perhaps directly caused by) the experiences I had yesterday, and they will be related to the experiences I will have tomorrow. There is a continuity of our experiences. In addition, no one lives in a vacuum; my experiences are related to those of many other people. Continuity and interaction are features of all experiences, but what is especially characteristic of artistic aesthetic experiences is that they are what Dewey called "consummatory." That is, with an aesthetic experience, there is a sense of immediate consummation, or fulfillment. We speak, then, said Dewey, not just of experiencing but, rather, of having "an experience." We separate off, so to speak, certain experiences as being particularly meaningful. So we use such expressions as "having a sublime experience" or "a profound experience" or "a moving experience." These are artistic aesthetic experiences, for Dewey, and this is why he remarks, "The enemies of the esthetic are neither the practical nor the intellectual. They are the humdrum; slackness of loose ends; submission to convention in practice and intellectual procedure." In the reading below, Dewey insists that to understand this experiential and interactive nature of art, we must see art as a process. Art is a verb.

JOHN DEWEY, *ART AS EXPERIENCE*[*]

By one of the ironic perversities that often attend the course of affairs, the existence of the works of art upon which formation of an esthetic theory depends has become an obstruction to theory about them. For one reason, these works are products that exist externally and physically. In common conception, the work of art is often identified with the building, book, painting, or statue in its existence apart from human experience. Since the actual work of art is what the product does with and in experience, the result is not favorable to understanding. In addition, the very perfection of some of these products, the prestige they possess because of a long history of unquestioned admiration, creates conventions that get in the way of fresh insight. When an art product once attains classic status, it somehow becomes isolated from the human conditions under which it was brought into being and from the human consequences it engenders in actual life-experience.

When artistic objects are separated from both conditions of origin and operation in experience, a wall is built around them that renders almost opaque their general significance, with which esthetic theory deals. Art is remitted to a separate realm, where it is cut off from that association with the materials and aims of every other form of human effort, undergoing, and achievement. A primary task is thus imposed upon one who undertakes to write upon the philoso-

[*]New York: Minton, Balch, 1934. Pages 3–4, 10–12, 22, 35, 37–38, 40–41, 46–48, 56–57.

phy of the fine arts. This task is to restore continuity between the refined and intensified forms of experience that are works of art and the everyday events, doings, and sufferings that are universally recognized to constitute experience.
Mountain peaks do not float unsupported; they do not even just rest upon the
earth. They *are* the earth in one of its manifest operations. It is the business of
those who are concerned with the theory of the earth, geographers and geologists, to make this fact evident in its various implications. The theorist who
would deal philosophically with fine art has a like task to accomplish.

If one is willing to grant this position, even if only by way of temporary experiment, he will see that there follows a conclusion at first sight surprising. In
order to understand the meaning of artistic products, we have to forget them for
a time, to turn aside from them and have recourse to the ordinary forces and
conditions of experience that we do not usually regard as esthetic. We must arrive at the theory of art by means of a detour. For theory is concerned with understanding, insight, not without exclamations of admiration, and stimulation of
that emotional outburst often called appreciation. It is quite possible to enjoy
flowers in their colored form and delicate fragrance without knowing anything
about plants theoretically. But if one sets out to *understand* the flowering of
plants, he is committed to finding out something about the interactions of soil,
air, water and sunlight that condition the growth of plants. . . .

My purpose . . . is to indicate that *theories* which isolate art and its appreciation by placing them in a realm of their own, disconnected from other modes of
experiencing, are not inherent in the subject-matter but arise because of specifiable extraneous conditions. Embedded as they are in institutions and in habits
of life, these conditions operate effectively because they work so unconsciously. Then the theorist assumes they are embedded in the nature of things.
Nevertheless, the influence of these conditions is not confined to theory. As I
have already indicated, it deeply affects the practice of living, driving away esthetic perceptions that are necessary ingredients of happiness, or reducing them
to the level of compensating transient pleasurable excitations.

Even to readers who are adversely inclined to what has been said, the implications of the statements that have been made may be useful in defining the nature of the problem: that of recovering the continuity of esthetic experience
with normal processes of living. The understanding of art and of its role in civilization is not furthered by setting out with eulogies of it nor by occupying ourselves exclusively at the outset with great works of art recognized as such. The
comprehension which theory essays will be arrived at by a detour; by going
back to experience of the common or mill run of things to discover the esthetic

quality such experience possesses. Theory can start with and from acknowl-edged works of art only when the esthetic is already compartmentalized, or only when works of art are set in a niche apart instead of being celebrations, recognized as such, of the things of ordinary experience. Even a crude experi-ence, if authentically an experience, is more fit to give a clue to the intrinsic na-ture of esthetic experience than is an object already set apart from any other mode of experience. Following this clue we can discover how the work of art develops and accentuates what is characteristically valuable in things of every-day enjoyment. The art product will then be seen to issue from the latter, when the full meaning of ordinary experience is expressed, as dyes come out of coal tar products when they receive special treatment.

Many theories about art already exist. If there is justification for proposing yet another philosophy of the esthetic, it must be found in a new mode of ap-proach. Combinations and permutations among existing theories can easily be brought forth by those so inclined. But, to my mind, the trouble with existing theories is that they start from a ready-made compartmentalization, or from a conception of art that "spiritualizes" it out of connection with the objects of concrete experience. The alternative, however, to such spiritualization is not a degrading and Philistinish materialization of works of fine art, but a conception that discloses the way in which these works idealize qualities found in common experience. Were works of art placed in a directly human context in popular es-teem, they would have a much wider appeal than they can have when pigeon-hole theories of art win general acceptance.

A conception of fine art that sets out from its connection with discovered qualities of ordinary experience will be able to indicate the factors and forces that favor the normal development of common human activities into matters of artistic value. It will also be able to point out those conditions that arrest its nor-mal growth. Writers on esthetic theory often raise the question of whether es-thetic philosophy can aid in cultivation of esthetic appreciation. The question is a branch of the general theory of criticism, which, it seems to me, fails to ac-complish its full office if it does not indicate what to look for and what to find in concrete esthetic objects. But, in any case, it is safe to say that a philosophy of art is sterilized unless it makes us aware of the function of art in relation to other modes of experience, and unless it indicates why this function is so inade-quately realized, and unless it suggests the conditions under which the office would be successfully performed.

The comparison of the emergence of works of art out of ordinary experi-ences to the refining of raw materials into valuable products may seem to some unworthy, if not an actual attempt to reduce works of art to the status of articles manufactured for commercial purposes. The point, however, is that no amount of ecstatic eulogy of finished works can of itself assist the understanding or the generation of such works. Flowers can be enjoyed without knowing about the interactions of soil, air, moisture, and seeds of which they are the result. But they cannot be *understood* without taking just these interactions into account— and theory is a matter of understanding. Theory is concerned with discovering the nature of the production of works of art and of their enjoyment in perception. How is it that the everyday making of things grows into that form of making which is genuinely artistic? How is it that our everyday enjoyment of scenes and situations develops into the peculiar satisfaction that attends the experience which is emphatically esthetic? These are the questions theory must answer. The answers cannot be found, unless we are willing to find the germs and roots in matters of experience that we do not currently regard as esthetic. Having discovered these active seeds, we may follow the course of their growth into the highest forms of finished and refined art. . . .

Experience is the result, the sign, and the reward of that interaction of organism and environment which, when it is carried to the full, is a transformation of interaction into participation and communication. . . . Experience occurs continuously, because the interaction of live creatures and environing conditions is involved in the very process of living. Under conditions of resistance and conflict, aspects and elements of the self and the world that are implicated in this interaction qualify experience with emotions and ideas so that conscious intent emerges. Oftentimes, however, the experience had is inchoate. Things are experienced but not in such a way that they are composed into *an* experience. There is distraction and dispersion; what we observe and what we think, what we desire and what we get, are at odds with each other. We put our hands to the plow and turn back; we start and then we stop, not because the experience has reached the end for the sake of which it was initiated but because of extraneous interruptions or of inner lethargy.

In contrast with such experience, we have *an* experience when the material experienced runs its course to fulfillment. Then and then only is it integrated within and demarcated in the general stream of experience from other experiences. A piece of work is finished in a way that is satisfactory; a problem receives its solution; a game is played through; a situation, whether that of eating a meal, playing a game of chess, carrying on a conversation, writing a book, or taking part in a political campaign, is so rounded out that its close is a consummation and not a cessation. Such an experience is a whole and carries with it its own individualizing quality and self-sufficiency. It is *an* experience.

Philosophers, even empirical philosophers, have spoken for the most part of experience at large. Idiomatic speech, however, refers to experiences each of which is singular, having its own beginning and end. For life is no uniform uninterrupted march or flow. It is a thing of histories, each with its own plot, its own inception and movement toward its close, each having its own particular rhythmic movement; each with its own unrepeated quality pervading it throughout. A flight of stairs, mechanical as it is, proceeds by individualized steps, not by undifferentiated progression, and an inclined plane is at least marked off from other things by abrupt discreteness. . . .

We say of an experience of thinking that we reach or draw a conclusion. Theoretical formulation of the process is often made in such terms as to conceal effectually the similarity of "conclusion" to the consummating phase of every developing integral experience. These formulations apparently take their cue from the separate propositions that are premises and the proposition that is the conclusion as they appear on the printed page. The impression is derived that there are first two independent and ready-made entities that are then manipulated so as to give rise to a third. In fact, in an experience of thinking, premises emerge only as a conclusion becomes manifest. The experience, like that of watching a storm reach its height and gradually subside, is one of continuous movement of subject-matters. Like the ocean in the storm, there are a series of waves; suggestions reaching out and being broken in a clash, or being carried onwards by a cooperative wave. If a conclusion is reached, it is that of a movement of anticipation and cumulation, one that finally comes to completion. A "conclusion" is no separate and independent thing; it is the consummation of a movement.

Hence *an* experience of thinking has its own esthetic quality. It differs from those experiences that are acknowledged to be esthetic, but only in its materials. The material of the fine arts consists of qualities; that of experience having intellectual conclusion are signs or symbols having no intrinsic quality of their own, but standing for things that may in another experience be qualitatively experienced. The difference is enormous. It is one reason why the strictly intellectual art will never be popular as music is popular. Nevertheless, the experience itself has a satisfying emotional quality because it possesses internal integration and fulfillment reached through ordered and organized movement. This artistic structure may be immediately felt. In so far, it is esthetic. What is even more important is that not only is this quality a significant motive in undertaking intellectual inquiry and in keeping it honest, but that no intellectual activity is an integral event (is *an* experience), unless it is rounded out with this quality. Without it, thinking is inconclusive. In short, esthetic cannot be sharply marked off from intellectual experience since the latter must bear an esthetic stamp to be itself complete. . . .

The enemies of the esthetic are neither the practical nor the intellectual. They are the humdrum; slackness of loose ends; submission to convention in practice and intellectual procedure. Rigid abstinence, coerced submission, tightness on one side and dissipation, incoherence and aimless indulgence on the other, are deviations in opposite directions from the unity of an experience. Some such considerations perhaps induced Aristotle to invoke the "mean proportional" as the proper designation of what is distinctive of both virtue and the esthetic. He was formally correct. "Mean" and "proportion" are, however, not self-explanatory, nor to be taken over in a prior mathematical sense, but are properties belonging to an experience that has a developing movement toward its own consummation. . . .

I have tried to show [here] that the esthetic is no intruder in experience from without, whether by way of idle luxury or transcendent ideality, but that it is the clarified and intensified development of traits that belong to every normally complete experience. This fact I take to be the only secure basis upon which esthetic theory can build. It remains to suggest some of the implications of the underlying fact. . . .

Art denotes a process of doing or making. This is as true of fine as of technological art. Art involves molding of clay, chipping of marble, casting of bronze, laying on of pigments, construction of buildings, singing of songs, playing of instruments, enacting roles on the stage, going through rhythmic movements in the dance. Every art does something with some physical material, the body or something outside the body, with or without the use of intervening tools, and with a view to production of something visible, audible, or tangible. So marked is the active or "doing" phase of art, that the dictionaries usually define it in terms of skilled action, ability in execution. The *Oxford Dictionary* illustrates by a quotation from John Stuart Mill: "Art is an endeavor after perfection in execution" while Matthew Arnold calls it "pure and flawless workmanship."

The word "esthetic" refers, as we have already noted, to experience as appreciative, perceiving, and enjoying. It denotes the consumer's rather than the producer's standpoint. It is Gusto, taste; and, as with cooking, overt skillful action is on the side of the cook who prepares, while taste is on the side of the consumer, as in gardening there is a distinction between the gardener who plants and tills and the householder who enjoys the finished product. . . .

Craftsmanship to be artistic in the final sense must be "loving"; it must care deeply for the subject matter upon which skill is exercised. A sculptor comes to mind whose busts are marvelously exact. It might be difficult to tell in the presence of a photograph of one of them and of a photograph of the original which was of the person himself. For virtuosity they are remarkable. But one doubts whether the maker of the busts had an experience of his own that he was concerned to have those share who look at his products. To be truly artistic, a work must also be esthetic—that is, framed for enjoyed receptive perception. Constant observation is, of course, necessary for the maker while he is producing. But if his perception is not also esthetic in nature, it is a colorless and cold recognition of what has been done, used as a stimulus to the next step in a process that is essentially mechanical.

In short, art, in its form, unites the very same relation of doing and undergoing, outgoing and incoming energy, that makes an experience to be an experience. Because of elimination of all that does not contribute to mutual organization of the factors of both action and reception into one another, and because of selection of just the aspects and traits that contribute to their interpenetration of each other, the product is a work of esthetic art. Man whittles, carves, sings, dances, gestures, molds, draws and paints. The doing or making is artistic when the perceived result is of such a nature that *its* qualities *as perceived* have controlled the question of production. The act of producing that is directed by intent to produce something that is enjoyed in the immediate experience of perceiving has qualities that a spontaneous or uncontrolled activity does not have. The artist embodies in himself the attitude of the perceiver while he works. . . .

The *form* of the whole is therefore present in every member. Fulfilling, consummating, are continuous functions, not mere ends, located at one place only. An engraver, painter, or writer is in process of completing at every stage of his work. He must at each point retain and sum up what has gone before as a whole and with reference to a whole to come. Otherwise there is no consistency and no security in his successive acts. The series of doings in the rhythm of experience give variety and movement; they save the work from monotony and useless repetitions. The undergoings are the corresponding elements in the rhythm, and they supply unity; they save the work from the aimlessness of a mere succession of excitations. An object is peculiarly and dominantly esthetic, yielding the enjoyment characteristic of esthetic perception, when the factors that determine anything which can be called *an* experience are lifted high above the threshold of perception and are made manifest for their own sake. ◣

Questions for Discussion

1. Is a stack of Brillo boxes in a grocery store art? Why or what not? Is Warhol's display art? If it is, why?

2. Can a painting by an elephant be art? Why or why not?

3. Is Weitz correct that art is an open concept? Is he correct, on the assumption it is an open concept, that it is in principle indefinable? If he is correct, then how can the concept of art have any meaning? What is being referred to when we speak of art?

4. Does Levinson's view of the nature of art depend upon an artist's intentions being a necessary condition for something to be art? If it does, is he correct? Are a person's intentions sufficient to make something art? Does Levinson's view presuppose that we already have a definition, or at least an understanding, of what art is in order to say that there is the intention to regard-as-a-work-of-art?

5. What exactly does it mean when Dewey says that art is experience? Assuming it means more than (or something different from) saying art is performance, what does it mean? Does his view imply that a person's intentions are necessary for an experience to be art? That is, could art as experience include someone's having an artistic aesthetic experience without intending to? Does his view imply that one could fail to have an artistic aesthetic experience if one tried to?

THE ARTWORK

Figure 3.1 is a picture of a sculpture. Let's assume that you have never seen this before and know nothing about it, such as who created it or when or why, what it is made of, or how large it is. Take a look at it and try to come up with what you think would be an appropriate title for this particular artwork—and don't use "Untitled." (Seriously . . . come up with a title for it.) Why did you choose that particular title for this particular artwork? What is it about this piece of sculpture that led you to select the title you did?

OK, here are four possible titles for it: (1) *Coat of Male*, (2) *Bird*, (3) *Opening the Fifth Seal*, and (4) *Constantine's Dream*. Now, if you had to guess which of those four possible titles is the actual title (that is, the title the sculptor gave it), which would you choose, and why? What is it about this particular artwork that you believe is best captured by that one title of those four? Perhaps later in this chapter I will tell you the actual title, but not yet. The point is not to guess the correct title, but to think about why you would give it the title you did or why you opted for one of the four possible titles rather than

one of the other three. I assume that whatever you came up with or whichever title you opted for was not simply random. You considered this particular
artwork's features in order to assign or select a particular title. Assuming, too,
that it was difficult to come up with your own title, and perhaps to select
among the four possible titles, why was that? What made it difficult? What
other information would you want or need to have in order to have made
this easier?

These questions, and this little exercise, point to issues that arise when we
focus on artworks. In Chapter 2, we looked at some broad and basic issues
that arise concerning the very nature of art. In Chapters 4 and 5 we will look
at some broad and basic issues that arise concerning art from the perspective
of the artist (that is, concerning the creation of artworks) and from the perspective of the audience (that is, concerning the experience of encountering
artworks). This chapter, however, will focus on issues that arise when considering artworks themselves. Of course, these various perspectives are not mutually exclusive, and some issues will overlap. But just as we could focus on,
say, the color of a lamp rather than on its shape or on its placement in a
room or on its function, so, too, we can focus on aesthetic and conceptual issues about artworks rather than on the artist's or audience's perspectives. The
lamp is still a lamp (with its color and shape and placement and function),
but for certain purposes we might want to focus on one of those aspects;
likewise, art is art, but we might want to focus on particular aspects and hold
off for the time being on considering the other aspects. This chapter, then,
will delay most considerations of the artist and the audience and zero in on
aspects of artworks themselves.

THE UNIQUENESS OF ART

In Chapter 2 we looked at some issues about what constitutes art. For instance, for something to be art, is it necessary that it be created by a human
who had certain intentions? We were considering, in part, what makes anything art. Here, however, we will be looking at issues related to artworks, under the assumption that we indeed have artworks. So the issue here is not
what makes something art, but rather, given that we have art, what are its
salient features?

One way of addressing this question is to consider the phenomenon of
forgery. What makes something, with respect to art, a forgery? A forgery is
not simply a copy or reproduction of something. After all, two people can
each have his or her own copy of some musical recording or movie on a

DVD, but neither of those copies is a forgery of the other. Clearly, a forgery is a copy, at least in a sense, but it must be something else than simply being a copy. In the case of a forgery, there is the intention to have others believe that this instance of some artwork is the original instance and not a later copy or reproduction. In the case of multiple copies of a song or movie, no one is trying to deceive others that any particular copy is the original. This points to an interesting aspect of artworks, namely, that some of them can be forged but others cannot. This is because some artworks, but not all, have what philosophers call *hecceity*. Hecceity refers to the "this-ness" or uniqueness of something. Think of the *Mona Lisa*: you might say that there is only one "real" *Mona Lisa*. Even if another painting existed that was exactly like it in all respects, that second painting is not *this* painting; it is not the *Mona Lisa*. A way of putting this is that there is only one embodiment of an artwork, at least for some artworks, such as the *Mona Lisa*. Other artworks, however, such as a musical composition or a film, can have multiple embodiments. Whereas the *Mona Lisa* is a physical object, and there is indeed an original painting (or embodiment), Beethoven's Fifth Symphony is an abstract object. The written score, even if it were the one that was actually written down by Beethoven, is just a representation of the musical composition. Destroying that written score, for instance, does not destroy the music any more than destroying a recording of the composition destroys the music.

The fact of the possibility (or impossibility) of forgery points to differences among artworks: that is, by their very nature, some artworks, but only some, have hecceity. This speaks to what kinds of things artworks are but itself leads to further questions. For example, just what makes the *Mona Lisa* the *Mona Lisa*, or Beethoven's Fifth Symphony Beethoven's Fifth Symphony, or the film *Casablanca* the film *Casablanca*? As philosophers would put it: what are the criteria of identity? A way of getting at this question is to ask what would have to change or be different for that thing—in this case, that particular artwork—not to be that thing. Beethoven's Fifth Symphony was scored to be played by lots of different instruments; each instrument has its own relevant notes to play. Would it still be Beethoven's Fifth Symphony if some orchestra performed it using only tubas or only violins? Would it still be Beethoven's Fifth Symphony if it were performed at twice the tempo at which it was scored? Would it still be Beethoven's Fifth Symphony if it were performed by a group of musicians who were not together in the same locale but, rather, spread ten miles apart from each other (but all playing their assigned respective parts at the "proper" time, that is, in a sequence that, if they were together in a concert hall, would sound as it was scored)? Likewise, what if one second of filming were removed from the original production of *Casablanca*? Would it be the same film? Or what if the *Mona Lisa* had been painted by Leonardo except for one brushstroke in the very tip of the bottom-left-hand corner? Would it be the *Mona Lisa*? The question here is, what constitutes a given artwork, and what, if anything, would need to be different about it for it not to be that given artwork? Like (the possibility of) forgery, this points to what is the very nature of an artwork—independent of aspects that we will look at later in this chapter, such as the context in which the artworks were created.

In the reading below, Joseph Margolis discusses what he calls the "ontological peculiarity" of artworks. By "ontological" he simply means what kind of thing an artwork is. Philosophers often speak of *particulars* and *universals*. A particular is some specific, individual thing, where *thing* can mean a physical object but can also mean an abstract object or an event. For instance, Stanford University (an abstract object) is a particular, and so is the Battle of Waterloo (an event). A universal is a type of thing. So, whereas Felix is a particular cat, cats are universals (or kinds of things). The word *cat* refers to the entire type or class, so it is said to be a universal term. Margolis claims that artworks are particulars, not universals. As part of his argument for this claim, he distinguishes what are called *types* and *tokens*. A type, as we just noted, is a kind of thing; a token is an instance of a type. For example, Felix is a token of the type cat. Or the three numerals 2, 2, and 2 are all tokens of the number two, which is a type. (A number is not the same thing as a numeral; we could, say, erase those three numerals from this piece of paper, but we cannot erase the number two because it is an abstract thing.) Margolis says that artworks are tokens, but they are a unique kind of token. As such, artworks are a truly distinctive kind of thing, different from universals and different from other kinds of particulars.

JOSEPH MARGOLIS, "THE ONTOLOGICAL PECULIARITY OF WORKS OF ART"*

In the context of discussing the nature of artistic creativity, Jack Glickman [in his article "Creativity in the Arts"] offers the intriguing comment, "Particulars are made, types created." The remark is a strategic one, but it is either false or mis-

Journal of Aesthetics and Art Criticism 36 (1977): 45–50.

leading; and its recovery illuminates in a most economical way some of the complexities of the creative process and of the ontology of art. Glickman offers as an instance of the distinction he has in mind, the following: "If the chef created a new soup, he created a new kind of soup, a new recipe; he may not have made the soup [that is, some particular pot of soup]." *If,* by "kind," Glickman means to signify a universal of some sort, then, since universals are not created (or destroyed), it could not be the case that the chef "created" a new soup, a new kind of soup. It must be the case that the chef, in making a particular (new) soup, created (to use Glickman's idiom) a kind of soup; otherwise, of course, that the chef created a new (kind of) soup may be evidenced by his having formulated a relevant recipe (which locution, in its own turn, shows the same ambiguity between type and token).

What is important, here, may not meet the eye at once. But if he can be said to create (to invent) a (new kind of) soup and if universals cannot be created or destroyed, then in creating a kind of soup, a chef must be creating something other than a universal. The odd thing is that a kind of soup thus created is thought to be individuated among related creations; hence, it appears to be a particular of some sort. But it also seems to be an abstract entity if it is a particular at all. Hence, although it may be possible to admit abstract particulars in principle, it is difficult to concede that what the chef created is an abstract particular *if* one may be said to have *tasted* what the chef created. The analogy with art is plain. If Picasso created a new kind of painting, in painting *Les Demoiselles d'Avignon,* it would appear that he could not have done so *by using oils.*

There is only one solution *if* we mean to speak in this way. It must be possible to instantiate particulars (of a certain kind or of certain kinds) as well as to instantiate universals or properties. I suggest that the term "type"—in all contexts in which the type/token ambiguity arises—signifies abstract particulars of a kind that can be instantiated. Let us offer a specimen instance. Paintings properly pulled from Dürer's etching plate for *Melancholia I* are instances of *that* etching; but bona fide instances of *Melancholia I* need not have all their relevant properties in common, since later printings and printings that follow a touching up of the plate or printings that are themselves touched up may be genuine instances of *Melancholia I* and still differ markedly from one another—at least to the sensitive eye. Nothing, however, can instantiate a property without actually instantiating that property. So to think of types as particulars (of a distinctive kind) accommodates the fact that we individuate works of art in unusual ways—performances of the same music, printings of the same etching, copies of the same novel—and that works of art may be created and destroyed. If, further, we grant that, in creating a new soup, a chef stirred the ingredients in his pot and that, in creating a new kind of painting, in painting *Les Demoiselles*, Picasso applied paint to canvas, we see that it is at least normally the case that one does not create a new kind of soup or a new kind of painting without (in Glickman's words) making a particular soup or a particular painting.

A great many questions intrude at this point. But we may bring this much at least to bear on an ingenious thesis of Glickman's. Glickman wishes to say that, though driftwood may be construed as a creation of "beach art," it remains true that driftwood was *made* by no one, is in fact a natural object, and hence that "the condition of artificiality" so often claimed to be a necessary condition of being a work of art, is simply "superfluous." "I see no conclusive conceptual block," says Glickman, "to allowing that the artwork [may] be a natural object." Correspondingly, Duchamp's "readymades" are created out of artifacts, but the artist who created them did not actually make them. Glickman's thesis depends on the tenability of his distinction between making and creating; and as we have just seen, one does not, in the normal case at least, create a new kind of art (type) without making a particular work of that kind (that is, an instance of that particular, the type, not merely an instance of that kind, the universal). In other words, when an artist *creates* (allowing Glickman's terms) "beach art," a new kind of art, the artist *makes* a particular instance (or token) of a particular type— much as with wood sculpture, *this unique token of this driftwood composition*. He cannot create the universals that are newly instantiated since universals cannot be created. He can create a new type-particular, a particular of the kind "beach art" but he can do so only by making a token-particular of that type. What this shows is that we were unnecessarily tentative about the relation between types and tokens. We may credit an artist with having created a new type of art; but there are no types of art that are not instantiated by some token-instances or for which we lack a notation by reference to which (as in the performing arts) admissible token-instances of the particular type-work may be generated.

The reason for this strengthened conclusion has already been given. When an artist creates his work using the materials of his craft, the work he produces must have some perceptible physical properties at least; but it could not have such properties if the work were merely an abstract particular (or, of course, a universal). Hence, whenever an artist produces his work directly, even a new kind of work, he cannot be producing an abstract particular. Alternatively put, to credit an artist with having created a new *type* of art—a particular art-type—

we must (normally) be thus crediting him in virtue of the particular (token) work he has made. In wood sculpture, the particular piece an artist makes is normally the unique instance of his work; in bronzes, it is more usually true that, as in Rodin's peculiarly industrious way, there are several or numerous tokens of the very same (type) sculpture. But though we may credit the artist with having created the type, the type does not exist except instantiated in its proper tokens. We may, by a kind of courtesy, say that an artist who has produced the cast for a set of bronzes has created an artwork-type; but the fact is: (i) he has *made* a particular cast, and (ii) the cast he's made is not the work *created*. Similar considerations apply to an artist's preparing a musical notation for the sonata he has created: (i) the artist makes a token instance of a type created; and (ii) all admissible instances of his sonata are so identified by reference to the notation. The result is that, insofar as he creates a type, an artist must make a token. A chef's assistant may actually make the first pot of soup—of the soup the chef has created, but the actual soup exists only when the pot is made. Credit to the chef in virtue of his recipe is partly an assurance that his authorship is to be acknowledged in each and every pot of soup that is properly an instance of his creation, whether he makes it or not; and it is partly a device for individuating proper token instances of particular type objects. But only the token instances *of* a type actually exist and aesthetic interest in the type is a given point only in virtue of one's aesthetic interest in actual or possible tokens—as in actual or contemplated performances of a particular sonata.

But if these distinctions be granted, then, normally, an artist makes a token of the type he has created. He could not create the type unless he made a proper token or, by the courtesy intended in notations and the like, he provided a schema *for* making proper tokens of a particular type. Hence, what is normally made, in the relevant sense, is a token of a type. It must be the case, then, that when Duchamp created his *Bottle Rack*, although he did not make a bottle rack—that is, although he did not manufacture a bottle rack, although he did not first bring it about that an object instantiate a bottle rack—nevertheless, *he did make a token of the Bottle Rack*. Similarly, although driftwood is not a manufactured thing, when an artist creates (if an artist can create) a piece of "beach art," *he makes a token of that piece of "beach art."* He need not have made the driftwood. But that shows (i) that artificiality is not superfluous, though it is indeed puzzling (when displaying otherwise untouched driftwood in accord with the developed sensibilities of a society can count as the creation of an artwork); and (ii) it is not the case (contrary to Glickman's claims) that a natural object can *be* a work of art or that a work can be created though *nothing* be made.

We may summarize the ontological peculiarities of the type/token distinction in the following way: (i) types and tokens are individuated as particulars; (ii) types and tokens are not separable and cannot exist separately from one another; (iii) types are instantiated by tokens and "token" is an ellipse for "token-of-a-type"; (iv) types and tokens may be generated and destroyed in the sense that actual tokens of a novel type may be generated, the actual tokens of a given type may be destroyed, and whatever contingencies may be necessary to the generation of actual tokens may be destroyed or disabled; (v) types are actual abstract particulars in the sense only that a set of actual entities may be individuated as tokens of a particular type; (vi) it is incoherent to speak of comparing the properties of actual token- and type-particulars as opposed to comparing the properties of actual particular tokens-of-a-type; (vii) reference to types as particulars serves exclusively to facilitate reference to actual and possible tokens-of-a-type. These distinctions are sufficient to mark the type/token concept as different from the kind/instance concept and the set/member concept.

Here, a second ontological oddity must be conceded. The driftwood that is made by no one is not the (unique) token that is made of the "beach art" creation; and the artifact, the bottle rack, that Duchamp did not make is not identical with the (probably but not necessarily unique) token that Duchamp did make of the creation called *Bottle Rack*. What Duchamp made was a token of *Bottle Rack*; and what the manufacturer of bottleracks made was a particular bottlerack that served as the material out of which Duchamp created *Bottle Rack* by making a (probably unique) instance of *Bottle Rack*. For, consider that Duchamp made something when he created *Bottle Rack* but he did not make a bottle rack; also, that no one made the driftwood though someone (on the thesis) made a particular composition of art using the driftwood. If the bottle rack were said to be identical with Duchamp's *Bottle Rack* (the token or the type), we should be contradicting ourselves; the same would be true of the driftwood case. Hence, in spite of appearances, there must be an ontological difference between tokens of artwork-types and such physical objects as bottle racks and driftwood that can serve as the materials out of which they are made.

My own suggestion is that (token) works of art are *embodied* in physical objects, not identical with them. I should argue, though this is not the place for it, that persons, similarly, are embodied in physical bodies but not identical with them. The idea is that not only can one particular instantiate another particular in a certain way (tokens or types) but one particular can embody or be embodied in another particular with which it is (necessarily) not identical. The important point is that identity cannot work in the anomalous cases here considered (nor in the usual cases of art) and that what would otherwise be related by way of identity are, obviously, particulars. Furthermore, the embodiment relationship does not invite dualism though it does require a distinction among kinds of things and among the kinds of properties of things of such kinds. For example, a particular printing of Dürer's *Melancholia I* has the property of being a particular token of *Melancholia I* (the artwork type), but the physical paper and physical print do not, on any familiar view, have the property of being a token of a type. Only objects having such intentional properties as that of "being created" or, as with words, having meaning or the like can have the property of being a token of a type.

What is meant in saying that one particular is embodied in another is this: (i) that the two particulars are not identical; (ii) that the existence of the embodied particular presupposes the existence of the embodying particular; (iii) that the embodied particular possesses some of the properties of the embodying particular; (iv) that the embodied particular possesses properties that the embodying particular does not possess; (v) that the embodied particular possesses properties of a kind that the embodying particular cannot possess; (vi) that the individuation of the embodied particular presupposes the individuation of the embodying particular. The "is" of embodiment, then, like the "is" of identity and the "is" of composition is a logically distinctive use. On a theory, for instance a theory about the nature of a work of art, a particular physical object will be taken to embody a particular object of another kind in such a way that a certain systematic relationship will hold between them. Thus, for instance, a sculptor will be said to make a particular sculpture by cutting a block of marble: Michelangelo's *Pietà* will exhibit certain of the physical properties of the marble and certain representational and purposive properties as well; it will also have the property of being a unique token of the creation *Pietà*. The reason for theorizing thus is, quite simply, that works of art are the products of culturally informed labor and that physical objects are not. So seen, they must possess properties that physical objects, *qua* physical objects, do not and cannot possess. Hence, an identity thesis leads to palpable contradictions. Furthermore, the conception of embodiment promises to facilitate a non-reductive account of the relationship between physical nature and human culture, without dualistic assumptions. What this suggests is that the so-called mind/body problem is essentially a form of a more general culture/nature problem. But that is another story.

A work of art, then, is a particular. It cannot be a universal because it is created and can be destroyed; also, because it possesses physical and perceptual properties. But it is a peculiar sort of particular, unlike physical bodies, because (i) it can instantiate another particular; and (ii) it can be embodied in another particular. The suggestion here is that all and only culturally emergent and culturally produced entities exhibit these traits. So the ontological characteristics assigned are no more than the most generic characteristics of art; its distinctive nature remains unanalyzed. Nevertheless, we can discern an important difference between these two properties, as far as art is concerned. For, the first property, that of being able to instantiate another particular, has only to do with individuating works of art and whatever may, contingently, depend upon that; while the second property has to do with the ontologically dependent nature of actual works of art. This is the reason we may speak of type artworks as particulars. They are heuristically introduced for purposes of individuation, though they cannot exist except in the sense in which particular tokens of particular type artworks exist. So we can never properly *compare* the properties of a token work and a type work. What we may compare are alternative tokens of the same type—different printings of the same etching or different performances of the same sonata. In short, every work of art is a token-of-a-type; there are no tokens or types *tout court*. Again, this is not to say that there are no types or that an artist cannot create a new kind of painting. It is only to say that so speaking is an ellipse for saying that a certain set of particulars are tokens of a type and that the artist is credited with so working with the properties of things, instantiated by the members of that set, that they are construed as tokens of a particular type.

So the dependencies of the two ontological traits mentioned are quite different. There are no types that are separable from tokens because there are no tokens except tokens-of-a-type. The very process for individuating tokens entails individuating types, that is, entails individuating different sets of particulars as the alternative tokens of this or that type. There is nothing left over to discuss. What may mislead is this: the concept of different tokens of the same type is intended, in the arts, to accommodate the fact that the aesthetically often decisive differences among tokens of the same type (alternative performances of a sonata, for instance) need not matter as far as the individuation of the (type) work is concerned. But particular works of art cannot exist except as embodied in physical objects. This is simply another way of saying that works of art are culturally emergent entities; that is, that works of art exhibit properties that physical objects cannot exhibit, but do so in a way that does not depend on the presence of any substance other than what may be ascribed to purely physical objects. Broadly speaking, those properties are what may be characterized as functional or intentional properties and include design, expressiveness, symbolism, representation, meaning, style, and the like. Without prejudice to the nature of either art or persons, this way of viewing art suggests a very convenient linkup with the functional theory of mental traits. Be that as it may, a reasonable theory of art could hold that when physical materials are worked in accord with a certain artistic craft then there emerges, culturally, an object embodied in the former that possesses a certain orderly array of functional properties of the kind just mentioned. Any object so produced may be treated as an artifact. Hence, works of art exist as fully as physical objects but the condition on which they do so depends on the independent existence of some physical object itself. Works of art, then, are culturally emergent entities, tokens-of-a-type that exist embodied in physical objects. ◣

ARTWORKS AND AESTHETICS

Whatever their ontological status, artworks are *art*works. They are different from works that are not works of art. In one sense, the Eiffel Tower is just a large metal structure, but in another sense it is a work of architecture. An intuitive and reasonable sense of what makes certain things artworks, as opposed to some other kind of works, is that there is something aesthetic about them. But what, exactly, is the aesthetic-ness about them?

In the reading below, art critic Frank Sibley claims that artworks have various kinds of features, some aesthetic and some nonaesthetic. For example, we can note that Picasso's *Guernica* is a certain size (approximately 138 inches by 305 inches), that it consists of the colors black, white, and gray, and that it contains representations of various figures (some human and some animal). We might also note that it is frenzied or disturbing or that it contains movement. Or, alternatively, we might note that it is certainly not serene or calming or flat. The features in the first group (its size and colors and content) are all straightforwardly descriptive. These are features that are perceivably true about the painting, and different people would agree with these descriptions. The features in the second group, however (being frenzied or disturbing or not serene), are not straightforwardly descriptive. Different people might or might not agree with these descriptions. Even if they did agree, it is not as if the lack of serenity is the same thing as being black, white, and gray. The features in the first group are nonaesthetic features, whereas those in the second group are aesthetic features.

Although it is relatively easy to recognize aesthetic features (even if we do not agree on them; that is, even if some people think *Guernica* is frenzied and others do not), it is not so easy to enunciate what makes certain features aesthetic. The difference between aesthetic features and nonaesthetic features is not simply that there is agreement by people about the nonaesthetic and possible disagreement about the aesthetic. We might all agree that certain features of artworks are indeed aesthetic, but disagree on how we "receive" them. That is, we might agree that certain features of *Guernica* are indeed aesthetic features even if we disagree in how those features relate to us (again, one person might find the painting boring and another person might find it disturbing, in a negative sense, and a third person might find it disturbing and therefore very profound). So we might all agree on the nonaesthetic features of an artwork, and we might even all agree on what the aesthetic features of an artwork are in the sense of identifying the features that are aesthetic, although our particular aesthetic experience might vary.

The Greek philosopher Aristotle remarked that an important difference between history and poetry is that history is concerned with particulars, but poetry is concerned with universals. That is, history focuses on understanding specific people, places, things, and events, but poetry focuses on what transcends specific people, places, things, and events. These remarks, of course, are not merely about poetry; rather, they are about art generally. So this view essentially holds that, say, Shakespeare's *Hamlet* is not simply a story about a particular person or character but, rather, speaks to general human concerns. Not everyone agrees with Aristotle on this, but the point here is that one notion of what constitutes the aesthetic features of art is that those features transcend the specific particularities of the artwork. *Guernica*'s physical size (a nonaesthetic feature) is specific; it is what it is. But *Guernica*'s frenzied quality, representing or portraying the suffering and terrors of war, is not specific. Even if the painting was created in response to specific historical events, its aesthetic nature is not merely a reporting of those specific events; it speaks to something that transcends those specific events.

Furthermore, what makes some features of artworks aesthetic features is that they are intended as such. As we saw in Chapter 2, Jerrold Levinson argued that what makes something art at all is that there is an intention for the artwork to be regarded as art. Some philosophers (and artists) have claimed that the presence of aesthetic features in something, what makes it art, is that the artist is trying to do something artistic; there is an intention to represent or express or communicate in an aesthetic way. In Chapter 4 we will consider these notions much more, but for now the point is that one claim about what makes certain features of artworks aesthetic features is that they are intended that way by the creators of those artworks. However, this view does not seem to bear scrutiny. Something can be perceived by others as having aesthetic features even if that was not the intent of the work's creator. For instance, a piece of pottery might exhibit the (aesthetic) feature of being graceful even if the person who made it was not intending that at all. The potter may simply have wanted a functioning pot; whether it turned out to be graceful or not was really irrelevant.

The nature of that which makes something aesthetic and the relationship between aesthetic and nonaesthetic features of artworks are long-standing conundrums in the philosophy of art. In the reading on page 76, Sibley notes that aesthetic features, although not reducible to nonaesthetic ones, are dependent upon them. That is, what makes a given artwork, say, graceful or dynamic or disturbing is a function of the work's nonaesthetic features. For example, if *Guernica* is frenzied or disturbing, that is because of the way the figures in it are painted or because the painting is made up of stark colors rather than, say, soft pastels. However, the frenzied or disturbing nature of *Guernica* (again, assuming it is frenzied or disturbing) is not reducible to the figures or colors; not all starkly colored paintings are disturbing, for example.

A way of making Sibley's point is to say that the aesthetic features of artworks are *emergent* features, or emergent properties. All this means is that the aesthetic features emerge out of the nonaesthetic features. They are dependent upon those nonaesthetic features, but they are also, in a sense, independent of them. Consider the sculpture pictured at the beginning of this chapter. (Oh, by the way, its title is *Coat of Male* and the sculptor was Fritz Bultman.) Would you describe it as delicate? Would you call it flowing? Balanced? Tense? If so, why; if not, why not? Just as with giving it a title, there are reasons you would say that it does or does not have the aesthetic feature of being, say, delicate. The reasons are dependent upon the sculpture's nonaesthetic features. (Perhaps it seems too thick or metallic for you to call it delicate, but even with its thickness or metallic nature you might still consider it flowing.) Some emergent features are aesthetic, but not all are. For example, being harmonious (a feature of, say, a musical composition or even a painting or a dance) is aesthetic. Harmony involves some sort of balance and structure that is dependent upon the features of those things that make up the harmony, such as a group of particular musical notes or, in the case of dance, specific movements juxtaposed with one another. No individual note or movement is harmonious; it is just a specific note or movement. But when brought together with others, harmony emerges. Harmony, then, is an aesthetic emergent feature. However, being edible is a feature of table salt (sodium chloride), which is itself a particular structure resulting from the combination of sodium and chlorine. Being edible (at least by humans) is not a feature of either sodium or chlorine, but being edible is a feature that emerges when sodium and chlorine are brought together to make sodium chloride. So with respect to artworks and their aesthetic features, yes, it certainly seems that aesthetic features are emergent features, dependent upon (yet independent of) nonaesthetic features. Unfortunately, knowing this does not seem to tell us much more about aesthetic features. Nonetheless, Sibley points out that these are just the sorts of things that critics focus on when they interpret and evaluate artworks. (We will have more to say about interpretation and evaluation of art in Chapter 5.)

There are two other aspects related to aesthetic features of artworks to be considered before we see what Sibley has to say. One of these aspects relates back to the issue of forgery. Earlier in this chapter we saw that some artworks, at least, seem to have a uniqueness about them. Copies of *Guernica* are not "the" *Guernica*. However, if what is essential about artworks is their aesthetic features—after all, what makes them *art*works rather than some other kind of works is their aesthetic features—then what can we say about copies of artworks that have exactly the same aesthetic features as the original artwork? If a copy of *Guernica* was "good" enough to truly duplicate and capture the aesthetic features of the original, then what? If the aesthetic experience that someone had were the same when encountering the copy and the original, then in what sense is there any relevant difference between them? How is the original a "genuine" artwork, while the forged copy is not? If we think that somehow there is still an important difference, does this imply or suggest that the aesthetic features of an artwork are not as significant or crucial to the thing's status as art as we might have thought? If we think there is an important difference between an original and a "perfect" copy of it, then it seems that something other than the intrinsic features of the artwork is crucial. (By *intrinsic* features we mean here those features of the artwork itself, independent of features about the artist, about the context of its creation, and so on.) We will take up this point again following Sibley's remarks.

A second, and final, aspect related to aesthetic features and art is that we speak of and acknowledge aesthetic features outside of art. For example, at least some people speak of the beauty of, say, a given mathematical proof.

Even more, we often speak of aesthetic features of nature. We often use terms like *beautiful, moving, delicate, graceful,* or *haunting* when describing aspects of nature, such as a beautiful sunset or the graceful flight of some bird or the haunting sound of a whale call. (We sometimes also use "negative" aesthetic terms for things and events in nature, such as *disturbing* or *frenzied*.) Assuming that we do not consider things in nature as artworks, then it is obvious that aesthetic features apply outside of art.

We won't get into the question of whether or not things in nature are appropriately considered to be artworks, other than to make a few comments here. First, the aesthetics of nature has certainly been something that aestheticians and artists have dealt with historically. For instance, many of the Romanticist artists and philosophers of the eighteenth and nineteenth centuries wrote volumes about the aesthetics of nature and how that relates to artworks, as well as about our aesthetic understanding and appreciation and the nature of aesthetic experience generally. Many of them spoke of our encounter with "the sublime" when we experience the beauty of nature and said that this was a more immediate and direct aesthetic experience than any aesthetic experience we could ever have with human artworks. So the issue of the aesthetics of nature and the nature of aesthetics has a long and respectable history. In addition, of course, some people have argued that things in nature can be considered artworks. One version of this view is that there are what are called "found" artworks, for instance, some aesthetically appealing piece of driftwood or shell or floral pattern. Another version of the view that there is art in nature is a religious one; nature itself is God's artwork. Many people, however, see this as a metaphor, holding that we should understand and appreciate and experience nature in ways that we would understand and appreciate and experience human artworks, only knowing that humans did not create nature (and its beauty). The aesthetician Allen Carlson, in particular, has noted that when we speak of nature and aesthetics we have various notions (whether implicit or explicit) that we employ. Sometimes we treat things in nature (or the natural environment itself) as if they are artworks; other times we treat those things as ways of helping us think about human artworks, and yet other times as not artworks at all. The issue of the aesthetics of nature and the nature of aesthetics is important and enlightening, but it is beyond what we are considering here. For now, we will return to Frank Sibley and the issue of aesthetic features in (human) artworks.

▌ FRANK SIBLEY, "AESTHETIC CONCEPTS"*

The remarks we make about works of art are of many kinds. For the purpose of this paper I wish to indicate two broad groups. I shall do this by examples. We say that a novel has a great number of characters and deals with life in a manufacturing town; that a painting uses pale colors, predominantly blues and greens, and has kneeling figures in the foreground; that the theme in a fugue is inverted at such a point and that there is a stretto at the close; that the action of a play takes place in the span of one day and that there is a reconciliation scene in the fifth act. Such remarks may be made by, and such features pointed out to, anyone with normal eyes, ears, and intelligence. On the other hand, we also say that a poem is highly-knit or deeply moving; that a picture lacks balance, or has a certain serenity and repose, or that the grouping of the figures sets up an exciting tension; that the characters in a novel never really come to life, or that a certain episode strikes a false note. It would be neutral enough to say that the making of such judgments as these requires the exercise of taste, perceptiveness, or sensitivity, of aesthetic discrimination or appreciation; one would not say this of my first group. Accordingly, when a word or expression is such that taste or perceptiveness is required in order to apply it, I shall call it an *aesthetic* term or expression, and I shall, correspondingly, speak of *aesthetic* concepts or *taste* concepts.

Aesthetic terms span a great range of types and could be grouped into various kinds of sub-species. But it is not my present purpose to attempt any such grouping; I am interested in what they all have in common. Their almost endless variety is adequately displayed in the following list: *unified, balanced, integrated, lifeless, serene, somber, dynamic, powerful, vivid, delicate, moving, trite, sentimental, tragic.* The list of course is not limited to adjectives; expressions in artistic contexts like *telling contrast, sets up a tension, conveys a sense of,* or *holds it together* are equally good illustrations. It includes terms used by both layman and critic alike, as well as some which are mainly the property of professional critics and specialists.

I have gone for my examples of aesthetic expressions in the first place to critical and evaluative discourse about works of art because it is there particularly that they abound. But now I wish to widen the topic; we employ terms the use of which requires an exercise of taste not only when discussing the arts but

---

Philosophical Review 68 (1959): 421–426, 437–439, 442–445.

quite liberally throughout discourse in everyday life. The examples given above are expressions which, appearing in critical contexts, most usually, if not invariably, have an aesthetic use; outside critical discourse the majority of them more frequently have some other use unconnected with taste. But many expressions do double duty even in everyday discourse, sometimes being used as aesthetic expressions and sometimes not. Other words again, whether in artistic or daily discourse, function only or predominantly as aesthetic terms; of this kind are *graceful, delicate, dainty, handsome, comely, elegant, garish*. Finally, to make the contrast with all the preceding examples, there are many words which are seldom used as aesthetic terms at all: *red, noisy, brackish, clammy, square, docile, cured, evanescent, intelligent, faithful, derelict, tardy, freakish*. . . .

The foregoing has marked out the area I wish to discuss. One warning should perhaps be given. When I speak of taste in this paper, I shall not be dealing with questions which center upon expressions like "a matter of taste" (meaning, roughly, a matter of personal preference or liking). It is with an ability to *notice* or *see* or *tell* that things have certain qualities that I am concerned.

I

In order to support our application of an aesthetic term, we often refer to features the mention of which involves other aesthetic terms: "it has an extraordinary vitality because of its free and vigorous style of drawing," "graceful in the smooth flow of its lines," "dainty because of the delicacy and harmony of its coloring." It is as normal to do this as it is to justify one mental epithet by other epithets of the same general type, *intelligence* by *ingenious, inventive, acute*, and so on. But often when we apply aesthetic terms, we explain why by referring to features which do *not* depend for their recognition upon an exercise of taste: "delicate because of its pastel shades and curving lines," or "it lacks balance because one group of figures is so far off to the left and is so brightly illuminated." When no explanation of this latter kind is offered, it is legitimate to ask or search for one. Finding a satisfactory answer may sometimes be difficult, but one cannot ordinarily reject the question. When we cannot ourselves quite say what non-aesthetic features make something delicate or unbalanced or powerful or moving, the good critic often puts his finger on something which strikes us as the right explanation. In short, aesthetic terms always ultimately apply because of, and aesthetic qualities always ultimately depend upon, the presence of features which, like curving or angular lines, color contrasts, placing of masses, or speed of movement, are visible, audible, or otherwise discernible without any exercise of taste or sensibility. Whatever kind of dependence this is, and there are various relationships between aesthetic qualities and non-aesthetic features, what I want to make clear in this paper is that there are no non-aesthetic features which serve in *any* circumstances as logically *sufficient conditions* for applying aesthetic terms. Aesthetic or taste concepts are not in *this* respect condition-governed at all.

There is little temptation to suppose that aesthetic terms resemble words which, like "square," are applied in accordance with a set of necessary and sufficient conditions. For whereas each square is square in virtue of the *same* set of conditions, four equal sides and four right angles, aesthetic terms apply to widely varied objects; one thing is graceful because of these features, another because of those, and so one almost endlessly. In recent times philosophers have broken the spell of the strict necessary-and-sufficient model by showing that many everyday concepts are not of that type. Instead, they have described various other types of concepts which are governed only in a much looser way by conditions. However, since these newer models provide satisfactory accounts of many familiar concepts, it might plausibly be thought that aesthetic concepts are of the same such kind and that they similarly are governed in some looser way by conditions. I want to argue that aesthetic concepts differ radically from any of these other concepts. . . .

No doubt there are some respects in which aesthetic terms *are* governed by conditions or rules. For instance, it may be impossible that a thing should be garish if all its colors are pale pastels, or flamboyant if all its lines are straight. There may be, that is, descriptions using only non-aesthetic terms which are incompatible with descriptions employing certain aesthetic terms. If I am told that a painting in the next room consists solely of one or two bars of very pale blue and very pale grey set at right angles on a pale fawn ground, I can be sure that it cannot be fiery or garish or gaudy or flamboyant. A description of this sort may make certain aesthetic terms *in*applicable or *in*appropriate; and if from this description I inferred that the picture was, or even might be, fiery or gaudy or flamboyant, this might be taken as showing a failure to understand those words. I do not wish to deny therefore that taste concepts may be governed *negatively* by conditions. What I am emphasizing is that they quite lack governing conditions of a sort many other concepts possess. Though on *seeing* the picture we might say, and rightly, that it is delicate or serene or restful or sickly or insipid, no *description* in non-aesthetic terms permits us to claim that these or any other aesthetic terms must undeniably apply to it.

I have said that if an object is characterized *solely* by certain sorts of features this may count decisively against the possibility of applying to it certain aesthetic terms. But of course the presence of *some* such features need not count decisively; other features may be enough to outweigh those which, on their own, would render the aesthetic terms inapplicable. A painting might be garish even though much of its color is pale. . . . Although there is this sense in which slimness, lightness, lack of intensity of color, and so on, count only towards, not against, delicacy, these features, I shall say, at best count only *typically* or *characteristically* towards delicacy; they do not count towards in the same sense as condition-features count towards laziness or intelligence; that is, no group of them is ever logically sufficient. . . .

II

A great deal of work remains to be done on aesthetic concepts. In the remainder of this paper I shall offer some further suggestions which may help towards an understanding of them. . . .

In the first place, while our ability to discern aesthetic features is dependent upon our possession of good eyesight, hearing, and so on, people normally endowed with senses and understanding may nevertheless fail to discern them. "Those who listen to a concert, walk round a gallery, read a poem may have roughly similar sense perceptions, but some get a great deal more than others," Miss [Margaret] McDonald says, but she adds that she is "puzzled by this feature 'in the object' which can be seen only by a specially qualified observer" and asks, "What is this 'something more'?"

It is this difference between aesthetic and perceptual qualities which in part leads to the view that "works of art are esoteric objects . . . not simple objects of sense perception." But there is no good reason for calling an object esoteric simply because we discern aesthetic qualities in it. The *objects* to which we apply aesthetic words are of the most diverse kinds and by no means esoteric: people and buildings, flowers and gardens, vases and furniture, as well as poems and music. Nor does there seem to be any good reason for calling the *qualities* themselves esoteric. . . .

The second notable difference between the exercise of taste and the use of the five senses lies in the way we support those judgments in which aesthetic concepts are employed. Although we use these concepts without rules or conditions, we do defend or support our judgments, and convince others of their rightness, by talking; "disputation about art is not futile," as Miss McDonald says, for critics do "attempt a certain kind of explanation of works of art with the object of establishing correct judgments." Thus even though this disputation does not consist in "deductive or inductive inferences" or "reasoning," its occurrence is enough to show how very different these judgments are from those of a simple perceptual sort.

Now the critic's talk, it is clear, frequently consists in mentioning or pointing out the features, including easily discernible non-aesthetic ones, upon which the aesthetic qualities depend. But the puzzling question remains how, by mentioning these features, the critic is thereby justifying or supporting his judgments. . . . The critic's talk . . . often serves to support his judgments in a special way; it helps us to *see* what he has seen, namely, the aesthetic qualities of the object. But even when it is agreed that this is one of the main things that critics do, puzzlement tends to break out again over *how* they do it. How is it that by talking about features of the work (largely non-aesthetic ones) we can manage to bring others to see what they had not seen? . . .

To help understand what the critic does, then, how he supports his judgments and gets his audience to see what he sees, I shall attempt a brief description of the methods we use as critics.

(1) We may simply mention or point out non-aesthetic features: "Notice these flecks of color, that dark mass there, those lines." By merely drawing attention to those easily discernible features which make the painting luminous or warm or dynamic, we often succeed in bringing someone to see these aesthetic qualities. We get him to see B by mentioning something different, A. Sometimes in doing this we are drawing attention to features which may have gone unnoticed by an untrained or insufficiently attentive eye or ear: "Just listen for the repeated figure in the left hand." "Did you notice the figure of Icarus in the Breughel? It is very small." Sometimes they are features which have been seen or heard but of which the significance or purpose has been missed in any of a variety of ways: "Notice how much darker he has made the central figure, how much brighter these colors are than the adjacent ones." "Of course, you've observed the ploughman in the foreground, but had you considered how he, like everyone else in the picture, is going about his business without noticing the fall of Icarus?" In mentioning features which may be discerned by anyone with normal eyes, ears, and intelligence, we are singling out what may serve as a kind of key to grasping or seeing something else (and the key may not be the same for each person).

(2) On the other hand we often simply mention the very qualities we want people to see. We point to a painting and say, "Notice how nervous and delicate the drawing is," or "See what energy and vitality it has." The use of the aesthetic term itself may do the trick; we say what the quality or character is, and people who had not seen it before see it.

(3) Most often, there is a linking of remarks about aesthetic and non-aesthetic features: "Have you noticed this line and that, and the points of bright
color here and there . . . don't they give it vitality, energy?"

(4) We do, in addition, often make extensive and helpful use of similes and
genuine metaphors: "It's as if there were small points of light burning," "as
though he had thrown on the paint violently and in anger," "the light shim-
mers, the lines dance, everything is air, lightness, and gaiety," "his canvases are
fires, they crackle, burn, and blaze, even at their most subdued always restlessly
flickering, but often bursting into flame, great pyrotechnic displays," and so on.

(5) We make use of contrasts, comparisons, and reminiscences: "Suppose he
had made that a lighter yellow, moved it to the right, how flat it would have
been," "Don't you think it has something of the quality of a Rembrandt?,"
"Hasn't it the same serenity, peace, and quality of light of those summer
evenings in Norfolk?" We use what keys we have to the known sensitivity, sus-
ceptibilities, and experience of our audience.

Critics and commentators may range, in their methods, from one extreme to
the other, from painstaking concentration on points of detail, line and color,
vowels and rhymes, to more or less flowery and luxuriant metaphor. Even the
enthusiastic biographical sketch decorated with suitable epithet and metaphor
may serve. What is best depends on both the audience and the work under discussion. But this would not be a complete sketch unless certain other notes
were added.

(6) Repetition and reiteration often play an important role. When we are in
front of a canvas we may come back time and again to the same points, drawing attention to the same lines and shapes, repeating the same words,
"swirling," "balance," "luminosity," or the same similes and metaphors, as if
time and familiarity, looking harder, listening more carefully, paying closer attention may help. So again with variation; it often helps to talk round what we
have said, to build up, supplement with more talk *of the same kind*. When
someone misses the swirling quality, when one epithet or one metaphor does
not work, we throw in related ones; we speak of its wild movement, how it
twists and turns, writhes and whirls, as though, failing to score a direct hit, we
may succeed with a barrage of near-synonyms.

(7) Finally, besides our verbal performances, the rest of our behavior is important. We accompany our talk with appropriate tones of voice, expressions,
nods, looks, and gestures. A critic may sometimes do more with a sweep of the
arm than by talking. An appropriate gesture may make us see the violence in a
painting or the character of a melodic line.

These ways of acting and talking are not significantly different whether we are dealing with a particular work, paragraph, or line, or speaking of an artist's work as a whole, or even drawing attention to a sunset or scenery. But even with the speaker doing all this, we may fail to see what he sees. There may be a point, though there need be no limit except that imposed by time and patience, at which he gives up and sets us (or himself) down as lacking in some way, defective in sensibility. He may tell us to look or read again, or to read or look at other things and then come back again to this; he may suspect there are experiences in life we have missed. But these are the things he does. This is what succeeds if anything does; indeed it is all that can be done.

By realizing clearly that, whether we are dealing with art or scenery or people or natural objects, this is how we operate with aesthetic concepts, we may recognize this sphere of human activity for what it is. We operate with different kinds of concepts in different ways. If we want someone to agree that a color is red we may take it into a good light and ask him to look. . . . But the ways we get someone to see aesthetic qualities are different; they are of the kind I have described. With each kind of concept we can describe what we do and how we do it. But the methods suited to these other concepts will not do for aesthetic ones, or vice versa. We cannot prove by argument or by assembling a sufficiency of conditions that something is graceful; but this is no more puzzling than our inability to prove, by using the methods, metaphors, and gestures of the art critic, that it will be mate [in chess] in ten moves. . . . Aesthetic concepts are as natural, as little esoteric, as any others. It is against the background of different and philosophically more familiar models that they seem queer or puzzling. ◣

FORM VERSUS CONTENT OR CONTEXT

In Chapter 2 we encountered two paintings (Figures 2.1 and 2.2), one painted by an elephant and the other by a human. Both are quite different from Picasso's *Guernica*. Although *Guernica* is hardly a photographic mirror of things or events, it does have content that we can recognize; we see figures of people and animals. We might want to call Figures 2.1 and 2.2 abstract paintings, but whether we do or not, they certainly do not seem to have any recognizable content. Nevertheless, we can identify features of those paintings, including aesthetic features. Whatever our response to them, as basic as a positive or negative response, we recognize them as artworks (ignoring for the moment that one of them was painted by an elephant). With no discernible content, what makes them artworks? The most common answer is:

form. As with the sculpture at the beginning of this chapter, we might know nothing at all about the paintings in Figures 2.1 and 2.2, but we can still recognize them as artworks and can speak about their aesthetic and nonaesthetic features because of their form (or forms). On page 86, in the final reading of this chapter, Clive Bell argues that form, or what he calls "significant form," is what is fundamental to art. Bell is straightforward. He asks what quality (or feature) is shared by all objects that provoke our aesthetic emotions; his answer is: significant form. This view is shared by many aestheticians and is called *formalism*. Formalists claim that it is the formal features of artworks that are essential to their character as art; whatever content an artwork has is secondary to its nature as art.

That form is fundamental to art goes without saying. In ballet, for example, there are a series of positions that dancers know and employ and can be choreographed into various dances. In poetry, there can be structured patterns or forms, such as an iambic pentameter pattern of stresses, regardless of the specific content of the words. Haiku poetry requires seventeen syllables. Musical compositions often have highly structured features, such as rhythm, meter, and time signatures. In film or theater, we can recognize and identify certain plot structures, sequences of events, and pacing for the resolution of conflict, again, regardless of the particular story line of that film or play. (Indeed, we sometimes remark that we have "seen that movie before," meaning that the plot, characters, and so on were so similar to some other movie that it felt like "the same" movie with only surface features changed.) All these examples refer to what we might call the *general* form of artworks. Haiku, for example, has a definite form or structure, so any example of haiku must have that form. Or blues, as a kind of music, has certain sound structures, such as being played in minor keys or in a slow tempo, that are characteristic (perhaps even defining) for a song to be a blues song. (Imagine "Stormy Monday" played at the tempo of a John Philip Sousa march!) In addition to general form, we might speak of the *specific* form of a particular artwork. For instance, we might point to the spatial pattern of the figures in *Guernica* as part of its specific form. Likewise, Beethoven's Fifth Symphony has formal features that are unlike those of his other symphonies, and the Eiffel Tower has formal features that are unlike those of the Empire State Building.

The "form of an artwork" can mean various things, in the sense that form can be compared or contrasted with various other things. For instance, we might contrast form and function. This distinction is obvious outside the sphere of art. For example, someone might say, "It's cold in here; will you shut the window?" The form of this remark is a question; however, it functions not as a question but, rather, as a request or even a command. It would be odd, or perhaps funny, if someone made that remark to you and you thought about it for a moment and then replied, "I don't know if I will; let's wait and find out," or "Hmm, no, I guess I won't shut it." In the context of art, form and function are not often confused, but they can blend into each other and complement each other. For instance, a particular statue might be carved in such a way as to honor someone as being "larger than life" (and so the statue itself is huge). Or a cathedral might be designed and constructed with especially high ceilings so as to remind people that, relative to the grand scheme of things, they are rather small and dependent upon some higher power.

The form of an artwork might also be contrasted to the elements of an artwork. So the specific colors or figures themselves in *Guernica* do not constitute the formal features of *Guernica*. Colors are just colors and figures are just figures; as themselves they are not forms. Of course, this holds for other arts as well. In music, notes are just notes; in literature, words are just words; in dance, movements are just movements. It is the arrangement and relations among the elements that constitute the form.

And as we have already noted, the form of an artwork can also be contrasted with its content. However, that is easier said than done. Aristotle pointed out that there is no form without content and no content without form. What he meant is that no particular thing has only form (that is, without any content) or only content (that is, without any form). His actual focus was on the notion of form and matter, and what he said was that there can be no matter (that is, no material thing) without some form or other and that there can be no form that exists in the world without any content. Yes, we can speak of forms such as circles, but no circles by themselves exist in the world; rather, there are things that are circular. Forms, as abstractions, are conceivable in the sense that we can think about them, but for anything to actually exist in the world, he said, requires matter. So, with respect to artworks, this is the view that no artwork exists as only form, without content. Even abstract art, such as Figures 2.1 and 2.2, has some content, however indistinguishable or amorphous it might be. Furthermore, this points to the issue of what, exactly, form is. What is the form (or forms) of *Guernica*? Is it even possible to encounter the form(s) of *Guernica* absent any of its content?

With respect to the issue of form versus content, Bell, of course, claims that only form constitutes the aesthetics and "artness" of an artwork. Others have rejected this view. Like Aristotle, some philosophers and artists have said that, of course, we could focus our attention on some formal features of an artwork, just as we could focus our attention on certain elements of the artwork. However, they say, those formal features are not what *make* it art. In addition, say other critics of formalism, content matters! It is the content of *Guernica*—what is depicted or represented—as well as how and why it is depicted or represented that is fundamental and important about the painting. It is the content that speaks to the horrors of war, not the form (whatever form or forms *Guernica* might have). In Chapter 4 we will look at various claims about what is important about art from the perspective of artists, those who create art. These include the notions that artists want to represent something or other, or that via art they want to express or communicate to others their feelings or thoughts, or that by creating art artists want to change the world in some way. So perhaps with *Guernica*, Picasso wanted to represent the horrors of war and to communicate this to viewers so that they would be repulsed by war and not wage it. In any case, none of these things make sense, say critics of formalism, if one says that form is what constitutes *Guernica* as an artwork. Granted, the form or forms that *Guernica* has are no doubt part of its aesthetic nature, but they are only a part.

In their turn, formalists respond by acknowledging that artworks do have content, but, they say, the content is not what makes the artwork art. The aesthetic quality and power of art is the result, they say, not (just) of the content, but of the form. One could try to represent or communicate the horrors of war in ways that are not aesthetically frenzied or disturbing by simply stating that war causes suffering. But the artistic "punch" comes from how this is represented or communicated. The same content can be aesthetically moving or not moving, depending on form.

Yet another notion that contrasts with form is context. Many philosophers and artists argue that context is a feature of artworks as much as form and content are. This is especially clear, they say, with respect to understanding and appreciating an artwork. For example, it makes a difference if we know about when an artwork was created or why or by whom. The French philosopher Roland Barthes speaks of the significance of a particular cover of the French magazine *Paris Match*. It showed a close-up picture of a young soldier and behind him was the French flag. The soldier seemed to be looking at the flag with respect. However, the picture was not as simple as it might have seemed. The soldier was a young black man who was serving in Algeria (in northern Africa), which at the time was a French colony. During the late 1950s and early 1960s, the Algerians rebelled against the French in order to become an independent country. So this seemingly simple picture actually carried a lot of meaning in it because of the context. For Barthes (and many others), it was French propaganda. Knowing the historical and political context, say the critics of formalism, is not simply relevant to understanding and appreciating the artwork; that context is part of the artwork.

Formalists respond to what they call "contextualism" by claiming that the very notion of context is too vague to be useful. Of course, artworks exist in a multitude of contexts: they are created by certain artists for certain reasons at certain times. However, they claim, the aesthetic features of artworks are not constituted by these multiple contexts. As was noted at the beginning of this chapter, we can encounter a given sculpture in a vacuum, so to speak (that is, not knowing any contexts), and we still can have an aesthetic experience because the artwork itself has aesthetic features. If the sculpture in Figure 3.1 is delicate, say, then it is delicate regardless of who happened to create it. If *Guernica* is frenzied, then it is frenzied whether or not it was Picasso who painted it and it is frenzied whether it was painted in 1937 or 1037 or 2007. It is frenzied, say formalists, whether Picasso wanted to point out the horrors of war or whether he wanted to warn others that, unless you bend to his will, this will also happen to you. The point, of course, is that formalists claim that context might be informative or useful in understanding or cognitively appreciating or perhaps even emotionally responding to an artwork, but context is not (or contexts are not) basic or fundamental in what makes artworks art. The issues of interpreting and evaluating art will be taken up in Chapter 5. For now, here is Bell's view in favor of formalism.

CLIVE BELL, "ART AND SIGNIFICANT FORM"*

It is improbable that more nonsense has been written about aesthetics than about anything else: the literature of the subject is not large enough for that. It is certain, however, that about no subject with which I am acquainted has so little been said that is at all to the purpose. The explanation is discoverable. He who would elaborate a plausible theory of aesthetics must possess two qualities—artistic sensibility and a turn for clear thinking. Without sensibility a man can

---

*In *Art*. New York: Capricorn Books, 1958. Pages 15–20, 22, 28–30, 34. (Original: New York: Frederick A. Stokes, 1913.)

have no aesthetic experience, and, obviously, theories not based on broad and deep aesthetic experience are worthless. Only those for whom art is a constant source of passionate emotion can possess the data from which profitable theories may be deduced; but to deduce profitable theories even from accurate data involves a certain amount of brain-work, and, unfortunately, robust intellects and delicate sensibilities are not inseparable. As often as not, the hardest thinkers have had no aesthetic experience whatever. I have a friend blessed with an intellect as keen as a drill, who, though he takes an interest in aesthetics, has never during a life of almost forty years been guilty of an aesthetic emotion. So, having no faculty for distinguishing a work of art from a handsaw, he is apt to rear up a pyramid of irrefragable argument on the hypothesis that a handsaw is a work of art. This defect robs his perspicuous and subtle reasoning of much of its value; for it has ever been a maxim that faultless logic can win but little credit for conclusions that are based on premises notoriously false. Every cloud, however, has its silver lining, and this insensibility, though unlucky in that it makes my friend incapable of choosing a sound basis for his argument, mercifully blinds him to the absurdity of his conclusions while leaving him in full enjoyment of his masterly dialectic. . . .

On the other hand, people who respond immediately and surely to works of art, though, in my judgment, more enviable than men of massive intellect but slight sensibility, are often quite as incapable of talking sense about aesthetics. Their heads are not always very clear. They possess the data on which any system must be based; but, generally, they want the power that draws correct inferences from true data. Having received aesthetic emotions from works of art, they are in a position to seek out the quality common to all that have moved them, but, in fact, they do nothing of the sort. I do not blame them. Why should they bother to examine their feelings when for them to feel is enough? Why should they stop to think when they are not very good at thinking? Why should they hunt for a common quality in all objects that move them in a particular way when they can linger over the many delicious and peculiar charms of each as it comes? So, if they write criticism and call it aesthetics, if they imagine that they are talking about Art when they are talking about particular works of art or even about the technique of painting, if, loving particular works they find tedious the consideration of art in general, perhaps they have chosen the better part. If they are not curious about the nature of their emotion, nor about the quality common to all objects that provoke it, they have my sympathy, and, as what they say is often charming and suggestive, my admiration too. Only let no one suppose that what they write and talk is aesthetics; it is criticism, or just "shop."

The starting-point for all systems of aesthetics must be the personal experience of a peculiar emotion. The objects that provoke this emotion we call works of art. All sensitive people agree that there is a peculiar emotion provoked by works of art. I do not mean, of course, that all works provoke the same emotion. On the contrary, every work produces a different emotion. But all these emotions are recognizably the same in kind; so far, at any rate, the best opinion is on my side. That there is a particular kind of emotion provoked by works of visual art, and that this emotion is provoked by every kind of visual art, by pictures, sculptures, buildings, pots, carvings, textiles, etc., etc., is not disputed, I think, by anyone capable of feeling it. This emotion is called the aesthetic emotion; and if we can discover some quality common and peculiar to all the objects that provoke it, we shall have solved what I take to be the central problem of aesthetics. We shall have discovered the essential quality in a work of art, the quality that distinguishes works of art from all other classes of objects.

For either all works of visual art have some common quality, or when we speak of "works of art" we gibber. Everyone speaks of "art," making a mental classification by which he distinguishes the class "works of art" from all other classes. What is the justification of this classification? What is the quality common and peculiar to all members of this class? Whatever it be, no doubt it is often found in company with other qualities; but they are adventitious—it is essential. There must be some one quality without which a work of art cannot exist; possessing which, in the least degree, no work is altogether worthless. What is this quality? What quality is shared by all objects that provoke our aesthetic emotions? What quality is common to Sta. Sophia and the windows at Chartres, Mexican sculpture, a Persian bowl, Chinese carpets, Giotto's frescoes at Padua, and the masterpieces of Poussin, Piero della Francesca, and Cézanne? Only one answer seems possible—significant form. In each, lines and colors combined in a particular way, certain forms and relations of forms, stir our aesthetic emotions. These relations and combinations of lines and colors, these aesthetically moving forms, I call "Significant Form"; and "Significant Form" is the one quality common to all works of visual art.

At this point it may be objected that I am making aesthetics a purely subjective business, since my only data are personal experiences of a particular emotion. It will be said that the objects that provoke this emotion vary with each individual, and that therefore a system of aesthetics can have no objective validity. It must be replied that any system of aesthetics which pretends to be based on some objective truth is so palpably ridiculous as not to be worth discussing. We have no other means of recognizing a work of art than our feeling for it. The objects that provoke aesthetic emotion vary with each individual. Aesthetic judgments are, as the saying goes, matters of taste; and about tastes, as everyone is proud to admit, there is no disputing. A good critic may be able to make me see in a picture that had left me cold things that I had overlooked, till at last, receiving the aesthetic emotion, I recognize it as a work of art. To be continually pointing out those parts, the sum, or rather the combination, of which unite to produce significant form, is the function of criticism. But it is useless for a critic to tell me that something is a work of art; he must make me feel it for myself. This he can do only by making me see; he must get at my emotions through my eyes. Unless he can make me see something that moves me, he cannot force my emotions. I have no right to consider anything a work of art to which I cannot react emotionally; and I have no right to look for the essential quality in anything that I have not *felt* to be a work of art. The critic can affect my aesthetic theories only by affecting my aesthetic experience. All systems of aesthetics must be based on personal experience; that is to say, they must be subjective.

Yet, though all aesthetic theories must be based on aesthetic judgments, and ultimately all aesthetic judgments must be matters of personal taste, it would be rash to assert that no theory of aesthetics can have general validity. For, though A, B, C, D are the works that move me, and A, D, E, F the works that move you, it may well be that *x* is the only quality believed by either of us to be common to all the works in his list. We may all agree about aesthetics, and yet differ about particular works of art. We may differ as to the presence or absence of the quality *x*. My immediate object will be to show that significant form is the only quality common and peculiar to all the works of visual art that move me; and I will ask those whose aesthetic experience does not tally with mine to see whether this quality is not also, in their judgment, common to all works that move them, and whether they can discover any other quality of which the same can be said.

Also at this point a query arises, irrelevant indeed, but hardly to be suppressed: "Why are we so profoundly moved by forms related in a particular way?" The question is extremely interesting, but irrelevant to aesthetics. In pure aesthetics we have only to consider our emotion and its object: for the purposes of aesthetics we have no right, neither is there any necessity, to pry behind the object into the state of mind of him who made it. . . . For a discussion of aesthetics, it need be agreed only that forms arranged and combined according to certain unknown and mysterious laws do move us in a particular way, and that it is the business of an artist so to combine and arrange them that they shall move us. These moving combinations and arrangements I have called, for the sake of convenience and for a reason that will appear later, "Significant Form."

A third interpretation has to be met.

"Are you forgetting about color?" someone inquires. Certainly not; my term "significant form" included combinations of lines and of colors. The distinction between form and color is an unreal one; you cannot conceive a colorless line or a colorless space; neither can you conceive a formless relation of colors. In a black and white drawing the spaces are all white and all are bounded by black lines; in most oil paintings the spaces are multi-colored and so are the boundaries; you cannot imagine a boundary line without any content, or a content without any boundary lines. Therefore, when I speak of significant form, I mean a combination of lines and colors (counting white and black as colors) that moves me aesthetically. . . .

On the other hand, with those who judge it more exact to call these combinations and arrangements of form that provoke our aesthetic emotions, not "significant form," but "significant relations of form," and then try to make the best of two worlds, the aesthetic and the metaphysical, by calling these relations "rhythm," I have no quarrel whatever. Having made it clear that by "significant form" I mean arrangements and combinations that move us in a particular way, I willingly join hands with those who prefer to give a different name to the same thing.

The hypothesis that significant form is the essential quality in a work of art has at least one merit denied to many more famous and more striking—it does help to explain things. We are all familiar with pictures that interest us and excite our admiration, but do not move us as works of art. To this class belongs what I call "Descriptive Painting"—that is, painting in which forms are used not as objects of emotion, but as means of suggesting emotion or conveying information. Portraits of psychological and historical value, topographical works, pictures that tell stories and suggest situations, illustrations of all sorts, belong to this class. That we all recognize the distinction is clear, for who has not said that such and such a drawing was excellent as illustration, but as a work of art worthless? Of course many descriptive pictures possess, amongst other qualities, formal significance, and are therefore works of art; but many more do not. They interest us; they may move us too in a hundred different ways, but they do not move us aesthetically. According to my hypothesis they are not works of art. They leave untouched our aesthetic emotions because it is not their forms but the ideas or information suggested or conveyed by their forms that affect us. . . .

To appreciate a work of art we need bring with us nothing but a sense of form and color and a knowledge of three-dimensional space. That bit of knowledge, I admit, is essential to the appreciation of many great works, since many of the most moving forms ever created are in three dimensions. To see a cube or rhomboid as a flat pattern is to lower its significance, and a sense of three-dimensional space is essential to the full appreciation of most architectural forms. Pictures which would be insignificant if we saw them as flat patterns are profoundly moving because, in fact, we see them as related planes. If the representation of three-dimensional space is to be called "representation," then I agree that there is one kind of representation which is not irrelevant. Also, I agree that along with our feeling for line and color we must bring with us our knowledge of space if we are to make the most of every kind of form. Nevertheless, there are magnificent designs to an appreciation of which this knowledge is not necessary: so, though it is not irrelevant to the appreciation of some works of art it is not essential to the appreciation of all. What we must say is that the representation of three-dimensional space is neither irrelevant nor essential to all art, and that every other sort of representation is irrelevant.

That there is an irrelevant representative or descriptive element in many great works of art is not in the least surprising. Why it is not surprising I shall try to show elsewhere. Representation is not of necessity baneful, and highly realistic forms may be extremely significant. Very often, however, representation is a sign of weakness in an artist. A painter too feeble to create forms that provoke more than a little aesthetic emotion will try to eke that little out by suggesting the emotions of life. To evoke the emotions of life he must use representation. Thus a man will paint an execution, and, fearing to miss with his first barrel of significant form, will try to hit with his second by raising an emotion of fear or pity. But if in the artist an inclination to play upon the emotions of life is often the sign of a flickering inspiration, in the spectator a tendency to seek, behind form, the emotions of life is a sign of defective sensibility always. It means that his aesthetic emotions are weak or, at any rate, imperfect. Before a work of art people who feel little or no emotion for pure form find themselves at a loss. They are deaf men at a concert. They know that they are in the presence of something great, but they lack the power of apprehending it. They know that they ought to feel for it a tremendous emotion, but it happens that the particular kind of emotion it can raise is one that they can feel hardly or not at all. And so they read into the forms of the work those facts and ideas for which they are capable of feeling emotion, and feel for them the emotions that they can feel—the ordinary emotions of life. When confronted by a picture, instinctively they refer back its forms to the world from which they came. They treat created form as though it were imitated form, a picture as though it were a photograph. Instead of going out on the stream of art into a new world of aesthetic experience, they turn a sharp corner and come straight home to the world of human interests. For them the significance of a work of art depends on what they bring to it; no new thing is added to their lives, only the old material is stirred. A good work of visual art carries a person who is capable of appreciating it out of life into ecstasy: to use art as a means to the emotions of life is to use a telescope for reading the news. You will notice that people who cannot feel pure aesthetic emotions remember pictures by their subjects; whereas people who can, as often as not, have no idea what the subject of a picture is. They have never noticed the representative element, and so when they discuss pictures they talk about the shapes of forms and the relations and quantities of colors. Often they can tell by the quality of a single line whether or not a man is a good artist. They are concerned only with lines and colors, their relations and quantities and qualities; but from these they win an emotion more profound and far more sublime than any that can be given by the description of facts and ideas. . . .

If the forms of a work are significant its provenance is irrelevant. . . . Great art remains stable and unobscure because the feelings that it awakens are independent of time and place, because its kingdom is not of this world. To those who have and hold a sense of the significance of form what does it matter whether the forms that move them were created in Paris the day before yesterday or in Babylon fifty centuries ago? The forms of art are inexhaustible; but all lead by the same road of aesthetic emotion to the same world of aesthetic ecstasy. ◣

Questions for Discussion

1. Are there really aesthetic features in artworks, or do we impose aesthetic features on artworks?

2. What is the function or functions, if any, of titles of artworks?

3. Are artworks truly unique sorts of particulars, as Margolis claims? He also says that they are "culturally emergent entities." What, exactly, does that mean? If they are, does that imply that the features of artworks, whether aesthetic or nonaesthetic, are not inherent in the artworks themselves?

4. Why aren't the aesthetic features of artworks reducible to the nonaesthetic features of artworks? If nonaesthetic features are only a necessary condi-

tion for aesthetic features, what else is needed for aesthetic features to be realized?

5. Critics of formalism say that the notion of form, at least of artistic or aesthetic form, is vague at best and so is not useful in understanding artworks. Is Sibley wrong to counter this claim by saying that the same thing could be said about content and context, that they, too, are vague at best and so not useful in understanding artworks?

CHAPTER 4

THE ARTIST

The twentieth-century writer Ayn Rand once remarked at a lecture that there was not a single word in her novels that she could not explain. A spectator at the lecture challenged her by quoting the following (randomly chosen?) paragraph from Rand's novel *Atlas Shrugged*:

> Clouds had wrapped the sky and had descended as fog to wrap the streets below, as if the sky were engulfing the city. She could see the whole of Manhattan Island, a long, triangular shape cutting into an invisible ocean. It looked like the prow of a sinking ship; a few tall buildings still rose above it, like funnels, but the rest was disappearing under gray-blue coils, going down slowly into vapor and space. This was how they had gone—she thought—Atlantis, the city that sank into the ocean, and all the other kingdoms that vanished, leaving the same legend in all the languages of men, and the same longing.

Rand then gave her analysis of this paragraph:

> This description had four purposes: (1) to give an image of the view from Dagny's window, namely: an image of what New York looks like on a foggy evening; (2) to suggest the meaning of the events which have been taking place, namely: the city as a symbol of greatness doomed to destruction; (3) to connect New York with the legend of Atlantis; (4) to

convey Dagny's mood. So the description had to be written on four levels: literal—connotative—symbolic—emotional.

The opening sentence of the description sets the key for all four levels: "*Clouds had wrapped the sky and had descended as fog to wrap the streets below, as if the sky were engulfing the city.*" On the literal level, the sentence is exact: it describes a foggy evening. But had I said something like: "There were clouds in the sky, and the streets were full of fog"—the sentence would have achieved nothing more. By casting the sentence into an active form, by wording it as if the clouds were pursuing some goal, I achieve the following: (1) on a literal level, a more graphic image of the view, because the sentence suggests the motion, the progressive thickening of the fog; (2) on the connotative level, it suggests the conflict of two adversaries and the grandeur of the conflict, since the adversaries are *sky* and *city*, and it suggests that the city is doomed, since it is being engulfed; (3) on the symbolic level, the word "*engulfed*" strikes the keynote for the tie to Atlantis, suggesting the act of sinking and, by connotation, blending the motion of the fog with the motion of waves; (4) on the emotional level, the use of so quiet a verb as "*to wrap,*" in the context of an ominous "*engulfing*" conflict, establishes a mood of quiet, desolate hopelessness.

Rand went on to describe and analyze in equal detail each of the other sentences in the paragraph and then concluded by saying:

No, I do not expect the reader of that paragraph to grasp consciously all the specific considerations listed above. I expect him to get a general impression, an emotional sum—the particular sum that I intended. A reader has to be concerned only with the end result; unless he chooses to analyze it, he does not have to know by what means that result was achieved—but it is *my* job to know. . . . One must hold all the basic elements of the book's theme, plot and main characters so firmly in one's mind that they become automatic and almost "instinctual." Then, as one approaches the actual writing of any given scene or paragraph, one has the sense of "feel" of what it has to be by the logic of the context—and one's subconscious makes the right selections to express it. Later, one checks and improves the result by means of conscious editing."

INTENTION

As Rand's remarks demonstrate, art does not just happen; artists put a great deal of effort and care into creating an artwork. They are thoughtful and purposeful in their acts of creation. Of course, there can be spontaneity in these acts of creation, for instance, with impromptu musical performances, but even in such cases the artistic act of creation is not simply random. Artistic imagination and creativity are not the result of magically waving a wand; rather, they require hard work and disciplined action, often involving a great deal of rigorous and sustained training and practice. Furthermore, art—at least, much art—is *about* something. In the act of creating an artwork, the artist is trying to do or say something by creating that artwork. That is, artists intend something or other by creating an artwork, in terms of both the creative process itself and the result, or product, of that process (namely, the artwork). As we've already seen in previous chapters, the nature and role of intention is a basic issue in the question of what the very nature of art is, as well as of what constitutes an artwork. In Chapter 5 we will also see how intention is relevant to issues related to the perspective of the audience of art, that is, to questions about interpreting and critiquing art. For now, the point is that much (perhaps all) art is about something; artworks convey meaning, and those meanings are intimately and inescapably tied up with what artists are doing or intending in and by creating artworks. Whereas in Chapter 3, the focus was on issues relating directly to artworks themselves, issues such as form and content or form and context, the focus in this chapter is on issues relating to artists, particularly to what artists are doing when they do art.

Different artists, of course, say that they are doing different things; there are a multitude of reasons and causes for what artists do. For instance, some artists are commissioned to create specific products. Advertising agencies hire artists to compose catchy jingles to encourage consumers to purchase their products, institutions or organizations hire artists to create artworks to adorn their buildings, governments commission artists to produce artworks for public spaces or for political agendas, and so on. Less commercially, individuals hire artists to paint portraits of particular subjects. In all these examples, the reason for the artist to create an artwork is, in a sense, external to the personal motivations of the artist. But when we ask ourselves why artists do what they do, we usually think about their personal intentions, what they mean by trying to create artworks.

Although there might be many different reasons and causes for artists doing what they do, philosophers (and artists) have tended to speak of a few broad kinds of reasons or causes. This chapter will consider three broad kinds: *representation*, *expression*, and *change*. Art as representation focuses on the notion that artists, by creating artworks, are trying to represent something or other (for example, perhaps something of value to them). Art as expression focuses on the notion that artists, by creating artworks, are trying to express something or other (for example, perhaps their feelings about something or some event). A variation of this view is that artists are trying to communicate to others or perhaps to evoke something from an audience. Art as change focuses on the notion that artists, by creating artworks, are trying to change something or other (for example, perhaps themselves or perhaps social conditions). Each of these will be considered here, with the representation view first.

REPRESENTATION

Obviously, many artworks represent. Portraits portray their subjects; photographs record what they the camera "sees"; some dance movements resemble, and are intended to resemble, the movements of, say, swans (as in *Swan Lake*) or waves (as in a hula). Not all artworks represent, at least in any obvious visual way—for instance, abstract paintings or architectural structures or collections of musical tones do not necessarily represent anything—but many do. In philosophical concerns about art, one of the oldest conceptions of art takes it as (primarily) representation. Indeed, one of the most famous views about art is Plato's criticisms of art, based on the notion that art is representation. Plato spoke of various levels of reality. Some things that are real are particular and fleeting. For instance, a tree might cast a shadow if it is in the sunlight. The shadow is certainly real; it exists. However, if the sun goes behind a cloud or the sun sets beyond the horizon, the shadow goes away; it no longer exists. The physical tree that casts that shadow is also real, in fact, it is "more" real, said Plato, than the shadow, since the physical tree continues to exist even when the sun goes behind a cloud or it sets. Just as the physical tree is more real than the shadow of a tree, the Idea, or essence, of Tree is even more real than the physical tree, said Plato. This is because the Idea of Tree can exist even if that tree dies or is cut down. In fact, even if all trees somehow went away, the Idea of Tree would still exist, just as the Idea of Dinosaur can exist even though there are no dinosaurs any more, or the Idea of Circle exists even if there are no perfect circles in the world.

It is against this background of the doctrine of Ideas that Plato formulated his views of art and aesthetics. Although he practiced art himself—his writings were essentially dramatic literary works—and he often included myths and fables in his writings, he is renowned for his criticisms of art and artists. For the most part, Plato saw art as a particular form of what the Greeks called *techné*, or knowledge related to doing or making something. Arts, in effect, were a form of craft, so Plato (and others) spoke of the art of horsemanship or the art of political statesmanship. The arts—that is, poetry, drama, and the like—were seen as a kind of craft. However, to the extent that art was a matter not of production (such as the art of horsemanship, in which someone produced a good rider or a tame horse) but, rather, of imitation (such as writing a poem or a play about horses), then art was imitation (the Greek term was *mimesis*, from which English gets the word *mimic*). Art as imitation was, for Plato, a matter of representing something. For instance, a painting of a horse represents a horse (or, perhaps, horses generally); it imitates them in the sense of being an image of them. Obviously, a painting of a horse is only like a real horse in the sense of looking like one. Just as a shadow of a person is real, but less real than a real person, for Plato, so, too, a painting of a horse is less real than an actual, physical horse. In addition, as just noted, for Plato, an actual, physical horse is real, but less real than the Idea of Horse. In a sense, an actual, physical horse is just a copy or representation of the more real Idea of Horse. Thus, a painting of a horse is a copy of a copy! It is even more removed from the Idea of Horse than is the physical object it represents. Art, then, for Plato, is akin to shadows and images; it is a low level of reality. To the extent that people might experience art as representing reality, then, it can be deceptive and hence bad. Whether intended or not, art can lead people away from seeking and knowing what is truly real (namely, Ideas).

Now, over the years many philosophers, as well as many artists, have rejected Plato's claims, but in doing so they have had to address a number of the issues he raised (whether he intended to or not). Those issues are metaphysical, epistemological, and axiological; they speak to what is represented, how it is represented, and why it is represented. But first, there is the issue of what, exactly, artistic representation is.

Clearly, in one sense, a representation is a copy or imitation of something. So a portrait of someone can represent a particular person because the portrait "looks like" the person. In a sense, it is a replication of that person. However, not all replications are representations. For example, if you have two copies of the same book, neither copy is thought to represent the other; they are simply two copies of the same book. In addition, something can represent something else without being a replica of it. For instance, at breakfast on some Monday morning, while describing some particularly noteworthy sporting event that happened over the weekend, someone might use a saltshaker to represent the local quarterback (even though the saltshaker does not look like the quarterback). So representation is not the same thing as duplication or replication or even physical resemblance. What, exactly, representation is—and whether or not there is any core set of necessary or sufficient conditions for something to be a representation—is something that philosophers and artists have argued about ever since Plato.

Still, we can ask, when there is artistic representation, *what* is being represented? It might be something in the world (say, a sunset or a person) or it might be some event (say, a wedding or a battle). In addition, it might be an attitude or value or abstract concept. Throughout history, certain objects have been taken to be representative of something based not on physical resemblance but on shared, understood social connotations. For example, in many paintings, dogs have been used to represent loyalty, so in a painting that portrayed a king or prince, a dog might be shown lying near his feet. Or in much of medieval religious art, a white rose was intended to represent purity and a red rose to represent martyrdom. A painting of a horse, then, contrary to Plato's notion, might not at all be (or be intended as) a representation of any given horse or even of horses generally; rather, it might be intended as, say, a representation of the sun (in ancient mythology) or lust (in much of Renaissance painting).

Likewise, *how* something is represented can be far more complex than what Plato seemed to suggest. As noted above, something might represent by mirroring or copying physical features of something, but that is neither necessary nor sufficient. In many cases of representation, symbolic idealizations are the means of representing. Imagine how one might represent, say, innocence in painting. Well, one might portray a baby, because we often think of babies as innocent and that connotation would probably be understood. How about in music? We would be unlikely to use "heavy" tones or slow, plodding tempos to represent innocence. And we would probably not score a passage representing innocence by having tubas play the notes. Rather, we might have, say, a flute playing simple phrases, perhaps with rising pitches.

How about in dance? Muscular, athletic leaps would probably not be the way we would represent innocence. In all these cases, we would use the materials at hand to portray or depict innocence, but they would rely on some symbolic, shared understandings much more than on physical resemblance. Nevertheless, some sense of resemblance would be there, which is why we would use a flute (for its light and gentle tonal qualities) rather than a tuba to musically represent innocence.

Also, there are questions of *why* something is represented. What is the artist trying to accomplish or achieve? This question speaks both to what motivates the artist and also to what goal(s) or purpose(s) the artist has. These are not necessarily the same thing. Getting paid might be what motivates an artist who has been commissioned to create an artwork that represents innocence. But that artist's goal might be to portray the subject of the artwork in a certain way so as to sway the targeted audience. Put more broadly, "why" in the sense of motivation has to do with reasons and causes, whereas "why" in the sense of goals or purposes has to do with intended results or outcomes. In any case, representation in art pertains to both denotation (that is, what features in the artwork relate to features in whatever is being represented) and connotation (that is, what associations and symbolic connections the artist and audience have or make). The reading below is selections from a classic discussion of some of the complexities of representation, written by a noted art theorist and historian, E. H. Gombrich.

▌ E. H. GOMBRICH, "TRUTH AND THE STEREOTYPE"*

In his charming autobiography, the German illustrator Ludwig Richter relates how he and his friends, all young art students in Rome in the 1820s, visited the famous beauty spot of Tivoli and sat down to draw. They looked with surprise, but hardly with approval, at a group of French artists who approached the place with enormous baggage, carrying large quantities of paint which they applied to the canvas with big, coarse brushes. The Germans, perhaps aroused by this self-confident artiness, were determined on the opposite approach. They selected the hardest, best-pointed pencils, which could render the motif firmly and minutely to its finest detail, and each bent down over his small piece of

---

*In *Art and Illusion*. Princeton: Princeton University Press, 1960. Pages 63–74, 87–90.

paper, trying to transcribe what he saw with the utmost fidelity. "We all fell in love with every blade of grass, every tiny twig, and refused to let anything escape us. Everyone tried to render the motif as objectively as possible."

Nevertheless, when they compared the fruits of their efforts in the evening, their transcripts differed to a surprising extent. The mood, the color, even the outline of the motif had undergone a subtle transformation in each of them. Richter goes on to describe how these different versions reflected the different dispositions of the four friends, for instance, how the melancholy painter had straightened the exuberant contours and emphasized the blue tinges. We might say he gives an illustration of the famous definition of Emile Zola, who called a work of art "a corner of nature seen through a temperament."

It is precisely because we are interested in this definition that we must probe it a little further. The "temperament" or "personality" of the artist, his selective preferences, may be one of the reasons for the transformation which the motif undergoes under the artist's hands, but there must be others—everything, in fact, which we bundle together into the word "style," the style of the period and the style of the artist. When this transformation is very noticeable we say the motif has been greatly "stylized," and the corollary to this observation is that those who happen to be interested in the motif, for one reason or another, must learn to discount the style. This is part of the natural adjustment, the change in what I call "mental set," which we all perform quite automatically when looking at old illustrations. We can "read" the Bayeux tapestry without reflecting on its countless "deviations from reality." We are not tempted for a moment to think the trees at Hastings in 1066 looked like palmettes and the ground at the time consisted of scrolls. It is an extreme example, but it brings out the all-important fact that the word "stylized" somehow tends to beg the question. It implies there was a special activity by which the artist transformed the trees, much as the Victorian designer was taught to study the forms of flowers before he turned them into patterns. It was a practice which chimed in well with ideas of Victorian architecture, when railways and factories were built first and then adorned with the marks of a style. It was not the practice of earlier times.

The very point of Richter's story, after all, is that style rules even where the artist wishes to reproduce nature faithfully, and trying to analyze these limits to objectivity may help us get nearer to the riddle of style. One of these limits . . . is indicated in Richter's story by the contrast between coarse brush and fine pencil. The artist, clearly, can render only what his tool and his medium are capable of rendering. His technique restricts his freedom of choice. The features and relationships the pencil picks out will differ from those the brush can indicate.

Sitting in front of his motif, pencil in hand, the artist will, therefore, look out for those aspects which can be rendered in lines—as we say in a pardonable abbreviation, he will tend to see his motif in lines, while, brush in hand, he sees it in terms of masses.

The question of why style should impose similar limitations is less easily answered, least of all when we do not know whether the artist's intentions were the same as those of Richter and his friends.

Historians of art have explored the regions where Cézanne and van Gogh set up their easels and have photographed their motifs. Such comparisons will always retain their fascination since they almost allow us to look over the artist's shoulder—and who does not wish he had this privilege? But however instructive such confrontations may be when handled with care, we must clearly beware of the fallacy of "stylization." Should we believe the photograph represents the "objective truth" while the painting records the artist's subjective vision—the way he transformed "what he saw"? Can we here compare "the image on the retina" with the "image in the mind"? Such speculations easily lead into a morass of unprovables. Take the image on the artist's retina. It sounds scientific enough, but actually there never was *one* such image which we could single out for comparison with either photograph or painting. What there was was an endless succession of innumerable images as the painter scanned the landscape in front of him, and these images sent a complex pattern of impulses through the optic nerves to his brain. Even the artist knew nothing of these events, and we know even less. How far the picture that formed in his mind corresponded to or deviated from the photograph it is even less profitable to ask. What we do know is that these artists went out into nature to look for material for a picture and their artistic wisdom led them to organize the elements of the landscape into works of art of marvelous complexity that bear as much relationship to a surveyor's record as a poem does to a police report.

Does this mean, then, that we are altogether on a useless quest? That artistic truth differs so much from prosaic truth that the question of objectivity must never be asked? I do not think so. We must only be a little more circumspect in our formulation of the question.

II

The National Gallery in Washington possesses a landscape painting by a nineteenth-century artist which almost seems made to clarify this issue.

It is an attractive picture by George Inness of "The Lackawanna Valley," which we know from the master's son was commissioned in 1855 as an advertisement for a railroad. At the time there was only one track running into the round-house, "but the president insisted on having four or five painted in, easing his conscience by explaining that the road would eventually have them." Inness protested, and we can see that when he finally gave in for the sake of his family, he shamefacedly hid the patch with the nonexistent tracks behind puffs of smoke. To him this patch was a lie, and no esthetic explanation about mental images or higher truth could have disputed this away.

But, strictly speaking, the lie was not in the painting. It was in the advertise-ment, if it claimed by caption or implication that the painting gave accurate in-formation about the facilities of the railway's roundhouses. In a different context the same picture might have illustrated a true statement—for instance, if the president had taken it to a shareholders' meeting to demonstrate improvements he was anxious to make. Indeed in that case, Inness' rendering of the nonexis-tent tracks might conceivably have given the engineer some hints about where to lay them. It would have served as a sketch or blueprint.

Logicians tell us—and they are not people to be easily gainsaid—that the terms "true" and "false" can only be applied to statements, propositions. And whatever may be the usage of critical parlance, a picture is never a statement in that sense of the term. It can no more be true or false than a statement can be blue or green. Much confusion has been caused in esthetics by disregarding this simple fact. It is an understandable confusion because in our culture pic-tures are usually labeled, and labels, or captions, can be understood as abbrevi-ated statements. When it is said "the camera cannot lie," this confusion is apparent. Propaganda in wartime often made use of photographs falsely labeled to accuse or exculpate one of the warring parties. Even in scientific illustrations it is the caption which determines the truth of the picture. . . . Without much re-flection, we can all expand into statements the laconic captions we find in mu-seums and books. When we read the name "Ludwig Richter" under a landscape painting, we know we are thus informed that he painted it and can begin argu-ing whether this information is true or false. When we read "Tivoli," we infer the picture is to be taken as a view of that spot, and we can again agree or dis-agree with the label. How and when we agree, in such a case, will largely de-pend on what we want to know about the object represented. The Bayeux tapestry, for instance, tells us there was a battle at Hastings. It does not tell us what Hastings "looked like." . . .

Varying standards of illustration and documentation are of interest to the histo-rian of representation precisely because he can soberly test the information sup-plied by picture and caption without becoming entangled too soon in problems of esthetics. Where it is a question of information imparted by the image, the comparison with the correctly labeled photograph should be of obvious value. . . .

An example from the seventeenth century, from the views of Paris by that well-known and skillful topographical artist Matthäus Merian, represents Notre Dame and gives, at first, quite a convincing rendering of that famous church. . . . As a child of the seventeenth century, his notion of a church is that of a lofty symmetrical building with large, rounded windows, and that is how he designs Notre Dame. He places the transept in the center with four large, rounded windows on either side, while the actual view shows seven narrow, pointed Gothic windows to the west and six in the choir. Once more portrayal means for Merian the adaptation or adjustment of his formula or scheme for churches to a particular building through the addition of a number of distinctive features— enough to make it recognizable and even acceptable to those who are not in search of architectural information. If this happened to be the only document extant to tell us about the Cathedral of Paris, we would be very much misled.

One last example in this series: a nineteenth-century lithograph of Chartres Cathedral, done in the heyday of English topographical art. Here, surely, we might expect a faithful visual record. By comparison with the previous instances, the artist really gives a good deal of accurate information about that famous building. But he, too, it turns out, cannot escape the limitations which his time and interests impose on him. He is a romantic to whom the French cathedrals are the greatest flowers of the Gothic centuries, the true age of faith. And so he conceives of Chartres as a Gothic structure with pointed arches and fails to record the Romanesque rounded windows of the west façade, which have no place in his universe of form.

I do not want to be misunderstood here. I do not want to prove by these examples that all representation must be inaccurate or that all visual documents before the advent of photography must be misleading. Clearly, if we had pointed out to the artist his mistake, he could have further modified his scheme and rounded the windows. My point is rather that such matching will always be a step-by-step process—how long it takes and how hard it is will depend on the choice of the initial schema to be adapted to the task of serving as a portrait. I believe that in this respect these humble documents do indeed tell us a lot about the procedure of any artist who wants to make a truthful record of an individual form. He begins not with his visual impression but with his idea or concept[,] . . . Merian with his idea of a church, and the lithographer with his stereotype of a cathedral. The individual visual information, those distinctive features I have mentioned, are entered, as it were, upon a pre-existing blank or formulary. And, as often happens with blanks, if they have no provisions for certain kinds of information we consider essential, it is just too bad for the information.

. . . Copying . . . proceeds through the rhythms of schema and correction. The schema is not the product of a process of "abstraction," of a tendency to "simplify"; it represents the first approximate, loose category which is gradually tightened to fit the form it is to reproduce. . . .

VI

Everything points to the conclusion that the phrase the "language of art" is more than a loose metaphor, that even to describe the visible world in images we need a developed system of schemata. This conclusion rather clashes with the traditional distinction, often discussed in the eighteenth century, between spoken words which are conventional signs and painting which uses "natural" signs to "imitate" reality. It is a plausible distinction, but it has led to certain difficulties. If we assume, with this tradition, that natural signs can simply be copied from nature, the history of art represents a complete puzzle. It has become increasingly clear since the late nineteenth century that primitive art and child art use a language of symbols rather than "natural signs." To account for this fact it was postulated that there must be a special kind of art which operates with "conceptual images." The child—it is argued—does not look at trees; he is satisfied with the "conceptual" schema of a tree that fails to correspond to any reality since it does not embody the characteristics of, say, birch or beech, let alone those of individual trees. This reliance on construction rather than on imitation was attributed to the peculiar mentality of children and primitives who live in a world of their own.

But we have come to realize that this distinction is unreal. Gustaf Britsch and Rudolf Arnheim have stressed that there is no opposition between the crude map of the world made by a child and the richer map presented in naturalistic images. All art originates in the human mind, in our reactions to the world rather than in the visible world itself, and it is precisely because all art is "conceptual" that all representations are recognizable by their style. . . .

We seem to have drifted far from the discussion of portrayal. But it is certainly possible to look at a portrait as a schema of a head modified by the distinctive features about which we wish to convey information. The American police sometimes employ draftsmen to aid witnesses in the identification of criminals. They may draw any vague face, a random schema, and let witnesses guide their modifications of selected features simply by saying "yes" or "no" to various suggested standard alterations until the face is sufficiently individual-ized for a search in the files to be profitable. This account of portrait drawing by remote control may well be over-tidy, but as a parable it may serve its purpose. It reminds us that the staring point of a visual record is not knowledge but a guess conditioned by habit and tradition. . . .

From the point of view of information there is surely no difficulty in dis-cussing portrayal. To say of a drawing that it is a correct view of Tivoli does not mean, of course, that Tivoli is bounded by wiry lines. It means that those who understand the notation will derive *no false information* from the drawing—whether it gives the contour in a few lines or picks out "every blade of grass" as Richter's friends wanted to do. The complete portrayal might be one which gives as much correct information about the spot as we would obtain if we looked at it from the very spot where the artist stood.

Styles, like languages, differ in the sequence of articulation and in the num-ber of questions they allow the artist to ask; and so complex is the information that reaches us from the visible world that no picture will ever embody it all. This is not due to the subjectivity of vision but to its richness. Where the artist has to copy a human product he can, of course, produce a facsimile which is indistinguishable from the original. The forger of banknotes succeeds only too well in effacing his personality and the limitations of a period style.

But what matters to us is that the correct portrait, like the useful map, is an end product on a long road through schema and correction. It is not a faithful record of a visual experience but the fruitful construction of a relational model.

Neither the subjectivity of vision nor the sway of conventions need lead us to deny that such a model can be constructed to any required degree of accu-racy. What is decisive here is clearly the word "required." The form of represen-tation cannot be divorced from its purpose and the requirements of the society in which the given visual language gains currency. ◣

EXPRESSION

Some art, of course, does involve representation. Even abstract paintings or artworks that do not seem to be "about" anything, at least in terms of their content, can still represent something or other to an audience. With respect to representation, the artist's intentions do not seem to be necessary; an art-work can represent something to an audience independently of the artist. In-deed, this is an important aspect of the interpretation and evaluation of art, which is the subject of Chapter 5.

Regardless of the fact of artistic representation, many people, and certainly many artists, claim that representation is not the most salient feature of art, either in terms of art as process or art as product. Rather, the central aspect of art is expression. That is, when creating artworks, artists are engaged in expressing themselves through that art (again, whether in terms of process or product). The root of the term *expression* is, of course, *express*, which comes from the Latin words *ex*, "out," and *pressare*, "press" or "squeeze." To express oneself is to state or announce something, usually verbally but in the case of art, nonverbally as well.

In the context of art, and the philosophy of art, the view that the fundamental aspect of art is the creative expression of oneself is often called expressionism (or, also, expressivism). One of the most famous advocates of this view was the Russian novelist Leo Tolstoy. Tolstoy claimed that the defining aspect of art was the expression of emotion. Whereas, say, science expressed (or, to use his word, transmitted) thought, art expressed emotion. Good art is and should be something that moves us, not something that convinces us. Furthermore, good art should actually transmit the feelings of the artist through the artwork to the audience (that is, to the person or persons who experiences the artwork). A successful artist, he claimed, should be (and will be) able to make the audience feel what the artist felt when creating the artwork. In addition, for Tolstoy, the value of art is that it transmits emotion and thus enables people to be more strongly connected to each other.

As with the view that art is representation, the view that art is expression, although seemingly straightforward and perhaps obviously true, is more complex than it appears at first glance and, as we will see soon, is perhaps not so obviously true. Many philosophers of art, as well as artists, have questioned the view that art is essentially expression. For one thing, the simple fact of self-expression does not obviously constitute art. A young child in the midst of throwing a temper tantrum is engaged in (creative?) self-expression, but it is not at all obvious that this is art! So one question posed by philosophers is whether creative self-expression is by itself sufficient for something to be art (and the case of a screaming child suggests that it is not). Is creative self-expression even necessary for something to be art? That, too, is not obvious. An artist might be given very specific instructions and guidelines for creating an artwork, and this might involve little or no self-expression. For example, an artist might be commissioned to paint someone's portrait in such-and-such a way. The simple fact that actors can express emotions or beliefs in the context of a dramatic scene certainly does not imply that they feel those emotions or have those beliefs. The result might be an artwork, but it is not necessarily a case of self-expression.

Even if self-expression is important in the creation of art, there are questions of what is expressed, how it is expressed, and why it is expressed. When an artist creates a work of art, what is being expressed might be the artist's feelings or emotions, or the artist's thoughts or beliefs, or something else entirely. The immediate point is that what is being expressed does not have to be emotion. In the case of, say, architecture, an architect might, with the artistic design aspects of the building, be expressing connectedness to a specific landscape or local environment or local history. In addition, what is actually expressed might not be what the artist feels or thinks or intends to express. An artist might well be trying to express some particular state, whether emotional or cognitive, but that state might not be what gets expressed. As we all know, intention and outcome are not always a perfect match! This can be very obvious when we are speaking: I might intend to express my appreciation to you, but I blunder and end up expressing, say, annoyance. Or I intend to compliment you but end up insulting you. As we sometimes say, we express ourselves poorly. Clearly, this can happen with art, too.

An artist might express, say, feelings or beliefs about personal betrayal or about innocence and redemption in very concrete ways (such as putting in specific content in the artwork) or in less concrete ways (such as using certain colors or shapes or tones in the artwork). Above, in the discussion of representation, we considered how one might represent innocence via painting, music, and dance. The same considerations come into play if we ask how one might express innocence in these art forms. It is likely that the same aspects or techniques would be used to express innocence as to represent it. For instance, in dance it seems unlikely that one would express innocence via heavy, muscular movements; in music it seems unlikely that one would express innocence via large volume or via instruments such as tubas or drums. (This should at least nudge us toward the question, then, of what, exactly, is the relationship between representation and expression.)

In addition, there might be a variety of reasons or causes or motivations for this self-expression: perhaps for personal therapy or purging of feelings or thoughts, or perhaps to inform or entertain or even to shock others. As we saw, Tolstoy claimed that the purpose of artistic (self-) expression was to transmit one's emotions to others and, hence, to create a connection with them. This is different from a long-standing view originating with the Greek philosopher Aristotle that the point, or at least one important effect, of art (which for Aristotle meant tragic drama) was catharsis, or purging of an emotion. By expressing emotion through art, one "gets through" the emotion, so to speak.

Yet another reason given for expressing personal states via art is that it is a process of self-discovery. Artists sometimes remark on their surprise about how their own work turned out, or ended up; the end product, they sometimes claim, was not what they intended at the beginning of the process or what they expected would be the result. By expressing themselves through their art, then, they came to learn something about themselves, and that, they say, is what is important about artistic expression.

As philosophers of art, and artists, take a critical look at this view of art as expression, some of them say that there is an important difference between the expression of the artist and the expressiveness in the artwork and the impact on the audience. Artist might not express themselves very well in their art. It might be, for example, that an artist tries to express innocence in some work but fails to do so. Furthermore, the artwork might express something other than what the artist was expressing or intending to express. An artist might be expressing outrage or reverence by creating an artwork, or the artist might intend the painting to express outrage or reverence; however, the expressiveness in the artwork might be of something else. Even more, the arousal of some emotion in the audience often is quite separate and independent of the artist's expression. An artist might feel reverence and (try to) express that in a given artwork, but that artwork might well be received by an audience as insincere or self-indulgent and so arouse a feeling of mockery or disgust. (For those who advocate art as expression, cases such as this simply mean that it is bad art, rather than meaning that art is not expression.)

Another objection to the view that art is expression is that very often it takes a great deal of time and effort to create an artwork, which is inconsistent with the self-expression of emotion. Emotional states are, at least usually, somewhat fleeting; a person is joyous or sad for a short while, but creating an artwork can take days or months or even longer. Also, the process of actually working on a given piece of art is not continuous; artists may go to sleep each night, take time out to eat, or (as is likely) work a day job. Emotional states are a different sort of thing. So, say these critics, even if art is in some sense self-expression, it is something other than a spontaneous, inspired outpouring of emotion.

Beyond these concerns about the nature of expression and its relation to art, many philosophers, as well as many artists, claim that "mere" self-expression is not what is important in the creation of art; rather, communication is. That is, self-expression is a one-way statement; it is an artist expressing herself, and that is all. Perhaps no one will ever encounter or experience the work. There is a difference between a diary and a literary work. Real art, they claim, is about communication. It is a two-way statement; it involves an artist using art as a means of connecting to others, not merely stating or announcing feelings or beliefs. Communication with others is what many artists, including Tolstoy, as noted above, claim is valuable about art. Still others, as we will discuss later in this chapter, claim that the goal of creating art is not merely self-expression or even "merely" communication; instead, it is to have an impact on others. The goal is to evoke or even provoke feelings or thoughts or action in others as a result of the artist's artwork. Expression, that is, creative self-expression, then, is not what is important or valuable about art, but having an impact on others is.

In the following reading, the noted philosopher of art R. G. Collingwood argues that art is imaginative expression that communicates to an audience. The process of creating art is, for him, a process of self-discovery, indeed, of an artist discovering just what his or her emotions are. The very act of communicating (emotions) to an audience is also, for the artist, an act of self-communication. Collingwood distinguishes what he sees as art proper, which leads to self-discovery, from craft, which, for him, is artistic endeavor without the aspect of self-discovery. In addition, far from artistic emotional expression being primarily, or even simply, expressing one's feelings, he remarks that "the artist never rants." Just "being emotional" via art, for Collingwood, might be being an exhibitionist, but it is not being an artist. Art, even as emotional expression, is more than, and different from, bellowing; a tantrum-throwing child (or adult) is not an artist. Here, then, is Collingwood:

R. G. COLLINGWOOD, *PRINCIPLES OF ART*[*]

Expressing Emotion and Arousing Emotion

Nothing could be more entirely commonplace than to say [the artist] expresses [emotions]. The idea is familiar to every artist, and to everyone else who has

---

[*]Oxford: Oxford University Press, 1938. Pages 109–117, 121–123.

any acquaintance with the arts. To state it is not to state a philosophical theory of definition of art; it is to state a fact or supposed fact about which, when we have sufficiently identified it, we shall have later to theorize philosophically. For the present it does not matter whether the fact that is alleged, when it is said that the artist expresses emotion, is really a fact or is only supposed to be one. Whichever it is, we have to identify it, that is, to decide what it is that people are saying when they use the phrase. Later on, we shall have to see whether it will fit into a coherent theory.

They are referring to a situation, real or supposed, of a definite kind. When a man is said to express emotion, what is being said about him comes to this. At first, he is conscious of having an emotion, but not conscious of what this emotion is. All he is conscious of is a perturbation or excitement, which he feels going on within him, but of whose nature he is ignorant. While in this state, all he can say about his emotion is: "I feel . . . I don't know what I feel." From this helpless and oppressed condition he extricates himself by doing something which we call expressing himself. This is an activity which has something to do with the thing we call language: he expresses himself by speaking. It is also something to do with consciousness: the emotion expressed is an emotion of whose nature the person who feels it is no longer unconscious. It has also something to do with the way in which he feels the emotion. As unexpressed, he feels it in what we have called a helpless and oppressed way; as expressed, he feels it in a way from which the sense of oppression has vanished. His mind is somehow lightened and eased.

This lightening of emotions which is somehow connected with the expression of them has a certain resemblance to the "catharsis" by which emotions are earthed through being discharged into a make-believe situation; but the two things are not the same. Suppose the emotion is one of anger. If it is effectively earthed, for example by imagining oneself kicking someone down stairs, it is thereafter no longer present in the mind as anger at all: we have worked it off and are rid of it. If it is expressed, for example by putting it into hot and bitter words, it does not disappear from the mind; we remain angry; but instead of the sense of oppression which accompanies an emotion of anger not yet recognized as such, we have that sense of alleviation which comes when we are conscious of our own emotion as anger, instead of being conscious of it only as an unidentified perturbation. This is what we refer to when we say that it "does us good" to express our emotions.

This expression of an emotion by speech may be addressed to someone; but if so it is not done with the intention of arousing a like emotion in him. If there is any effect which we wish to produce in the hearer, it is only the effect which we call making him understand how we feel. But, as we have already seen, this is just the effect which expressing our emotions has on ourselves. It makes us, as well as the people to whom we talk, understand how we feel. A person arousing emotion sets out to affect his audience in a way in which he himself is not necessarily affected. He and his audience stand in quite different relations to the act, very much as physician and patient stand in quite different relations towards a drug administered by the one and taken by the other. A person expressing emotion, on the contrary, is treating himself and his audience in the same kind of way; he is making his emotions clear to his audience, and that is what he is doing to himself.

It follows from this that the expression of emotion, simply as expression, is not addressed to any particular audience. It is addressed primarily to the speaker himself, and secondarily to any one who can understand. Here again, the speaker's attitude towards his audience is quite unlike that of a person desiring to arouse in his audience a certain emotion. If that is what he wishes to do, he must know the audience he is addressing. He must know what type of stimulus will produce the desired kind of reaction in people of that particular sort; and he must adapt his language to his audience in the sense of making sure that it contains stimuli appropriate to their peculiarities. If what he wishes to do is to express his emotions intelligibly, he has to express them in such a way as to be intelligible to himself; his audience is then in the position of persons who overhear him doing this. Thus the stimulus-and-reaction terminology has no applicability to the situation.

The means-and-end, or technique, terminology too is inapplicable. Until a man has expressed his emotion, he does not yet know what emotion it is. The act of expressing it is therefore an exploration of his own emotions. He is trying to find out what these emotions are. There is certainly here a directed process: an effort, that is, directed upon a certain end; but the end is not something foreseen and preconceived, to which appropriate means can be thought out in the light of our knowledge of its special character. Expression is an activity of which there can be no technique.

Expression and Individualization

Expressing an emotion is not the same thing as describing it. To say "I am angry" is to describe one's emotion, not to express it. The words in which it is expressed need not contain any reference to anger as such at all. Indeed, so far as they simply and solely express it, they cannot contain any such reference. . . .

This is why, as literary critics well know, the use of epithets in poetry, or even in prose where expressiveness is aimed at, is a danger. If you want to express the terror which something causes, you must not give it an epithet like "dreadful." For that describes the emotion instead of expressing it, and your language becomes frigid, that is inexpressive, at once. A genuine poet, in his moments of genuine poetry, never mentions by name the emotions he is expressing.

The reason why description, so far from helping expression, actually damages it, is that description generalizes. To describe a thing is to call it a thing of such and such a kind: to bring it under a conception, to classify it. Expression, on the contrary, individualizes. The anger which I feel here and now, with a certain person, for a certain cause, is no doubt an instance of anger, and in describing it as anger one is telling truth about it; but it is much more than mere anger: it is a peculiar anger, not quite like any anger that I felt before, and probably not quite like any anger I shall ever feel again. To become fully conscious of it means becoming conscious of it not merely as an instance of anger, but as this quite peculiar anger. Expressing it, we saw, has something to do with becoming conscious of it; therefore, if being fully conscious of it means being conscious of all its peculiarities, fully expressing it means expressing all its peculiarities. The poet, therefore, in proportion as he understands his business, gets as far away as possible from merely labeling his emotions as instances of this or that general kind, and takes enormous pains to individualize them by expressing them in terms which reveal their difference from any other emotion of the same sort.

This is a point in which art proper, as the expression of emotion, differs sharply and obviously from any craft whose aim is to arouse emotion. The end which a craft sets out to realize is always conceived in general terms, never individualized. However accurately defined it may be, it is always defined as the production of a thing having characteristics that could be shared by other things. A joiner, making a table out of these pieces of wood and no others, makes it to measurements and specifications which, even if actually shared by no other table, might in principle be shared by other tables. A physician treating a patient for a certain complaint is trying to produce in him a condition which might be, and probably has been, often produced in others, namely, the condition of recovering from that complaint. So an "artist" setting out to produce a certain emotion in his audience is setting out to produce not an individual emotion, but an emotion of a certain kind. It follows that the means appropriate to its production will be not individual means but means of a certain kind: that is to say, means which are always in principle replaceable by other similar means.

As every good craftsman insists, there is always a "right way" of performing any operation. . . .

Art proper, as expression of emotion, has nothing to do with all this. The artist proper is a person who, grappling with the problem of expressing a certain emotion, says "I want to get this clear." It is no use to him to get something else clear, however like it this other thing may be. Nothing will serve as a substitute. He does not want a thing of a certain kind, he wants a certain thing. This is why the kind of person who takes his literature as psychology, saying "How admirably this writer depicts the feelings of women, or bus-drivers, or homosexuals . . . ," necessarily misunderstands every real work of art with which he comes into contact, and takes for good art, with infallible precision, what is not art at all. . . .

Selection and Aesthetic Emotion

It has sometimes been asked whether emotions can be divided into those suitable for expression by artists and those unsuitable. If by art one means art proper, and identifies this with expression, the only possible answer is that there can be no such distinction. . . . [In one sense,] it is true that there is a specific aesthetic emotion. As we have seen, an unexpressed emotion is accompanied by a feeling of oppression; when it is expressed and thus comes into consciousness the same emotion is accompanied by a new feeling of alleviation or easement, the sense that this oppression is removed. It resembles the feeling of relief that comes when a burdensome intellectual or moral problem has been solved. We may call it, if we like, the specific feeling of having successfully expressed ourselves; and there is no reason why it should not be called a specific aesthetic emotion. But it is not a specific kind of emotion pre-existing to the expression of it, and having the peculiarity that when it comes to be expressed it is expressed artistically. It is an emotional coloring which attends the expression of any emotion whatever. . . .

The Artist and the Ordinary Man

If art is not a kind of craft, but the expression of emotion, [the] distinction of kind between artist and audience disappears. For the artist has an audience only in so far as people hear him expressing himself, and understand what they hear him saying. Now, if one person says something by way of expressing what is in his mind, and another hears and understands him, the hearer who understands him has that same thing in his mind. The question whether he would have had it if the first had not spoken need not here be raised; however it is answered, what has just been said is equally true. If someone says "Twice two is four" in the hearing of some one incapable of carrying out the simplest arith-metical operation, he will be understood by himself, but not by his hearer. The hearer can understand only if he can add two and two in his own mind. Whether he could do it before he heard the speaker say those words makes no difference. What is here said of expressing thoughts is equally true of expressing emotions. If a poet expresses, for example, a certain kind of fear, the only hear-ers who can understand him are those who are capable of experiencing that kind of fear themselves. Hence, when someone reads and understands a poem, he is not merely understanding the poet's expression of his, the poet's, emo-tions, he is expressing emotions of his own in the poet's words, which have thus become his own words. As Coleridge put it, we know a man for a poet by the fact that he makes us poets. We know that he is expressing his emotions by the fact that he is enabling us to express ours.

Thus, if art is the activity of expressing emotions, the reader is an artist as well as the writer. There is no distinction of kind between artist and audience. This does not mean that there is no distinction at all. When Pope wrote that the poet's business was to say "what all have felt but none so well express'd," we may interpret his words as meaning (whether or not Pope himself consciously meant this when he wrote them) that the poet's difference from his audience lies in the fact that, though both do exactly the same thing, namely express this particular emotion in these particular words, the poet is a man who can solve for himself the problem of expressing it, whereas the audience can express it only when the poet has shown them how. The poet is not singular either in his having that emotion or in his power of expressing it; he is singular in his ability to take the initiative in expressing what all feel, and all can express. . . .

Expressing Emotion and Betraying Emotion

Finally, the expressing of emotion must not be confused with what may be called the betraying of it, that is, exhibiting symptoms of it. When it is said that the artist in the proper sense of that word is a person who expresses his emo-tions, this does not mean that if he is afraid he turns pale and stammers; if he is angry he turns red and bellows; and so forth. These things are no doubt called expressions; but just as we distinguish proper and improper senses of the word "art," so we must distinguish proper and improper senses of the word "expres-sion," and in the context of a discussion about art this sense of expression is an improper sense. The characteristic mark of expression proper is lucidity or intel-ligibility; a person who expresses something thereby becomes conscious of what it is that he is expressing, and enables others to become conscious of it in himself and in them. Turning pale and stammering is a natural accompaniment of fear, but a person who in addition to being afraid also turns pale and stammers does not thereby become conscious of the precise quality of his emotion. About that he is as much in the dark as he would be if (were that possible) he could feel fear without also exhibiting symptoms of it.

Confusion between these two senses of the word "expression" may easily lead to false critical estimates, and so to false aesthetic theory. It is sometimes thought a merit in an actress that when she is acting a pathetic scene she can work herself up to such an extent as to weep real tears. There may be some ground for that opinion if acting is not an art but a craft, and if the actress's object in that scene is to produce grief in her audience; and even then the conclusion would follow only if it were true that grief cannot be produced in the audience unless symptoms of grief are exhibited by the performer. And no doubt this is how most people think of the actor's work. But if his business is not amusement but art, the object at which he is aiming is not to produce a preconceived emotional effect on his audience but by means of a system of expressions, or language, composed partly of speech and partly of gesture, to explore his own emotions: to discover emotions in himself of which he was unaware, and, by permitting the audience to witness the discovery, enable them to make a similar discovery about themselves. In that case it is not her ability to weep real tears that would mark out a good actress; it is her ability to make it clear to herself and her audience what the tears are about.

This applies to every kind of art. The artist never rants. A person who writes or paints or the like in order to blow off steam, using the traditional materials of art as means for exhibiting the symptoms of emotion, may deserve praise as an exhibitionist, but loses for the moment all claim to the title of artist. Exhibitionists have their uses; they may serve as an amusement, or they may be doing magic. The second category will contain, for example, those young men who, learning in the torment of their own bodies and minds what war is like, have stammered their indignation in verses, and published them in the hope of infecting others and causing them to abolish it. But these verses have nothing to do with poetry. ◣

CHANGE

In his essay entitled, "Why I Write," George Orwell, known widely as the author of two famous works of social and political commentary, *1984* and *Animal Farm*, commented:

Putting aside the need to earn a living, I think there are four great motives for writing, at any rate for writing prose. They exist in different degrees in every writer, and in any one writer the proportions will vary from time to time, according to the atmosphere in which he is living. They are: *(i) Sheer egoism.* Desire to seem clever, to be talked about, to be remembered after death, to get your own back on the grown-ups who snubbed you in childhood, etc., etc. . . . *(ii) Aesthetic enthusiasm.* Perception of beauty in the external world, or, on the other hand, in words and their right arrangement. Pleasure in the impact of one sound on another, in the firmness of good prose or the rhythm of a good story. . . . *(iii) Historical impulse.* Desire to see things as they are, to find out true facts and store them up for the use of posterity. *(iv) Political purpose.*—Using the word "political" in the widest possible sense. Desire to push the world in a certain direction, to alter other peoples' idea of the kind of society that they should strive after. Once again, no book is genuinely free from political bias. The opinion that art should have nothing to do with politics is itself a political attitude. . . .

What I have most wanted to do throughout the past ten years is to make political writing into an art. My starting point is always a feeling of partisanship, a sense of injustice. When I sit down to write a book, I do not say to myself, "I am going to produce a work of art." I write it because there is some lie that I want to expose, some fact to which I want to draw attention, and my initial concern is to get a hearing.

As noted earlier in this chapter, some artists intend to represent something or other with their art. That representation can be made through the content of their work or through the style and form of their work. For instance, at the beginning of this chapter we saw that Rand intended to use the image of fog engulfing Manhattan, as well as the very term *engulf*, in order to convey both a mood and a meaning. Also, whether or not an artist intends to represent anything, an artwork might represent something or other for an audience. In his painting *Guernica*, Picasso might or might not have intended to represent something (no doubt he did intend to represent a particular historical event and the trauma of that event), but for a viewer, the work might represent a variety of things, independent of Picasso's intentions. Likewise, as we just saw, there can be no question that artists express things with their work. As with representation, expression can be made through the content of the work or through the style and form of the work. As we saw above, many things can be expressed in and through an artwork, some intended and some not.

Despite the fact that representation and expression are relevant to art and artists, many artists claim that these aspects of art—both of the process of creating an artwork and of the product, or artwork, itself—are not what are foremost for them. The point of engaging in the creation of art, they say, is not merely to represent something or to express something; it is not simply to reflect on the world or on themselves. Rather, the point is to change the world in some way, to make a difference via their creation of art. For instance, Anne Bogart, theater director and professor at Columbia University, speaks of the transformative power of theater as an art form as well as of the basic purpose and nature of art generally to be transformative:

> Artists are individuals willing to articulate in the face of flux and transformation. And the successful artist finds new shapes for our present ambiguities and uncertainties. The artist becomes the creator of the future through the violent act of articulation. I say violent because articulation is a forceful act. It demands an aggressiveness and an ability to enter into the fray and translate that experience into expression. In the articulation begins a new organization of the inherited landscape. . . . [As] societies develop, it is the artists who articulate the necessary myths that embody our experience of life and provide parameters for ethics and values.

This change and making a difference can be either internal or external. The notion of internal change refers to the personal discovery and growth that the artist says comes about by the act of creating art. They come to discover things about themselves, they say, as a result of having gone through the creative process of "doing art." Whether intended or not, one result of doing art is self-discovery.

The notion of external change refers to art, and the endeavors of artists, as a way to change the world outside themselves in some way. The goal of art, or at least of their own work as artists, they say, is to make a difference in the world, to change things for the better. Art, they argue, can and should be a vehicle for social change. This concept is certainly not new. Art has long been a means of reflecting on social, political, and human concerns, with the intention that by such reflection, people will be led to take action to change their circumstances. As just one example: the novels of Charles Dickens have long been recognized not simply as illustrations of the difficult and harsh conditions of life for many in nineteenth-century England, but also as a form of protest intending to instigate change. Other well-known examples include Jonathan Swift's *Gulliver's Travels*, Harriet Beecher Stowe's *Uncle Tom's Cabin*, Upton Sinclair's *The Jungle*, and Ralph Ellison's *Invisible Man*. Politically motivated art, of course, goes beyond literary arts. For instance, in the area of visual art, the works of feminist artists Judy Chicago and Martha Rosler were influential. Another example, which had widespread recognition and appeal, was much of the music of the 1960s that was consciously intended as protest, with the goal of changing social attitudes and practices. In addition, art has long been used as a means to influence social and political agendas in the form of propaganda. Especially today, in an age of widespread "mass art," we are inundated, via television, musical recordings, film, and videos, with examples of art forms that have the open intent of shaping people's attitudes and behaviors.

Also among aestheticians, art as a means of social and political change has been acknowledged and embraced. For example, the twentieth-century art critic Sidney Finkelstein argued that the function of art is to humanize or liberate people. Art, he claimed, is a means of exploring the world and also of changing the world, at least the social world. He claimed not only that art is a means of changing the conditions of social existence, but also that that is its primary role. Art that fails to do this, regardless of the aesthetic qualities of the artwork, was, for him, not good art. In Chapter 6 we will look more closely at the role(s) of art in society; here the point is that many artists claim that representation or expression are not the significant concerns for artists or that, to the extent they are significant, it is only as means toward bringing about change.

Art, then, is clearly a form of social and political activism. Today many artists speak of interventionist art, that is, of art used as a mode of directly intervening into people's lives with the explicit purpose of advancing a particular agenda. Although this is not new, it became more and more prominent in the late twentieth century and into the twenty-first, with popular projects such as Culture Jamming, Reclaim the Streets, Art Attack, and other similar art-focused and art-inspired social activism. Culture Jamming, for instance, attempts to change people's environments by "jamming" (diverting, changing, exposing, disrupting, or "messing up") dominant cultural forms such as advertising. Reclaim the Streets uses art to physically transform spaces (for example, by planting a tree in the middle of a street or hanging art from an overpass) with the goal of changing people's ideas about those spaces and their possibilities and potential uses.

One of the major forms of such art today is often called eco-art. As Amy Lipton says in her work *Ecovention*:

> [Artists] are reaching out across disciplines and helping to bridge the gap between art and life by raising awareness and appreciation of our natural resources. By giving aesthetic form to restored natural areas and urban sites, these artists are engaging in a collaborative process with nature, practicing a socially relevant art. They are helping to create a new paradigm by proving that art can contribute to society as a whole, not merely in the politically correct sense or as a social critique, but rather by participating directly in the world. By focusing on the interrelationships between the biological, cultural, political, or historical aspects of ecosystems, these artists are working to extend environmental principles and practices directly into the community.

An example of such interventionist art is the work of Toronto artist Melanie Kramer, who, beginning in 2002, initiated her Garden the City project. This was an effort to try to get more people in Toronto to use urban spaces to have gardens in order to grow their own food. Kramer and her cohorts designed and distributed artistic postcards throughout the city. The postcards were dropped or left for others to come across in random places throughout the city, including libraries, subways, free newspaper boxes, and coffee shops. The postcards were intended to intervene in people's daily lives, encouraging those who found them to grow food in the city or at least to visit the Garden the City Website, where they could learn about gardening in the city, ask questions, and offer their feedback on the project.

As with representation and expression, when considering art as change we must ask what, how, and why. What is changed (or discovered or learned) as a result of the process and the product of art? Is actual change a necessary or sufficient feature for something to be art? If an artist intends a work to create change, say, to get people to plant an urban garden, but the result is that no one does, does this make the "artwork" not really art? Is the failure to create change then a failure to create art? Or what if the change that results is not the intended change? For example, if distributing postcards in random places throughout the city was received by most people (or by those with social power) as an annoyance or as littering and the result was that people saw this project negatively, what would this say about the project as art? What if the result was personal, inner growth or discovery for the artist, but little, no, or even negative impact on others?

There are also questions about how and why change (or discovery or learning) occurs or is sought. Does art, whether in terms of the product (that is, the artwork that is created) or the process (that is, the act of creating the artwork), create new facts about the world, or does art (only) stimulate new interpretations of existing facts? Is art (or should it be) a means toward social and political agendas? If it is (or should be), then how is that different from propaganda? Also, does that mean that nonpolitical art is bad art? If art is not (or should not be) a means toward social and political agendas, then in what senses is change the (or a) function of art? Are there appropriate or inappropriate social and political agendas for art? This concern about the relation of art and social change, in terms both of responding to social change and of creating social change, is the subject of the reading below by theater director Anne Bogart. Echoing Orwell's remark that the artist's desire is "to push the world in a certain direction, to alter other peoples' idea of the kind of society that they should strive after," she speaks of what she sees as the important transformative role of art at any time, but especially at the beginning of the twenty-first century, in an era of mass-produced culture and values.

ANNE BOGART, INTRODUCTION TO *AND THEN, YOU ACT: MAKING ART IN AN UNPREDICTABLE WORLD*[*]

> I always took for granted that the best art was political and was revolutionary. It doesn't mean that art has an agenda or a politics to argue: it means the questions being raised were explorations into kinds of anarchy, kinds of change, identifying errors, flaws, vulnerabilities in systems. (TONI MORRISON)

The South African writer Antjie Krog described meeting a nomadic desert poet in Senegal who described the role of poets in his culture. The job of the poet, he explained to her, is to remember where the water holes are. The survival of the whole group depends on a few water holes scattered around the desert. When his people forget where the water is, the poet can lead them to it.

[*]New York: Routledge, 2007. Pages 1–6.

What an apt metaphor for the role of the artist in any culture. The water is the history, the memory, the juice, and elixir of shared experience. I want to keep this notion in mind while examining the role of the artist in our present climate.

My previous book of essays, *A Director Prepares*, detailed the process of preparation and groundwork for an artist. But preparation is only useful in relation to the ensuing action. This book is about action during times of difficulty, whether personal or political.

Love is not a feeling. No matter how much you feel, love means nothing when unrelated to action. Love is action. In order to engage in effective action you must first find something that you value and put it at the center of your life. When you put your life into the service of what you value, that action will engender other values and beliefs. Through engagement, things happen. Movement is all. Keep moving and yet slow down simultaneously. In Latin this is known as *festina lente*, "make haste slowly." Inside of this paradox, you make a space where growth and art can happen. Within the framework of art and theater you will find a special freedom and the space and time to explore complexities. It does not cost you anything. It costs you your life.

You cannot expect other people to create meaning for you. You cannot wait for someone else to define your life. You make meaning by forging it with your hands. It requires sweat and commitment. Working toward the creation of meaning is the point. It is action that forges the meaning and the significance of a life.

And it is critical to have some direction and be clear about certain impossible goals that you are trying to achieve if you hope to achieve some of the possible goals. And you must be bold enough to speculate, postulate and imagine on the basis of partial knowledge. At the same time you must remain open to the very strong possibility that in fact you are way off the mark.

We are living in very particular times that demand a very specific kind of response. No matter the immensity of the obstacles—political, financial or spiritual—the one thing we cannot afford is inaction due to despair.

In the immediate aftermath of 9/11, people in the United States awoke in a profound and palpable silence. In German the word *Betroffenheit* aptly describes the feeling. Simply translated, the word means shock, bewilderment, perplexity, or impact. The root of the word *treffen* "to meet" and *betroffen* is "to be met" and *Betroffenheit* is the state of having been met, stopped, struck, or perplexed. I see it as the shock of having been met, stopped abruptly in the face of a particular event.

Don Saliers, a professor of theology at Emory University suggests that the silence that follows a violent event is similar in quality to the speechlessness of a powerful aesthetic experience. He describes a space and time engendered by the shock of the event where language ceases. We are left only with an awareness of the limits of language and the limits of what can be taken in. In this gap definitions disappear and certainty vanishes. Anything is possible—any response, any action or inaction. Nothing is prescribed. Nothing is certain. Everything is up for grabs.

In the case of post-9/11, patriotism rushed in to fill the gap of this fertile and palpable silence. Patriotism served as a way to replace disorientation and *Betroffenheit* with certainty. And certainty, if taken to its extreme, always ends in violence.

As it turns out, this manufactured certainty did, in fact, lead to violence and more violence. Self-perpetuating aggression became its own *raison d'etre* and the battle is worldwide, ugly, and nearly impossible to stop. U.S. citizens were told that any criticism of the War on Terror was unpatriotic. And yet, the concept of an open society is based on the recognition that nobody is in possession of the ultimate truth. When one is in touch with the complexities, it is impossible to be certain. If we fail to recognize that we might be wrong, we can only undermine any action done in the world.

The artist's job is to stay alive and awake in the space between convictions and certainties. The truth in art exists in the tension between contrasting realities. You try to find shapes that embody current ambiguities and uncertainties. While resisting certainty, you try to be as lucid and exact as possible from the state of imbalance and uncertainty. You act from a direct experience of the environment.

Significant political events always drop a lens between the environment and the perceiver. Generations view the world according to the most dominant lens. The Great Depression, for example, permanently altered the way that vast numbers of Americans saw their own lives and fortunes. The McCarthy era produced insidious paranoia and a general suspicion about left-wing political convictions. The events of September 11th 2001 also changed the lens. For many, the event intensified the feeling of separation from the rest of the world. For others, the sense of isolation was replaced with an acute sensitivity to the globe's interconnective tissues. If, as the Buddhists suggest, the art of life is the art of adjustment, then what are the necessary adjustments for artists working in the present climate? What needs to change in light of the new lens? How can we stay connected to our own culture and remember where the water is? How can we work in the theater within an atmosphere of fear and hostility and constantly attempt to reveal the water supply of our humanity? How can we nurture the necessary courage, energy, and expression in the face of adversity?

I look to history, literature, science, and aesthetics in order to figure out how to function positively and effectively within the present environment. I have found many practical ideas and stimulating encouragement in the process. The research has been helpful and gives me courage and hope in the day-to-day reality of running a theater company and directing new productions.

Leonard Bernstein, the composer and conductor, suggested that a musician's response to violence should be to "make the music more intense." This is what I want to do. I want to make the music more intense. Not just loud but also eloquent, expressive, magnetic, and powerful. I look around at the American theater, and I see it mostly steeped in an old-fashioned aesthetic and performed on weak knees. I want it strengthened, emboldened, wild, persuasive, and relevant to the issues of our time. We need courage and a love of the art form. Powerful theatrical productions, brave writing, and radiant acting can galvanize and profoundly transform expectations about how broad the spectrum of life can be beyond daily survival. In a culture where daily human hopes have shrunk to the myriad opiates of self-centered satisfaction, art is more necessary and powerful than ever.

Rather than the experience of life as a shard, art can unite and connect the strands of the universe. When you are in touch with art, borders vanish and the world opens up. Art can expand the definitions of what it means to be human. So if we agree to hold ourselves to higher standards and make more rigorous demands on ourselves, then we can say in our work, "We have asked ourselves these questions and we are trying to answer them, and that effort earns us the right to ask you, the audience, to face these issues too." Art demands action from the midst of living and makes a space where growth can happen.

One day, particularly discouraged about the global environment, I asked my friend the playwright Charles L. Mee, Jr., "How are we supposed to function in these difficult times? How can we contribute anything useful in this climate?" "Well," he answered, "You have a choice of two possible directions. Either you convince yourself that these are terrible times and things will never get better and so you decide to give up, or you choose to believe that there will be a better time in the future. If that is the case, your job in these dark political and social times is to gather together everything you value and become a transport bridge. Pack up what you cherish and carry it on your back to the future."

Near the end of the twentieth century, the Dalai Lama was asked if he would want to return to the earth in another century, even though it is certain that poverty, pollution, and overpopulation will make the planet a miserable environment to inhabit. "If I could be useful," was his response.

In a violent culture sidetracked by the attraction of fame, success, and individuality, this notion of being useful feels radical. Can art intend to be useful? Art is an exquisite and extravagant waste of time and space in a world complete unto itself. The product contains the process of engagement, struggle, and achievement that made it come to life. And yet the irony is that art is indeed useful in deep and enduring ways.

The poet Joseph Brodsky describes art as the oxygen that might arrive when the last breath has been expended:

A great writer is one who elongates the perspective of human sensibility, who shows a man at the end of his wits an opening, a pattern to follow. . . . Art is not a better, but an alternative existence; it is not an attempt to escape reality but the opposite, an attempt to animate it.

In the United States, we are the targets of mass distraction. We are the objects of constant flattery and manufactured desire. I believe that the only possible resistance to a culture of banality is quality. To me, the world often feels unjust, vicious, and even unbearable. And yet, I know that my development as a person is directly proportional to my capacity for discomfort. I see pain, destructive behavior, entropy, and suffering. I dislike the damaging behavior and blindness of the political sphere. I watch wars declared, social injustices that inhabit the streets of my hometown, and a planet in danger of pollution and genocide. I have to *do* something. My chosen field of action is the theater.

In order to "make the music more intense," you must first examine your intentions. If the motivation for action does not transcend the desire for fame and success, the quality of the results will be inferior. If your aim is intense engagement rather than self-aggrandizement, the results will be richer, denser, and more energetic. The outcome of an artistic process contains the energy of your commitment to it.

Next, recognize the basic ingredients. The classic recipe for effective theater is threefold:

1. you need something to say;
2. you need technique; and
3. you need passion.

Like a milking stool, if one of the three legs is missing, the stool will topple over and be ineffectual. It is as simple as that. ◣

Questions for Discussion

1. Given that something can represent pretty much anything, depending upon the context—for example, in some religious art a goat can (and did) represent lust—is there any art that is not representation?

2. What is the difference (or differences) between how one could *represent* in art—for example, represent betrayal or innocence—and how one could *express* in art?

3. Aristotle claimed that art is universal (as opposed to history, which is particular). Collingwood claimed that art is particular, that it is particular emotional expression. In what ways is art universal and in what ways is it particular?

4. Must art be political? If, say, van Gogh's paintings did not (or do not) create social change, does this mean it is bad art; does it mean it is not art? If art is not created for the purpose of social change, what purpose(s) does or should it have?

5. What is the relation between an artist's intentions and representation, expression, or change? For example, if an artist intends to express some feeling or idea but it is not communicated to an audience, that is, if they do not recognize that feeling or idea, does this mean that the artwork is bad art?

CHAPTER 5

THE AUDIENCE

In act 2, scene 2 of Shakespeare's *Hamlet*, the title character remarks:

> *Is it not monstrous that this player here,*
> *But in a fiction, a dream of passion,*
> *Could force his soul so to his own conceit*
> *That from her working all the visage wann'd,*
> *Tears in his eyes, distraction in his aspect,*
> *A broken voice, an' his whole function suiting*
> *With forms to his conceit? And all for nothing,*
> *For Hecuba!*
> *What's Hecuba to him, or he to Hecuba,*
> *That he should weep for her?*

Hecuba was a queen of Troy and the subject of a tragedy written by the Greek playwright Euripides. In Shakespeare's play, Hamlet is speaking of the impact of this character on his own life. "What's Hecuba to him?" has come to function, for some people at least, as a slogan for addressing the impact that art can have on us. (It is also the title of a fine analysis of this topic by E. M. Dadlez.) We have all had the experience of seeing a painting, hearing a song, reading a novel or poem, watching a film or play, or having some sort of encounter with an artwork that moved us deeply and profoundly. Yet at the same time, we knew it was "only" art. For instance, in the case of a novel, we know it is fiction, not real life, yet we can be moved, perhaps even in life-altering ways, by the events of the story. People can be brought to tears watching a movie (while at the same time perhaps be munching on snacks!). It is, in a word, an aesthetic experience. Of course, not all aesthetic experiences are so profound. Sometimes we encounter an artwork and we find it mildly interesting, thought provoking, inspiring, disturbing, puzzling, or some such. But the point is that we have a response to it that, for lack of a better term, we call aesthetic. And we recognize that others might not have the same response; the movie I find to be stirring and sad, you might find to be maudlin and sappy.

In Chapter 4 we noted that there are a variety of things that artists might be doing, or trying to do, via the creation of art; they might be representing something or expressing or communicating something or prodding us in some way. We noted, too, that whatever artists might be doing via art, audiences might receive art in very different ways. In this chapter we will consider three issues that arise in the context of the audience's perspective in art. The first issue is the very notion of an aesthetic experience, the simple (or not so simple) act of encountering art. The second issue is the interpretation of art. We do not just encounter art, we also often wonder what it means, how we should interpret what it is. The third issue is the critique of art. Some art we think is great (perhaps it moves us emotionally) and some art we think stinks and some art just leaves us cold (we think, "Meh, so?"). For each of these issues, we can ask about the what, the how, and the why. That is, we might want to consider what is experienced in the context of an aesthetic experience, or we might want to consider how an artwork is best interpreted, or perhaps why (toward what goal or purpose) one would critique an artwork. First, then, what about aesthetic experience?

One long-standing view about aesthetic experience is associated with Aristotle, who wrote about the notion of *catharsis*. Catharsis is a purging or purification, in particular in an emotional sense. Aristotle specifically wrote about tragedies, but his remarks and view can be, and have been, extended to art generally. According to this view, when we encounter art and have an aesthetic experience, we have (or might have) a cathartic experience. By the process of encountering art we can be purged of certain kinds of emotions or emotional responses. So, for example, viewing tragedies allows us to rid ourselves of these emotions, and in this way viewing tragedies brings a certain relief and cleansing. Or viewing tragedies allows emotions such as fear and pity to be purified; tragedy does not allow us to rid ourselves of these emotions, but it makes them purer than they were. In any case, the nature of the aesthetic experience we have encountering art is cathartic. For Aristotle, this cathartic effect was a good thing; it was one reason he thought that art, and our experiencing art, was beneficial. (Aristotle's discussion of art was, in part, a response to his teacher Plato, who was far more critical of art, in part because of its power to affect people emotionally.) As we have noted, however, art is not received equally by everyone. The artwork that I find profound, you might find boring. Also, for many artists, purging or purification is the last thing they want an audience to undergo when encountering their art. If anything, they want to incite and provoke audiences to action. So whether or not art does produce a cathartic effect, that is at best only part of the story of aesthetic experience.

Another influential notion about the nature of aesthetic experience was enunciated by the aesthetician Edward Bullough, who spoke of aesthetic experience as involving the proper "psychic distance" from art. By this notion he meant that people can experience an artwork in various ways, not all of them being aesthetic. For instance, suppose three people are watching a play. (Let's hope there are more than three people watching it, but we will focus on these three!) The first person, Smith, is just a regular person who enjoys going to the theater. The second person, Jones, is the producer of the play, who has put up a large sum of money in hopes that it will be a good investment and return a nice financial profit. The third person, Brown, is the husband of one of the actors in the play and is very jealous about his wife. Now, as the play proceeds, and all three are watching it, Smith has an enjoyable, perhaps enthralling, experience. Jones, however, noticing many empty seats in the house, is dejected by the thought that the play will not return a profit. Brown, watching his wife's character kissing another character on stage, gets more and more enraged by the minute. All three are having experiences, of course, but for Bullough, only Smith is having an aesthetic experience. Jones experiences the play only as an investment venture, and Brown cannot separate his wife from the character she is playing on stage. For Bullough, only Smith has the proper psychic distance to truly have an aesthetic experience in this case. Of the three, only Smith is experiencing the play as art. (Jones is experiencing it as an investment venture, and Brown is experiencing it as real life. Jones "overdistances," and Brown "underdistances.")

Bullough's notion of proper psychic distance is, of course, a metaphor, and other aestheticians as well as artists have criticized it. It is related to a broader conception of aesthetic experience that is often labeled *disinterestedness*. The point is not that when we encounter art we are not interested in it. Rather, the point is that other sorts of interests are not relevant to the aesthetic experience. So, in the story above, Jones's financial interests interfered with his ability to have an aesthetic experience, and, likewise, Brown's personal interests prevented him from having an aesthetic experience. This view has also been associated with a view that has been called *aestheticism*, the notion of "art for art's sake." That is, whether or not art has personal, financial, moral, political, social, or any other sort of value associated with it, the essence of it as art is its aesthetic value and its aesthetic nature. *As art* it should be experienced appropriately, that is, aesthetically. All other sorts of interests or values are secondary; they might be important, but not with respect to the nature of artworks as art. Again, many aestheticians and artists (as well as others) have claimed that being disinterested (or having the "proper" psychic distance) is mistaken. Art, they say, cannot be and should not be experienced in a vacuum, so to speak. We will look more specifically at this issue in Chapter 6.

Besides the influential views of Aristotle and Bullough, Marcia Muelder Eaton has identified three broad conceptions of aesthetic experience. One is that an aesthetic experience is a matter of having some sort of special sense. This idea is found in many historical views about art and aesthetics, especially those of the early modern period (roughly the seventeenth, eighteenth, and early nineteenth centuries). It has to do with the notion of having good taste, of being discriminating. Indeed, for many years the term *taste* was used in this aesthetic sense. Just as people have physical senses (such as sight and hearing), they also have an aesthetic sense, namely, taste. It is, in effect, an aesthetic perception. A philosopher who was particularly known for supporting this view is the eighteenth-century British philosopher David Hume. For Hume, we "perceive" beauty or other aesthetic features in art (and in nature) because we have the sense of taste. Just as some people have better or worse senses of smell or sight or hearing than other people, so, too, Hume said, some people have better senses of aesthetic taste than others. People with better aesthetic sense—that is, better taste—can appreciate art better than others can. Although aesthetic sense, or taste, might be inborn (just as some people are born with better hearing or sight), taste can be trained and improved (or diminished). For instance, someone can be taught to distinguish various features of fine wines and come to be a sophisticated wine taster. So, too, with exposure to fine arts, one can develop one's aesthetic sense.

Another way of understanding aesthetic experience is as involving not a special sense or sensitivity, but a special attitude or way of encountering an artwork. For instance, many people claim that there is an important difference between nudity and nakedness. Many paintings are said to be nudes, that is, the content portrays a person (almost always a woman) who is not wearing clothes. But, they say, there is a difference between a painting of a nude and a painting of someone who is "merely" naked, and that difference, they say, is that there is a different attitude taken toward the two. Or the difference in attitude or way of encountering might be that for an experience to be an aesthetic one, the encounter must be primarily on an emotional level. To see a play, for example, from the perspective of someone interested in optics and lighting might be to see it with one's attention on the technical aspects of lighting the stage. However, to see that same play from an aesthetic perspective is to "feel" the light, so to speak. The point is not optics but emotional effect. This is much like Bullough's view of proper psychic distance, or the view of disinterestedness.

Yet a third way of understanding an aesthetic experience is as involving a special focus on aesthetic features of the artwork. For example, one might focus (whether intellectually or emotionally) on the unity or harmony of a painting or dance rather than on the color of the costume. Or one might focus on the balance or intensity or complexity of elements in a painting rather than on its subject matter. This, in effect, is the view of the formalists, such as Clive Bell, whose work we saw in Chapter 3. In this understanding, what makes for an aesthetic experience, as opposed to some other kind of experience, is what we focus on with respect to an artwork. Bell happened to insist that the necessary focus was the formal features of artworks, but one could (and some do) claim that formalism is not required, or even important, for holding this broader view that aesthetic experience is a matter of special focus. It could be claimed, for example, that one could or should focus on the content of artworks rather than the form(s).

In the reading on the next page, aesthetician and art educator David Fenner spells out an array of aspects that are in place for an aesthetic experience to be possible and for us to better understand the nature of aesthetic experience. As we noted earlier in the chapter, when considering the nature of aesthetic experience, we can zero in on questions of what is experience, how it is experienced, and why it is experienced. In addition, Fenner points out that we also need to consider who is experiencing and the fact that there are many contexts and factors (some subjective and some not) that are involved in any given person's having an aesthetic experience.

DAVID E. W. FENNER, "AESTHETIC EXPERIENCE AND AESTHETIC ANALYSIS"

The "raw data" that aesthetics is meant to explain is the aesthetic experience. People have experiences that they class off from other experiences and label, as a class, the aesthetic ones. Aesthetic experience is basic, and all other things aesthetic—aesthetic properties, aesthetic objects, aesthetic attitudes—are secondary in their importance to aesthetic experiences. . . .

Considering aesthetic experience as the raw data that philosophical aesthetics seeks to explain is a relatively recent phenomenon. This was certainly not the focus in the seventeenth and eighteenth centuries. Aesthetic judgment was the focus of Shaftesbury, Hutcheson, Hume, and Kant: "How do we make meaningful judgments (hopefully real ones) about the aesthetic quality of (certain) objects and events?" But with George Santayana, John Dewey, and Jerome Stolnitz, the focus changes. Now the interest is in the aesthetic experience: what makes those experiences we label "aesthetic" special? Why do we separate those experiences from others? . . .

Aesthetic experiences, if we are to treat them as "raw data," must be explored without pre-conception, prejudice, or limitation. And, truly enough, the vast majority of aesthetic experiences are not focused exclusively, in terms of their contents, on formal or simple-sensory matters. Aesthetic experiences are, first, experiences. They are complex things, having to do with things as tidy as the formal qualities of the object under consideration and with things as messy as whether one had enough sleep the night before, whether one just had a fight with his roommate, whether one is carrying psychological baggage that is brought to consciousness by this particular aesthetic object. . . .

Experiences and analyses are different, the latter only one part of the former. So to speak of each as the basis of the philosophical exploration of aesthetics is to conflate. Once more for the record, I want to state that this tension is not a new one. The substance of this conflation goes back to an attempt to do service in the history of this discipline to the two energies, one toward judgment and articulation of the proper subjects and proper methods of judgment, the other toward the psychological, to the "raw data" of pure and complex experience that we seek to taxonomize into aesthetic experiences and nonaesthetic experiences. . . .

Journal of Aesthetic Education 37 (2003): 40–42, 44–51, 52.

Aesthetic Experience

Following is an attempt to analyze the complexity we normally find in aesthetic experience.

Formal Analysis

If we understand aesthetics as having essentially to do with the sensuous or sensory aspects of experiences—with other considerations (such as information about the object or associations the viewer makes in attendance to the object) being of secondary concern—then we understand that in some fashion these purely sensory aspects can be bracketed off from other parts of the complex aesthetic experience. This sort of thing is illustrated in the use of the rich aesthetic vocabulary that we have to describe the purely sensory aspects. We talk about balance, elegance, grace, harmony, excess, order, delicacy, grandeur, simplicity, modesty, subtlety, openness, authority, gentility, charm, garishness, and vulgarity when talking about aesthetic objects, and we in most cases are not talking about the subject matter of the object but rather about how the subject matter is presented. Or, more simply, about the presentation itself. We use aesthetic terms to reference what immediately hits our eyes, ears, or noses. From the basic objective properties of lines, colors, proportions, contrasts, and so forth, we develop a view of an object's aesthetic qualities (the metaphysical story of how not presently at point), and from an aesthetic description of the object, we determine the object's aesthetic worth. This is to say, of course, that aesthetic judgments tend to take as their substance the formal qualities of aesthetic objects. This is not always the case, but it is frequently so. Aesthetic evaluations are regularly evidenced by reference to the object's aesthetic properties, and these properties are said to be present on the evidence of the presence of basic properties of line and color.

The argument still stands, however, that an aesthetic analysis is not the full story when it comes to aesthetic experience; this is a lesson we learned from [Archibald] Alison. A formal treatment of an aesthetic object is not to explain fully, in the vast majority of cases, exactly what went into a particular aesthetic experience.

Associations

Alison claimed that it was imagination, or certain associations, which made for aesthetic experiencing. The mere presentation of beauty was not enough to stimulate the spectator into feeling pleasure over the beauty; the spectator becomes a more active participant. He exercises his mind, his imagination, and his attentive contemplation, in order to experience more fully the nature of the object, and in so doing experience the object as fully aesthetically as he can. Without this mindful/imaginative activity, the experience is not aesthetic, but one of mere pleasure.

> The emotions of taste may therefore be considered as distinguished from the emotions of simple pleasure by their being dependent upon the exercises of imagination; and though founded in all cases upon some simple emotion, as yet further requiring the employment of this faculty for their existence.

. . . The associations Alison spoke of are not cognitive in type; they are imaginative. There are many different sorts of association—emotional and cognitive alike—but the point is that, first, in all cases these are psychological phenomena, and, second, whenever they arise, they are as much a part of the experience as any other part. They have as much claim to being a part of an aesthetic experience as, say, the formal parts discussed above.

There is a range of associations which we may make in having an aesthetic experience. These could include:

1. Recollective: One recalls some past experience.
2. Emotional: One associates a certain emotion with the object under attendance. This emotion could be very general ("the Blues make one feel sad"), somewhat general ("Merchant-Ivory films make me feel melancholy"), somewhat specific ("I think of Scotland on very windy days"), or very specific ("Mexican ballad music reminds me of my mother when I was young").
3. Cognitive: One makes a connection, in thinking about the object under consideration, to another object or event that shares some property with the first. This is the essence, I think, of all the aesthetic-interpretative work that goes on in considering text (whatever sort: literary or filmic, for example). A friend of mine recently remarked that the power of Martin Scorsese's *Raging Bull* lies in how powerfully religiously thematic the film was. . . .

Contexts

The artworld of the twentieth century, if it must be reduced to a single word, would be reduced to the word "challenge." The early part of the century saw extensive and aggressive challenges to the very definition of art: Dadaism, the "Ready-mades," and Pop Art expanded academic definitions of art very broadly.

The middle part of the century saw a great deal of conceptual art, art that was to be understood, that was making a point or sending a message. The last part of the twentieth century challenged our values. Mapplethorpe, [Andres] Serrano, Richard Serra, Damien Hurst, Christopher Ofili, and a host of others have presented works that confront and provoke us. They are not merely cognitive vehicles; they are strongly emotional ones, assailing our values and the contexts in which we hold those particular values.

It must be the case that there are many individuals who see Mapplethorpe photographs who do not, perhaps cannot, "get beyond" the subject matter of those photos. This is understandable, to some degree or on some level, because aesthetic experiences, the "raw data" of experiences of viewing objects presented to us as objects primarily or merely just to be looked at, tend to include reactions based on seeing the object within a context, as seeing it as a challenge.

Surely this must be the case. Consider so many of the twentieth century's artworks, ones which have very little power as aesthetic objects if considered merely in terms of their formal properties. Marcel Duchamp would hardly be mentioned in the artworld today were his art objects considered merely in terms of their formal characteristics. *In Advance of a Broken Arm* (once a snow shovel) is visually very boring, as is *Fountain*. Consider John Cage's *4' 33''* or Robert Rauschenberg's *Erased De Kooning* or Andy Warhol's *Brillo Pad Boxes*. Each of these artists must have intended his work to be presented not in terms of their formal characteristics. Each of these items, taken as formal aesthetic objects, are remarkably dull. And that was the point (one of the points, at least). These works were meant to issue certain challenges. And this is where their value as aesthetic objects, as art objects, lies. . . .

Do we take these reactions, which are part and parcel of "first contact" with so many contemporary aesthetic objects, as bona fide parts of aesthetic experiences? Given that the meaningfulness of so many of these objects rests solely and squarely on their power for provoking us, the answer, it would seem, has to be "yes."

What are the various contexts under which we consider aesthetic objects— contexts which we bring as categories for dealing with aesthetic objects and experiencing them?

1. Social Contexts

A. *Ethnic and Racial Contexts*. Many objects, perhaps all objects, today can be understood (I do not say "should"—that would be a separate argument) as conveying, overtly or tacitly, some message about matters of race and heritage.

B. *Class Contexts*. The same can be said for class—of education, birth, or economic status.

C. *Gender Contexts*. Does my experience of a work hold for me some significance in terms of sex or gender? Do I see Ridley Scott's *Thelma & Louise* as a feminist manifesto? Do I see Milos Forman's *One Flew Over the Cuckoo's Nest* as essentially misogynist?

D. *National or Cultural Contexts*. Some aesthetic objects present strong nationalist messages. In the eighteenth century, Sir Joshua Reynolds and Benjamin West produced visual works of art that celebrate and support Great Britain. In nineteenth century America, we find the work of Winslow Homer and Thomas Eakins (and Gerald Murphy in the early twentieth), and, in the literary arts, the work of Ralph Waldo Emerson, Nathaniel Hawthorne, and Herman Melville. Germany sees perhaps its greatest nationalist artist in the nineteenth century: Richard Wagner. In the early twentieth century, Mexican artists such as Diego Rivera, José Clemente Orozco, and David Alfaro Siqueiros painted murals which focused on cultural nationalism and revolutionary politics.

E. *Political Contexts*. I believe the *New Yorker* to be the best example of popular applied aesthetics today, and I usually assign a copy of it as a required text for aesthetics courses I offer. . . . One student reacted strongly to being "forced" to read (part of) "that liberal rag." He pointed out that the *New Yorker* had that semester celebrated the humanity of Tipper Gore, while at the same time running an article on George W. Bush's ineptitude with the English language, and spending a good deal of time in several issues mocking the aesthetic and moral sensibilities of New York Major Rudy Giuliani. I had not seen these same things, or, better put, had not seen these things as my student had. He was looking at the magazine through political eyes.

2. Moral Contexts

A. *Religious Contexts*. It is understatement to say that Serrano's photograph of a crucifix suspended in a jar of urine (*Piss Christ*), Scorsese's *Last Temptation of Christ*, and Ofili's *Madonna*, complete with elephant dung, have been considered widely from religious contexts.

B. *Sexual Contexts*. The line between those objects created to satisfy prurient interests and those created to satisfy aesthetic ones has always been blurry. It is not a recent phenomenon. Michelangelo walked that line, apparently.

Rembrandt supposedly did, too. A good example is Edouard Manet's *Olympia*, thought to be morally unfit not due to the fact that the central figure was nude, but due to the defiance in the subject's face as she presented herself as a nude. . . .

C. *Violence Contexts.* There are those in the world whose thresholds for viewing violence are low, and there are some art objects which present deeply arresting portraits of violence (Kubrick's *Clockwork Orange*, Tarantino's *Reservoir Dogs*). When these come together, the influence of the latter on the former effectively halts aesthetic experience. As some people cannot see beyond the sexual content of a Mapplethorpe photo, some people cannot aesthetically appreciate *Clockwork Orange* or *Reservoir Dogs* because they cannot get beyond the violence. This is neither a fault in the viewer or the object; it is simply a matter of human psychology.

3. "Taste" Contexts

A. *"Good Taste."* [Richard Shusterman recently argued] that no case has been made against censorship which would preclude the propriety of censoring for reasons that are aesthetic in nature. Shusterman argues that (i) aesthetic censorship would have the effect of highlighting the best work; (ii) it would not dull our aesthetic sensibilities with less-good work; and (iii) if economic constraints will necessarily act as a censor, better we censor on aesthetic grounds so that the best work is assured support. There are a great number of artworks out in the world today that are aesthetically unmeritorious. They do not reward aesthetic attention, and may even be blamed for distracting our finite attention for works which we would find rewarding. This being said, there *are* also works out there which are aesthetically meritorious, but which get dumped into the aforementioned category simply because they are in "bad taste." Some artworks would reward aesthetic attention, but are not granted that opportunity—their potential goes unactualized—due to the fact that they are vulgar in some way.

B. *"My Taste."* Hume's attempt, the common wisdom holds, to balance the subjectivity and incorrigibility of taste with a realist account of aesthetic judgment fails. It fails on the probability that two equally well disposed aesthetic judges might finally disagree about the merits of a given object. This is usually chalked up to a difference in taste. Here we are not talking about "good taste" versus "bad," but about varieties of taste: some people like Mozart, some like John Lennon. Some people like David Lynch, some like

David Lean. Some people like Kandinsky, some like Sargent. If it is an irreducible fact about human aesthetic sensibility that tastes vary, then this constitutes a very present and very real context through which we view aesthetic objects.

External Factors

Not everything objective, with regard to an aesthetic experience, has to do with a formal analysis of the object under consideration. Some objective factors play a role in the creation of aesthetic experiences which we might call "secondary aspects."

1. **Informational Factors.** Above I referred to aesthetic analysis as focusing on the formal characters of aesthetic objects. I hope that I left open, and perhaps alluded to the existence of, secondary factors in aesthetic analyses. There are many facts, the knowing of which alters aesthetic experiences—sometimes only a bit, but sometimes a great deal.
   A. *Genetic Information:* What are the origins of the work? Who was the artist, what were her circumstances? What was the environment in which the work was created? When was it created? Where? What was the context of the work? What was the society in which it was created like? What were the religious, moral, social values of that time and place?
   B. *Comparative Information:* What was the genre of the work? How does it relate or compare to others of its kind? What is its kind?
   C. *Provenance Information:* What is the history of the work? Was it valued when it was first created? Who valued it? Who has owned it? How did it come to be in this museum, gallery, or collection? What awards has it won?
2. **Subjective Factors.** The analogy that philosophy of mind has used over the last few decades between the mind and a computer is apt here (once more). But instead of discussing hardware and software, the focus here will be on dust, magnets, and humidity. Just as a computer can be wildly affected by these sorts of things, so human experiences are subject to a variety of stimuli which on the surface have nothing at all to do with aesthetics, but which nonetheless can play a palpable role in the construction of (any) experience.
   A. *Psychological Factors.* If one is distracted, sad, or in a silly mood, one's experience will be affected. Indeed, psychological influences have a

huge effect on the way that we take in the contents of our experiences, the way we meaningfully shape them, and the way we record them in our memories. If one is distracted enough, what might at another time constitute a very powerful experience might on this viewing constitute a minor, even a forgettable, experience. If one feels sufficiently negative or negatively critical, what might be the substance of a very valuable experience might go entirely unnoticed.

B. *Physical Factors*. . . . Physical factors of temperature, comfort, and conflicting events can influence one's experience. If the theatre is too cold, if the seat is too small, if the person behind you spends five minutes getting the cellophane off a piece of peppermint, then one's experience of a performance is going to suffer for it.

C. *Maintenance of Distance.* Edward Bullough argued that in order to experience an object or event aesthetically, one must maintain a Psychical Distance between oneself and the object or event under attention. "Distance" is that state in which the viewer understands that she, her person, emotions, the potential of her action, is not actually engaged directly with the object. She is out of direct involvement with the object, experiencing it as if it were "out of reach" where she cannot affect any changes that would alter the object, and the object cannot affect any changes in her. One understands, for instance, that it is inappropriate to run on stage to stop Othello from strangling Desdemona. . . .

Conclusion

Aesthetic experiences and aesthetic analyses are different. They are each at different times the focus of philosophical aesthetics. The latter is purely a philosophical enterprise. The former is frequently, although certainly not always, studied from both the viewpoints of philosophy and psychology. Today, for the twentieth century, and for much of the nineteenth, the trend has been toward focusing, as the core to philosophizing about aesthetics, on aesthetic experience, and to do so in a way that incorporates a psychological perspective. The point of this essay is to highlight the difference between the judgment-oriented approach and the experience-oriented approach, and to enhance that focus by examining many of the various sorts of experiential factors that are as much a part of an aesthetic experience as any other experience we may have. ◢

AESTHETIC INTERPRETATION

In 1934 William Carlos Williams wrote the following poem:

This is just to say
I have eaten
the plums
that were in
the icebox

and which
you were probably
saving
for breakfast

Forgive me
they were delicious
so sweet
and so cold

Now, what in the world does that mean? Is this really about plums? Is it only about plums? For that matter, is it about anything at all? Upon reading this poem, what sort of aesthetic experience did you have, if any?

So far in this chapter, we have considered what it is to have an aesthetic experience. When thinking about art from the perspective of the audience, that issue (namely, the nature of aesthetic experience) is fundamental. In addition to that issue, and perhaps as part of that issue, is the topic of interpretation. Interpretation is related to the facts that art has meaning and that art is intentional (that is, about something). That is, artworks—at least, most artworks—do not "just happen" but are the result of conscious decisions and planning by artists. As we noted in Chapter 4, in the process of creating a work of art, an artist tries to do something: express herself or communicate some thought or feeling to others through the artwork or, perhaps, arouse or provoke some thought or feeling in whoever might encounter that artwork. The point is that art does not just pop into existence but, rather, is the result of someone's efforts. In addition, that work of art is about something or other. It might be about some particular thing or event, as in the case of portraits; it might be about some sense of what it is to be human, as in the case of a poem or novel; it might be about getting people to see things in a new or different way, as in the case of a controversial photograph; it might be about focusing on forms or patterns rather than on particular content, as in the case of abstract art. The point is that art is the result of someone's efforts and that there is meaning to a work of art. Indeed, often people encounter some artwork and ask, "What does it mean?" They ask because the meaning is not common or obvious, but there is the assumption that—having been the result of someone's efforts—it does mean something or other (and perhaps it means many things). Aesthetic interpretation is the topic of explaining art *as art*.

Because interpretation is a form of explanation, it is not merely a matter of describing art. Simply describing the colors and shapes in a particular painting is not giving an interpretation. Even describing the painting in aesthetic terms—for example, saying that the painting has balance or grace or movement—is still a description, not an explanation, and so is not an interpretation. Because interpretation is not mere description, it is similar to, although not the same thing as, criticism or critique, which involves evaluation. Later in this chapter we will look more closely at the issue of criticism. For now, we will just say that interpretation is between mere description and evaluative criticism.

Aestheticians usually speak of two broad goals or purposes of aesthetic interpretation. One is the goal of *understanding*. We might encounter some work of art, but not understand it. Sometimes this means that we might not understand what the artist was intending by creating the artwork. For example, as we have talked about previously, Picasso's *Guernica* came about as his response to the destruction of a town during the Spanish Civil War in the 1930s. Someone could see this painting and not know the history behind it, but knowing the history allows a person to understand it more than he or she would without knowing the history. A second goal of aesthetic interpretation is *appreciation*. Understanding is a cognitive, intellectual notion. Knowing the history behind *Guernica* might help someone understand it more (for example, why certain figures are portrayed or why certain colors were used), but that would not necessarily mean that the person had a new or different appreciation of the painting. A viewer who was unmoved by it before learning the history might still be unmoved afterward, even if more informed. Appreciation, then, is different from understanding, and it is a different goal of interpretation. With appreciation, the goal is to "understand" at an emotional level; it is to respond differently. With the aid of an interpretation (or, perhaps, multiple interpretations), one might come to perceive an artwork not only differently but also more fully and thus have an enhanced aesthetic experience. Some people have argued that interpretations do not enhance one's aesthetic experience but, rather, actually diminish it because an interpretation "pushes" one's understanding or appreciation in certain directions and not others. They have also claimed that, at least at the level of having an aesthetic experience (and perhaps appreciation), a botanist, for example, does not necessarily have an enhanced experience (or appreciation) compared to, say, a child's, even though the botanist obviously has enhanced understanding. Likewise, they say, art experts might have greater understanding of an artwork, but not necessarily greater appreciation. We will come back to this later in the chapter.

Besides the issue of the goals or purposes of aesthetic interpretation, there is also the issue of the process(es) or method(s) of interpretation, in other words, the issue not of *why* but of *how* a work of art should be interpreted. One common approach to interpretation is to focus on aspects of the artwork itself, ignoring everything else. For instance, with *Guernica*, one might focus on the colors that were used (blacks and grays), as well as pointing out what was not used (bright colors); one might focus on the figures that are portrayed in the painting (people and animals in contorted positions showing obvious pain and anguish). As we discussed in Chapter 3, this approach is often associated with formalism. And as we noted at that point, an alternative approach, contextualism, sees contextual information as relevant not only to what the artwork is but also to how it is interpreted. So, contextualists hold, we should not ignore what are seen as relevant facts and contexts about the artwork. For example, we should bring in the historical events that prompted Picasso to paint *Guernica*. Or one might bring in information about Picasso's other paintings to see if there is any commonality with *Guernica*. One might include any information about what Picasso said in speeches or lectures or letters, about *Guernica* in particular or about his views on art in general. This issue of *how* to interpret a work of art also speaks to *what* gets interpreted. Is it the artwork by itself, or is it the artist's intentions, personal history, cultural events, and so on?

An additional issue related to aesthetic interpretation is the question of what would count as (1) a correct or incorrect interpretation, and also (2) a better or worse interpretation. At just a commonsense level, some interpretations seem to be incorrect. For example, to say that Shakespeare's play *Hamlet* is about snowboarding clearly seems to be a misinterpretation. After all, Shakespeare did not know about snowboarding, so how could *Hamlet* be about it? However, this assumes that an artwork must be, or should be, interpreted in terms of the artist's intentions. Yet many people have argued that an artist's intentions are not the only factor that is relevant to interpreting a work of art (and perhaps are not relevant at all, because a work of art can mean many different things to different people). Among philosophers of art, there is a lot of disagreement about what standards or criteria are appropriate for determining or evaluating aesthetic interpretation (that is, for saying what would count as a correct or incorrect interpretation, as well as a better or worse interpretation).

A major topic within the issue of interpretation is the role or significance of the artist's intentions. Two questions arise here. The first is, Where is the locus of meaning in an artwork? What this question is asking is this: If interpretation is to give us the meaning (or a meaning or even multiple meanings) of an artwork, then where does that meaning lie? There is an expression: "Every generation has its *Hamlet*." This expression is getting at the point that different people interpret *Hamlet* differently, not only as individuals, but also as people from different eras: across time people get different meanings out of the same artwork. People in the twenty-first century live in different contexts (at least some different contexts) than did people in the seventeenth century; it makes sense that we would (or at least might) understand a given artwork differently than did those who lived in earlier centuries. Whatever *Hamlet* might mean, or however we should understand it, does its meaning (or does a good or correct understanding of it) depend upon what Shakespeare intended? A great many people have argued that the artist's intentions are not necessary (or even relevant) to whatever meaning an artwork has. They speak of "the intentional fallacy" and claim that the locus of meaning of an artwork lies not in the artist but in the audience. (In literary theory, this has sometimes been referred to as "reader response.") The view is that the meaning of an artwork, and so any appropriate interpretation, is a relation between the artwork and the audience. So we hear people remark, "This is what it means to me (whatever the artist might have had in mind)." Many other people, however, have defended the importance of artists' intentions. They claim that artworks do not just happen; they are created as intentional objects by artists. *Hamlet* simply is not and cannot be about snowboarding! There might well be multiple interpretations regarding an artwork, but there are clearly limits to interpretation. There are facts, whether internal to the artwork or external, in the sense of contextual information, that must constrain appropriate interpretation.

The second question that arises here is, Who is the artist? This is another way at getting at the nature of (appropriate) interpretation. The point is in part about the locus of meaning (is it in the author's head, so to speak, from whence it comes out in the artwork?) and also in part about the nature of meaning generally. The French philosopher Michel Foucault once famously asked, What is an author? For him, meaning is not private or static; it is social and fluid. Regardless of what I personally might mean when I use a term or when I interpret an artwork, if everyone else used that term or interpreted that artwork in some other way, they would, in effect, trump me. The meaning of an artwork is the way it is interpreted, for Foucault; there is no sharp division between the artist and the audience. The individual who happened to create the artwork is one component, but only one, in determining the artwork's meaning(s). Other aestheticians and artists have responded by claiming that there is a difference between an artwork *having* meaning and an artwork *generating* meaning. That is, there is a difference between what one reads *out of* an artwork and what one reads *into* an artwork. If you tell me something, I might get information out of what you say, but I might also read into your remarks something more than or different from what was actually said. Likewise, one might interpret an artwork as meaning X, but that does not necessarily mean that X is what was there.

Below, Richard Wollheim speaks to various issues related to interpretation. Although he uses the term "criticism," he really is speaking more about interpretation than about evaluation. He argues that the point of interpretation is to better perceive what is there in the artwork. As he puts it, interpretation is retrieval, that is, it is a matter of retrieving what went into the creation of the artwork. In order to (better) understand and appreciate an artwork, we need to know how it came to be. We need to reconstruct, as best we can, the creative process that resulted in the artwork. Only by doing that can we be in a position to interpret, whether or not there ends up being only one appropriate interpretation or multiple appropriate ones.

RICHARD WOLLHEIM, "CRITICISM AS RETRIEVAL"*

It is a deficiency of at least the English language that there is no single word, applicable over all the arts, for the process of coming to understand a particular

*In *Art and Its Objects, Second Edition with Six Supplementary Essays.* Cambridge: Cambridge University Press, 1980. Pages 185–192, 199–203.

work of art. To make good this deficiency I shall appropriate the word "criticism," but in doing so I know that, though this concurs with the way the word is normally used in connection with, say, literature, it violates usage in, at any rate, the domain of the visual arts, where "criticism" is the name of a purely evaluative activity.

The central question to be asked of criticism is, What does it do? How is a piece of criticism to be assessed, and what determines whether it is adequate? To my mind the best brief answer, of which this essay will offer an exposition and limited defense, is, Criticism is *retrieval*. The task of criticism is the reconstruction of the creative process, where the creative process must in turn be thought of as something not stopping short of, but terminating on, the work of art itself. The creative process reconstructed, or retrieval complete, the work is then open to understanding.

To the view advanced, that criticism is retrieval, several objections are raised.

1. The first objection is that, by and large, this view makes criticism impossible: and this is so because, except in exceptional circumstances, it is beyond the bounds of practical possibility to reconstruct the creative process.

Any argument to any such conclusion makes use of further premises—either about the nature of knowledge and its limits, or about the nature of the mind and its accessibility—and the character of these further premises comes out in the precise way the conclusion is formulated or how it is qualified. For, though an extreme form of the objection would be that the creative process can never be reconstructed, the conclusion is likelier to take some such form as that criticism is impossible unless the critic and the artist are one and the same person, or the work was created in the ambience of the critic, or the creative process was fully, unambiguously, and contemporaneously documented by the artist. . . .

A step further, and it is asserted that from these same premises an alternative view of criticism follows. This alternative view may be expressed as, Criticism as *revision*, and it holds that the task of criticism is so to interpret the work that it says most to the critic there and then. Assuming the critical role, we must make the work of art speak "to us today."

It is clear that this derivation too must require further premises, though less clear what they would be. One thing seems certain, though it is often ignored by adherents of the revisionary view, and that is this: If criticism is justifiably revision when we lack the necessary evidence for reconstructing the creative process, then it must also be revision when we have, if we ever do, adequate evidence for retrieval. We cannot as critics be entitled to make the work of art relate to us when we are in a state of ignorance about its history without our having an obligation to do so, and this obligation must continue to hold in the face of knowledge. Otherwise revision is never a critical undertaking: it is only, sometimes, a *pis-aller* [that is, last resort or stop-gap], or a second best to criticism. Indeed, the strongest case for the revisionary view of criticism draws support from a thesis which appears to dispense with skepticism or, at any rate, cuts across it.

The thesis I have in mind, which is generally called "radical historicism" and is best known through the advocacy of Eliot, holds that works of art actually change their meaning over history. On this thesis the task of the critic at any given historical moment is not so much to impose a new meaning upon, as to extract the new meaning from, the work of art. That works of art are semantically mobile in this way is to be explained not simply—to take the case of a literary work—by reference to linguistic change or to shifts in the meaning of words and idioms, but, more fundamentally, more radically, by appeal to the way in which every new work of art rewrites to some degree or other every related, or maybe every known, work of art in the same tradition. To this central contention that thesis adds the corollary that, as some particular meaning of a work of art becomes invalid or obsolete, it also becomes inaccessible: it ceases to be a possible object of knowledge. . . .

2. A second objection to the retrieval view of criticism goes deeper in that it concentrates upon the view itself and not merely upon its consequences. According to this objection, retrieval is, from the critical point of view, on any given occasion either misleading or otiose. From the outset the objection contrasts retrieval with its own favored view of criticism, which may be expressed as, Criticism is *scrutiny*—scrutiny of the literary text, of the musical score, of the painted surface—and it holds that retrieval is misleading when its results deviate from the findings of scrutiny and it is otiose when its results concur with the findings of scrutiny. In this latter case it is (note) retrieval that is reckoned otiose, not scrutiny, and the reason given is that reliance upon retrieval presupposes scrutiny and not *vice versa*. Scrutiny is presupposed because it is only with the findings of scrutiny before us that we can be certain that we are dealing with a case where the results of retrieval merely duplicate those of scrutiny, and hence that retrieval is not misleading. So, overall, retrieval can never do better than scrutiny, sometimes it can do worse, and which is the case cannot be determined without the benefit of scrutiny. . . .

This objection to the retrieval view shows itself vulnerable on a number of counts.

In the first place, though it is indubitably true that the creative process either is or is not realized in the work of art, nevertheless, if "realized" means (as it presumably does) "fully realized," this is not, from the point of view of criticism, the best way of setting out the alternatives. For critically it is a highly relevant fact that the creative process may be realized in the work of art to varying degrees. (There are, indeed, theoretical reasons of some strength, which I shall not assess, for thinking that the creative process is never realized in a work of art either to degree 1 or to degree 0: realization must always be to some indeterminate degree.) But, it might be thought, this presents no real problem. For the objection can surely concede that the creative process may be realized to varying degrees, and can further concede that sometimes, even when the creative process has not been fully realized, retrieval may not be misleading. All that it has to insist upon, surely, is that, if the creative process may be harmlessly, though otiosely, reconstructed up to the point to which it was realized in the work of art, retrieval is misleading if, and as soon as, it is carried beyond this point. However, as we shall see, this concession brings its difficulties in train.

Secondly: Suppose we confine ourselves (as the objection says) to that part of the creative process which is realized in the work of art. It becomes clear that there is something that reconstruction of this part of the process can bring to light which scrutiny of the corresponding part of the work cannot. It can show that that part of the work which came about through design did indeed come about through design and not through accident or error. Scrutiny, which *ex hypothesi* limits itself to the outcome, cannot show this. (A parallel in the philosophy of action: If an action is intentional, then, it might be thought, reconstruction of the agent's mental process will not tell us more about it than we could learn from observation of the action: but we can learn this from observation of the action only if we already or independently know that the action was intentional.) Accordingly—and as yet the point can be made only hypothetically—if criticism is concerned to find out not just what the work of art is like but what the work of art is like by design, then, contrary to what the objection asserts, scrutiny, to be a source of knowledge, must presuppose retrieval.

Thirdly: The objection, as emended, states that that part of the creative process which is not realized in the work of art is not to be reconstructed. But how is this part of the process to be identified? There are two distinct grounds on which the distinction could be effected, and they give different results. We could exclude from critical consideration any part of the creative process in which the work of art is not (subject to the necessary qualifications) more or less directly prefigured: alternatively, we might exclude only that part of the creative process which has no bearing at all upon the character of the work. Two kinds of case show how crucial it is which way the distinction is effected. The first case is where the artist changes his mind. Rodin's *Monument to Balzac* started off as a nude sculpture. Is the critically relevant part of the creative process only that which includes Rodin's change of mind to, and his subsequent concentration upon, the draped Balzac: or should it also embrace his concentration upon, and his subsequent change of mind from, the naked Balzac? The second case is where an artist sticks to his intention but fails in it. In writing *The Idiot* Dostoyevsky set out to portray a totally good man. Prince Myshkin is not a totally good man, but Dostoyevsky's depiction of him is clearly unaffected by the original aim: it is the failed depiction of a totally good man. Should we, or should we not, regard Dostoyevsky's original aim, unsuccessfully realized though it is in the work of art, as a critically relevant part of the creative process?

In the light of the next, or fourth, point, the previous two points can be sharpened. For the objection, in claiming that scrutiny can establish everything that at one and the same time is critically relevant and can be established by retrieval, totally misconceives the nature of the interest that criticism might take in the creative process and, therefore, what it stands to gain from reconstructing it. For the objection appears to assume that, if the critic is interested in the creative process, this is because, or is to be accounted for by the degree to which, it provides him with good evidence for the character of the work. The critic seeks to infer from how the work was brought about how it is. Now, of course, if this were so, then there would, on the face of it at any rate, be reason to think that retrieval was at best a detour to a destination to which scrutiny could be a short cut. But that this is a misconception is revealed by the fact that the critic committed to retrieval is not committed to any assumption about the likely degree of match between the creative process and the resultant work and he will continue to be interested in the creative process even in the case when he knows that there is a mismatch between the two. The critic who tries to reconstruct the creative process has a quite different aim from that which the objection to the retrieval view assumes. He does so in order to understand the work of art—though it would be wrong to say, as some philosophers of art tend to, that he seeks understanding rather than description. Understanding is reached through description, but through profound description, or description profounder than scrutiny can provide, and such description may be expected to include such issues as how much of the character of the work is by design, how much has come about through changes of intention, and what were the ambitions that went to its making but were not realized in the final product. . . .

3. A third objection to the retrieval view, which is open to adherents of both the revisionary view and the scrutiny view and also to others, is that it confuses the meaning of the work of art and the meaning of the artist, and it encourages the critic to pursue the second at the expense of the first. The distinction upon which this objection rests is initially not hard to grasp. Eliot has pointed out the mistake that Poe evidently made when he wrote "My most immemorial year," and in *Crome Yellow* Aldous Huxley describes a poet who is inordinately satisfied with the line "Carminative as wine" until the next morning he looks up the first word in a dictionary. Neither poet meant what his words mean. But these are very simple cases, and problems arise as soon as we try to project the distinction into areas of interest.

The basic problem is this: In order to determine the meaning of a work of art we have first to determine what the meaning-bearing properties of the work are, and it is only on a very naïve view of the matter that we can do this without invoking the creative process itself and thus losing the clarity of the distinction which the simple cases promised. A typical naïve view would be one that equated the meaning-bearing properties of a poem with the ordered and aligned words, or the "text." . . . [To] say that we have to invoke the creative process in order to fix the meaning-bearing properties of the work of art does not commit us to the view . . . that every work of art has every meaning-bearing property that the artist wished it to have. The retrieval view concedes that an artist may fail. The objection then misfires. The retrieval view has no difficulty in distinguishing—in principle, that is—between the meaning of the work of art and the meaning of the artist, and it identifies the former as the proper object of critical attention.

All objections apart, and I shall consider no more, the retrieval view invites, in one significant respect, clarification. For the arguments that I have been considering for and against the view that the creative process is the proper critical object bear a close resemblance to arguments advanced of recent years for and against the critical relevance of the artist's intentions. It, therefore, seems appropriate to ask, How are the creative process (as I have introduced it) and the artist's intention (as it figures in recent debate) related?

The creative process, as I envisage it, is a more inclusive phenomenon than the artist's intentions, and in two ways. In the first place, the creative process includes the various vicissitudes to which the artist's intentions are subject. Some of these will be themselves intentional—change of mind—but some will be chance or uncontrolled. Secondly, the creative process includes the many background beliefs, conventions, and modes of artistic production against which the artist forms his intentions: amongst these will be current aesthetic norms, innovations in the medium, rules of decorum, ideological or scientific world-pictures, current systems of symbolism or prosody, physiognomic conventions, and the state of the tradition.

A consequence follows which is of major importance for the process of retrieval. In recording an artist's intention the critic must state it from the artist's point of view or in terms to which the artist could give conscious or unconscious recognition. The critic must concur with the artist's intentionality. But the reconstruction of the creative process is not in general similarly restrained. The critic must certainly respect the artist's intentionality, but he does not have to concur with it. On the contrary he is justified in using both theory and hindsight unavailable to the artist if thereby he can arrive at an account of what the artist was doing that is maximally explanatory. Retrieval, like archaeology [which] provides many of the metaphors in which retrieval is best thought about, is simultaneously an investigation into past reality and an exploitation of present resources. Anachronism arises not when the critic characterizes the past in terms of his own day, but only when in doing so he falsifies it. There is no anachronism involved in tracing *Virgin and Child with St. Anne* to Leonardo's Oedipal strivings, or in describing Adolf Loos as bridging the gap between C. F. A. Voysey and Le Corbusier—if, that is, both these statements are true. . . .

A question remains: Is a limit set to retrieval? Obviously where evidence is lacking, our understanding stops short. The 30,000 years or so of Paleolithic art must remain ultimately a mystery to us, short of a landslide victory for archaeology. We shall probably never know the authentic rhythm or phrasing of medieval plainsong. But are there cases where both retrieval is impossible (or barely possible—for it must be conceded that, like the creative process itself, reconstruction of the creative process is realizable to varying degrees) and the explanation lies in a radical difference of perspective between the artist and us, the interpreters?

I suspect that there are, and an analogy gives us an insight into the situation. For an outward parallel to the reconstruction of the creative process is provided, at any rate in the case of the visual arts, by the physical restoration of the work of art. Admirers of French romanesque architecture, well aware that originally a great deal of the sculpture that adorns such buildings would have been brightly painted, are nevertheless likely, when confronted with attempts to restore it to its original condition—for instance, the historiated capitals at Issoire—to deplore the result. The heavy hand of the restorer is partly to blame, but not totally. For the modern spectator there seems to be no way of getting anything like the original colors to make anything like the intended impact upon him. We might restate the point in terms of the present discussion and say that he seems powerless to reconstruct the creative process in a way that at once meets the demands of internal coherence and seems naturally to terminate on the work before him. Maybe he can do so computationally but he cannot internalize the result, and the consequence is that here we may have reached the limits of retrieval. ◣

AESTHETIC CRITICISM

Consider the following two poems, both written in the twentieth century:

1. *I will not wash my face;*
    I will not brush my hair;
    I "pig" about the place—
    There's nobody to care.
    Nothing but rock and tree;
    Nothing but wood and stone.
    Oh, God, it's hell to be
    Alone, alone, alone.

2. *One must have a mind of winter*
    To regard the frost and the boughs
    Of the pine-trees crusted with snow;

    And have been cold a long time
    To behold the junipers shagged with ice,
    The spruces rough in the distant glitter

    Of the January sun; and not to think
    Of any misery in the sound of the wind,
    In the sound of a few leaves,

    Which is the sound of the land
    Full of the same wind
    That is blowing in the same bare place
    For the listener, who listens in the snow,

And, nothing himself, beholds,
Nothing that is not there and the nothing that is.

What did you think? What did you feel? What made either of them "good" or "bad"? Assuming that you had some sort of positive or negative response to them, what was it and why? If you were to talk about them to a friend, what would you say about them? Obviously, the point here is how you evaluated these poems. (By the way, the first poem is the first stanza of a poem entitled "The Telegraph Operator," by Robert W. Service; the second poem is entitled "The Snow Man," by Wallace Stevens.)

As with interpretation, and many other topics that we have touched on throughout this book, when considering the evaluation of art we can focus on what gets evaluated, how it gets evaluated, and why it gets evaluated. And, of course, these three foci can and do overlap. How we judge a particular artwork might depend upon what we know about its external contexts. For instance, if we knew (or even believed) that Picasso was trying to portray a young boy's fantasy vacation when he painted *Guernica*, we might evaluate it quite differently from the way we might if we knew (or believed) that he was trying to portray the horrors of war. Or if we knew (or believed) that Robert Service was trying to be funny or was trying to write lyrics to a song when he wrote "The Telegraph Operator," we might evaluate it quite differently from the way we might if we thought he was trying to be profound. Likewise, we might evaluate it quite differently if we knew (or believed) he was ten years old when he wrote it from the way we might if we knew (or believed) he was fifty years old when he wrote it.

Also, as with interpretation, we can ask, What would it mean to say that one has made a good or bad evaluation of an artwork? What would make one's judgment good or bad when it came to evaluating art? We said that someone who interpreted *Hamlet* as being about snowboarding has erred. Could we likewise say that someone has erred who says that *Hamlet* is a good (or bad) play? What would it mean to misevaluate an artwork? Are there facts about an artwork, whether internal to the work itself or external, that is, part of its context, that are relevant to an evaluation's being correct or incorrect (or good or bad)? (On page 156, we will see one answer to these questions by the aesthetician Monroe Beardsley.)

Clearly, the first thing to say here is that when it comes to critiquing or evaluating art, the point is not simply *what* you say, but *why* you say it. As Beardsley says in the reading, if a person offers no reasons for an evaluation, that judgment is merely dogmatic and also is not informative. If a person only says, in terms of evaluation, that he or she does or does not like an artwork, that is really a statement about the person, not about the artwork. Confession is not critique! Nevertheless, we all recognize that different people evaluate an artwork differently. We will come back to this point soon.

Earlier we said that an interpretation is something between a simple description and an evaluation. That is, an interpretation of an artwork gives an explanation, in a sense, of what is going on with the artwork without necessarily giving an evaluation of it. Giving an evaluation is also, indeed even more, like giving an explanation. As we just noted, when we give an evaluation of an artwork, we need to give reasons for that evaluation, or judgment. When we give an evaluation, or judgment, of an artwork, we are, in effect, answering a "why" question. As was pointed out back in Chapter 1, sometimes a "why" question can be answered with a simple description, but sometimes such a question requires an explanation as an answer. Imagine, for example, that your car will not start one morning. You wonder why. An appropriate answer to that question would be to give an explanation, say, that it is out of gas. Actually, for this to provide an explanation for (and an answer to) why the car won't start, more is needed, namely, some other facts about why gas is necessary for a car to start. (If your car is an electric car, then being out of gas would not really be an explanation or answer to why it did not start.) The same situation holds for giving an evaluation (or judgment). If "The Telegraph Operator" is a dreadful poem, then there are reasons why it is, and if *Guernica* is a triumphant painting, then there are reasons why it is.

We have acknowledged that people evaluate an artwork differently. Nevertheless, each person's evaluation or judgment is based on reasons. If I hate (or love) "The Telegraph Operator," it is quite appropriate for you to ask why. Even if the evaluation is my personal, subjective evaluation, I still have (and need) reasons why I find it to be such a bad poem. So the fact of personal, subjective preferences does not speak against the necessity of reasons for evaluations. In addition, as we remarked in Chapter 1, there is a difference between subjectivity and relativism. Being relative always means being relative to some standard or criterion. So even if we say that aesthetic evaluation is relative, we still require some sort of standard or criterion against which we measure the artwork. At the risk of beating this point into the ground, whatever one's view about the subjectivity or relativism of aesthetics and art, evaluation requires reasons. Granted those reasons might (and probably will) vary, reasons are still needed.

Below, Beardsley claims that there are three basic criteria by which artworks should be evaluated: unity, complexity, and intensity. You will see why he argues for these. For now, it is important to know that underlying his view is the notion that (for him) there is a fundamental function to art. That function is to produce aesthetic experience. If that is so, then, he says, art can appropriately be evaluated according to its capacity to fulfill that function (and, perhaps, according to its actual success in doing so). So Beardsley provides a basis (that is, a standard or criterion) for evaluating art in general and particular artworks. Does an artwork produce an aesthetic experience? Good art does and better art does it better. Also, bad art, even if it is art, produces a bad aesthetic experience. (Now, one might question, or disagree with, his claims that there is a function to art and that the function is to produce aesthetic experience, but that issue is separate from, although related to, the issue of what the basis is for evaluating art.)

Another aspect of Beardsley's view is that it is the aesthetic features of an artwork that are the basis for evaluation. We have already noted in previous chapters that artworks also have nonaesthetic features. In Chapter 6 we will focus much more explicitly on this issue, because among the nonaesthetic features of artworks are their moral aspects. Many aestheticians have claimed that these nonaesthetic features, especially moral ones, are relevant in evaluating artworks. We will look at that view in Chapter 6, but for now the issue is what role, if any, these nonaesthetic features have, given Beardsley's view. That is, if the aesthetic experience produced by an artwork that one finds morally repugnant is an experience of, say, repulsion, then that seems relevant, given Beardsley's own view, to evaluating the artwork. The experience produced in this case seems negative, so it would seem that one would have to evaluate the artwork negatively. Yet, say many critics, the strength of much art is that it does create discomfort. Good art, they say, should challenge us and move us out of our comfort zones. Again, we will return to this issue in the next chapter. For now, here is Beardsley:

▌ MONROE C. BEARDSLEY, "THE CLASSIFICATION OF CRITICAL REASONS"*

When a critic makes a value-judgment about a work of art, he is generally expected to give reasons for it—not necessarily a conclusive argument, but at

*Journal of Aesthetic Education 2 (1968): 55–63.

least an indication of the main grounds on which his judgment rests. Without the reasons, the judgment is dogmatic, and also uninformative: it is hard to tell how much is being asserted in "This painting is quite good," unless we understand why it is being asserted.

These reasons offered by critics (or "critical reasons") are, of course, extremely varied. Here is a small sampling:

[On Joseph Haydn's *Creation*:] "The work can be praised unconditionally for its boldness, originality, and unified conception. But what remains so remarkable in this day and age is its overall spirit of joy, to which a serene religious faith, a love of this world and a sense of drama contribute." (Raymond Ericson)

[On the finale of Anton Bruckner's Fifth Symphony:] "Perhaps this movement is the greatest of all symphonic finales" because "It is a vision of apocalyptic splendor such as no other composer, in my experience, has ever painted." (Winthrop Sargeant)

[On a novel by Max Frisch:] "Rarely has a provocative idea been spoiled more efficiently by excessive detail and overdecoration." (Richard Plant)

[On a motion picture of Pier Paolo Pasolini's:] "The sleeper of the year is a bone-bare, simple, and convincingly honest treatment of the life of Jesus, *The Gospel According to St. Matthew*." (Ernest Schier)

[On Edvard Munch's lithograph and oil painting, *The Cry*:] "This cry of terror lives in most of Munch's pictures. But I have seen faces like this in life—in the concentration camp of Dachau. . . . With 'The Cry,' the Age of Anxiety found its first and, perhaps to this very day, its unmatched expression." (Alfred Werner)

Probably the first question that will occur to a philosopher who looks over such a list of reasons is this: which of them are relevant? That is, which of them really are grounds on which the judgment can legitimately and defensibly be based? Just because "The Cry" is an "unmatched expression" of the Age of Anxiety, does that make it a good painting (or lithograph)? What reasons are there for supporting that this reason counts in favor of the painting?

Many large and difficult issues in esthetics will look ahead whenever this line of inquiry is pursued very far—too many to cope with here. The task can be somewhat simplified and clarified, however, if we sort these issues into two main categories with the help of an important distinction having to do with reasons. There are *reasons why* something is a good work of art (or a poor one), and *reasons for supposing that* something is a good work of art (or a poor one); in other words, there are reasons that serve to explain why the work of art is good or poor, and reasons that constitute logical support for a belief that the work of art is good or poor. That these are not the same can easily be shown. If Hayden's

[sic] *Creation* has a "unified conception," that would help to explain why it is a good musical composition. On the other hand, if we know that a large-scale musical work was composed by Hayden in his mature years, this fact is in itself a reason to belief that the work is probably very good, even though we have not yet heard it; but this fact does not provide any explanation of its goodness— being composed by Hayden is not one of the things that is good about the work.

One way of setting aside some of the reasons offered by critics as irrelevant to the value-judgment they accompany would then be to insist that relevant crit- ical reasons (or critical reasons in a strict sense) be those that are reasons in both of the senses just distinguished. A relevant reason is one that provides sup- port to the value-judgment for which it is a reason and also helps to explain why the judgment is true. If the critic judges that a novel is poor, or at least less good than some other novel with which he compares it, and gives as one rea- son that there is a great deal of "detail" and "decoration," then this reason not only helps to lower our estimate of the work's value but also points out part of what is wrong with it.

If we insist that a relevant critical reason must have both of these functions, it follows that in order to be relevant, reasons must be statements about the work itself, either descriptive statements about its parts or internal relations (in- cluding its form and regional qualities) or interpretive statements about its "meaning" (taking this term loosely enough to include such things as what it represents, symbolizes, signifies, expresses, says, etc.). For statements about ex- ternal matters, although they may serve as indications of probable goodness or poorness, do not explain that goodness or poorness by telling us what in the work itself makes it good or poor. . . .

Some estheticians . . . say that by its very nature, art criticism is too compli- cated and too loose for any such attempt at classification to be feasible. But why not see how far we can go, if we are careful not to force reasons into cate- gories where they don't fit? If it should in fact turn out to be the case (astonish- ingly, perhaps) that all relevant critical reasons in the strict sense fall into a few basic categories, that would not be without interest, and it might suggest further lines of inquiry of considerable philosophic importance. . . .

My procedure for constructing [a classification] is based on the observation that critical reasons are not all on the same level—that some are subordinate to others. We ask the critic, for example, "What makes the Max Frisch novel so poor?" He replies, "Among other things, excessive detail." We ask again, "What is so bad about the detail? Why is it excessive? How does it help to make the work poor?" If he is cooperative, the critic may reply once more: "The detail is excessive because it distracts the reader from those elements in the work (elements of plot, perhaps) that would otherwise give it a fairly high degree of unity," or perhaps, "The detail is excessive because it dissipates what would otherwise be strong dramatic and emotional qualities of the work." So it seems that the objectionableness of the detail is itself explained by an appeal to a more fundamental and general principle: that unity is desirable in the work, or that intensity of regional quality [that is, a quality or feature that belongs to the work as a whole, but not to any of the parts of that work] is desirable in the work.

If we press farther, however, and ask the critic why greater unity would help to make the work a better one, this question too, deserves an answer, but it would have to be of a quite different sort. In explaining why excessive detail and overdecoration are objectionable, the critic appeals to other features of the work itself, which these features either increase or diminish. But what makes unity desirable is not what it does to other features of the work; thus, as far as the work itself is concerned, unity is a basic criterion. The fine arts critic could reasonably say that a particular group of shapes and colors in a painting is good because it creates a very subtle balance, and he could also say that balance is good because it is one way of unifying the painting; but he could not say that unity in a painting is a good thing because it makes the painting contain these particular shapes and colors.

In my view, there are exactly three basic criteria that are appealed to in relevant critical reasons, and all of the other features of works of art that are appealed to in such reasons are subordinate to these, or can be subsumed under them. There is unity, which is specifically mentioned in connection with Hayden's *Creation* and presupposed in the criticism of the Max Frisch novel. There is complexity, which I think is part of what Winthrop Sargeant admires in Bruckner's *Fifth*. (Insofar as the simplicity of Pasolini's film is regarded as a positive merit, I take it not as a low degree of complexity but as absence of "excessive detail and overdecoration.") And there is intensity of regional quality: the "overall spirit of joy" in Hayden, the "cry of terror" in Edvard Munch.

Any such simplifying scheme as this ought to arouse immediate skepticism and protest. It is obviously too neat to be correct. It is tempting, no doubt, because it really does embrace and tidy up a very large number of critical reasons, and it enables us to distinguish the relevant ones from the irrelevant ones on a fairly clear principle. But certainly it needs to be examined and tested severely before it can be accepted.

Some searching questions can be asked about the three proposed criteria of judgment. First, are they sufficiently clear? Some estheticians who have considered unity, for example, have expressed doubt (1) that it has a sufficiently well-defined meaning to be used in this highly general way, and (2) that it has the same meaning across the arts (the same, that is, for painting as for poetry or music). I do not know how to prove that I am right in rejecting both of these doubts. We can surely find examples of pairs of paintings or prints where it is perfectly evident that one is more unified than the other. And even though what tends to unify a painting is, of course, not identical to what tends to unify a poem or a musical composition, as far as I can tell I mean the same thing when I say that one poem is more unified than another or when I say that one painting is more unified than another.

I do not mean to imply, of course, that we can estimate infallibly the degree to which a basic esthetic property (such as unity) is present in a particular painting. When we look at a painting and it fails to hang together, that may be because we are tired, or our perceptions are dulled by an adverse mode, or we are not attending close enough, or we have had too little acquaintance with works of that sort. A negative conclusion must usually be somewhat tentative and rebuttable; for it may well be that if later we come to the painting again, in a more serene mood, with sharper faculties, and with greater willingness to give in to whatever the painting wishes to do to us, we may find that in fact it has a tight though subtle unity that is perfectly apparent to the prepared eye. But if we return again and again, under what we take to be the most favorable conditions, and it still looks incoherent, we have reasonable grounds for concluding that probably the painting cannot be seen as unified. . . .

Second, are the three basic criteria really basic? One of the marks of being basic (as I have said) is that the question "Why is X good (or poor) in the work?" seems to come to a turning-point in them, for at that point it takes one outside of the work itself. Another mark is that the subordinate reasons are contextually limited. That is, the features they allude to may be desirable in some works but not necessarily in all. A particular cluster of shapes and colors may work well in one setting but badly in another; balance is not necessarily always a good thing; and details that would be excessive in one novel might not be excessive in another. But the basic criteria, I would claim, are all one-way. Unity, complexity, and intensity of regional quality never count against a work of art (we cannot say the painting is good because its regional quality is so insipid, or because it is so elementary a design, or because it falls apart into messiness), but always count in favor of it, to the extent to which they are present. The example of simplicity, which I mentioned earlier, might seem to refute at least part of this claim; but it seems to me that whenever simplicity is held up as a desirable feature, either it is not strictly simplicity (the opposite of complexity) that is referred to, but some sort of unity, or it is not the simplicity that is admired, but the intensity of some regional quality that happens to be obtainable in this case only by accepting simplicity.

Third, are the three proposed criteria really adequate to cover the entire range of relevant critical reasons? Consider "boldness" or "originality," for example, which are cited in the praise of Hayden's *Creation*. "Boldness" could no doubt benefit from further clarification: it could refer to a regional quality of the work, or it could refer in a somewhat roundabout way to originality (perhaps Hayden was bold to try out certain hitherto unheard of, or at least unfamiliar, ideas in it). But originality does not seem to fit under the three basic criteria. Or consider the description of Pasolini's film as "convincingly honest." Honesty, again, might be a certain quality of the work—absence of sentimentality and melodrama, etc. But it might be a correspondence between the film itself and the actual feelings of the film maker (even though he is a Communist, he could still have certain feelings about the story, which he sincerely puts into his work); and honesty in that sense, like sincerity, does not seem relevant to unity or complexity or intensity of regional quality. . . .

This challenge leads into the fourth question I intend to raise here: What good (philosophical) reason is there for holding that any particular (critical) reason is relevant or irrelevant to the judgment of a particular work? If someone says that the Bruckner *Fifth* is great because it presents a "vision of apocalyptic splendor," there are always two questions we can ask: First, is it true that the work presents such a vision? (Granted that the music is splendid, and therefore splendor can be heard in it, how do we know that it is "apocalyptic?") Second, if the statement is true, why is it a ground for saying that the work is great? (How does apocalypticity make the music good?) . . .

Anything so complex as a work of art can usually be regarded from more than one point of view: It is (let us say) a visual design, an example of skilled workmanship, a source of income for the painter and (even more) for the art dealer, a political document, an excellent example of a certain historical style, and so forth. And one very broad way of sorting out all the various remarks that people might want to make about the painting is to say that they are made from different points of view: economic, or art-historical, or political, or other. Then how are we to distinguish between one point of view and another? According to some philosophers, one point of view can be distinguished from another only in terms of the sort of reason given: thus, if one says that the painting is costly, we can classify this point of view as economic; and if another says that the painting is a good example of Mannerism, we can classify his point of view as that of the art historian. But in that case, we would not use points of view to help us sort out the reasons, or we would be going in a circle. I would prefer to distinguish between one point of view and another in terms of a kind of value that one might take an interest in: market value or art-historical value (that is, usefulness in illuminating some phase of art history).

Speaking very broadly (and for some purposes too sweepingly), the various kinds of value that may be found in works of art can be classified under three headings. There is cognitive value (of which art-historical value would be a species). We often speak well of works of art if they contribute in some way to our knowledge. Perhaps Winthrop Sargeant is suggesting that Bruckner gives us a kind of insight into the nature of apocalypses, and perhaps Alfred Werner is suggesting that Munch gives us a better understanding of our Age of Anxiety. In any case, claims like these are frequently made, and if they are valid claims, then they certainly do show that the work is worth creating and preserving. But I do not think they are relevant reasons for saying that the work is good music or good painting—only that it is good as religious intuition or a social document.

Next there is what might be called moral and social value. Someone might follow Winthrop Sargeant's suggestion (and his remarks elsewhere) by saying that Bruckner's music is religiously significant, and under suitable circumstances can strengthen religious faith (assuming that this is desirable). Someone else might praise Pasolini's film because it can produce moral uplift or strengthen character. And, quite apart from whether or not "The Cry" is a good painting, it may be of great social worth as an "unmatched expression," a minatory reminder, of the ills of our age. But again, even if all these claims are admitted, they would not properly lead us to say that these works are good works of art.

Finally, there is esthetic value. This is the kind of value that we look for most especially and suitably in works of art, and the kind of value whose presence and degree we report when we say that the work is good or poor. If we set aside all those reasons that clearly depend upon a cognitive or a moral/social point of view, we may consider those that remain to be peculiarly esthetic. They are, however, not all equally relevant. Relevance depends on our theory of esthetic value. If we hold, as I do, that the esthetic value of an object is that value which it possesses in virtue of its capacity to provide esthetic experience, then certain consequences follow. For the only way to support such a judgment relevantly and cogently would be to point out features of the work that enable it to provide an experience having an esthetic character. And thus the relevant reasons, as I assumed above, will be those that both support and explain. ◣

Questions for Discussion

1. Can there be a correct interpretation of an artwork? Can there be an incorrect interpretation? What would make an interpretation correct or incorrect?

2. Can there be a correct evaluation of an artwork? Can there be an incorrect evaluation of an artwork? What would make an evaluation correct or incorrect?

3. In what respects, if any, is an aesthetic experience a function of interpretation? Is it the case that a child could have the "same" aesthetic experience of, say, Beethoven's Fifth Symphony as a trained musician could? Why or why not?

4. Wollheim argues that interpretation (or, for him, criticism) is retrieval; it is being able to, as best one can, reproduce the creative process that led to the artwork. Is he right? Does this presuppose, or not, that the artist's intentions are at least necessary for having a correct or good interpretation of an artwork?

5. What would make a criterion of evaluation a good (or bad) criterion? Are Beardsley's three criteria for evaluation good criteria? Do his criteria allow for factors external to the artwork itself to be relevant in terms of evaluation? Should they?

CHAPTER 6

RELATIONSHIPS BETWEEN ART AND SOCIETY: ETHICS, EDUCATION, CULTURE

At the very beginning of this book we looked at the case of the 9/11 photograph and the clay model of a proposed statue that was based on, but varied from, that photograph. We noted that the statue itself was never created, given the outcry from people who were upset about the proposed design. No doubt you also know of the controversy created by the Danish cartoonist Kurt Westergaard, who drew a cartoon in 2005 depicting the prophet Muhammad wearing a turban with a bomb in it. Many Muslims treated this as blasphemy, and many violent protests resulted, as did an attack on Westergaard himself. In 1987 the Honduran-Cuban photographer Andres Serrano exhibited an artwork entitled *Piss Christ* that showed a Christian crucifix encased in a jar of what Serrano said was his own urine. In 2002, US Attorney General John Ashcroft announced that he had spent $8,000 of taxpayer's money for drapes to cover up the exposed breast of *Spirit of Justice*, an eighteen-foot-tall aluminum statue of a woman that stands in the Hall of Justice. Later in this chapter we will discuss art and education, but you are probably already aware of cases in which artworks in the context of schooling were embroiled in controversy, such as two children's books from the 1980s (*Heather Has Two Mommies* and *Daddy's Roommate*) that portrayed gay homes in positive ways, or Mark Twain's *Tom Sawyer*, which contains racial terms that have deeply

165

offended some people. There are, of course, countless other examples of art being seen as socially or morally controversial. In addition, there are countless examples of art seen as positive, that is, as uplifting or empowering or liberating.

Art is connected to society in many ways. Especially today, because of technology, art is everywhere. Millions of songs are downloaded from iTunes or the Internet every year, and billions of dollars are spent by moviegoers every year. The Harry Potter books were a worldwide phenomenon. Thousands, even millions, of people can and do encounter artworks every day, and they are often the same artworks; that is, on any given day, thousands, perhaps millions, of people can be listening to the same song or watching the same movie or video. There are celebrity artists, such as pop singers or movie stars, who are known around the world and are recognized by millions of people. Because of the availability and presence of art that technology has made possible, philosophers (and others) have expanded their aesthetic focus to include issues relating art and society.

An important issue here is the business of art and the role of art in business. Today movies are spoken of in terms of how much money they earn, not in terms of how aesthetically moving or profound they are. For instance, when people speak of the movie *Avatar*, they talk about its box-office draw, not its artistic integrity. We all recognize that art is fundamental to advertising. More people recognize musical jingles from television ads than recognize major political figures. In 2004, more Americans voted for the winner of *American Idol* than for the president of the United States. Art is part of business because it is seen as affecting how people behave, in particular what they will spend their money on. Some philosophers argue that advertising jingles are not artworks because their purpose is to sell a product, not to be a work of art. However, many advertisements use already-recognized musical compositions in them, for instance, clips from popular songs. It would be strange to claim that these stopped being songs (and art) because they are included within a television ad. Their use might not be artistic, but they are still artworks. Indeed, they are used in advertisements because of their power as artworks; they speak to people (consumers), and businesses want their products to be associated with them. It is this very commodification of art—that is, treating art as an economic commodity—that was the focus of some philosophers, such as Walter Benjamin, who critiqued and criticized such uses of art, and Theodor Adorno, who spoke of the creation of a "culture industry." Later in this chapter we will look more directly at these sorts of concerns.

Another significant area in which art is connected to society at large is with respect to social and political values. This often comes up in the context of questions about public funding for certain art and censorship issues. Should the government have a role in the funding of art? Many people argue that this is not an appropriate use of taxpayer money (which is how the government can fund anything), usually because they say that such funds should go to other, more important, matters, such as national defense or health issues. Others, who might believe that there is some legitimate role for the government in the funding of art, insist on accountability for such funding. They say, for example, that the National Endowment for the Arts needs to be responsive to public wishes and attitudes, so the government has a legitimate role in deciding and overseeing what particular artistic projects get funded.

The issue of accountability also speaks to the issue of censorship and the place and role of art in society, especially in connection to morality and social values. There is, of course, a spectrum of views about this issue. Some people argue that artistic expression is protected by the right to free expression, so no censorship is appropriate, regardless of how offensive some artwork might be. This view is sometimes put forth with the sentiment, If you don't like what you see, then don't look at it! If some work of art offends you, proponents of this view say, then walk away (or if you don't like what you see on television, change the channel). Others, however, have argued that this view is too simplistic. Some things are too offensive simply to walk away from. More than that, however, they claim that some works of art are not merely offensive; they are harmful. For instance, pornography, they say, is not merely offensive but, rather, leads to women being harmed (either from direct assault or from the promotion of general attitudes that dehumanize women). Or, they say, works of art that glorify the degradation of certain people go beyond being offensive to being harmful. The general point, of course, is that to the extent that art is a social phenomenon, it is related to social, political, and moral values. Given the fact that art is so prevalent in today's society, these value issues have become more and more immediate and widespread. There is no question that art is connected to social and moral values in a number of ways. Here we will look at three broad topics that come up when we examine the relation of art and society. First, we will look at art and values generally, especially moral values. Second, we will look at art and education. Third, we will look at art in culture, that is, the broad cultural meaning of art.

ART AND VALUES

In one sense we have already covered the topic of art and values in earlier chapters, but they were values *within* art. For example, we saw Monroe Beardsley speak of three basic criteria connected to the evaluation of art: unity, complexity, and intensity. Although he calls these criteria for evaluating art, they can also be seen as values within artworks. Other criteria might be added to this list, such as originality, authenticity, creativity, or ability to provoke. In addition, in earlier chapters we spoke of value questions related to artists and audiences. For instance, when we ask why an artist expresses some feeling or belief or value via an artwork, we are asking about the relation between art and values. Or when we ask why an artist represents something or other via the artwork, we again are asking about the relation between art and values. So, too, when we ask why people experience art (for instance, why do they go to concerts or museums or purchase artworks), we are asking about the relation between art and values.

Here, however, we will focus on values not within art, but *about* art. One of the most discussed and most important topics related to values about art is the nature of the relationship between aesthetic values and nonaesthetic values. We have already touched on this: Was the clay model of the 9/11 fire-fighters controversial because of its aesthetic features? Not at all! No one talked about the unity or complexity or intensity of the (proposed) statue. On the other hand, when Clive Bell argued in favor of formalism (in Chapter 3), he directly advocated separating aesthetic features and nonaesthetic features when considering the nature of art. The view of aestheticism is in large part just that: aesthetic features are separate and separable from nonaesthetic features, and art should be viewed, understood, and evaluated in terms of its aesthetic features only. Indeed, there are well-known examples of artworks that have been found objectionable from a moral perspective but praiseworthy from an aesthetic perspective. Two such examples are the 1915 film *The Birth of a Nation*, directed by D. W. Griffith, and the 1935 film *Triumph of the Will*, directed by Leni Riefenstahl. The first film was quite openly racist (certainly by today's standards), and the second was a glowing tribute to Adolf Hitler.

Aestheticism, in effect, says that aesthetic values and nonaesthetic values (including moral values) are mutually exclusive. Whatever moral values an artwork might have is secondary and is irrelevant to its status as art. Only aesthetic values matter with respect to an artwork *as art*, although we might acknowledge other values within and about the artwork. *Guernica* might have economic value; if someone wanted to buy it, it would cost a lot of money. It might have historical value; to someone interested in attitudes about the Spanish Civil War, it might provide useful and valuable information. But, as an artwork, say the aestheticists, those issues and values are irrelevant.

Others claim that art and nonaesthetic values are related, either negatively, meaning the values are (or should be) in conflict, or positively, meaning the values are (or should be) in tandem.

Those who say there is a negative relation mean that art should challenge "current" values and provoke people to question their values and beliefs. The purpose, or at least a purpose, of art is to question and upset people's complacency about what they believe and value. It should prod people out of their comfort zones. For example, by portraying the devastating consequences of war on a young man's life, Dalton Trumbo's novel *Johnny Got His Gun* was a direct challenge to the value of patriotism.

Those who see a positive relation between art and nonaesthetic values, particularly moral values, usually mean this prescriptively, not descriptively. That is, they do not usually simply say that art *does* go hand in hand with moral values; rather, they hold that it *should*. If it does not, then the art is bad. John Ashcroft believed that nudity in the Hall of Justice was inappropriate morally, so artwork that portrayed nudity there was not acceptable. People who found *Piss Christ* or images of Muhammad to be sacrilegious objected not to the aesthetic features of the artworks—they did not complain about a lack of unity or complexity or intensity—but to their moral content.

The view that moral nonaesthetic features of art are relevant to the evaluation of art is sometimes referred to as *ethicism*. To repeat, there are various types of nonaesthetic values associated with art, including economic, historical, political, religious, and cultural ones. Among those nonaesthetic values are moral values. The moral values usually have to do with the content of the artwork (for example, *Piss Christ* or the portrayal of Muhammad), but they might have to do with other aspects. For example, some people argue that any artwork produced by certain people, regardless of its content (or form), is objectionable. Before entering politics, Hitler went to art school and hoped to be a painter. Some people would consider any artwork by Hitler bad, no matter what its aesthetic features were. They would object, for instance, to a museum having a public display of his artworks. The point is that some people find the source of an artwork to be relevant to its value as art. Usually, however, when people have focused on the moral aspects of an artwork, they have focused on the content of the artwork.

In the reading below, Berys Gaut argues in favor of ethicism. As he says from the very start, "The ethical assessment of attitudes manifested by works of art is a legitimate aspect of the aesthetic evaluation of those works." He is also explicit that his view is not that aesthetic values and moral values are identical, either generally speaking or in terms of their relation to art. Some artworks can be, for him, ethically or morally flawed, yet have such aesthetic virtue that the moral flaws are outweighed in our total evaluation or judgment of the artwork. As you read his essay, keep in mind that when considering the moral and aesthetic values and the relationship between them, these values can be in regard to what is "in" the artwork (that is, its content), and "in" the artist, so to speak (that is, the intentions of the artist), and also "in" the audience (that is, the work's impact on others). So it could be the case that an artist does not intend a work to be morally offensive, but it is; or it could be the case that an artist does intend a work to be morally offensive (or at least provocative) but fails, so that no one is offended (or provoked) by it. Nevertheless, there might be a relation between moral and aesthetic values in such cases. Again, when reading Gaut, it is important to be aware of just what he is claiming about the relation between art and morality and what he is not claiming. He tried to be very clear about the difference.

BERYS GAUT, "THE ETHICAL CRITICISM OF ART"*

Ethicism

This essay argues that the ethical criticism of art is a proper and legitimate aesthetic activity. More precisely, it defends a view I term *ethicism*. Ethicism is the thesis that the ethical assessment of attitudes manifested by works of art is a legitimate aspect of the aesthetic evaluation of those works, such that, if a work manifests ethically reprehensible attitudes, it is to that extent aesthetically defective, and if a work manifests ethically commendable attitudes, it is to that extent aesthetically meritorious.

This thesis needs elucidation. The ethicist principle is a pro tanto one: it holds that a work is aesthetically meritorious (or defective) *insofar as* it mani-

_____

*In *Aesthetics and Ethics: Essays at the Intersection*. Edited by Jerrold Levinson. Cambridge: Cambridge University Press, 1998. Pages 182–189, 192–196.

fests ethically admirable (or reprehensible) attitudes. (The claim could also be put like this: manifesting ethically admirable attitudes *counts toward* the aesthetic merit of a work, and manifesting ethically reprehensible attitudes *counts against* its aesthetic merit.) The ethicist does not hold that manifesting ethically commendable attitudes is a necessary condition for a work to be aesthetically good: there can be good, even great, works of art that are ethically flawed. Examples include Wagner's Ring Cycle, which is marred by the anti-Semitism displayed in the portrayal of the *Nibelungen*; some of T. S. Eliot's poems, such as *Sweeney among the Nightingales*, which are similarly tainted by anti-Semitism; and Leni Riefenstahl's striking propaganda film, *The Triumph of the Will*, deeply flawed by its craven adulation of Hitler. Nor does the ethicist thesis hold that manifesting ethically good attitudes is a sufficient condition for a work to be aesthetically good: there are works such as Harriet Beecher Stowe's *Uncle Tom's Cabin* which, though the ethical attitudes they display are admirable, are in many ways uninspired and disappointing. The ethicist can deny these necessity and sufficiency claims, because she holds that there are a plurality of aesthetic values, of which the ethical values of artworks are but a single kind. So, for instance, a work of art may be judged to be aesthetically good *insofar as* it is beautiful, is formally unified and strongly expressive, but aesthetically bad *insofar as* it trivializes the issues with which it deals and manifests ethically reprehensible attitudes. We then need to make an *all-things-considered* judgment, balancing these aesthetic merits and demerits one against another to determine whether the work is, all things considered, good. And we should not suppose that there is any mechanically applicable weighing method that could determine the truth of such a judgment: overall judgments are plausibly ones that resist any form of codification in terms of mechanically applicable principles. These kinds of pro tanto and all-things-considered judgments are common in other evaluative domains, notably the moral domain.

The notion of the aesthetic adopted here should be construed broadly. In the narrow sense of the term, aesthetic value properties are those that ground a certain kind of sensory or contemplative pleasure or displeasure. In this sense, beauty, elegance, gracefulness, and their contraries are aesthetic value properties. However, the sense adopted here is broader: I mean by "aesthetic value" that value of an object *qua* work of art, that is, its artistic value. This broader sense is required, since not all of the values of an object *qua* work of art are narrowly aesthetic. Besides a work's beauty, we may, for instance, aesthetically admire it for its cognitive insight (subject, as we shall see, to certain conditions), its articulated expression of joy, the fact that it is deeply moving, and so on.

However, this broader sense of "aesthetic" does not mean that just any property of a work of art counts as aesthetic. Works of art may have many other sorts of value properties that are not values of them *qua* works of art: they can have investment value, value as status symbols, and so forth.

The notion of manifesting an attitude should be construed in terms of a work's displaying pro or con attitudes toward some state of affairs or things, which the work may do in many ways besides explicitly stating an opinion about them. . . . What is relevant for ethicism are the attitudes *really* possessed by a work, not those it merely claims to possess; so the attitudes manifested may be correctly attributable only by subtle and informed critical judgment. . . .

Ethicism does not entail the causal thesis that good art ethically improves people. Since the ethicist principle is a pro tanto one, it allows for the existence of great but ethically flawed works; and even if all aesthetically good works were ethically sound, it would not follow that they improve people, any more than it follows that earnest ethical advice improves people, for they may be unmoved by even the most heartfelt exhortation. Much of the ethical discussion about art, particularly concerning the supposedly pernicious effects of some popular films and music genres, has been concerned with the question of whether such art morally corrupts. This is a version of the causal thesis and should be kept distinct from ethicism. Further, ethicism has nothing to say about the issue of censorship, nor does it give any grounds of support to either the friends or foes of artistic censorship. All that follows from ethicism is that if a work manifests morally bad attitudes it is to that extent aesthetically flawed, flawed as a work of art. The fact that a work of art is aesthetically flawed is not grounds for its censorship: if it were, the art museums of the world would suffer serious depletion.

Objections to Ethicism

1. Ethicism fails to distinguish sharply enough between ethical and aesthetic evaluation. There is an aesthetic attitude in terms of which we aesthetically evaluate works; this aesthetic attitude is distinct from the ethical attitude we may adopt toward works; and ethical assessment is never a concern of the aesthetic attitude. So the ethical criticism of works is irrelevant to their aesthetic value.

The existence of the aesthetic attitude has, of course, been much disputed. But, even if we accept its existence, its adoption is compatible with ethicism. To see why, we need to specify in more detail what the aesthetic attitude is. There are two basic ways of doing this: the aesthetic attitude may be individuated by some feature intrinsic to it or by its formal objects.

Consider the case in which the attitude is individuated by its formal objects: these may be understood in narrow aesthetic fashion, as beauty and its subspecies, such as grace and elegance, or characterized more broadly by the criteria to which formalists appeal, such as Beardsley's unity, complexity, and intensity. Since the presence of these properties arguably does not require, or suffice for, the presence of ethical properties, it may be held that ethical assessment is irrelevant to aesthetic evaluation. Yet this objection is unconvincing, for the list of properties deployed is too narrow to embrace all those of aesthetic relevance. In the assessment of art, appeal is made to such properties as raw expressive power and deep cognitive insight as well as to beauty, elegance, and grace; and the relevance of these expressive and cognitive values explains how there can be great works, such as *Les Desmoiselles d'Avignon*, that are militantly ugly. So the narrow aesthetic view fails. In more sophisticated fashion, the formalist appeals to purely intrinsic properties of works as aesthetically relevant, an appeal motivated by a conception of the work of art as autonomous from its context. But that conception is flawed, for a work can be fully interpreted only by situating it within its generative context. . . .

The alternative is to individuate the aesthetic attitude by some features intrinsic to it, and for the opponent of ethicism the most promising feature is the detachment or disengagement we purportedly display toward fictional events. Since it is logically impossible to intervene in such events, the will is detached, practical concerns are quiescent, an attitude of contemplation is adopted. Given the practical character of morality, it follows that ethical assessment plays no role in aesthetic attitude and therefore no role in aesthetic evaluation. But the step from the claim that the will is disengaged and therefore that ethical assessment has no role to play does not follow: there is similarly no possibility of altering historical events, and we are in this sense forced to have a detached or contemplative attitude toward them, but we still ethically assess historical characters and actions. If it is objected that we are ethically engaged in history because we hope to draw from its lessons for our current practice, the same may be said of the lessons we can draw from fiction, such as the psychological insights that Freud discovered there. . . .

2. A more radical objection holds that ethical assessment has no place in the assessment of art. Works of art can at best manifest attitudes toward those fictional characters and situations they describe, and such attitudes are not ethically assessable, since they are directed toward merely imagined objects—such objects cannot be harmed or hurt in reality, for they do not exist. What is ethically assessable, in contrast, are attitudes directed toward real characters and

situations, but works of art do not manifest attitudes toward such things, for they do not describe them. Hence, there is no place left for the ethical assessment of art.

Even at first blush, the objection is hyperbolic, since not all works of art are fictions: Riefenstahl's film is a documentary of the 1934 Nuremberg rally, and Hitler was not a fictional character. So, at best, the argument would apply only to a subclass of works of art. Second, attitudes directed toward only imagined states of affairs can in fact properly be ethically assessed. Consider a man whose sexual life consists entirely of rape fantasies, fantasies he has not about women he sees in real life, but about women he only imagines. Would we say that there is nothing to be said from an ethical point of view about the attitude he manifests in his imaginings of these fictional women? Clearly, what a person imagines and how he responds to those imaginings play an important part in the ethical assessment of his character. . . . When the rape fantasist imagines his fictional women, he is imagining them *as women*, that is, as beings of a kind that also has instances in the real world; and that he imagines them as women is, of course, essential to his imaginative project. Thus, by virtue of adopting such an attitude toward his imagined women, he implicitly adopts that attitude toward their real-life counterparts—and so reveals something of his attitude toward real-life women. . . . So the attitudes manifested toward fictional entities will have many implications for attitudes manifested toward real entities.

3. Ethical assessment is relevant to a work's aesthetic merit, but ethicism gives the connection the wrong valence: works can be good precisely *because* they violate our sense of moral rectitude. Often the most fascinating characters in works are the evil ones, such as Satan in *Paradise Lost*. And recall the passage in *King Lear* in which blind Gloucester asks Lear, "Does thou know me?" and Lear replies, "I remember thine eyes well enough. Does thou squiny at me? / No, do thy worst, blind Cupid, I'll not love." As Lawrence Hyman writes, "The dramatic effect requires our moral disapproval," but Shakespeare manages to "transfigure that moral shock into aesthetic pleasure."

It is important to distinguish between the evil or insensitive characters represented by a work and the attitude the work displays toward those characters. Only the latter is relevant to the ethicist thesis. Satan is indeed fascinating because evil, but the work represents him as such, showing the seductive power of evil, and does not approve of his actions. Milton was not a Satanist. And while the power of Lear's bad joke does rest on its hearty heartlessness, it is part of the point of *Lear* that the flamboyant insensitivity displayed by Lear in his derangement is of a piece with the gross egoism that leads to disaster, an egoism overcome only by grief and loss, and transmuted into a finer moral wisdom. Lear's attitude toward Gloucester is represented by the play, but not shared by it. It is true that some works, such as de Sade's *Juliette*, not merely represent evil, but also manifest approval toward that evil. If this work has indeed any serious aesthetic merit, it can in part be traced to the literary skill with which it represents the attitude of finding sexual torture erotically attractive; yet the ethicist can consistently and plausibly maintain that the novel's own espousal of this attitude is an aesthetic defect in it. . . .

The Merited-Response Argument

Ethicism is a thesis about a work's manifestation of certain attitudes, but in what does this manifestation of attitudes consist? It is obvious that works prescribe the imagining of certain events: a horror film may prescribe imagining teenagers being assaulted by a monster; *Juliette* prescribes imagining that acts of sexual torture occur. Perhaps less obviously, works also prescribe certain responses to these fictional events: the loud, atonal music of the horror film prescribes us to react to the represented events with fear, *Juliette* invites the reader to find sexual torture erotically attractive, to be aroused by it, to be amused by the contortions described, to admire the intricacy of their implementation, and so forth. The approbatory attitude that *Juliette* exhibits toward sexual torture, then, is manifested in the responses it prescribes its readers to have toward such torture. The attitudes of works are manifested in the responses they prescribe to their audiences.

It is important to construe this claim correctly to avoid an objection. Consider a novel that prescribes its readers to be amused at a character's undeserved suffering but that does so in order to show the ease with which the reader can be seduced into callous responses. Then one response (amusement) is prescribed, but a very different attitude is manifested by the work (disapproval of the ease with which we can be morally seduced); hence, the manifestation of attitudes is wholly distinct from and independent of the prescription of responses. What this objection reveals is that prescriptions, like attitudes, come in a hierarchy, with higher-order prescriptions taking lower-order ones as their objects. Thus, my amusement at the character's suffering is prescribed, but there is a higher-order prescription that this amusement itself be regarded as callous and therefore as unmerited. . . . Similar remarks apply to paintings, films, and other representational arts. Music without a text is also subject to ethical criticism if we can properly ascribe to the music a presented situation and a prescribed response to it. If Shostakovich's symphonies are a musical protest against the Stalinist regime, we can ethically assess them.

The notion of a response is to be understood broadly, covering a wide range of states directed at represented events and characters, including being pleased at something, feeling an emotion toward it, being amused about it, and desiring something with respect to it—wanting it to continue or stop, wanting to know what happens next. Such states are characteristically affective, some essentially so, such as pleasure and the emotions, while in the case of others, such as desires, there is no necessity that they be felt, although they generally are. . . .

Though a work may prescribe a response, it does not follow that it succeeds in making this response merited: horror fictions may be unfrightening, comedies unamusing, thrillers unthrilling. This is not just to say that fear, amusement, and thrills are not produced in the audience; for people may respond in a way that is inappropriate. Rather, the question is whether it is appropriate or inappropriate to respond in the way the work prescribes. If I am afraid of a harmless victim in a horror movie because of her passing resemblance to an old tormentor of mine, my fear is inappropriate. And my admiration for a character in a novel can be criticized for being based on a misunderstanding of what he did in the story. So prescribed responses are subject to evaluative criteria.

Some of these criteria are ethical ones. As noted earlier, responses outside the context of art are subject to ethical evaluation. I can criticize someone for taking pleasure in others' pain, for being amused by sadistic cruelty, for being angry at someone when she has done no wrong, for desiring the bad. The same is true when responses are directed at fictional events, for these responses are actual, not just imagined ones. If we actually enjoy or are amused by some exhibition of sadistic cruelty in a novel, that shows us in a bad light, reflects ill on our ethical character, and we can properly be criticized for responding in this fashion. . . .

The aesthetic relevance of prescribed responses wins further support from noting that much of the value of art derives from its deployment of an affective mode of cognition—derives from the way works teach us, not by giving us merely intellectual knowledge, but by bringing that knowledge home to us. This teaching is not just about how the world is, but can reveal new conceptions of the world in the light of which we can experience our situation, can teach us new ideals, can impart new concepts and discriminatory skills—having read Dickens, we can recognize the Micawbers of the world. And the way knowledge is brought home to us is by making it vividly present, so disposing us to reorder our thoughts, feelings, and motivations in the light of it. . . .

These observations can be assembled into an argument for ethicism. A work's manifestation of an attitude is a matter of the work's prescribing certain responses toward the events described. If these responses are unmerited, because unethical, we have reason not to respond in the way prescribed. Our having reason not to respond in the way prescribed is a failure of the work. What responses the work prescribes is of aesthetic relevance. So the fact that we have reason not to respond in the way prescribed is an *aesthetic* failure of the work, that is to say, is an aesthetic defect. So a work's manifestation of ethically bad attitudes is an aesthetic defect in it. Mutatis mutandis, a parallel argument shows that a work's manifestation of ethically commendable attitudes is an aesthetic merit in it, since we have reason to adopt a prescribed response that is ethically commendable. So ethicism is true. ◣

AESTHETICS (AND) EDUCATION

Plato famously criticized art in his book *The Republic*. Art that is meant to be representative, he said, was at best a copy of reality. Just as a shadow of a person is real, but it is less real than the actual person, a painting of a person is real, but it is less real than an actual person. To the extent, then, that we focus on art, we focus on a "low" level of reality. Such a focus is a distraction, he said, from seeking or knowing truth. In addition, Plato also claimed that art is passionate, and this was of concern to him for two reasons. The first reason was that art, he held, arises from passion, rather than from reason or rationality. Artists are inspired; they are enthusiastic (literally, "filled with gods"), so even if they manage to produce a work of beauty (meaning that they produce an artwork that is merely a shadow of the Idea of Beauty), they do so not from knowledge but from passion. The second reason this was a concern to Plato was that art can also evoke or provoke passion—as opposed to reason—in the person who encounters it. Art can stir people up! For Plato, this feature of art could be dangerous, because it is passionate and not reasoned.

Plato's third concern about art, and a concern that is related to its nature as being both imitative and passionate, was that art can (and, he said, often does) portray things and people that are bad in ways that make them appear not so bad. (This is probably even truer today than during Plato's time; it is not at all uncommon that the "hero" of a movie is someone who tricks and deceives others for purely selfish gain.) Quite simply, for Plato, art can make what is bad appear to be good, and a possible result of that is that art can lead people to confuse the bad with the good and to pursue what is bad.

Despite the concerns that Plato had about art—that it is at best a shadow of reality, that it derives from passion rather than reason, that it can mislead people—he nonetheless recognized and appreciated the power of art. Also, he acknowledged that art was a basic human way of approaching Beauty and, as such, could be important and (morally) valuable. Indeed, the power of art, why it can be so moving, stems from its relation to Beauty and to Goodness. Further, in other passages in *The Republic*, he speaks of the importance and value of art as part of the education of a state's leaders.

That art is educationally important and valuable is a message that today has a mixed reception. On the one hand, many people see art (or the arts) as less important or valuable than other forms of knowledge or skill. We have all heard of the basis of education as "the three Rs": reading, (w)riting, and (a)rithmetic. When budget cuts are required by schools, especially publicly funded schools, frequently the first areas of the curriculum to be jettisoned are the arts, because they are seen as less necessary (and so less important or valuable) for the education of students. On the other hand, many educators have strongly argued the contrary. For instance, Harvard University's Project Zero, founded in 1967, has for decades been promoting and demonstrating the educational importance and value of art (and the arts). Arts, say these educators, are a basic and natural component of a person's maturation. With no prodding at all, children naturally and spontaneously relish in singing and dancing and drawing; they choose to make up stories and act out imaginative roles; they build sandcastles and Lego structures. Children are, they argue, natural actors, playwrights, architects, artists, and so on.

When aestheticians speak of aesthetic education, they usually do so in two respects. First, they speak of the role of the arts in education, and second, they speak of the role of aesthetics (that is, philosophy of art) in art education. The first emphasizes why art, and studying art, is important and valuable generally speaking; the second emphasizes why philosophy of art and studying aesthetics is important and valuable. We will look at these respects in more detail, but first we will consider the "education" aspect of aesthetic education (because general philosophical aspects and concerns about education are directly relevant to aesthetic education).

The philosophy of education involves the investigation and analysis of fundamental concepts and issues within and about education. Included among these concepts and issues are the basic notions of school and schooling, formal and nonformal education, and teacher and student. For instance, there are basic questions about what, exactly, a school is or what, exactly, a teacher is. In addition to these basic notions, there are questions about what is taught (or learned), how it is taught (or learned), and why it is taught (or learned). For example, in the context of formal education (meaning the structured program of schooling that is expected of youth, usually outside the home), what should make up the curriculum for students? Or, given some curriculum, how should it be taught? Perhaps most important, why should a given curriculum be taught? What are the goals of formal schooling?

The very concept of education is related to the notion of raising or rearing someone. The word *educate* is said to derive from the Latin word *educare*, meaning "to rear" or "to bring forth." At the same time, the concept of education is related to the notion of moving or going from one place to another. The word *educate* is also said to derive from another Latin term, *ex-ducere*, meaning "to move from or out of." The point of both these notions is that to become educated, a person is moved (usually by others) from one state of being to another state of being, in particular from the state of being "ignorance" to the state of being "knowledge." Education is a process of transformation. A school, then, is not the physical building where students go; a school is not a schoolhouse. Rather, a school is an abstract notion of "where" this process of transformation occurs. While it is certainly true that most students go to a schoolhouse in order to go to school, what makes it a case of going to school is not the schoolhouse. (Many students are home-schooled, and long-distance education uses technology such as the Internet; both are examples of schooling that takes place away from the traditional schoolhouse.)

When philosophers and educational theorists speak of education, they almost always mean formal education. That is, they mean a structured program of schooling, with a fairly set curriculum along with standards and criteria for what counts as successful educative achievement. Teaching and learning can and do occur outside formal education. For instance, students learn things from siblings and friends and from television and the Internet; they learn things on their own, sometimes by design and sometimes by accident (say, on playgrounds). The point is that learning (and, perhaps, teaching) occurs simply by a person being alive and interacting with others. Formal education, however, involves more than a collection of learning experiences; it involves structure and purpose, again, with stated standards and criteria for achievement.

Given these very basic notions, three broad, fundamental questions arise about education: What is taught (or learned) in the context of formal education? How is it taught (or learned)? Why is it taught (or learned)? These questions point to the issues of curriculum (what is taught/learned), peda- gogical methods (how is it taught/learned), and educative goals (why is it taught/learned). These three questions—and their answers—overlap. For ex- ample, in asking what should be taught, that is, what the curriculum should be for some (or any) student, appropriate answers depend upon what goal(s) one has in mind. If the goal is to enable a student to bake a cake, then the appropriate curriculum would be different than it would be if the goal is to enable a student to fly an airplane or to perform heart surgery.

The first question, then, would appear to be, What are the goals of formal education? Even this question, however, leads to another question, Goals for whom? Because formal education is a social phenomenon—that is, it is a structure that goes beyond individual students—one view of the goal(s) of formal education is that it exists in order to benefit society generally, not sim- ply individual students. So some people claim that the basic goal of formal education is to produce good future workers, people who have the knowl- edge and skills to perform jobs that are needed and wanted by society. If learning English grammar is useful toward that goal, then, under this view, learning English grammar is an appropriate part of the formal curriculum; if it is not useful toward that goal, then it is not an appropriate part.

Others claim that the goals should be centered on students themselves, not simply on students as future workers. A person, they claim, is more than merely an employee or worker; one's job is not one's life. Of course, having the knowledge and skills that enable one to perform socially useful work is important, but the goals of formal education should not (only) be to pro- duce workers.

Still others see no necessary conflict between these different goals. They claim that the kinds of knowledge and skills that come from learning things like English grammar in fact produce the best future workers, because they learn knowledge and skills that transcend any single given job or workplace. Learning how to learn, learning how to be a lifelong learner, is what is most valuable and useful for anyone, both with respect to employment and with respect to one's identity. Long-term goals, they say, might not be the same as short-term goals. John Dewey, whom we encountered in Chapter 2, for ex- ample, argued that the ultimate goal of formal education is to enhance the autonomy of students, by which he meant the abilities of persons to set their own life goals and to know how to go about achieving those goals.

As noted above, the goals of formal education relate directly to the issue of curriculum, that is, to what should be taught (or learned)—an issue that philosophers and educational theorists have long focused on. Concerns include broad notions of knowledge (that is, what should be taught or learned), as well as more specific knowledge. Broad notions of knowledge cover content, skills, and values. Content refers to the specific information included in the curriculum. For example, a school's curriculum might include specific courses in science, arts, math, and so on. Here the issue is, What content should be included in a school's curriculum? What information does "the school" want students to learn? Besides the notion of knowledge as information (that is, bits of facts), a second broad notion of knowledge covers skills. Knowing that a whale is a mammal is one type of knowledge (factual information); knowing how to construct a mathematical proof is another type of knowledge. Learning the rules of English grammar, most language teachers will say, is not merely about learning specific facts of English; it is about learning certain skills, say, of recognizing structures and patterns, a skill that goes beyond the classroom and beyond looking only at languages. And a third broad notion of knowledge addresses—for lack of a better term—values. In other words, part of a school's curriculum is teaching certain attitudes or aspects of appreciation and respect. Learning how to "step into someone else's shoes" is not the same as learning factual information or learning specific skills. It is more of a matter of learning values. This, say many educational theorists and others, is as much an appropriate part of a school's curriculum as are content and skills.

Along with these broad types of knowledge that are of curricular concern, there are more specific curricular matters. These come down to the specific courses that are seen as appropriate or not for formal education. For instance, should arts courses (such as music, painting, drama, and so on) be required of students? What content, skills, or values result from students' being taught arts? Likewise, should math be required of students—and, if so, at what levels? What content, skills, or values result from students' being taught math? These are the basic sorts of curricular questions. They lead immediately to other questions, for example, Who should determine the curriculum for a school? How much should parents, as opposed to teachers, as opposed to school administrators, as opposed to politicians, be the ones to determine curriculum?

In addition to questions about the goals of formal education (why something should be taught/learned) and about the curriculum (what should be taught/learned), there are questions of method (how something should be taught/learned). These issues include matters of technique—for instance, lectures, student classroom presentations, group activities—as well as matters of assessing and evaluating styles of teaching and learning and also standards and criteria for what it means to say that something has been taught or learned. One measure of whether something has been learned is having students take tests. If a student can repeat some bit of information at a later time, this could be a sign that the student has indeed learned that information. If a student can perform some task, this could be a sign that the student has indeed learned some skill. If a student can express via some creative project or activity a change in herself, this could be a sign that the student has indeed learned some attitude or value. For philosophers and educational theorists, the question is, What would count as evidence of successful teaching or successful learning? Merely writing down a correct answer on a test would not, in itself, demonstrate successful learning (since the answer might be a lucky guess). Being able to perform some task would not, in itself, demonstrate successful learning (since that skill might have been the result not of the intended teaching but of something or someone else). Nonetheless, great attention has been paid by educational theorists on how to identify, assess, and evaluate both teaching and learning.

I hope it is obvious how these issues about education in general relate to aesthetic education in particular. Those same questions of what should be taught/learned, along with how and why it should be taught/learned, are paramount for art and aesthetics. The most basic of these questions is the "why" question, as it speaks to the goals and purposes of such education. This is the question that Maxine Greene addresses on the next page, as part of what she calls the "artistic-aesthetic curriculum." She directly speaks of many (positive) effects of aesthetic education, and so, indirectly of goals and purposes. Aesthetic education, that is, the opportunity to engage with arts—both in the sense of being exposed to art and creating art—helps students develop in many ways: giving students the courage to explore new ideas and feelings, giving them the power to create something, allowing (even forcing) them to reflect on themselves, fostering imagination, demonstrating and promoting connectedness to others, encouraging (even forcing) attention to the meaning of their own work and that of others, and so on. For Greene, aesthetic education is far from being impractical or "just fun," far from simply putting a finish or veneer on students; aesthetic education is deeply and fundamentally practical. The knowledge and skills and values that are learned are applicable far beyond the art classroom.

MAXINE GREENE, "THE ARTISTIC-AESTHETIC CURRICULUM: LEAVING IMPRINTS ON THE CHANGING FACE OF THE WORLD"*

You have undoubtedly heard me, over the years, exploring some of the meaning of "art," of "aesthetic education," and you are as aware as I that the search can never be complete. There are . . . two lectures I gave this summer [concerning] a continuing effort to communicate a sense of what informed encounters with the several arts can make possible for people young and old, whoever they are. . . . I started with an account of the photography exhibition at the Metropolitan Museum of Art, "The Waking Dream." Part of what I said was, as always, an account of my personal response to what I saw on the several occasions I visited the exhibition. Part of it was an attempt to use the show and the experiences it provoked as a kind of metaphor for the awakenings, the unexpected disclosures, the new vistas made possible by what happens and what can happen during the days spent at Lincoln Center Institute. And, yes, I used it all as a lead-in to a discussion of imagination (which I should like to pursue a little further today), the cognitive capacity which has been so overlooked or ignored or denied by both the political leaders and the educational leaders working to define "Goals 2000" and the various "outcomes" considered necessary for this country's economic and technological growth.

Precisely what is this capacity? Why do so-called "postmodern" thinkers give the imagination a centrality when they talk about the ways in which we become involved with our worlds? Why is it overlooked, either deliberately or unthinkingly, by those expressing interest in the "active learner," in enhanced literacy on every level? Is there not some sense in which the investments, the innovations presumably sought in a technological society are related to imagination? Why is the activation of imagination (*your* imagination, your colleagues', your students) so crucial in the realization of works of art? If it is indeed the case that an aesthetic experience requires aware participation on the part of the perceiver, the listener, the reader, how can there be such participation without the ability to bring an "as-if" into being, to look through the windows of the actual to what might be and what ought to be? . . .

---

*In *Variations on a Blue Guitar: The Lincoln Center Institute Lectures on Aesthetic Education*. New York: Teachers College Press, 2001. Pages 177–183.

To speak of imagination in relation to encounters with the arts is not to talk of fantasy or castles in the air or false hopes. As I view it (and I know you may not see it in the same way), imagination is what enables us to enter into the created world of, yes, *Charlotte's Web* and *Winnie the Pooh* and *Don Juan*, and Toni Morrison's *The Bluest Eye*, and Shakespeare's *Much Ado About Nothing*, and George Eliot's *Middlemarch*, and Marquez's *Love in the Time of Cholera*, and Puig's *Kiss of the Spider Woman* as novel, film, or musical play. Doing so, we find ourselves creating new patterns, finding new connections in our experience. I quoted Dewey a few days ago on the ways in which art clarifies and concentrates the meanings of things ordinarily dumb and inchoate, and the ways in which works of art can keep alive "the power to experience the common world in all its fullness." This would not happen, I am sure, if it were not for the ability to pull aside the curtains of habit, automatism, banality, so that alternative possibilities can be perceived. And it is imagination that makes this kind of experience attainable for people—this break with literalism, this summoning up of the "as-if," the "not yet," the "might be." I think back in my own history and try to recapture what all this has meant and still means for me: the problem of alienation and emancipation in some manner enhanced by my lending Hawthorne's Hester Prynne my life; the matter of the "soul's slavery" generating all sorts of questions after reading *The Awakening*; the new experiences created by those scenes in the Hebrides in *To the Lighthouse*; the startling and renewed vision of Stravinsky's *The Firebird* in the Harlem Dance Theater's production of the ballet; the peculiar realization made palpable by Pecola's wanting to look like Shirley Temple in *The Bluest Eye* and the remembered girl-child wanting the same thing in Tillie Olsen's "I Stand Here Ironing"; the ideas of invisibility and nobodiness etched into my consciousness by James Baldwin and Ralph Ellison; the alternatives to my standard views of time and history discovered in *A Hundred Years of Solitude*. I could go on and on trying to recapture the ways in which encounters with art forms opened windows in experience for a little girl from Brooklyn, and then for a bigger girl continually (although indirectly) taught to accept things as they were and make the best of them. Indeed, I am not sure even now that thinking of that sort may partially explain why the arts are treated as frivolities and thrust, as they so frequently are these days, quite aside in our schools.

In any case, I want to urge you to go back in your own life narratives and try to recover those moments when imagination, released through certain encounters with the arts, opened worlds for you, disclosed new vistas (not always pleasant ones, I grant), helped you look at things as if they could be otherwise.

And, yes, helped you play somehow with language, with the thought of carnival, with having (as James Joyce once said) "two thinks at the same time." Then, I believe, you might ask yourself how you actually understand what "art" is and what "aesthetic" means. . . . Again, do you cherish the arts because they seem to you to bring you in touch with something transcendent, even some universal value, something that moves you to aspire, to strain upwards, beyond yourself? (When I say that, I think of *King Lear*, of Beethoven's Ninth Symphony, of Verdi's *Requiem*, of Martha Graham's *Night Journey*, of the Sistine Chapel, of certain spirituals.) Is this what you hope for your students—why you wish to initiate them into something grand and lustrous, beyond the everyday? Or do you value art forms because they express (or embody) the feelings and perceptions of certain peculiarly sensitive and observant women and men—Wordsworth, say, Mary Cassatt, Toni Morrison, Nikki Giovanni, Emily Dickenson, Tennessee Williams, Vincent Van Gogh—who saw and heard more, felt more acutely, were more in touch than ordinary folks like thee and me? Or is it the marvelous perfection of certain magically wrought forms—a Mozart symphony, a Yeats poem, a Joyce novel, Flaubert's *Madame Bovary*, T. S. Eliot's *Four Quartets*, Mark Rothko's mysterious washes opening to unimaginable depths?

Or do you value the art experiences you have had here and in other places because of what they have signified for your own sense of the world around, your own pursuits of meaning? Do you take what we think of as a "participatory" approach to the arts, one based on the belief that the active participation of the perceiver or reader or listener is required for the completion of the artistic process, and that this completion is essential for the aesthetic effect? When you, for example, encounter a work as presumably remote in time and space as Molière's *Don Juan*, according to this view, you will not be likely to have a full experience with it if you take a disinterested, distanced view. Here, too, connections have to be found, can be found, to your own lived experience and your own choices and your own activities. This view (sometimes called "pragmatic") is closely related to what is called the "reader response" theory in the study of literature. The emphasis here is on the qualities of the play and on the lived experience of those who attend to it and work to make it, in its enactment, an object of their experience—something to be grasped in its detail and its fullness. And grasped by the total person, not by a particular subjective cast of mind. As you have seen or will soon see, it is difficult to watch *Don Juan* in what would seem a total amorality without being moved to ponder your own moral choices and the standards governing them, especially at a time when there appear to be no objective standards recognized and acknowledged by all. Our feelings about class and power cannot but be affected, as must our feelings about fidelity and purity and "the war between men and women." In my own case (and I am sure in some of yours), I cannot quite set aside the Mozart opera, nor the Shaw play about Don Juan, the same Don Juan, "in hell." Nor can I set aside the philosopher Kierkegaard, because he cannot gain the "courage to be." I know this is the Molière version and not Mozart or da Ponte or Shaw or any of the many who rendered noncommittal, irresponsible behavior; but all the other things I have read and heard and seen play into the lived experience I have with this *Don Juan*, as I work to make it—physically, dialogically, imaginatively, conceptually—an event in the life I live with others. The meaning of the play is not hidden somewhere in the work; it is not predetermined. According to this view, it emerges more and more clearly in the audience involvement or by means of that involvement, and diverse persons achieve what they look upon as meaningful through their particular attentiveness, their willingness to look through the various perspectives the play presents, and against their own lived worlds.

Now there is no requirement that you take this view of how to render a work of art open to yourself and, in time, to others. You may well think an appreciation has no "right" to appropriate a work in this fashion. You may think that to focus on experience this way is to lose sight of the work of art, glowing there in its own peculiar space, free of the mundane world. You may think that, for all the talk of context, this approach sacrifices the wonder, the glory, even the "sacred" character of the arts. Or that too little is done to bring the appreciator in touch with the creative impulse that burns like a candle in the artist, a candle that may help those coming close to light their own. In the last analysis, it is a choice you have to make as individual and as teacher, struggling to be true to what you know and have encountered in your life, trying at once to communicate to others in a manner than allows them to reach out freely and make Molière's work and Mozart's and Morrison's and, yes, Madonna's authentically and reflectively and critically their own.

One of the reasons for trying to make this clear in your own terms and in accord with your own philosophy is that only then will you be able to communicate to colleagues or administrators or school boards the relevance of what we call aesthetic education or its significance for school restructuring and school reform. And, indeed, this may be one of our central responsibilities: to clarify for ourselves and others how what we do here does relate and might relate to what is commonly described as "active learning" and to the emergence of communities in school. Last time, I quoted Dewey on the ways in which works of art that are widely enjoyed in a community are, he said, "marvelous aids in the creation of such a life." Naturally, we hope (as you yourselves do) that—in your own encounters with others in your schools—you can enable people to recognize that.

All you need to do is picture your life in workshops in previous years and how, through your mutual participation in learning the languages of the various arts and bringing particular works alive, you did indeed bring a community into being. Not only was it one that brought you together with other people, very often very different people, in shared learning and shared creating; it may well have been a community that enabled you to recover a lost spontaneity in yourself—to feel yourself in the process of shaping a more distinctive identity for yourself because of your being among and in the presence of others. I have seen this over and over, as participant teachers here have sung in ensembles they created, or orchestrated their diverse verses in spirituals or other forms, brought a dramatic scene into existence out of what seemed a discordant variety of voices and improvised gestures, discovered not only how dance movement carves out different designs in space, but how a plurality of movements can be ordered into new patterns—sometimes symmetrical, sometimes not—new relations in space and time.

How, on the various levels at which you teach, can you create the kinds of situations where involvement with the arts not only enables you and your students to combat boredom and banality, but develops among all of you the sense of agency that is most apparent (or so it seems to me) in encounters with the arts? This takes me back, of course, to the participatory approach or to the "reader response" approach. I have in mind the notion that works of art can never be realized by a merely passive attention. There has to be an active, energetic, reaching out—so that the noticing we have so often described will take place, so that diverse perspectives can be looked through when it comes to a poem or painting or play, and diverse frequencies can be attended to when it comes to a musical piece. It is with this in mind, of course, that we attach so much importance to the work done with teaching artists—to the moving, and sounding, and rendering that engage you with the actual languages of the arts, with the perceptual landscapes, the landscapes of pattern and shape and color and sound where our lives began. How can we think of this in connection with the teaching of history, of social studies, or of the interdisciplinary humanities course we begin to see in the so-called "coalition" schools? How can we show the connection between our attentiveness to the concrete particularities of things in the domains of the arts and the posing of investigative, curious, sometimes impassioned questions that lead to the general descriptions, the overarching explanations of the sciences? How can the problem-solving of the choreographer, of the painter, of any of those who deal with relation, with design, with the shifting shapes of organization, be at once appreciated, participated in, and connected with what it is to "do" math? How can involvement with Hudson River landscapes, and Tuscan landscapes, and British Midlands landscapes, and French impressionist landscapes release visual imagination—and at once provoke questions that lead to doing geography? How can we in public schools play our part in the "blurring of the disciplines," so that aesthetic education becomes resource and provocation, so that the arts become centrally significant even as they open spaces on the "margin" where moments of freedom and presence occur? Here is where your inventiveness—along with that of your teaching artists—comes in. We all have a world to make, in a larger world that does not always understand. ◤

AESTHETICS AND CULTURE

Art is everywhere, not only across geographical space but also across time. Cave paintings have been found in numerous places around the world, some dating back more than 17,000 years. Probably the most famous are in Lascaux, France, but they have also been found in Spain, South Africa, India, Argentina, the United States, and elsewhere. Artworks, such as the cave paintings, along with art implements, such as flutes and drums, have appeared throughout human history and are part of every society and culture across the globe. In spite of the variation across different cultures, anthropologists often speak of certain human universals. For example, every society and culture identifies such things as age grading, bodily adornment, eschatology, food taboos, gift giving, kinship nomenclature, penal sanctions, residence rules, and many others. Every culture exhibits these features. The particulars vary (for example, different cultures identify different things as appropriate or inappropriate as food), but the underlying features are universal across human cultures. One of those human cultural universals is art.

There are many aspects of the relationships between art and culture. Here we can briefly look at only a few. One broad aspect is the relationship between art and politics. We have already noted above the issue of censorship and the interrelation of art and morality. The issue of censorship is just one example of what has been called the "politicization of aesthetics" and the "aestheticization of politics." Although the emphasis is somewhat different in each of these terms, they both speak to the blending and use (or misuse) of one in relation to the other. A prime example is art in the context of political propaganda. Think of how different political ads portray their chosen candidate and their opponents via the use of images, colors, background music, and so on. In addition, as we saw in Chapter 4, many artists are open and explicit about creating and using art as a political tool. Art is a means of social and political change for them.

This art-politics connection clearly blends into a related and broader art-culture connection. For instance, think of the way various groups or cultures are often portrayed in popular arts: how often, in American films at least, are Arabs portrayed as "normal" rather than as fanatical or hyperreligious? So not only is art closely bound with politics, but (as in the case of portraying other peoples) it is also bund with culture broadly. This is not meant as a division between politics and culture. Indeed, those two arenas obviously overlap and do so in connection with art. For example, many people have claimed that art reflects and perpetuates attitudes about race and gender, sometimes intentionally and sometimes not. One example of race in art is the claim that we (whoever "we" is) often display art from nonwhite cultures as being either downright primitive or, at least, other than our own. To take another example: many hip-hop artists have claimed that rap and hip-hop music reflect a nonmainstream culture, which explains why they have often been criticized and dismissed. A well-known artist and academician, Adrian Piper, has created numerous artworks and written numerous essays enunciating such concerns. Likewise, many feminists have argued that mainstream art reflects male perspectives and interests and power, again, whether deliberately or not. In film, for instance, they refer to "the male gaze" as reflective of those perspectives. Clearly, this issue—the relation of art to politics and culture—is worthy of a book-length treatment (and has been treated in many books). The point here is only to emphasize the fact of this interrelationship and to acknowledge the importance of art in social and cultural contexts.

In the following reading, anthropologist Clifford Geertz speaks of the "phenomenon of aesthetic force" and says that art at times can seem beyond language, or at least beyond our ability to fully describe or explain its significance for us. To get any sort of handle on art, he says, we need to place it within other modes of social activity. As he remarks in the midst of discussing a Moroccan poet, "The man who takes up the poet's role in Islam traffics, and not wholly legitimately, in the moral substance of his culture." Art and aesthetics, says Geertz, are signs that are part of larger semiotic systems; they are modes of thought and being, not just of communicating. We have seen other references to semiotic signs and systems in an earlier chapter (Joseph Margolis in Chapter 3) and will again later (Nelson Goodman in Chapter 7), but we should probably say something more explicit here about what semiotic systems are.

Semiotics is the study of signs. Signs are anything that can represent something. Although most people think of signs as things such as stop signs on street corners or "No exit" placards in buildings, practically anything can function as a sign. For example, there are natural signs, such as smoke being a sign of fire or dark clouds being a sign of (impending) rain. These are said to be natural signs because they are not the result of human actions or decisions. There are also conventional signs, that is, things that represent something on the basis of human actions and decisions, such as "No exit" signs. Even more broadly, languages themselves are systems of conventional signs.

The modern study of semiotics is usually associated with the work of Ferdinand de Saussure, a Swiss linguist, and Charles S. Peirce, an American philosopher. Saussure is most known for introducing the terms *signifier* and *signified*. A signifier is a word or phrase that is used as a sign of something else. For example, the word *cat* is a signifier of an animal. A signified is the object that the signifier relates to. One thing that Saussure emphasized about signs is that they have meaning not in themselves, but only in relation to other signs. The word *cat* does not have any significance by itself, but it does, he claimed, in terms of its relationship to other signs. Signs have meaning in terms of their differences from other signs, a point that later philosophers elaborated upon.

A major contribution of Peirce's was in introducing three basic terms that identify three different kinds of signs or ways that signs can in fact be signs and function as signs: *icon*, *index*, and *symbol*. An icon is something that represents something else in virtue of having a close resemblance to the thing being represented. Most people know icons as portraits of religious figures. For Peirce, what made something an icon, and why a portrait is a sign, is because it (the icon) shares relevant features with the object. Quite simply, a portrait represents someone in particular because it looks like that person. An index is something that represents something else because of a causal connection to that thing. For example, a scab is a sign of a wound or injury, not because a scab looks like a wound, but because it is caused by the healing process connected with a wound. A symbol represents something, and so is a sign of it, on conventional grounds. Again, the word *cat* is a sign of cats, but there is nothing about the particular sounds (or, in the case of writing the word, nothing about the particular squiggles of ink) that connects to that kind of animal. In Spanish, the word *gato*, not the word *cat*, is the conventional sign for cats. Almost all language is a matter of symbolic signs.

There is not a sharp distinction among these various kinds of signs. For instance, some symbolic signs, such as words, are used conventionally because there is a causal (indexical) connection to the object. A chickadee (a species of bird) is called that (at least in English) because the sounds it makes are very much like "chickadee." Likewise, there is not necessarily a sharp distinction between an icon and an index; although a portrait is an icon (because it looks like the person who is pictured in the painting), there is clearly a causal connection from how that person looks to how the portrait looks. In addition, there is not a sharp distinction between natural signs and conventional signs. For example, some colors are often associated with danger, such as red being associated with blood, which is why many conventional signs that are intended as warnings are made red. Those who study semiotics claim that signs are everywhere and that everything is at least potentially a sign. For instance, in the Sherlock Holmes story "Silver Blaze," the detective claims that the fact that a dog did *not* bark in the night was evidence of (that is, a sign of) the identity of the criminal; the absence of barking signified to Holmes that the dog recognized the person. So, even the absence of something can be a sign.

Most philosophers have focused on two subfields within semiotics: social semiotics and linguistic semiotics. Social semiotics is concerned with the social significance of signs. There are many nonverbal symbols of social status. For example, different styles of clothes represent different kinds of jobs (such as a nurse's uniform or a police officer's uniform) or different "levels" of jobs (such as a suit and tie versus jeans and T-shirts, or the number of stripes on a military uniform). In addition, even something like the relative placement of people in a gathering can be a sign of relative importance. For instance, how close a person stands to the president during an official ceremony often signifies that person's importance. Likewise, the very way that people carry themselves (for example, upright versus slumping) is taken as representing various things. Many social scientists, as well as social philosophers, investigate and analyze such social signs, often with respect to underlying issues of social status and power. It is social semiotics more than linguistic semiotics (which deals with the meaning and use of language) upon which social scientists, including Geertz, focus. Linguistic semiotics, however, can and does overlap with social semiotics. For instance, both social semioticians and linguistic semioticians look at what is involved in forms of address, for instance, calling people by first names versus nicknames versus titles, as well as who is expected and allowed to use certain forms of address and in what contexts. Given this background of social semiotics, Geertz speaks here of art as a set of cultural semiotic relations.

CLIFFORD GEERTZ, "ART AS A CULTURAL SYSTEM"*

I

Art is notoriously hard to talk about. It seems, even when made of words in the literary arts, all the more so when made of pigment, sound, stone or whatever in the non-literary ones, to exist in a world of its own, beyond the reach of discourse. It not only is hard to talk about it; it seems unnecessary to do so. It speaks, as we say, for itself: a poem must not mean but be; if you have to ask what jazz is you are never going to get to know. . . .

But anyone at all responsive to aesthetic forms feels it as well. Even those among us who are neither mystics nor sentimentalists, nor given to outbursts of aesthetic piety, feel uneasy when we have talked very long about a work of art in which we think we have seen something valuable. The excess of what we have seen, or imagine we have, over the stammerings we can manage to get out concerning it is so vast that our words seem hollow, flatulent, or false. After art talk "whereof one cannot speak, thereof one must be silent," seems like very attractive doctrine.

But, of course, hardly anyone, save the truly indifferent, is thus silent, artists included. On the contrary, the perception of something important in either particular works or in the arts generally moves people to talk (and write) about them incessantly. Something that meaningful to us cannot be left just to sit there bathed in pure significance, and so we describe, analyze, compare, judge, classify; we erect theories about creativity, form, perception; we characterize art as a language, a structure, a system, an act, a symbol, a pattern of feeling; we reach for scientific metaphors, spiritual ones, technological ones, political ones; and if all else fails, we string dark sayings together and hope someone else will elucidate them for us. The surface bootlessness of talking about art

*Modern Language Notes 91 (1976): 1473–1476, 1488–1494, 1497–1499.

seems matched by a depth necessity to talk about it endlessly. And it is this peculiar state of affairs that I want here to probe, in part to explain it but even
more to determine what difference it makes.

To some degree art is everywhere talked about in what may be called craft
terms—in terms of tonal progressions, color relations, or prosodic shapes. This
is especially true in the West where subjects like harmony or pictorial composition have been developed to the point of minor sciences, and the modern move
toward aesthetic formalism, best represented right now by structuralism, and by
those varieties of semiotics which seek to follow its lead, is but an attempt to
generalize this approach into a comprehensive one, to create a technical language capable of representing the internal relations of myths, poems, dances,
or melodies in abstract, transposable terms. But the craft approach to art talk is
hardly confined to either the West or the modern age, as the elaborate theories
of Indian musicology, Javanese choreography, Arabic versification, or Yoruba
embossment remind us. Even the Australian aborigines, everybody's favorite example of primitive peoples, analyze their body designs and ground paintings
into dozens of isolable and named formal elements, unit graphs in an iconic
grammar of representation.

But what is more interesting and I think more important is that it is perhaps
only in the modern age and in the West that some men (still a small minority,
and destined, one suspects, to remain such) have managed to convince themselves that technical talk about art, however developed, is sufficient to a complete understanding of it; that the whole secret of aesthetic power is located in
the formal relations among sounds, images, volumes, themes, or gestures.
Everywhere else—and, as I say, among most of us as well—other sorts of talk,
whose terms and conceptions derive from cultural concerns art may serve, or
reflect, or challenge, or describe but does not in itself create, collects about it to
connect its specific energies to the general dynamic of human experience. "The
purpose of a painter," Matisse, who can hardly be accused of undervaluing
form, wrote, "must not be conceived as separate from his pictorial means, and
these pictorial means must be more complete (I do not mean more complicated) the deeper his thought. I am unable to distinguish between the feeling I
have for life and my way of expressing it."

The feeling an individual, or what is more critical, because no man is an
island but a part of the main, the feeling a people has for life appears, of
course, in a great many other places than in their art. It appears in their religion, their morality, their science, their commerce, their technology, their politics, their amusements, their law, even in the way they organize their

everyday practical existence. The talk about art that is not merely technical or a spiritualization of the technical—that is, most of it—is largely directed to placing it within the context of these other expressions of human purpose and the pattern of experience they collectively sustain. No more than sexual passion or contact with the sacred, two more matters it is difficult to talk about, but yet somehow necessary, can confrontation with aesthetic objects be left to float, opaque anti hermetic, outside the general course of social life. They demand to be assimilated.

What this implies, among other things, is that the definition of art in any society is never wholly intra-aesthetic, and indeed but rarely more than marginally so. The chief problem presented by the sheer phenomenon of aesthetic force, in whatever form and in result of whatever skill it may come, is how to place it within the other modes of social activity, how to incorporate it into the texture of a particular pattern of life. And such placing, the giving to art objects a cultural significance, is always a local matter; what art is in classical China or classical Islam, what it is in the Pueblo southwest or highland New Guinea, is just not the same thing, no matter how universal the intrinsic qualities that actualize its emotional power (and I have no desire to deny them) may be. The variety that anthropologists have come to expect in the spirit beliefs, the classification systems, or the kinship structures of different people and not just in their immediate shapes, but in the way of being-in-the-world they both promote and exemplify, extends as well into their drummings, carvings, chants, and dances. . . .

III

There is hardly a better example of the fact that an artist works with signs that have a place in semiotic systems extending far beyond the craft he practices than the poet in Islam. A Muslim making verses faces a set of cultural realities as objective to his intentions as rocks or rainfall, no less substantial for being nonmaterial, and no less stubborn for being man-made. He operates, and always has operated, in a context where the instrument of his art, language, has a peculiar, heightened kind of status, as distinctive a significance, and as mysterious, as Abelam paint. Everything from metaphysics to morphology, scripture to calligraphy, the patterns of public recitation to the style of informal conversation conspires to make of speech and speaking a matter charged with an import if not unique in human history, certainly extraordinary. The man who takes up the poet's role in Islam traffics, and not wholly legitimately, in the moral substance of his culture.

In order even to begin to demonstrate this it is of course necessary first to cut the subject down to size. It is not my intention to survey the whole course of poetic development from the Prophecy forward, but just to make a few general, and rather unsystematic, remarks about the place of poetry in traditional Islamic society—most particularly Arabic poetry; most particularly in Morocco, where my wife, Hildred Geertz, has done an extensive study of it; most particularly on the popular, oral verse level. The relationship between poetry and the central impulses of Muslim culture is, I think, rather similar more or less everywhere, and more or less since the beginning. But rather than trying to establish that, I shall merely assume it and proceed, on the basis of somewhat special material, to suggest what the terms of that relationship—an uncertain and difficult one—seem to be. . . .

[A strong] sense for Quranic Arabic as the model of what speech should be . . . is reinforced by the whole pattern of traditional Muslim life. . . . [It leads] to everyday life being punctuated by lines from the Quran and other classical tags. Aside from the specifically religious contexts—the daily prayers, the Friday worship, the mosque sermons, the bead-telling cantations in the mystical brotherhoods, the recital of the whole book on special occasions such as the Fast month, the offering of verses at funerals, weddings, and circumcisions—ordinary conversation is laced with Quranic formulae to the point where even the most mundane subjects seem set in a sacred frame. The most important public speeches—those from the throne, for example—are cast in an Arabic so classicized that most who hear them but vaguely understand them. Arabic newspapers, magazines, and books are written in a similar manner, with the result that the number of people who can read them is small. The cry of Arabization—the popular demand, swept forward by religious passions, for conducting education in classical Arabic and using it in government and administration—is a potent ideological force, leading to a great deal of linguistic hypocrisy on the part of the political elite and to a certain amount of public disturbance when the hypocrisy grows too apparent. It is this sort of world, one in which language is as much symbol as medium, verbal style is a moral matter, and the experience of God's eloquence wars with the need to communicate, that the oral poet exists, and whose feeling for chants and formulas he exploits. . . . "I memorized the Quran," one such poet said, trying hard, to explain his art. "Then I forgot the verses and remembered the words."

He forgot the verses during a three-day meditation at the tomb of a saint renowned for inspiring poets, but he remembers the words in the context of performance. Poetry here is not first composed and then recited; it is composed in the recitation, put together in the act of singing it in a public place. . . .

Of course . . . he does not create his text out of sheer fancy, but builds it up, molecularly, a piece at a time, like some artistic Markov process, out of a limited number of established formulae. Some are thematic: the inevitability of death ("even if you live on a prayer rug"); the unreliability of women ("God help you, O lover, who is carried away by the eyes"); the hopelessness of passion ("so many people gone to the grave because of the burning"); the vanity of religious learning ("where is the schoolman who can whitewash the air?"). Some are figurative: girls as gardens, wealth as cloth, worldliness as markets, wisdom as travel, love as jewelry, poets as horses. And some are formal—strict, mechanical schemes of rhyme, meter, line, and stanza. The singing, the tambourines, the dancing men, the genre demands, and the audience sending up you-yous of approval or whistles of censure, as these things either come effectively together or do not, make up an integral whole from which the poem can no more be abstracted than can the Quran from the reciting of it. It, too, is an event, an act, constantly new, constantly renewable.

And, as with the Quran, individuals, or at least many of them, punctuate their ordinary speech with lines, verses, tropes, allusions taken from oral poetry, sometimes from a particular poem, sometimes one associated with a particular poet whose work they know, sometimes from the general corpus, which though large, is, as I say, contained within quite definite formulaic limits. In that sense, taken as a whole, poetry, the performance of which is widespread and regular, most especially in the countryside and among the common classes in the towns, forms a kind of "recitation" of its own, another collection, less exalted but not necessarily less valuable, of memorizable truths: lust is an incurable disease, women an illusory cure; contention is the foundation of society, assertiveness the master virtue; pride is the spring of action, unworldliness moral hypocrisy; pleasure is the flower of life, death the end of pleasure. Indeed, the word for poetry, $š^c ir$, means "knowledge," and though no Muslim would explicitly put it that way, it stands as a kind of secular counterpoise, a worldly footnote, to the Revelation itself. What man hears about God and the duties owed Him in the Quran, fix-worded facts, he hears about human beings and the consequences of being one in poetry.

The performance frame of poetry, its character as a collective speech act, only reinforces this betwixt and between quality of it—half ritual song, half plain talk—because if its formal, quasi-liturgical dimensions cause it to resemble Quranic chanting, its rhetorical, quasi-social ones cause it to resemble everyday speech. As I have said, it is not possible to describe here the general tone of interpersonal relations in Morocco with any concreteness; one can only claim, and hope to be believed, that it is before anything else combative, a constant testing of wills as individuals struggle to seize what they covet, defend what they have, and recover what they have lost. So far as speech is concerned, this gives to all but the most idle conversation the quality of a catch-as-catch-can in words, a head-on collision of curses, promises, lies, excuses, pleading, commands, proverbs, arguments, analogies, quotations, threats, evasion, flatteries, which not only puts an enormous premium on verbal fluency but gives to rhetoric a directly coercive force; ͨandu klām, "he has words, speech, maxims, eloquence," means also, and not just metaphorically, "he has power, influence, weight, authority." . . .

In short, in speech terms, or more exactly speech-act terms, poetry lies in between the divine imperatives of the Quran and the rhetorical thrust and counterthrust of everyday life, and it is that which gives it its uncertain status and strange force. On the one hand, it forms a kind of para-Quran, sung truths more than transitory and less than eternal in a language style more studied than the colloquial and less arcane than the classical. On the other, it projects the spirit of everyday life into the realm of, if not the holy, at least the inspired. Poetry is morally ambiguous because it is not sacred enough to justify the power it actually has and not secular enough for that power to be equated to ordinary eloquence. The Moroccan oral poet inhabits a region between speech types which is at the same time a region between worlds, between the discourse of God and the wrangle of men. And unless that is understood neither he nor his poetry can be understood, no matter how much ferreting out of latent structures or parsing of verse forms one engages in. Poetry, or anyway this poetry, constructs a voice out of the voices that surround it. If it can be said to have a "function," that is it.

"Art," says my dictionary, a usefully mediocre one, is "the conscious production or arrangement of colors, forms, movements, sounds or other elements in a manner that affects the sense of beauty," a way of putting the matter which seems to suggest that men are born with the power to appreciate, as they are born with the power to see jokes, and have only to be provided with the occasions to exercise it. As what I have said here ought to indicate, I do not think that this is true (I do not think that it is true for humor either); but, rather, that "the sense of beauty," or whatever the ability to respond intelligently to face scars, painted ovals, domed pavilions, or rhymed insults should be called, is no less a cultural artifact than the objects and devices concocted to "affect" it. The artist works with his audience's capacities—capacities to see, or hear, or touch, sometimes even to taste and smell, with understanding. And though elements of these capacities are indeed innate—it usually helps not to be color-blind—they are brought into actual existence by the experience of living in the midst of certain sorts of things to look at, listen to, handle, think about, cope with, and react to; particular varieties of cabbages, particular sorts of kings. Art and the equipment to grasp it are made in the same shop. . . .

If we are to have a semiotics of art (or for that matter, of any sign system not axiomatically self-contained), we are going to have to engage in a kind of natural history of signs and symbols, an ethnography of the vehicles of meaning. Such signs and symbols, such vehicles of meaning, play a role in the life of a society, or some part of a society, and it is that which in fact gives them their life. Here, too, meaning is use, or more carefully, arises from use, and it is by tracing out such uses as exhaustively as we are accustomed to for irrigation techniques or marriage customs that we are going to be able to find out anything general about them. . . .

It is, after all, not just statues (or paintings, or poems) that we have to do with but the factors that cause these things to seem important—that is, affected with import—to those who make or possess them, and these are as various as life itself. If there is any commonality among all the arts in all the places that one finds them (in Bali they make statues out of coins, in Australia drawings out of dirt) that justifies including them under a single, Western-made rubric, it is not that they appeal to some universal sense of beauty. That may or may not exist, but if it does it does not seem, in my experience, to enable people to respond to exotic arts with more than an ethnocentric sentimentalism in the absence of a knowledge of what those arts are about or an understanding of the culture out of which they come. . . .

To be of effective use in the study of art, semiotics must move beyond the consideration of signs as means of communication, code to be deciphered, to a consideration of them as modes of thought, idiom to be interpreted. It is not a new cryptography that we need, especially when it consists of replacing one cipher by another less intelligible, but a new diagnostics, a science that can determine the meaning of things for the life that surrounds them. It will have, of course, to be trained on signification, not pathology, and treat with ideas, not with symptoms. But by connecting incised statues, pigmented sago palms, frescoed walls, and chanted verse to jungle clearing, totem rites, commercial inference, or street argument, it can perhaps begin at last to locate in the tenor of their setting the sources of their spell. ◣

Questions for Discussion

1. Is it ever appropriate for art to be censored by the state? Why or why not?
2. If art is educationally important, should it be required of all students? Why or why not?
3. Who should decide whether or not art projects should receive public funding? If it is obvious that some artwork is deemed inappropriate by a majority of people, is that sufficient to say it should not receive public funding? Why or why not?
4. Just how pervasive and pernicious is "mass art" or the "culture industry"? Are you swayed by the presence and use of art by businesses or politicians? If you recognize that they are using art in an effort to influence you, does it still do so?
5. Geertz says that art is a set of cultural semiotic relations. If that is correct, what does that imply about the importance, or lack of importance, of artists' intentions or aims in the creation of artworks?

CHAPTER 7

RELATIONSHIPS BETWEEN ART AND SCIENCE: METHOD, UNDERSTANDING, KNOWLEDGE

In 1959, C. P. Snow, who was both a physicist and a novelist, gave a lecture titled "The Two Cultures and the Scientific Revolution." He used the term *two cultures* to refer to what he saw as a present and widening gap between the sciences and the humanities (including the arts). This gap, he said, was revealed through the ignorance that each had about the other:

> During the war [World War II] and in the years since, my colleagues and I have had to interview somewhere between thirty and forty thousand of these [professional engineers and applied scientists]—that is, about 25 per cent. The number is large enough to give us a fair sample, though of the men we talked to most would still be under forty. We were able to find out a certain amount of what they read and thought about. I confess that even I, who am fond of them and respect them, was a bit shaken. We hadn't quite expected that the link with the traditional culture should be so tenuous, nothing more than a formal touch of the cap.
>
> As one would expect, some of the very best scientists had and have plenty of energy and interest to spare, and we came across several who had read everything that literary people talk about. But that's very rare. Most of the rest, when one tried to probe for what books they had read,

would modestly confess, "Well, I've *tried* a bit of Dickens," rather as though Dickens were an extraordinarily esoteric, tangled and dubiously rewarding author. . . .

But what about the other side? They are impoverished too—perhaps more seriously, because they are vainer about it. They still like to pretend that the traditional culture is the whole of "culture," as though the natural order didn't exist. . . . They gave a pitying chuckle at the news of the scientists who have never read a major work of English literature. They dismiss them as ignorant specialists. Yet their own ignorance and their own specialization is just as startling. A good many times I have been present at gatherings of people who, by the standards of the traditional culture, are thought highly educated and who have with considerable gusto been expressing their incredulity at the illiteracy of scientists. Once or twice I have been provoked and have asked the company how many of them could describe the Second Law of Thermodynamics. The response was cold: it was also negative. Yet I was asking something which is about the scientific equivalent of: *Have you read a work of Shakespeare's?*

However representative this anecdote is of the general state of sciences and humanities or arts, it certainly is not altogether shocking or unfamiliar. It is standard in colleges and universities to speak of "arts and sciences," both curricularly and administratively, usually with the understanding that these are separate. In most colleges and universities, students can receive, depending upon their particular courses of study, a bachelor of arts degree or a bachelor of science degree. And although historically courses of study that were called "liberal arts" included much of what we today would think of as science, many schools today now speak of "liberal arts and sciences" to ensure that both areas are given full credit and recognition.

RELATIONS OF ART AND SCIENCE

What is the relationship between art and science? Because there are many different arts and many different sciences, probably a better question is, What are the relationships between arts and sciences? As we have already noted in previous chapters, the great variation among different arts makes it difficult to say with much authority what (if anything) makes them all instances of art. The same, of course, holds for the many disciplines and fields of study within science. Although there is overlap, much of what physicists study is quite different from what biologists study, and both are different from what sociologists study. Likewise, although there is overlap, the methods used by physicists and biologists and sociologists are often quite different, to such an extent that the methods of one discipline may even be inapplicable in another. So, just as with the arts, there is great variation within the sciences. What this says is that questions about the relationships between arts and sciences are difficult to address, because the relations between, say, physics and music are quite different from those between geology and music, not to mention between geology and dance.

A further concern, besides the fact that there are many different arts and sciences, is that these areas can be characterized in different ways. For instance, we might want to focus on *what* they deal with. We might want to say that what science investigates is the natural world and the things or processes within it. Under that focus, what is defining of science is the content of its investigations. Physics deals with certain aspects of the world, and sociology deals with different aspects of the world (and literature, perhaps, deals with yet different aspects of the world). Or we might want to say that what makes something science is not *what* it investigates but *how* it investigates it. That is, what is defining or characteristic of science is method(s). Both astronomers and poets might talk about the moon, but how they approach that topic is quite different. Finally, science is not something that just exists; it is an endeavor (or set of endeavors) engaged in by people and institutions. There are purposes and aims to scientific investigation. We might, then, want to say that *why* scientists investigate the things they do, as well as why they use the methods they do, is fundamental to what science is (and the same would be said about art). These concerns—the what, the how, and the why—should seem familiar by now; they relate to metaphysical issues, epistemological issues, and axiological issues. Any and all of these issues and concerns are relevant to addressing the question of the nature of the relationships between arts and sciences, and, indeed, we will see them all addressed as we look at various perspectives throughout this chapter.

We have seen that there are a number of factors to consider when asking about the relationships between arts and sciences: Which particular arts and sciences are we considering? Are the relationships we are asking about ones focused on content (the what) or on method and process (the how) or on aims and purposes (the why)? Although these many factors might seem to make it difficult to address, much less answer, the question about relationships, there is actually much that can and has been said.

One way of approaching this is by way of analogy. The American scholar Ian Barbour has written on the relations between science and religion (recognizing that there are different religions, just as there are different sciences). Although the complexity of issues noted above apply here, we can nonetheless see various ways that religious concerns and scientific concerns might and do relate. One basic mode of relation between them is that they *conflict*. That is, both religion and science make claims about the world or things in it, and those claims clash with each other. If a cosmologist says that the world is 13 billion years old and Bishop Ussher says it is 6,000 years old, and if they are both making factual claims about the real age of the world, then obviously they cannot both be true. They are making contrary claims, and they are rival views. Very often this is how religion and science are portrayed.

A second view of the relationship between religion and science is that they are *independent* of each other. Each has its appropriate, relevant sphere of concern. They do not contradict each other because they are talking about different things, even when they sometimes seem to be talking about the same thing. So, according to this view, when a theist says that God parted the waters or separated the land and the sea, that statement is not necessarily meant to contradict a scientific account of how such a thing could or did happen. The point is that religious claims are not necessarily meant as physical descriptions of the world. Instead, they are metaphorical or allegorical and are meant to speak about the meaning or significance of events in the world.

A third view is that there is and can be important *dialogue and integration* across the spheres of religion and science. There might well be "boundary questions" that both speak to, so they are not completely isolated from each other. For example, both religion and science wrestle with the question of the origin of humanity and the nature of who we are as persons (the notion of a soul). Much of the history of science is a testimony to religious believers trying to understand the physical world. This area of study is often called "natural theology," in which one studies God's creation in order to better understand God the creator. So there might well be areas of mutual concern between religion and science (they are not totally independent of each other), and yet they have separate concerns as well (they are not complete rivals).

The same sorts of views can be said to apply to the question of the relation between art and science. That is, they might be seen as being in conflict with each other, as being simply independent of each other, or as having some points of overlap (what Barbour called dialogue and integration).

These three views are not necessarily mutually exclusive. For example, many people see science as concerned with facts and knowledge and art as concerned with emotion and feeling. If that were true (but as we will see on the next page, this view is criticized), then the relationship between art and science might be seen either as one of independence (each has its respective concerns) or as one of conflict (each promotes the importance of one kind of concern over the other). The readings in this chapter exemplify various perspectives on these relationships. The first reading, by psychologist Howard Gardner, addresses the notion that both art and science are problem-solving activities. He claims that there are definitely points of contact and similarity between art and science, for instance that both are forms of communication, but it is also clear that he sees them as quite distinct, perhaps even in some ways incompatible. The other two readings, by Nelson Goodman and John Bender (both philosophers), downplay the differences between art and science. Neither author conflates art and science or denies that there are obvious differences between them; however, they see more similarity than difference, especially in terms of underlying assumptions about how both art and science proceed and about the primary goals of both.

First, Gardner makes his case that, like science, art is a form of problem solving. That is, both art and science engage in problem solving and, in addition, some of the ways that art problem solves are akin to some of the ways that science problem solves. The primary emphasis for him is with art at the level of creation; that is, his focus is on art from the perspective of artists (rather than, say, from the perspective of the audience, of someone perceiving an artwork). Gardner claims that for the most part scientific problem solving is a matter of conceptualization, whereas artistic problem solving is a matter of execution. In other words, he sees scientific problem solving as, in effect, finding the right concepts to describe and explain aspects of the world. There are factors and constraints on scientists that are external to them and that point to whether or not the particular problem is solved. With artists, he says, relevant factors and constraints are less external. With art, says Gardner, a particular problem is solved only when and if the artist actually executes something, that is, actually creates something that he or she finds (subjectively) to be satisfactory as a solution to the problem. With science, he says, it is a matter of communal fact checking and verification by other scientists that determines whether or not there has been a satisfactory solution to a problem. Tradition (that is, what has been accepted as established) and accumulation of facts or information is far more important to science than to art, according to Gardner. Nevertheless, he holds, despite all these differences, there are "affinities" between art and science, especially at the level of creativity and exploration. That is to say, some aspects of science focus on *explanation*, such as verifying some experimental data and accounting for why the data is what it is. However, other aspects of science focus on *exploration*, such as proposing some model for testing a hypothesis or suggesting a thought experiment. At these points of exploration, he claims, creativity is important in science, and it is here that scientists might rely on hunches or metaphors to push along some suggestive and fruitful hypothesis or model and are more akin to artists.

HOWARD GARDNER, *THE ARTS AND HUMAN DEVELOPMENT: A PSYCHOLOGICAL STUDY OF THE ARTISTIC PROCESS*[*]

Problem-Solving in a Medium

Given evidence of the hard labors and years of training and development even among the most fluent creators, it seems convincing to think of artistic creation as a practice of problem-solving within a given medium. . . .

Although the use of the term *problem-solving* seems natural in the realm of science or business, it may seem somewhat out of place in the arts, where one does not think of setting problems with correct answers, or looking up solutions in an answer book. Indeed, the procedure of the artist seems far removed from the logician or scientist who, in tackling a proof, must specify his steps precisely, abide by canons of logic, and allow for independent verification. Yet it is plausible to speak of problem-solving in the arts, not only because many involved with the arts so describe their activity, and because much of aesthetic education involves the setting and solving of problems, but also because a view of the arts as a problem-process obviates a number of difficulties. If the arts are construed as inspiration, as sheer creativity, as intuitions or uncontrolled spontaneity, the chance to gain an analytical handle on the aesthetic process is sacrificed. Viewing the arts as solely a product of unconscious processes effectively removes them from the realm of scientific investigation. If the notion of a prob-

---

[*]New York: Basic Books, 1994. Pages 270–274, 311–315.

lem is sufficiently broadened so it is no longer merely the textbook variety en-countered in grammar school, the analyst retains some assurance that he is still close to the phenomena of the arts, while at the same time he can entertain hope of analyzing the artistic process. . . .

I believe that the kind of problem-solving characteristic of scientists high-lights conceptualization. That is, the scientist generally has a specified problem that can be posed in a number of equivalent ways, at least a partial idea of what a solution would look like, and some experience working with the elements in-volved in the problem. His chief burden is to reanalyze the elements and to find a new configuration or arrangement that answers the demands or constraints of the problem. As a rule, he can discuss the problem with others and can benefit from their ideas. He can prepare an outline of the final report, lacking only the confirming or contradictory data. Once he has hit upon a conceptualization, the problem is effectively solved. He can either write out the answer himself in some form, or can convey the answer to someone else who can also attend to the final execution or embodiment of his conceptualization. The medium in which the solution is manifest is not crucial—words, symbols, figures, or draw-ings may each or all be acceptable, so long as the essential factors and insight are retained. This focal idea can be expressed in a number of ways, independ-ently verified by other investigations, and used as the basis for other problems. If the particular realization of the solution is forever lost, this is not crucial, pro-viding someone can remember the general idea. If the solver dies in the process of completing the problem, someone else can probably accomplish its execu-tion adequately. Once a problem has been solved, there is no point in others solving it independently (except as drill); rather, the solution should dictate ad-ditional problems which if solved will contribute to the *progress* of the science.

A contrast can readily be drawn with the typical operations of the artist. The artist less frequently borrows his problem from a tradition, generally cannot specify the solution ahead of time, nor can he depend on others to help him or to recognize a solution. Instead he begins with a vague idea and spends the bulk of his time exploring within a given medium. He may also devote consid-erable effort to conceptualization, but this "thought" is one step removed form his solution, which must eventually appear in the particular artistic medium in which he works. Rembrandt's sketches for a painting and Henry James's notes for a novel are worth little apart from their particular realization. A composer may indeed be able to think out his whole work in his head, but except for the most preliminary phase he will do this in terms of specific notes, rhythms, and harmonies, and not merely in terms of a "slow section, a "crescendo," or a "rondo." He "hears" the work. The artist generally defines his problem as he goes along, discovering new possibilities, and adding new constraints as the materials and his maneuvers dictate. Which problem(s) he has solved is apparent only after he has completed the work. Nor will others necessarily concur on the appropriateness of the solution; since there is no possibility of translation in the arts, since a solution must remain within the particular medium and cannot be converted by logical operations into equivalent forms, individuals may well disagree on the artist's goals and his success in realizing them. The artist's work is, in part, a rhetorical creation, which furnishes its own argument as a valid "solution" or "product." Since the artistic work has only an executionary, and not a conceptualized status, collaboration is only of limited help; the artist cannot readily share his problem with another individual and expect him to produce the same solution. . . . Problem-solving in the arts is closely tied to the particular execution, and only those factors associated with a given realization in a given medium are relevant to the problem-solving process. . . .

The Artistic and the Scientific Processes

. . . To as great an extent as art, science is a form of communication; the information it conveys is of a different order, however. Whereas the artist is interested in the subjective world, and is intent upon conveying his understanding and feeling for the world of human individuals or the "living" aspects of objects, the scientist more typically investigates the world of objects or treats individuals as objects. The scientist does not create an object in which aspects of himself are embodied so that the beholder can obtain subjective information about the scientist and his ideas. At least, so artistic a view of science is far from the intention of most scientists, who indeed take pains to exorcise traces of themselves from their works. The scientist has set up a series of questions about the world of objects; he seeks to communicate in as simple and unambiguous fashion as possible just what he has discovered about those objects or facets of the world. Further, the scientist does not need to exemplify his message in the object nor to make the form of the message attractive in itself; instead he desires to have the message maximally translatable so it can fit into a variety of contexts, illustrating and elucidating a number of phenomena. The artist . . . communicates (often wittingly) a part of himself, and is vitally concerned with the *form* of the message. It is perhaps for such reasons that many individuals have questioned the validity of applying the methods and practice of science to the arts. William James cautioned in a letter:

It strikes me that no good will ever come to Art as such from the analytic study of Aesthetics—harm rather, if the abstraction could in any way be made the basis of practice. The difference between the first and second best things in art, absolutely seem to escape verbal definition—it is a matter of a hair, a shade, an inner quiver of some kind—yet what miles away in point of persuasiveness. . . . [Gardner's ellipsis]Absolutely the same verbal formula applies to the supreme success and to the thing that just misses and yet the verbal formulas are all that your aesthetic will give.

And Wolf Kahn speaks of the incompatibility of artists and academe:

The university cannot provide (future artists) with the proper climate altogether. The academic climate is formed by the prevailing rationalism, verbal modes, and abstract symbols as well as a regard for the intellect and its categories. Artists are dedicated to the irrational, to unconscious processes, to intuition and to the unique particular. Traditionally artists have been allied with the trades not the scholar. Their audiences existed and still exist in the market place rather than the academy.

Whereas the scientist has need of formal operations in order to contribute to and appreciate the work of the scientific community, the artist may pursue his own work without the ability to reason in proportions and without a coherent philosophy, so long as he is able to handle his medium competently. Eliot said of Shakespeare and Dante, "neither did any real thinking—that was not their job," and he said of Henry James that "his mind was so fine, it was never violated by thought." Eliot is here questioning the artist's need to reason like a critic or scientist. Why should the artist describe objects in proportion and then evaluate the proportions with respect to another? Such an exercise is irrelevant to the artist's practice—only his abilities to create objects, to perceive flaws, and to correct them through an alteration in the medium matter. . . .

While in the education of scientists efforts are made to provide as many principles as possible and to bring students closely in contact with the work of their teachers, the proximity of a teacher's work and the formalization of artistic principles is thought by many art educators to be damaging. Rules are ultimately there to be imaginatively transformed, deliberately violated, or subtly altered.

Despite these differences, one can discern an approximate isomorphism between the scientific and artistic processes. In each domain there is a message

from a creator—in the case of the sciences, the originator of the scientific the-
orem or the experimenter reporting his result. The audience of the sciences is
primarily composed of critics, individuals who share a knowledge of the field
and can ascertain whether the creator has made a legitimate contribution to the
scientific canons. One could postulate an audience analogous to the audience
for *objets d'art*, which reads the scientific journals and scours the newspaper
reports chiefly for the pleasurable feeling such reading affords. Although such
an audience—composed of readers of *Scientific American* and the *New York
Times*—may actually exist, it differs from the aesthetic audience in several
ways. First of all, it is limited in size: Despite the magazine's attention to presentation, fewer individuals presumably read the *Scientific American* for its entertainment or arousal value than would read a novel. Then, too, while the art
audience must be exposed directly to the aesthetic object—hearing about a
performance or painting is scarcely equivalent to seeing them—scientific audiences can be informed second-hand about an interesting discovery. Indeed the
original papers might well not be comprehensible to the layman. Furthermore,
one may enjoy the audience role simply by hearing a poem (or viewing a painting) which, though not completely understood, can nonetheless elicit pleasant
feelings, but comprehension is essential in the select audience of the scientific
process. The meaning, rather than the surface features of sound or sight, is of
overriding import in the scientific process.

The central dyad of creator-audience seems to be replaced in the scientific
process by the tighter network of fellow creators and critics. These roles are
often combined and interchangeable—most scientists competent enough to
appreciate a scientific investigation are themselves creators. Furthermore, the
ability to criticize a piece of science competently is in itself creative, for a
penetrating critique of a scientific object may contain within it seeds of a
more satisfactory formulation. (In this sense, most academic disciplines—and
predominantly, philosophy—involve a merging of creative and critical roles.) In
the arts, a critique that surpasses the original object is rare.

The discrepancy between creator and performer does, I think, exist in the
sciences, but not in the same way as in the arts. The artistic performer generally
examines the plan or score of the creator and seeks to realize it in a way faithful
to the creator's intention, while at the same time inducing appropriate response
in the audience. Only by an unreasonable stretch of the imagination does a scientific creator of this type exist, though the engineer's role may indeed be
viewed in this way. On the other hand, there is certainly a division of labor
within the scientific community between those who formulate questions and

problems—strictly cognitive and notational steps—and those who go to the laboratory or the world to test such hypotheses. In the one instance, discrimination and conceptualization are primary; in the other instances, careful experimental techniques and, in many cases, a specific manual and making skills are required. That different temperaments and personalities characterize the researcher and the theoretician in the sciences is clear; in fact, the qualities of the researcher—the less pensive, more dogged, outgoing, rugged, extroverted scientist—may well approach the traits of the artistic performer, who is also, in a sense, realizing someone else's notions. Still the role of performer and creator are far more frequently united in the sciences than in the arts, because the lack of audience and the relatively straightforward procedures of most experimental tasks enables a relatively larger proportion of scientists to "perform" in their field.

Some remarks have already been made about problem-solving in the sciences and the arts. The scientist generally takes his problem from a commonly recognized area on which other scientists may well be working, and he draws on a variety of acceptable methods to solve it. He has some notion of his goal, and some checks along the way as to his success. In most cases he and his fellow scientists will agree when the problem has been solved, the formula derived, the model constructed. Conceptualization is vital, execution often delegable. The artist, on the other hand, only rarely tries to solve a particular problem that the tradition has handed him and that others are also tackling (except some highly general problems as "imitating nature"; more specific tasks are assigned chiefly as drill). The artist's problem is more likely to be the representation or articulation of a modal/vectoral quality. He will rely on his own rather than on "established" methods or techniques to accomplish the problem, he will encounter a variety of unanticipated problems along the way, and will have only intuitive notions of his success in execution. While the solution of scientific problems will usually be apparent, there may be disputes about the artist's accomplishment. The tensions of problem-solving, followed by a release at the resolution, nevertheless characterize both processes.

Interestingly enough, while the problem-solving behavior of the average scientist and artist are not strikingly similar, there are stronger affinities at the poles of scientific and artistic creation. The purely commercial artist may follow formulas to such an extent that he is akin to the scientist performing routine calculations. At the other extreme, the most original scientist, such as Darwin or Freud, who is charting out a wholly new area of investigation, shares characteristics with the revolutionary artist. He too must "convince others" of his orientation, devise fresh language and novel procedures, conceptualize a field anew, and rely heavily on subjective intuitions. And, like good works of art, pioneering works in a new scientific area often defy translation. Probably the chief difference between science and art at this level is that the scientist is still intent upon objectifying what he is studying and retains as his goal the eventual translation of his findings into some more general conceptual coin. He seeks agreement with his formulation rather than approval of its form or evocation of pleasurable affect. Even the most scientifically oriented artists, such as Leonardo, the Impressionists, or the Cubists, would not consider replacing their works by some kind of more conclusive and inclusive formula, and remain relatively uninterested in the audience's "agreement" with their views.

Although the scientist who wants to propagandize his views or launch a new field requires the creative, communicative qualities of his aesthetic counterparts, his relation to the scientific tradition is more stringently dictated. The scientist works within a paradigm that has been fairly well established in his field, and he tries to answer questions raised by that paradigm. His problems are dictated by recent research in the field, permissible operations are legislated, and only the foolhardy researcher remains ignorant of what his colleagues have accomplished. To be sure, the artist belongs to a tradition as well; few artists create objects that, when viewed from sufficient perspective, appear radically different from those of their contemporaries or immediate predecessors.

Unless he chooses to do so, the artist need not strive to answer problems that others about him are seeking to solve, immerse himself in the most recent work of the field, nor choose a genre with strong constraints. The arts are not cumulative, at least not in the same way as the sciences. An artist can master the medium and get a feeling for what is possible by studying the literature, painting, or music of the sixteenth century, as readily as by immersing himself in contemporary productions. Some might think him peculiar, but ultimately he will be judged on how well he deploys aesthetic materials, and not on the contemporaneousness of his achievement. And if his tastes happen to attach more to the sixteenth than to the twentieth century, this factor will not deter others from considering his works. But the prospect of a scientist familiar only with past centuries or especially attached to the sixteenth century is patently ludicrous, and would rightly be rejected by those colleagues interested in a systematic cumulation rather than in a hodge-podge of scientific knowledge. Should a scientist die while in the midst of a work, it is likely that others could finish it; if all his works were destroyed, they could be reconstructed by those privy to his conceptualization. But who can finish a dead artist's work? The work inheres in his execution, and an approximate re-creation of a burnt painting or fragmentary score is unacceptable. ◢

ART, SCIENCE, AND UNDERSTANDING

Earlier we noted that there are a number of ways in which art and science might be related: conflict, independence, dialogue, and integration. We also noted that we could think of art and science each in terms of content, methods, or aims and purposes. Finally, we also noted what Nelson Goodman calls the "domineering dichotomy" between art and science, namely, that art is emotive and focused on feeling whereas science is cognitive and focused on knowing. As will become evident in his selection on page 217, Goodman rejects this dichotomy, arguing that even though there are certainly differences between art and science, there is much more likeness and affinity than is usually recognized. As he says, "The difference between art and science is not that between feeling and fact, intuition and inference, delight and deliberation, synthesis and analysis, sensation and cerebration, concreteness and abstraction, passion and action, mediacy and immediacy, or truth and beauty, but rather a difference in domination of certain specific characteristics of symbols." We will very soon unpack just what he means by "domination of certain specific characteristics of symbols," but first we will look more closely at some features of science that show it to be more akin to art than is often acknowledged.

Science, for all its rigor and objectivity, is steeped in values. There are values about science and values within science. That is, there are values associated with the results of scientific investigations, about what those results mean and how they affect us. For instance, medical research has obvious and often immediate impacts that matter to us. In addition, the more that geologists and seismologists learn about the structure and movement of the geologic plates, the more they will be able to help warn us about potential earthquakes. Basic research into the nature of light and sound have led to time-saving and life-saving technologies, such as lasers and microwave ovens. Of course, scientific investigations have also made possible weapons of mass destruction. It is obvious, then, that there are values related to science through its impact on our lives.

However, there are also values within science, values that are inherent to the "doing" of good scientific research. Among these values are—for lack of a better term—moral or social values. For example, the philosopher of science Nicholas Rescher has argued that moral values are inherent in scientific research. That is, he has claimed, scientific research simply cannot take place absent many moral decisions being made. These are not moral decisions regarding the uses of scientific information once it has been attained; rather, moral decisions permeate the very possibility of doing scientific research at all. Rescher identifies at least seven areas of scientific research in which values are an inherent part: (1) choice of research goals, (2) staffing of research activities, (3) research methods, (4) standards of proof, (5) dissemination of research findings, (6) control of misinformation, and (7) allocation of credit for research achievements. Rescher argues that, far from values being in conflict with good science, values are inescapable for scientific research ("The Ethical Dimension of Scientific Research," in *Beyond the Edge of Certainty*, ed. R. Colodny [Englewood Cliffs, NJ: Prentice-Hall, 1965], 261–276). Another philosopher of science, Richard Rudner, claimed that no hypothesis of science is ever completely verified ("The Scientists qua Scientist Makes Value Judgments," *Philosophy of Science* 20 (1953): 1–6). By accepting a hypothesis, scientists must make the decision that the evidence that supports the hypothesis is good enough to justify accepting the hypothesis. This decision of what counts as being "good enough evidence" is a function of the importance—and, for Rudner, this importance is inescapably a matter of morality—of accepting or rejecting the hypothesis. If the hypothesis under consideration is about the effectiveness of some drug for treating a disease or ailment and could have potentially serious health consequences, then we would desire a very high degree of confidence in the level of support before accepting the hypothesis that the drug is safe for consumption. On the other hand, if the hypothesis is about whether or not one dye for fabrics is longer lasting than an alternative dye, the level of desired degree of confidence in the hypothesis would be less. How sure we need to be before we accept a hypothesis, said Rudner, will depend on how serious a mistake would be. Scientists *must* make a value decision about the required level of confidence in the acceptability of evidence regarding any hypothesis. This is integral to the doing of scientific research. The main point of this argument is that values *within* science—and, yes, within good science—are inescapable.

Rudner's claims point to another kind of value that is fundamental and inherent in any scientific investigation. It is what philosophers refer to as *epistemic values*. Epistemic values are aspects of science, according to philosopher of science Ernan McMullin, that are presumed to promote the truth-like character of science, its character as the most secure knowledge available to us of the world we seek to understand. An epistemic value is one we have reason to believe will, if pursued, help toward the attainment of such knowledge. For example, we want reliable scientific data to be replicable, to be precise and accurate. It is usual in science to expect the results of experiments to be clearly quantifiable. Yet these features of being replicable, precise, accurate, and quantifiable (among others) are not "in the data themselves." They are values that we hold regarding the validity and reliability of the data. Such values, says McMullin, are inherent and inescapable for science ("Values in Science," in *PSA 1982*, vol. 2, ed. P. D. Asquith and T. Nickle [East Lansing, MI: Philosophy of Science Association, 1983], 3–28).

Now, a crucial concern in talking about values in science, especially epistemic values, is that they are basic to the content and methods and aims of science. Science simply is not possible without making value decisions regarding what to investigate, how to investigate it, and why. Furthermore, any scientific investigation requires interpretation of the data that is forthcoming. Regardless of the result, as scientists themselves will say, the data do not speak for themselves; they must be interpreted. And interpretation requires appealing to epistemic values. This by no means "downgrades" the verifiability or reliability or even objectivity of scientific research; if anything, it acknowledges the creativity that is inherent in much scientific exploration. But it also points to a rejection of the "domineering dichotomy" between art and science that Goodman and others speak of.

Above we noted that epistemic values are called that because they are presumed to promote the "truth-like character" of science. McMullin means two related things. First, truth itself is an epistemic value. That is, we can have results of scientific research that "work" even though they are not true, and the history of science reveals many examples of this. For instance, the Ptolemaic system of astronomy, which holds that the earth is at the center of everything and the sun, moon, planets, and stars revolve around the earth, can actually work quite well for many mundane purposes. If we simply want a calendar that helps predict seasons or a system that allows us to navigate ships across the oceans, the Ptolemaic astronomical system works just fine. Depending upon one's purposes, this system is a "useful fiction." Likewise, for many purposes, but not all, the ideal gas laws (which describe how gases respond to changes in temperature and pressure) work fine, even though they are not literally true (that is, there are contexts in which those laws fail to hold). The point here is that to say that something is true is not merely descriptive, but also evaluative, much like saying that something is verified or precise or even replicated.

The second thing McMullin means about truth as an epistemic value is that, even in science, truth is not always the aim. In part this is because it is never obvious when we can say that we know something is true. We can say that something has been verified or replicated over and over and that, as best we know, it is true, but there is always the possibility that some test or experiment could come along in the future that shows what we thought was true was not. To use the same example, for centuries it seemed obvious that the earth was stationary, and lots of evidence seemed to verify this view. But we now say that it was not true, that we were wrong. The point here is that the goal of scientific investigation might not be the accumulation of what seems to be true; rather, the goal of scientific investigation is understanding and predictability. If we have a hypothesis that we test and we get results that seem to confirm that hypothesis, we might not know for sure that it is true, but we do know that it has been confirmed. On the basis of that confirmation, it might lead to further hypotheses, which, if they, too, are confirmed, might make us say that our original hypothesis is even more confirmed. The result is that we might well have greater and greater understanding of things. But that understanding, along with its usefulness in making future predictions, is not necessarily the same thing as truth. So, as McMullin says, epistemic values help promote the *truth-like* character of science. However, understanding is what is key.

The assertion that understanding is the basic aim of research is the core of Goodman's claims about the relationship between art and science. He claims that it is mistaken both to think that truth is the fundamental value of science and also to think that truth is not an important value of art. In fact, for both, understanding is the fundamental value. In any case, both art and science include numerous and various epistemic values. Whereas Gardner, in the reading above, focused on art from the perspective of the artist, Goodman, in the reading below, focuses on art from the perspective of aesthetic experience (which could be for the artist, but could also be for the audience). Aesthetic experience, he says, is dynamic and involves symbol systems. Symbols are anything that, via convention, stand for something or other. Words, for instance, are symbols that stand for things beyond themselves. (*Cat* stands for particular critters; *dog*, for other critters.) Different arts have different sorts of symbols, and different sciences have different sorts of symbols. In all these cases, interpretation is necessary, and it is symbols that are being interpreted in the light of a structured system. In dance, certain movements are the "medium," whereas in music, the medium is sounds and rhythms; sciences use other symbol systems (for instance, blips on a radar screen or rates of particle decay). Once again, Goodman is not saying that art and science are identical or that there are no differences between them (either in terms of what they focus on, how they do so, or why). What he is saying is that both are endeavors within symbol systems and both are primarily concerned with interpretation of symbols and the understanding that results from interpretation.

NELSON GOODMAN, "ART AND THE UNDERSTANDING"*

Action and Attitude

A persistent tradition pictures the aesthetic attitude as passive contemplation of the immediately given, direct apprehension of what is presented, uncontaminated by any conceptualization, isolated from all the echoes of the past and all the threats and promises of the future, exempt from all enterprise. By purification rites of disengagement and disinterpretation we are to seek a pristine, unsullied vision of the world. I need hardly recount the philosophic faults and aesthetic absurdities of such a view until someone seriously goes so far as to maintain that the appropriate aesthetic attitude toward a poem amounts to gazing at the printed page without reading it.

I have held, on the contrary, that we have to read the painting as well as the poem, and that aesthetic experience is dynamic rather than static. It involves making delicate discriminations and discerning subtle relationships, identifying symbol systems and characters within these systems and what these characters denote and exemplify, interpreting works and reorganizing the world in terms of works and works in terms of the world. Much of our experience and many of our skills are brought to bear and may be transformed by the encounter. The aesthetic "attitude" is restless, searching, testing—is less attitude than action: creation and re-creation.

---

*In *Languages of Art,* 2nd ed. Indianapolis: Hackett Publishing Company, Inc., 1976. Indianapolis: Bobbs-Merrill, 1968. Pages 241–249, 251–252, 262–265.

What, though, distinguishes such aesthetic activity from other intelligent be-havior such as perception, ordinary conduct, and scientific inquiry? One instant answer is that the aesthetic is directed toward no practical end, is unconcerned with self-defense or conquest, with acquisition of necessities or luxuries, with prediction and control of nature. But if the aesthetic attitude disowns practical aims, still aimlessness is hardly enough. The aesthetic attitude is inquisitive as contrasted with the acquisitive and self-preservative, but not all nonpractical inquiry is aesthetic. To think of science as motivated ultimately by practical goals, as judged or justified by bridges and bombs and the control of nature, is to confuse science with technology. Science seeks knowledge without regard to practical consequences, and is concerned with prediction not as a guide for be-havior but as a test of truth. Disinterested inquiry embraces both scientific and aesthetic experience.

Attempts are often made to distinguish the aesthetic in terms of immediate pleasure; but troubles arise and multiply here. Obviously, sheer quantity or in-tensity of pleasure cannot be the criterion. That a picture or poem provides more pleasure than does a proof is by no means clear; and some human activi-ties unrelated to any of these provide enough more pleasure to render insignifi-cant any differences in amount or degree among various types of inquiry. The claim that aesthetic pleasure is of a different and superior *quality* is by now too transparent a dodge to be taken seriously.

The inevitable next suggestion—that aesthetic experience is distinguished not by pleasure at all but by a special aesthetic emotion—can be dropped on the waste-pile of "dormitive virtue" explanation.

This clears the way for the sophisticated theory that what counts is not plea-sure yielded but pleasure "objectified," pleasure read into the object as a prop-erty thereof. Apart from images of some grotesque process of transfusion, what can this mean? To consider the pleasure as possessed rather than occasioned by the object—to say in effect that the object is pleased—may amount to saying that the object expresses the pleasure. But since some aesthetic objects are sad—express sadness rather than pleasure—this comes nowhere near distin-guishing in general between aesthetic and nonaesthetic objects or experience.

Some of these difficulties are diminished and others obscured if we speak of satisfaction rather than pleasure. "Satisfaction" is colorless enough to pass in contexts where "pleasure" is ludicrous, lazy enough to blur counterinstances, and flexible enough to tolerate convenient vacillation in interpretation. Thus we may hope to lessen the temptation to conjure up a special quality or kind of feeling or to indulge in mumbo-jumbo about objectification. Nevertheless, satisfaction pretty plainly fails to distinguish aesthetic from nonaesthetic objects and experiences. Not only does some scientific inquiry yield much satisfaction, but some aesthetic objects and experiences yield none. Music and our listening, pictures and our looking, do not fluctuate between aesthetic and nonaesthetic as the playing or painting varies from exalted to excruciating. Being aesthetic does not exclude being unsatisfactory or being aesthetically bad.

The distinguishing feature, some say, is not satisfaction secured by satisfaction sought; in science, satisfaction is a mere by-product of inquiry; in art, inquiry is a mere means of obtaining satisfaction. The difference is held to be neither in process performed nor in satisfaction enjoyed but in attitude maintained. On this view the scientific aim is knowledge, the aesthetic *aim* satisfaction.

But how cleanly can these aims be separated? Does the scholar seek knowledge or the satisfaction of knowing? Obtaining knowledge and satisfying curiosity are so much the same that trying to do either without trying to do the other surely demands a precarious poise. And anyone who does manage to seek the satisfaction without seeking the knowledge will pretty surely get neither, while on the other hand abstention from all anticipation of satisfaction is unlikely to stimulate research. One may indeed be so absorbed in working on a problem as never to think of the satisfaction to be had from solving it; or one may dwell so fondly on the delights of finding a solution as to take no steps toward arriving at one. But if the latter attitude is aesthetic, aesthetic understanding of anything is foredoomed. And I cannot see that these tenuous, ephemeral, and idiosyncratic states of mind mark any significant difference between the aesthetic and the scientific.

The Function of Feeling

All of these failures to arrive at an acceptable formulation in terms of pleasure or satisfaction, yielded or "objectified" or anticipated, will hardly dislodge the conviction that the distinction between the scientific and the aesthetic is somehow rooted in the difference between knowing and feeling, between the cognitive and the emotive. This latter deeply entrenched dichotomy is in itself dubious on many grounds, and its application here becomes especially puzzling when aesthetic and scientific experience alike are seen to be fundamentally cognitive in character. But we do not easily part with the idea that art is in some way or other more emotive than science.

The shift from pleasure or satisfaction to emotion-in-general softens some of the crudities of the hedonistic formulas but leaves us with trouble enough. Paintings and concerts, and the viewing and hearing of them, need not arouse emotion, any more than they need give satisfaction, to be aesthetic; and antici-pated emotion is no better criterion than anticipated satisfaction. If the aesthetic is characteristically emotive in some way, we have yet to say in what way.

Any picture of aesthetic experience as a sort of emotional bath or orgy is plainly preposterous. The emotions involved tend to be muted and oblique as compared, for example, with the fear or sorrow or depression or exultation that arises from actual battle or bereavement or defeat or victory, and are not in gen-eral keener than the excitement or despair or elation that accompanies scien-tific exploration and discovery. What the inert spectator feels falls far short of what the characters portrayed on the stage feel, and even of what he himself would feel on witnessing real-life events. And if he leaps on the stage to partici-pate, his response can no longer be called aesthetic. That art is concerned with simulated emotion suggests, as does the copy theory of representation, that art is a poor substitute for reality: that art is imitation, and aesthetic experience is a pacifier that only partly compensates for lack of direct acquaintance and con-tact with the Real. . . .

Again, even among works of art and aesthetic experiences of evident excel-lence, the emotive component varies widely—from, say, a late Rembrandt to a late Mondrian, or from a Brahms to a Webern quartet. The Mondrian and the Webern are not obviously more emotive than Newton's or Einstein's laws; and a line between emotive and cognitive is less likely to mark off the aesthetic neatly from the scientific than to mark off some aesthetic objects and experiences from others. . . .

Most of the troubles that have been plaguing us can, I have suggested, be blamed on the domineering dichotomy between the cognitive and the emotive. On the one side, we put sensation, perception, inference, conjecture, all nerve-less inspection and investigation, fact, and truth; on the other, pleasure, pain, interest, satisfaction, disappointment, all brainless affective response, liking, and loathing. This pretty effectively keeps us from seeing that in aesthetic expe-rience the *emotions function cognitively*. The work of art is apprehended through the feelings as well as through the senses. Emotional numbness dis-ables here as definitely if not as completely as blindness or deafness. Nor are the feelings used exclusively for exploring the emotional content of a work. To some extent, we may feel how a painting looks as we may see how it feels. The actor or dancer—or the spectator—sometimes notes and remembers the feeling of a movement rather than its pattern, insofar as the two can be distinguished at all. Emotion in aesthetic experience is a means of discerning what properties a work has and expresses.

To say this is to invite hot denunciation for cold over-intellectualization; but rather than aesthetic experience being here deprived of emotions, the understanding is being endowed with them. The fact that emotions participate in cognition no more implies that they are not felt than the fact that vision helps us discover properties of objects implies that color-sensations do not occur. Indeed, emotions must be felt—that is, must occur, as sensations must—if they are to be used cognitively. Cognitive use involves discriminating and relating them in order to gauge and grasp the work and integrate it with the rest of our experience and the world. If this is the opposite of passive absorption in sensations and emotions, it by no means amounts to canceling them. Yet it explains the modifications that emotions may undergo in aesthetic experience. . . .

Cognitive employment of the emotions is neither present in every aesthetic nor absent from every nonaesthetic experience. We have already noted that some works of art have little or no emotive content, and that even where the emotive content is appreciable, it may sometimes be apprehended by nonemotive means. In daily life, classification of things by feeling is often more vital than classification by other properties: we are likely to be better off if we are skilled in fearing, wanting, braving, or distrusting the right things, animate or inanimate, than if we perceive only their shapes, sizes, weights, etc. And the importance of discernment by feeling does not vanish when the motivation becomes theoretic rather than practical. The zoologist, psychologist, sociologist, even when his aims are purely theoretic, legitimately employs emotion in his investigations. Indeed, in any science, while the requisite objectivity forbids wishful thinking, prejudicial reading of evidence, rejection of unwanted results, avoidance of ominous lines of inquiry, it does not forbid use of feeling in exploration and discovery, the impetus of inspiration and curiosity, or the cues given by excitement over intriguing problems and promising hypotheses. And the more we discuss these matters, the more we come to realize that emotions are not so clearly differentiated or so sharply separable from other elements in cognition that the distinction can provide a firm basis for answering any moot questions. . . .

Art and the Understanding

In saying that aesthetic experience is cognitive experience distinguished by the dominance of certain symbolic characteristics and judged by standards of cognitive efficiency, have I overlooked the sharpest contrast: that in science, unlike art, the ultimate test is truth? Do not the two domains differ most drastically in that truth means all for the one, nothing for the other?

Despite rife doctrine, truth by itself matters very little in science. We can generate volumes of dependable truths at will so long as we are unconcerned with their importance; the multiplication tables are inexhaustible, and empirical truths abound. Scientific hypotheses, however true, are worthless unless they meet minimal demands of scope or specificity imposed by our inquiry, unless they effect some telling analysis or synthesis, unless they raise or answer significant questions. Truth is not enough; it is at most a necessary condition. But even this concedes too much; the noblest scientific laws are seldom quite true. Minor discrepancies are overridden in the interest of breadth or power or simplicity. Science denies its data as the statesman denies his constituents—within the limits of prudence.

Yet neither is truth one among competing criteria involved in the rating of scientific hypotheses. Given any assemblage of evidence, countless alternative hypotheses conform to it. We cannot choose among them on grounds of truth; for we have no direct access to their truth. Rather, we judge them by such features as their simplicity and strength. These criteria are not supplemental to truth but applied hopefully as a means for arriving at the nearest approximation to truth that is compatible with our other interests.

Does this leave us with the cardinal residual difference that truth—though not enough, not necessary, and not a touchstone for choosing among hypotheses—is nevertheless a consideration relevant in science but not in art? Even so meek a formulation suggests too strong a contrast. Truth of a hypothesis after all is a matter of fit—fit with a body of theory, and fit of hypothesis and theory to the data at hand and the facts to be encountered. And as Philipp Frank liked to remind us, goodness of fit takes a two-way adjustment—of theory to facts and of facts to theory—with the double aim of comfort and a new look. But such fitness, such aptness in conforming to and reforming our knowledge and our world, is equally relevant for the aesthetic symbol. Truth and its aesthetic counterpart amount to appropriateness under different names. If we speak of hypotheses but not of works of art as true, that is because we reserve the terms "true" and "false" for symbols in sentential form. I do not say this difference is negligible, but it is specific rather than generic, a difference in field of application rather than in formula, and marks no schism between the scientific and aesthetic.

None of this is directed toward obliterating the distinction between art and science. Declarations of indissoluble unity—whether of the sciences, the arts, the arts and sciences together, or of mankind—tend anyway to focus attention upon the differences. What I am stressing is that the affinities here are deeper, and the significant differentia other than is often supposed. The difference between art and science is not that between feeling and fact, intuition and inference, delight and deliberation, synthesis and analysis, sensation and cerebration, concreteness and abstraction, passion and action, mediacy and immediacy, or truth and beauty, but rather a difference in domination of certain specific characteristics of symbols.

The implications of this reconception may go beyond philosophy. We hear a good deal about how the aptitudes and training needed for the arts and for the sciences contrast or even conflict with one another. Earnest and elaborate efforts to devise and test means of finding and fostering aesthetic abilities are always being initiated. But none of this talk or these trials can come to much without an adequate conceptual framework for designing crucial experiments and interpreting their results. Once the arts and sciences are seen to involve working with—inventing, applying, reading, transforming, manipulating—symbol systems that agree and differ in certain specific ways, we can perhaps undertake pointed psychological investigation of how the pertinent skills inhibit or enhance one another; and the outcome might well call for changes in educational technology. Our preliminary study suggests, for example, that some processes requisite for a science are less akin to each other than to some requisite for an art. But let us forego foregone conclusions. Firm and usable results are as far off as badly needed; and the time has come in this field for the false truism and the plangent platitude to give way to the elementary experiment and the hesitant hypothesis.

Whatever consequences might eventually be forthcoming for psychology or education would in any case count as by-products of the theoretical inquiry begun here. My aim has been to take some steps toward a systematic study of symbols and symbol systems and the ways they function in our perceptions and actions and arts and sciences, and thus in the creation and comprehension of our worlds. ◣

ART AND KNOWLEDGE

As we have just seen, Goodman rejects the notion that art is essentially emotive and is primarily (or only) about feeling whereas science is cognitive and about knowing. In the reading on page 228, John Bender goes even further and argues not only that art is concerned with cognition and knowing, but also that art is in fact a source of knowledge. Bender claims that art gives us knowledge, including what philosophers call propositional knowledge. Art gives us knowledge, he says, because art involves intentional objects and symbols that ground various inferences and from which we draw inferences. That will need to be unpacked! First, some general remarks should be made about how philosophers have dealt with the nature of knowledge.

In Chapter 1 we looked at some basic issues about epistemology (the study of knowledge). We saw there that philosophers often speak of various types of knowledge: knowledge by acquaintance (that is, some immediate awareness of something, such as knowing you have a toothache), propositional knowledge (that is, knowledge of the content of propositions, such as knowing that the earth is smaller than the sun), and practical knowledge (that is, knowledge involving some practice, such as knowing how to ride a bike). We also saw that there are metaphysical questions about knowledge (such as what kinds of things we can know), epistemological questions about knowledge (such as how we know what we know), and axiological questions about knowledge (such as why knowledge is valuable). These various kinds of questions can all come into play when we consider some aspect of our lives. For example, we might wonder about moral knowledge; can we *know* (rather than merely believe) what is right or wrong, what is good or bad? What would moral knowledge be? Are there moral facts about the world that we could encounter that might settle the issue of whether, say, abortion on demand is good or bad? Obviously, there are biological and social facts, but are there moral facts? How could we know (again, rather than merely believe) that, say, abortion is good or bad? What could we appeal to in order to settle that question? Why does it matter whether or not there is moral knowledge (as opposed to moral beliefs)? These are the kinds of questions that would be involved in asking about moral knowledge.

Similarly, there are questions about artistic or aesthetic knowledge. Can we *know* that something is art or *know* that something is good art? And, if so, how? Are there artistic or aesthetic facts? Is it important to know artistically or aesthetically, and, if so, why? With respect to the relationships between art and science, are these questions relevant to exploring or explaining those relationships? We will get at these questions by considering what Bender has to say.

First, as mentioned above, he claims that art gives us knowledge because it involves intentional objects and symbols that ground inferences and from which we draw other inferences. So, what does he mean? By "intentional objects," Bender means art is about something or other. For philosophers, one meaning of *intentional* is simply "about something." My hope that you like this book is intentional; it is about your response. Likewise, if I think about my cat, that is said to be intentional; my state of thinking is about something (in this case, my cat). So Bender is simply saying that art is about something or other; it involves intentional objects (where "objects" might not be physical objects but could be, say, states of affairs or possibilities). Also, like Goodman, Bender says that art involves symbols; we use certain sounds, colors, movements, and the like to represent or exemplify things beyond themselves. In addition, we use these (artistic) symbols and make inferences because of them. For example, I might look at Picasso's *Guernica* and, because of having looked at it, think about any number of things and even draw conclusions about something or other.

One aspect of knowledge, whether artistic or otherwise, is the issue of whose knowledge is meant. I just remarked that, having viewed *Guernica*, I might draw some inferences and even learn something. But even if that were so, would it follow that the same would be true if you viewed *Guernica*? One claim often made about art and knowledge is that artists, through the process of creating some artwork, learn something about themselves. However, even if, say, Picasso learned something about himself because of having painted *Guernica*, the question remains whether he learned anything about anything else (much less whether someone viewing *Guernica* actually learns anything). The point here is simply to highlight that when such knowledge claims are made, it is important to ask, Knowledge for whom? With respect to the relationship between art and science, this comes back to Gardner's reading earlier in this chapter: namely, Gardner notes that science is said to give us knowledge about the world and that this knowledge is general and communal. That is, the knowledge resulting from scientific investigation yields knowledge not only for the investigator but for others. In addition, the content of the knowledge is not about the investigator but about the world. Does the content of *Guernica* tell us anything about the world? For Goodman and Bender, yes, because, as with any "piece of knowledge," it involves interpretation within symbol systems (as does the result of any scientific investigation).

Bender also speaks of "modal knowledge." When philosophers speak of *modalities*, they mean notions of possibility and necessity (and also actuality). We often encounter the view that the value of art is that it can show us what is possible, that it can help us think about how things could be, not just about how things are. This is what Bender means by speaking of art as a source of modal knowledge. For example, classical Greek tragedy might show us what can happen if someone exhibits hubris, that is, if someone acts as if he is too important or above the social and moral constraints that most of us abide by. (For that matter, simple children's fairy tales do much the same!) Art can show us what might be possible; it can give us knowledge, at least in the sense of some form of guidance in the world.

Repeating a message from Goodman, Bender also claims that art requires interpretation, but so too does science. In this context, he notes that there is an underdetermination of interpretation, given the sensory data of an artwork. This means that the features of an artwork (for instance, the particular colors of a painting or the rhythm of a musical phrase) are not sufficient to determine one, final correct interpretation of that artwork. However, underdetermination of facts is also true of science, according to Bender (and many others). That is, a set of factual information might have many competing explanations. For instance, there is a particularly high level of the element iridium in certain geological formations that were formed approximately 65 million years ago (when the dinosaurs died out). Some geologists point to that information and claim that the cause was a meteor slamming into the earth, while other geologists point to that same information and claim that the cause was enhanced volcanic activity on the earth. The facts of the iridium level underdetermine which account is correct. For Bender, underdetermination of facts (whether about scientific objects or artistic objects) is true of both science and art.

Nonetheless, when speaking of knowledge, philosophers are usually concerned with justified true belief. We noted in Chapter 1 that to say that someone knows X (for instance, knows that the earth is smaller than the sun) entails that the person believes X, that X is true, and that the person has some justification for believing X. Each of these conditions (belief, truth, and justification) is necessary in order for the person to know X. Bender points out that some people have argued that these notions simply do not apply to art, so art cannot be a source of knowledge. For example, what would it mean to say that an artwork is true? And how can an artwork provide justification for some belief? We certainly do not think that Sherlock Holmes existed and solved mysteries simply because there are stories written that portray such events. We cannot point to Sherlock Holmes stories to justify a belief that nineteenth-century London was a hotbed of crime. To many people, then, the notions of truth and justification are simply irrelevant to what art is and also to why art matters. But if so, then art cannot be a source of knowledge.

Bender's response to this is that there are various conceptions of truth and justification and that all of them require interpretation. As was noted in Chapter 1, one conception of truth is correspondence: what makes a belief true is that it corresponds to facts in the world (and what makes a belief false is that it does not correspond to facts in the world). Another conception of truth is coherence: what makes a belief true is that it coheres with other beliefs that have been established or accepted. Yet another conception is the pragmatic view of truth: what makes a belief true is that it has practical consequences that are borne out in our future actions and beliefs. Whatever conception of truth one might employ, according to Bender, there must be interpretation, and this is the case for scientific claims as well as for artistic or aesthetic claims. For example, take truth as correspondence. according to Bender, to say that a belief corresponds to facts in the world presupposes that we can specify exactly what the belief is and also what things and events in the world constitute the relevant facts. However, relevance is not "given" but is, rather, a matter of interpretation. Clearly, many interpretations can be wrong, or at least unhelpful, but that does not mean that there is only one correct interpretation. The same concerns apply, for Bender, to the issue of justification: what is relevant in any proposed justification depends on interpretation. Again, not any interpretation will do; some interpretations are good and others are bad, but they are interpretations nonetheless.

Finally, one more aspect of knowledge that speaks to the nature of art and of science concerns something that cognitive scientists have pointed out recently, namely, that there are inherent and necessary "emotive" aspects of cognition. In other words, when we believe, or know, something, this is never a case of simply having facts. There is always some interpretive component and also some, often inexplicit, evaluative component to believing or knowing. We sometimes speak of having a "gut feeling" or a "hunch" about things. Such feelings, of course, can often be misleading (our gut feelings might be wrong), but they are, say cognitive scientists, natural and inherent in how we encounter the world. If this is so, then, as Goodman and Bender have claimed, the dichotomy between cognition and emotion, or between knowing and feeling, is not a sharp line at all and is not a fruitful basis for making distinctions between art and science.

None of these issues has been directed toward saying that there are no differences between art and science. Clearly, there are differences. Art does not necessarily try to explain things in the world, but science (often) does. Art is not intended to predict what will happen in the world, but science (often) is. Art is not expected to be either verified or replicated, but science (often) is. The issue is more a question of what it is about art and about science that make them similar or different, of how we know, and of why, and to whom, this matters. Here, then, is Bender:

JOHN W. BENDER, "ART AS A SOURCE OF KNOWLEDGE: LINKING ANALYTIC AESTHETICS AND EPISTEMOLOGY"*

Art, Knowledge, and Philosophers

It is in no way remarkable that, as an epistemologist and aesthetician, I happen to think that not enough has been done by philosophers to relate aesthetic experience and aesthetic appreciation to epistemic states such as knowledge and justified belief. It is of more interest, perhaps, that as an epistemologist and aesthetician, I am puzzled and dissatisfied by our tradition's handling of the question, "Does art give us knowledge?" . . . It is ironic that philosophers, so often liable to charges of overintellectualizing an issue, have for so long been reluctant to validate their enjoyment and valuing of art, even partially, in terms of the knowledge it can impart. . . .

The claim I wish to defend . . . is the claim that art, in general, functions in a multiplicity of cognitive, perceptual, and expressive ways, and frequently, though certainly not always, this includes, or should include, the conveyance of propositional knowledge, when those appreciating the works are sufficiently thoughtful. I wish to suggest that viewing art as a source of knowledge (whether it is unique knowledge available only through art, as Martha Nussbaum seems to suggest, I doubt but leave aside) is a natural supposition if we see artworks as intentional objects and symbols which ground various inferences and from which we draw (many more) inferences. The picture I propose we paint of art is one of a complex intentional object suspended in an even more complex inferential web, some strands of which lead to knowledge.

The knowledge which art can give us is sometimes empirical and about the world; it can be general or specific in scope, abstract or concrete in its content. It is sometimes psychological or social and about ourselves; often it is of a nor-

*In *Contemporary Philosophy of Art: Readings in Analytic Aesthetics.* Edited by John W. Bender and H. Gene Blocker. Upper River, NJ: Prentice Hall, 1993. Pages 593–595, 597–602, 604–606.

mative, value-oriented nature or, in some other way, is a version of what I will call "modal" knowledge, knowledge that something is necessary, lawful, probable, possible, or impossible. Modal knowledge tells us about how things could or would or should be, under certain conditions or in a certain context, and often concerns tendencies, potentialities, and generalities. . . .

Notwithstanding Objections, Art Can Yield Knowledge

In the remainder of this paper, I will elaborate on my positive view that art can be the source of important and valuable propositional knowledge, but I will do so from the defensive posture of answering three complex and interrelated objections. . . .

1. *Art, surely, provides us with valuable and pleasurable experiences of rather vast variety, but not knowledge per se, except in trivial or secondary ways. In this, our experience of art is similar to other types of aesthetic or enjoyable experiences. When one drives a fast car fast, or attends a tennis match, for example, one may be after the exciting experience but is not, except in peculiar circumstances, after knowledge; even Saturday's "thoughtful" hike in a subalpine meadow is not a botanical hunt for knowledge. Likewise, the gaining of knowledge is not the point or heart of aesthetic experience. Let's not overintellectualize art or view it too didactically.*

The complete answer to this objection will require the whole of this paper. But we can begin with a few points. Construed as a statement of the naïve idea that art is a source of pleasure and little more, this is not a serious objection and, at any rate, has already been thoroughly trounced by many writers. . . . Art is far too cognitive and serious an intellectual pursuit to be treated as a simple stimulus for pleasure. It is true that some warm themselves with music as well as with a fire in the den, or relax with a novel, but it is also true that this is a simple-minded use of art.

It is much more interesting to view this first objection in a different way . . . namely, that art should not be subordinated to science and treated like a mere "truth vehicle." That is, of course, correct, but it is not my intention to scientize art or to claim that knowledge is art's sole goal or that its function is always didactic; rather it is to take art seriously and on its own terms—terms, however, that sometimes include truth and knowledge, I argue. This is strikingly different from viewing art as a neutral conduit or messenger of cold facts, itself to be "factored out" once the information is received. . . . Significant art comes to us *only* when we pay the greatest attention to the work itself. Unlike science, where it is possible (if unadvisable) to learn the conclusions of experiments and ignore their design, with art there is no way to ignore the aesthetics and absorb the knowledge. *Having* the experience is, indeed, crucial. But this in no way negates the fact that, as in science, the knowledge to be found in art comes to us through the process of inference. . . .

To learn anything from the work, indeed, to be in the position to learn, requires that we engage in *interpreting* the work. We first must hear the music as exemplifying the relevant properties such as profundity and depth, lightness and innocent joyfulness, and hear (or cognize) these various elements as being related to each other in specific ways. For example, we must interpret the profound and light passages as contrasting but not in opposition, and we must judge that the piece exhibits a convincing and natural way of moving from one to the other, if we are going to claim that ultimately we have learned something. . . .

It is an accepted fact of art criticism that such inferences and interpretations are *underdetermined* by the basic sensory data of an artwork. This means that our inferences are in for competition and that justification is not a deductive matter, but epistemologists know these lessons well from other knowledge areas and yet do not conclude (at least *some* do not conclude) that standards of justification are hopeless. The underdetermination thesis also, I think, argues in favor of the relevance of certain kinds of background, contextual, historical, and biographical information to the justifiability of our inferences. Any strong claim of the "autonomy of art" is untenable, in my view, because it denies obvious facts such as that we often make valuable inferences from art to artist and from artist to art, and that what an artist intends to do or not to do, as well as the contexts in which he or she is working, affects what the artist in fact accomplishes. It is only when we take seriously the picture of the work of art as a presentational symbol (a symbol exhibiting some of the properties it refers to) centered in a complex inferential web that we come to accept the demand for inferential justification as itself legitimate, and the possibility that knowledge is communicated as real.

Our discussion thus far has only suggested that, in regard to art and aesthetic experience, we can appropriately talk of inferences and justification without fear of necessarily neutering, overscientizing, or overintellectualizing the experience. We can rejoin the argument now by taking up another objection, closely related to the first.

2. *The cognitive nature of art's functions can be granted, certainly. There have been, after all, numerous theories emphasizing this: [Susanne] Langer conceived of artworks as presentational symbols that articulate the human emo-*

tional landscape, and Charles Morris before her saw art as iconic signs that sig-
nify certain properties by exhibiting them. Nelson Goodman, the leading cur-
rent cognitivist, takes art to literally and metaphorically exemplify many
properties, some formal, some emotional, and claims that art's value is a matter
of its cognitive, symbolic efficacy. But when we experience these functions of
art, we can feel or understand what they express without formulating some les-
son, some truth, something propositional. You may be right that in experiencing
art we are involved in cognitive inferences about it, and that our claims about
this content are open to and in need of justification in some sense of that term.
But what we "know" through art we "know" in experiencing it; it is knowledge
by acquaintance, as it were; it is more like knowing how the Eiffel Tower looks
at night than it is like knowing that the Eiffel Tower is a symbol of modernity or
that it is riveted together. The upshot of the processes of aesthetic appreciation
and interpretation is an enriched experience, not a propositional conclusion.

There is much truth to this objection, but also much romance. Artworks *are*
experienced and can be entered into, lived, even "inhabited," as Steven Smith
has suggested. Art can "create worlds," as Goodman would say, or at least create
parts or aspects of worlds, in which we can immerse ourselves. One does indeed
sense the overwhelming depth of the *Cavatina* from Beethoven's B-flat quartet,
Op. 130, and *feel* its reflective peace. And, I would admit, in many cases, one's
work is done when the formal and expressive features and relationships of a
piece of art have been noticed and experienced. But sometimes, it seems to me,
there is more to do, more to be had. There is a difference between being trans-
ported into Beethoven's world and knowing where you are, or, perhaps more accurately, there are varying degrees of understanding of that world. It is possible
to *feel* Beethoven's music intelligently, to inhabit *The World According to Garp*
with familiarity, but not know what to make of it. Learning more and more what
to make of it is a process which, at least in part, involves making intricate and
unobvious inferences to propositional conclusions, some of which, to my mind,
constitute knowledge. It is no threat to this knowledge that the artworks which
can yield it are often themselves not composed of propositions. Vast reaches of
our propositional knowledge are grounded in the nonpropositional, and the
most natural of signs . . . can give us propositional knowledge.

When we understand the symbolic intent of an image, the metaphorical
force of a poetic line, the thematic content of a literary work, the "depth meaning" of a passage . . . we are inferring content.

Sometimes we stop at the point of understanding that the piece contains
a visual or verbal metaphor for death or pleasure, a damning representation of a

person, an ambiguous depiction of two lovers, and so on, but often we are motivated to ask *why* these features are present and feel justified in drawing some
conclusions, hazarding a guess about a unifying theme or about the work's significance or "meaning." It has been common (prior to recent postmodern de-
nials to the contrary) to agree to this thesis in regard to the literary and
theoretical arts, but its force is more general, applying, I believe, to every art
form, although not to every artwork. Superb as pure abstractionist art can be,
for example, I admit that the "knowledge" we derive from a certain example
may be nothing more than an acquaintance with *this* particular way of achieving balance or intensity, *this* way of exemplifying energy, tension, or void.

But even here, we must be careful not to be too "minimalist" about knowledge. Maybe there is nothing more to do in front of a Morris Louis painting than
to absorb its cool sensuality, or, while viewing the Rothko triptych, to feel
"metaphysical" or contemplative. But would it be wrong to say that through
Mondrian's compositions in his reduced style of the 1920s and 1930s we can
come to know that our sense of physical structure and unity is as much *created*
by color as it is filled in by it? "But the unifying principles internal to a Mondrian do not apply generally to objects," one may object. A quick, justificatory
reply may be, "Have you noticed how many everyday objects and structures
can be seen as one sees a Mondrian?" Again, one can hardly fail to sense and
marvel at the exquisite balance of a Mozart middle symphony, such as *Symphony #25 in G minor, K. 183*—it is the property most clearly and resoundingly
exemplified by this work. But one can go beyond simply feeling this symmetry
and discover through repeated attention that this feature is not adequately explained in the usual terms of the Classical symmetry of the composition's
melodic lines, but also and more strikingly is due to the shapes, lengths, and or-
chestral "weights" of the four movements and the relations among these abstract values. That is to say, one can learn something *architectural* from Mozart:
that the perceived weight, shape, and length of component and noncontiguous
elements of a whole can contribute to a subtle sense of balance.

Consequently, it is not at all clear to me that aesthetic apprehension and appreciation is more like knowing what the Eiffel Tower looks like than it is like
knowing that it is a symbol of modernity. The situation may better be described
by saying that aesthetic experiences with significant epistemic content are like
recognizing that the Eiffel Tower is a symbol of modernity *through* knowing,
among other things, how it looks.

3. *But, surely, there remain two very large obstacles in the way of your thesis,
not surprisingly, one having to do with truth and the other with justification. If*

we put aside certain analytic niceties, we can think of knowledge as justified true belief. The problem over truth is this: What art expresses, presents, communicates to us, implies, insinuates, or "argues for" must be construed as one point of view, one perspective, one "way the world is," and, in some cases, perhaps, as a statement of the artist's beliefs, attitudes, outlook, fears, and aspirations. But all this belongs to the Platonic realm of "opinion," as it were, not to the realm of truth. The second problem, about justification, is related to the truth problem: Even if we grant that analyses and interpretations of an artwork's content can be justified, that only provides us with grounds for conclusions of the form, "The painting expresses the importance of x," "The novel's most important claim is p," "The symphony seems to be the composer's most concise statement of the fear that q and of his confidence that r." Having justification for conclusions such as these is a wholly different matter from being justified in believing that x is important, or that p, q, or r are true. But these latter beliefs are what are necessary if art gives us knowledge.

In her excellent, insightful, and now slightly greying article, "The Cognitive Content of Art," Dorothy Walsh makes an observation which seems to give weight to what I am calling the "truth problem." Even though artists and artworks put forward radically different and, according to Walsh, incompatible, views and visions, we do not treat them as competing truth claims, as we do when we encounter theoretical incompatibilities in science or philosophy. . . .

Walsh resists the proposal that would resolve the apparent incompatibility among artworks' cognitive content by claiming that each work is only a *partial* articulation of the world and human experience, and hence may each be true. She concludes, instead, that the solution lies in conceiving of art not as a *truth* vehicle but as a vehicle of *possibility*. Art's cognitive role, in this view, is to present us with certain diverse possibilities. . . . Given my earlier reference to art's conveyance of "modal" knowledge, one might expect that I must concur with Walsh on this point, but my agreement with her is limited. . . .

Indeed, as soon as we resist the evaporation of art's cognitive content into the realm of mere possibility, it also becomes wise to resist describing every difference as radical incompatibility. If we do not, it becomes difficult to explain, short of postulating a kind of aesthetic schizophrenia, the ease with which we embrace both Bach and Debussy, Shostokovich [*sic*] and Schubert. It is better, when we can do it, to say things like this: "Following Bach, Mozart, and Beethoven, as Brahms did, his emphases are as different and new as they are natural, and those earlier voices had their various influences on his focus and concern." . . .

What we are prepared to call or identify as the knowledge inherent in art clarifies itself only as we think critically about the work—not only trying to make sense of it, but also trying to place it, or what it seems to be teaching us, within the rest of our epistemic field. This is the process by which we can become *justified* in believing something that has been put forward to us in the context and form of art. Knowledge is not the same as the receipt of information, as Keith Lehrer and many other epistemologists are fond of pointing out, and, at least concerning the type of knowledge we are discussing here, it is safe to say that to have it, there must be some critical and conscious thought about, some epistemic evaluation of, the inferences we make in coming to grips with an artwork.

The problem of justification, as I stated earlier, is the correct observation that having a justified interpretation of what a work is "up to" is not the same thing as having reasons or justification for believing that what it "says" is true. But once we admit this, I think we can see how it is possible to be justified in accepting what the work offers. What is noteworthy here is that reaching a justified *interpretation of the work is a necessary part, and the uniquely aesthetic part of the process.* (This explains why art and literary criticism, which deal with the canons of interpretation, can correctly be said to add to the knowledge we derive from the arts.) We must notice the work's subtle features, weigh and evaluate different hypotheses about their interconnections, argue about their meanings, and engage in numerous other cognitive labors in casting a justifiable interpretation. *Evaluation* of the work's artistic prowess and merit is also relevant to the ultimate question of knowledge and justification. How convincingly a theme is handled in the work, and how natural and coherent the work's progress is toward its conclusions, can affect the warrant we have for our knowledge claims, though a detailed articulation of this procedure would be difficult at present. But surely the breathtaking clarity and seamless unity with which a great artwork can sometimes explore new horizons, new claims about the human condition, rightfully weighs in the positive toward our acceptance of its lessons. . . .

Conclusion: The Functions of Art

Here is a partial list of the possible functions of art, none of which I would deny. Art

Gives us unique perceptual and cognitive experiences;
Offers new ways of perceiving and conceiving things;

Exhibits, expresses, and evokes emotions in us;

Gives us pleasure—sensory, sensual, and intellectual in kind;

Represents things;

Communicates intentional states and attitudes of the artist;

Exemplifies properties and relations of very abstract sorts;

Functions as a presentational sign;

Creates "worlds" and points of view;

Is an exercise of and exercises the imagination;

Utilizes verbal, visual, auditory, and kinesthetic metaphors;

Matures and deepens our aesthetic sensibilities;

Is a "working out" of some problem or concern of the artist;

Portrays and manifests values, hopes, aspirations, ideals;

Gives us knowledge of the world, sometimes factual, sometimes normative, and
sometimes "modal."

Any theory of art which denies these functions is bound to fail, simply because, like life (which cannot be encompassed by one science), art is too varied and complex to be exhausted by a simple and singular view of its rewards and lessons. Art is perhaps more profitably viewed as more similar in its complexity to philosophy than to science, if only because it is a common mistake to assign science a singular function, the pursuit of, and accumulation of, truth or knowledge. It seems to many that more divergent things (sometimes embarrassingly divergent) go on in philosophy: seeing issues from different perspectives, meeting argument with counterargument, developing conceptual and analytical abilities, striving to understand a multiplicity of views, manipulating and relating concepts and abstractions. But philosophy's range of activities and functions has not caused us (not all of us, at least) to dismiss the idea that there is philosophical knowledge, and a similar conclusion is warranted, I believe, in the case of art. Among its many other values, art brings us knowledge—or so I have tried to argue. ◣

Questions for Discussion

1. Can artistic or aesthetic claims be tested? Can an artwork be false (or, for that matter, true)?

2. Scientific illustrations are useful in helping people learn scientific knowledge. Does this mean that illustration (art?) is genuinely a part of scientific knowledge?

3. Gardner claims that both art and science are forms of communication. However, what is communicated in each? Does fiction communicate false statements?

4. Are Goodman and Bender correct that art and science are seen as being dichotomous, that is, art as being essentially emotive and science as being essentially cognitive? Does this view fit with any or all of the views from Chapter 2 on the nature of art (for example, Dewey's view)?

5. Why aren't the differences between art and science sufficient to support the view that they are fundamentally separate, that their content and methods and aims are more different than alike?

PERFORMING ARTS

Although you might not have been around in 1969 for the famous Wood-stock festival that involved thousands of (mostly young) people coming to-gether in rural New York for several days of music, you have probably heard of, or even heard recordings of, the guitarist Jimi Hendrix performing the US national anthem, "The Star-Spangled Banner." It was a single, and for many people singular, performance of a particular song, a performance that was a rather unconventional rendering at the time. He performed the same song other times and, as we know, the same song has been performed millions of times; this was a specific, particular performance.

In Chapter 3 we remarked on the fact that some artworks are unique, in-dividual things, such as the *Mona Lisa*. There is one specific original. Copies and reproductions of it are just that, copies and reproductions. Other art-works are not like this. The many copies of *Hamlet* are all on a par; no one of them is the original. What about artworks that are performances as opposed to things? Each performance of "The Star Spangled Banner" is unique, even each performance of it by Hendrix. Nevertheless, we still say each perfor-mance is of *it*, that is, of the same song. The name "The Star Spangled Ban-ner" does not refer to specific performances the way *Mona Lisa* refers to a specific painting. What is the status and nature, then, of art as performance? In the reading on page 244, Francis Sparshott will address this issue by ask-ing about "the identity of a dance," but first there are background concerns to address, not only about dance but also about performances and perform-ing arts in general.

237

What is a performing art? We commonly speak of the performing arts, meaning art forms that characteristically require their existence in the form of some sort of performance or action. Typically, people speak of dance, music, theater, opera, and the like as performing arts. We might also include, say, poetry readings (as opposed to poems) as a performing art, since the act and context of reading to an audience is crucial. Although there might be a score for a musical composition or a script for a play, the score or script in itself is not the primary focus. The point of the score or script, so to speak, is to be performed. So, again, performing arts require performance, action, as opposed to what are sometimes called plastic arts. Plastic arts are comprised of "things," such as actual paintings or sculptures or buildings. (In this book, rather than speaking directly about plastic arts, Chapters 9 and 10 will look at visual arts, in which an artwork that is viewed is the focus, and literary arts, in which an artwork involving written language is the focus.)

One more comment about terminology here: Besides the term *performing arts*, you have no doubt also heard the term *performance art*. Performance art is, of course, a performing art, in the sense that performance, or action, is characteristic of it. However, performance art is often, perhaps usually, understood as a form of social commentary and critique carried out in the form of a performance. It is, then, a subset of the larger notion of performing art. All cases of performance art are cases of performing arts, but not all cases of performing arts—for example, a given performance of *Hamlet*—are cases of performance art. This chapter is about performing arts.

Performing arts, then, require performance. That seems straightforward enough, but it turns out not to be so straightforward to determine just what, exactly, a performance is. We will come to that soon. In addition to a performance, there is, of course, a performer (or performers). We might think that who is a performer is also straightforward, and usually it is, but not always. For instance, in John Cage's infamous musical composition *4'33''*, in which "the performer" sits at a piano and does not play any notes and then gets up after four minutes and thirty-three seconds and leaves, the pianist does not perform in the sense of playing notes, and if anything, the audience, via their responses and actions, are considered performers of the piece. There are also instances of productions of plays in which "the performers," that is, the cast members, go out into the audience and interact with audience members, in effect making them part of the performance and, in a sense, performers.

In the previous paragraph we mentioned that it is not quite so straightforward to say just what a performance is. This is because we might want to distinguish a performance from an act of performing. A performance is, in a sense, a completed product—Hendrix's performance of "The Star Spangled Banner," for instance. An act of performing, however, is a process. A performer performs a performance! For example, we might think of a particular musical score, in itself and unperformed, or a particular dramatic script, simply written down. That score or script can be performed. So the performance of, say, Beethoven's Fifth Symphony might involve certain sorts of directions by the conductor, or the performance of *Hamlet* might involve certain sorts of staging instructions by the director. Then there is the actual performing of the symphony or the play, which might or might not comply with the conductor's directions or the director's instructions.

These sorts of issues and concerns—about who, exactly, is the performer and what, exactly, is the performance—are matters that relate to performing arts, but not to plastic arts. Some of the complications are due to the fact that with performing arts there are often a multitude of artists involved. For instance, with theater there can be the playwright, the actors, the director, the stage manager, the lighting crew, the sound crew, and so on. Similarly musical or dance concerts can involve many people, and the "artwork," that is, the performance, involves many artists. Earlier in the book we noted that Michel Foucault asked, "What is an author?" Well, with a performance, who is the artist? The answer is, lots of people. Of course, not all performances involve many people. A person can perform a solo performance. However, many (perhaps most) instances of performing arts involve multiple parties.

The variety of issues that have been covered in the previous chapters in this book are relevant to performing arts in spite of their unique aspects. For example, in Chapter 3, when we looked at issues related to the artwork, we considered forgery. The *Mona Lisa* can be forged, but can Beethoven's Fifth Symphony be forged? Can *Hamlet* be forged? What would it mean to say that Hendrix's performance of "The Star Spangled Banner" was, or could be, forged? It seems impossible. If someone else performed that song exactly as Hendrix did (note for note, with exactly the same intonation and timbre and timing and so on), it would not be a forgery of Hendrix's performance but a cover of it, a performance by some other person. Yet Hendrix's performance was as individual and unique as the *Mona Lisa*, meaning there is only one of them. What, if anything, does this say about the nature of individual artworks (including performances) as well as the nature of forgery?

Another topic related to artworks discussed earlier is the distinction between, and relation of, the aesthetic features of an artwork and the nonaesthetic features of an artwork. We can recognize the gracefulness of a dancer (that is, of a dancer's dancing of a dance), but what are the nonaesthetic features that make up that gracefulness? What are the features from which the gracefulness emerges? Are there aesthetic features that are peculiar to performances? It certainly seems so. The same written lines of a script can be performed, say, majestically or pathetically, perhaps for no other reason than the resonance of the actor's voice (imagine Mickey Mouse doing a dramatic scene from *Hamlet*).

In addition, we looked at the issue of form versus content and form versus context for art generally. How do those issues play out for performing arts? Context, at least "local" context, is especially salient for performing arts. Local context refers to the immediate situation of the performance. A dance performed on a ten-foot-by-ten-foot stage will be a very different artwork from the same dance performed on a hundred-foot-by-hundred-foot stage. A play performed on a stage with no props at all and with the actors wearing street clothes will be a very different artwork from the same play performed on a Broadway stage with elaborate lighting and sound and costumes.

In Chapter 4 we looked at aesthetic issues that are especially of concern for artists. For instance, the issue of artist intention is important. Artworks do not just happen; artists create them and create them for certain reasons, with certain intentions. Obviously, that is true for performing arts as well. However, as we noted above, performing arts frequently involve a multitude of artists, each presumably with intentions and goals, intentions and goals possibly inconsistent with those of the other artists. This holds as well for the issues of representation, expression, and change, all of which we addressed in Chapter 4. That is, because of the nature of performances and the involvement of multiple artists, what is represented (expressed, changed), how it is represented, and why it is represented all become even more complex and complicated. As an example, in Sparshott's reading below, he notes what he calls "levels of intimacy" in a dance. This includes the necessity that the dancer follow the instructions (and intentions) of the choreographer (much as an actor needs to follow the instructions of the play's director). However, at the same time, because a dancer is also a creative artist, the choreographer must let the dancer (the actual performer) be an artist and have some creative freedom.

The same kinds of considerations arise in the context of the audience. In Chapter 5 we looked at the notions of aesthetic experience, interpretation, and evaluation. These topics are salient in performing arts as much as in plastic arts. Again, because of the added complexity of having multiple artists involved, these topics take on added dimensions. For instance, in addition to forming their own interpretations of a piece of music, musicians must interpret what the composer intended in a certain part of the score, and they must also interpret what the conductor intends with certain directions for the playing of that score. These are all matters of interpretation for the artists involved in the performance and the performing of the artwork; in addition, the audience members make their own interpretations. (What did the increasing tempo in that last passage mean? Was it scored by the composer? Was this a decision by the conductor to emphasize the passage, regardless of what the composer had scored? Was this a rogue wind section or bassoonist who got carried away? If it was scored by the composer, then why? What was the composer trying to do in that passage? And so on.) Obviously, the various aesthetic, philosophical issues touched on in earlier chapters are present and important for specific arts, including performing arts. It is now time to turn to some specific performing arts.

DANCE

The first performing art we will consider is dance. Dance as art is usually distinguished from what aestheticians call "social" dance. Dance as art is dance whose performance is intended as artwork. In social dance, the intention is bodily movement not as artwork but for some other reason, such as exercise, therapy, or the like. Dance is unique among the arts as being almost wholly about human bodily movement. Of course, other performing arts, such as theater and music, involve bodily movement, but their emphasis is not on the movement itself. Sometimes aestheticians and dancers will speak of dance as formalized movement and poses. Clearly, dance is not simply a matter of inspired movement. There is a great deal of regimentation involved in dance, however inspired dance movements might be. Dancers often speak of line, form, and repetition. The most formalized style of dance is ballet, which contains very specific and enunciated dance positions. There are, in fact, several versions of dance notation, systems for "recording" or "writing down" a dance. Dance involves more than the dancer (performer). There is often also a choreographer (much like a musical composer or scriptwriter), the person who creates the dance. There is also a regisseur, or stage director (much like a play director). A dance performance also, of course, usually involves music, lighting, staging, costuming, and so on.

Many aestheticians speak of dance as a sort of body language. That is, via movements and gestures, the dancer communicates with an audience. Certain sorts of movements represent and project identifiable messages. Slow, lumbering movements obviously mean something quite different from what fast, muscular leaps mean. Aestheticians, then, often speak of the semiotics of bodily movement when they speak of dance; they speak of the expressiveness of movements. Just as some authors are noted for their expressiveness with words, particular dancers are noted for being especially expressive in and with and through their movements, as well as for their creative interpretations (perhaps analogous to good authors being able to construct word images or make intriguing metaphors)—dancers such as Isadora Duncan, Rudolf Nureyev, George Balanchine, and Martha Graham.

This notion of dance as body language points to an aesthetic and artistic aspect of dance that is unique to dance among the arts. It is essentially and fundamentally via bodily movement that dance (or a dancer's dancing) functions as art. If a dance (or a dancer) is to express joy, for instance, it must be through bodily movement and nothing else. If sorrow is to be represented or communicated, it is through bodily movement and nothing else. Given that dance as art is usually conjoined with music (as well as lighting, staging, and so on), it is still bodily movement, not sounds or tones, that constitute the dance aspect. Of course, coordination of those movements with the sounds or lighting is important. It would be puzzling, to say the least, to have joyous sounding music along with slow, ponderous, dragging dance movements. The aesthetics of dance, then, are fully, if not completely, determined by bodily movement. (*Whose* movements is another matter. That is, if a choreographer calls for certain movements and those movements seem out of place with the music or lighting, but are embodied by the dancer just as the choreographer called for, then they are, in effect, the choreographer's movements, not the dancer's; the dancer is like an excellent actor speaking the lines of a terrible script.)

Another aspect of dance that is if not unique then at least pronounced is the fact that performance is even more central to dance than to other arts, including other performing arts. A musical score can be evaluated on its own, independently of being performed. Likewise, a dramatic script can be evaluated on its own, independently of being performed. In both cases, the product (that is, the score or the script) can be encountered and considered. Knowledgeable musicians and composers can read a musical score and have a good sense of what it will sound like if performed. They can know just from the score whether there is, say, harmony or appropriate tension "in the music." Likewise, readers can look at a script and critique it without it's ever having been acted out. Indeed, this is common practice for playwrights. Dance is different. Although there are systems of notation that function much like a score or a script, they are much less central as indicators of the artistic product that is likely to result upon performance. The actual dancing by dancers is much more constitutive of the artwork. Actual performing might not be a necessary condition, but it is far more central to dance as art than to other performing arts. In this sense, dance is closer to painting than to theater. One knows what one has only when one has it, and there are far fewer signposts along the way than there are with other performing arts. (Having said that, I will now retract it to a degree. In cases of, say, jazz or impromptu and improvisational performances, it is the actual performing that in large part determines the artwork.)

One aspect of dance that sometimes surprises people is that there are specific identified dances, not in the sense of a type of dance (such as the polka) but individual dances. A famous instance is Martha Graham's *Lamentation*; another is George Balanchine's *Jewels*. That is, there is such a thing as *a dance*, a unique, particular dance, just as there is a unique, particular painting that is *Guernica*.

In the reading below, Francis Sparshott addresses the topic of what the identity of a dance is. What, exactly, is a dance? Earlier in the book we spoke of types and tokens, where a type is a kind of thing (for example, a cat) and a token is a specific instance of that type (for example, Felix the cat). Sparshott notes that we can, and often do, speak of a certain dance as a type and each performance of that dance as a token. This is fine, as far as it goes, he says. However, because there is also a performing of a dance, that is, a performer's interpretation within a given performance, then the type/token account does not quite fully capture the complexity of the relation between a dance and a performance of that dance. A given dance is a complex of meaningful movements and we want to distinguish dance X from dance Y. In addition, the dancer is both a person and also a "character" (much like actors are who they are as persons, but also, in the context of plays, particular characters). For Sparshott, if we ask when two performances are tokens of the same dance type, which seems to be a simple question, the answer is not straightforward because it involves these multiple dimensions of a dancer being a person and a character, as well as of the various relevant artists relating their different intentions, aims, and so on. What makes two performances, or two performings of a performance, the same dance is that there is a set of interrelations among these various factors. As he puts it, a dancer must make Giselle *her* Giselle, while at the same time being true to what was choreographed. In the final analysis, for Sparshott a dance is a bundle of actual possibilities, that is, actual embodied, performed movements with no specifiable set of necessary or sufficient conditions as to exactly which movements, but not without boundaries or limits. A dance is, in a sense, a normative kind; it is a set of instructions for carrying out sets of meaningful movements.

FRANCIS SPARSHOTT, "THE IDENTITY OF A DANCE"*

When are we justified in saying that two performances are performances of "the same" dance? What are the conditions of identity of dances, and why are they what they are? . . .

Dance and Dancer

We can tell the dancer from the dance. The same dancer may dance both Odette and Odile in *Swan Lake*, but she must dance them differently; her audience will be specifically interested in how the one dancer expresses the duality in these linked roles. Another part of the interest lies in seeing how her rendering of the duality differs from other dancers' ways of rendering it.

Things are different when we are watching an improvised dance, or when we see unfamiliar dancers in an unfamiliar repertoire. We can still compare these dancers with other dancers, these dances with other dances; but we can do so only on the basis of a distinction between dancer and dance that we have to make within a single phenomenon, a single observed performance. It is then that we ask Yeats's famous question, how can we tell the dancer from the dance?

To recognize a dance as a dance at all, we must recognize it as an alternative to other possible dances. If we had no sense of what other dances there might be, we could not be recognizing it as a dance rather than something else—"moving around," perhaps. And to identify a dance as a particular dance is to recognize it as inherently repeatable. It is a distinct thing that has been

---

*In *A Measured Pace: Toward a Philosophical Understanding of the Arts of Dance*. Toronto: University of Toronto Press, 1995. Pages 397–408, 419.

done; so it is something that can be done, and therefore could be done again. . . .

To see a dance, I must see it as repeatable by the same person. But people keep changing. If the dance were repeated by the same person, it would be on a different occasion, or later on the same occasion. Between the two occurrences the dancer would have tired, or matured, or both, or would have got warmed up or invigorated. In any case, the dancer would have had the experience of doing the dance one more time and knowing it that much better—or becoming that much more bored with it. The changes might be too small to notice, but they would be real. . . . The dancer is the same, and the dance is the same, but the same dancer will not always do the same dance in the same way.

Dancers are beset by perils and promises of age, fatigue, injury, illness, enthusiasm, inspiration, dejection, and luck; occasions are beset by good and bad audiences, resilient or slippery floors, efficient or inadequate or ill-timed lighting, goodness knows what accidents of costuming; and the choreography of a dance is hedged around with a haze of expedients, emergencies, fallbacks, and options, as well as stylistic alternatives that the necessary variability of human affairs dictates. A choreographer can seldom be sure that the dance will always be danced by the same dancer (injuries cannot always lead to cancellations) and can never be sure just what the conditions of the dancers or the circumstances of the performance will be; whether consciously or not, every choreography must have variability built in. To know what "the same again" will be in a dance, we must have the same sort of sense that the choreographer had of the ideals of repeatability and the limits of variability.

In short, we know the dancer from the dance because we cannot know either dancer or dance without knowing the different but intimately related ways in which each may vary. . . .

The Choreographer's Performance

A choreographer's making of a dance is the performing of a performance in our sense. The dance as composed is a performance with a character that can be isolated for attention and criticized. But what the dancer dances is not necessarily identical with what the choreographer composed. In a sense, it can never be. A work for performance, as Paul Thom explains, is meant to be realized for and beheld by audiences; works differ in the flexibility they admit, choreographers differ in the rigidity of their stipulations; but in any case . . . what the choreographer composes can only be a series of dance movements which, because in principle danceable by many differently equipped dancers (and by dancers each of whom will be in different conditions on different occasions), must leave open options of manner and nuance. As in music, there are three levels of indeterminacy. Some composers are more persnickety than others in what they specify (by way of bowing, dynamics, accent, expression, and so on), but even the most obsessive must leave something to the performer, including the precise interpretation of the attempts to introduce precision. Here are two levels, then: the latitude necessary for the executant to make sense of the composition, and the extra leeway the composers allow or demand by leaving open options that they might not have left open. Things are made more complex, but not fundamentally different, by "aleatoric" practices, where some things are left to the performers' choice or chance; here, too, composers differ in how meticulous their instructions are as to when and how choice and chance are to enter, and here, too, the executants have to decide how to follow these instructions to produce a performance that will make sense—only they can actually *perform*.

There is, however, a third level of indeterminacy. Choreographers and composers are not, as such, producers or impresarios. Their task is to create, to prescribe a work, not to issue commands to performers. It is up to performers and directors to follow their directions or not, and it is a familiar fact that they do not always do so. They depart their script or score from necessity, or for convenience or economy, or for artistic reasons. What is permissible in this regard, or what is even noticeable, varies in very complex ways. It depends on the context of production, and on the wider cultural context that generates specific sorts of expectations about how scores will be used. Nicholas Wolterstorff has taught us to think of works of art (especially in performance arts) as normative kinds; the artist, in accordance with prevailing conventions, lays down what is to count and what is not to count as a performance of the work, leaving the rest indifferent. But many works are so complex that a production can fly in the face of many such prescriptions and still pass muster as a production of the work, and there may or may not be a consensus as to what is beyond the bounds of whatever it may be.

It is so obviously and inevitably true that what the dancers do need not coincide with what the choreographer proposed that in a new dance, where choreographer and regisseur [that is, stage manager or director] are the same, we expect that parts of the choreography will really count only as options, and that if the dance stays in repertoire it is unlikely to stay the same. The attempt to reconstruct the original performance of a work is a very special sort of undertaking, more archeology than art. (Notoriously, when choreographers are enlisted to help in such reconstructions, they often keep trying to change things.) . . .

Gregory Currie argues that a work of art is to be regarded neither as the outcome of a segment of the artist's biography, nor as a self-contained phenomenon, but as the terminus of a heuristic path, the rational process of production whereby the artist evolved a work from the problems faced and the antecedents confronted. A critic's task is to reconstruct that path and thus make the work fully intelligible. That's all very well; but, as we have just seen, in the performing arts the path has no determinate end. There are a multiplicity of contingencies and expedients, heuristic highways and bypaths leading to alternative classes of performance options, any or all of which may remain accessible for future opportunities or emergencies. A choreographed dance is a bundle of such actual possibilities, more or less determinate in scope, more or less loosely tied.

The Dancer's Performance

A dancer who takes on a role in a ballet works within limits imposed by artistic conscience and by the instructions of choreographer or regisseur. Within those limits, a dancer has to work up a way of dancing the part. The part, the role, then assumes the function of *task*, and the dancer's dancing is the performance of this task. But the performance itself is what has to be worked up, and when this is achieved it assumes the function of a secondary task. The dancer dances, again and again, not just Giselle, but *her* Giselle. We can tell her Giselle from another dancer's because of the different stylistic choices she consciously or unconsciously makes. And we can tell her performance on Thursday from her performance on Sunday, possibly by stylistic shifts as her understanding of the role changes, but more probably by whether she is on form, and by more specific variations in the way she looks and moves.

Like other signs, it can be held, a dance as dance is constituted entirely by its relevantly meaningful aspects. It is a complex of meaningful movements. But like all other signs, it can in principle be identically repeated, and exists only as token or tokens, as actual exemplar of its inherently repeatable features. But the actual movements of the dancers' bodies neither constitute nor are constituted by signs or their meaningful aspects; they are what the men and women are actually doing. What the "sign" in question is is a matter for interpretation; that being so, it could be many things at once. We have seen that, on each occasion, a dancer in the role of Giselle is dancing Giselle. From her point of view, though, that is not immediately relevant. What is relevant is that she is dancing *her* Giselle, giving a rendering of the interpretation of the role that she has got up for the current production. But that is not the whole story. On any given occasion, she is crafting that evening's performance, autarchically if not autonomously. The construction that is her Giselle functions, as does the role of Giselle itself, only regulatively: the actual object of her attention and endeavors is the performance she is giving right now—itself, of course, a sign constituted by its meaningful features. There is no mechanical process by which the dance is being produced, however much of it she has made automatic so that she can "dance it in her sleep." She is a thinking person, and the dance is necessarily a product of her thought at the time—necessarily, because at any moment her partners may falter, or some variation in her surroundings may call for instant adjustment. Just as the choreographer's Giselle allows for individual variations, so the dancer's Giselle admits of variations from evening to evening. Such variations do not make each performance what anyone would call a fresh creative act, but they do make it an achievement of craft and artistry, to be appreciated for its own sake and not merely as the trivially successful realization of a design on which the real interest is concentrated. . . .

Performance and Performing

In my artificial use of the terms, performer and performance are correlative. The performer is no more and no less than the agency of the performance as such, and the performance is just what the performer does in the doing of it. There is a third term: the performing of the performance by the performer. . . .

I have distinguished the dancer from the dance. Do I need to add anything about the third term in the relation, the dancer's dancing of the dance? Not necessarily. I began with the dancing, from which dancer and dance are projected as polarities and then identified, respectively, with the personal and product aspects of the existing institution of dance. To distinguish the dancing from the dance would be to differentiate the pattern of energies from its discernable outcome as a pattern of movement. To distinguish the dancer from the dancing would be to differentiate the intender and designer from the act of execution. These theoretical distinctions become real separations only when the artefact or performance has an embodiment that does not coincide with its production. To the extent that a dancer's dancing of her Giselle simply realizes the very same that she realizes whenever she dances it, the separation has some reality. But I have nothing more to say of it here. . . .

The Identity of a Dance

When do we think of a copied, or modified, or disguised, version or similitude of a work of art as actually being that work, and when do we not? I began by using Peirce's vocabulary of "type" and "token" to discuss this issue, saying that a performance is a token of a work of art, and hence is that work, in so far as it can be traced by the appropriate means to the design act originating the work, and in so far as the design is discernable in the performance; we have just seen how this must be modified in discussing the performing arts. Do we need to say anything different when we are talking specifically about dance?

One difference is that not all dance is art. Dance in general . . . tends to exist in the form of named dances that are recognized as scattered particulars within cultures, identified institutionally by various contextual and formal criteria. In such cases the concept of a "design act," activity coalescing in the generation of an aesthetic object, has no bite. We may say that someone must have invented the polka, or that it emerged from a definite consensus in a specific dance-making milieu, but who cares? What makes the polka the polka is the way it is taught and disseminated, the intercommunicative mass of dance practice within which it circulates. It is a historical entity like an epidemic. And since within our culture there is a rough and ready sense in which dancing is dancing, there may be something to be said for treating *Swan Lake*, another named dance, in the same way. What makes *Swan Lake Swan Lake* is the way its unity is recognized within a dancing, dance-making, and dance-going community that understands itself, for practical purposes, fairly well, and which has an extensive but not infinite tolerance for distortion and perversion. . . .

The complexities of the identity conditions of dances are notoriously exemplified by *Swan Lake*. What confronts us is a sort of family resemblance among dances that are linked by a complex set of intentions and references. Petipa and his colleagues (notably, in the second and canonical version, Ivanov) set about composing a ballet to music by Tchaikovsky, who (and whose colleagues and successors) more or less simultaneously set about constructing a score. After a while, a pattern in dance and music became more or less established, but was still subject to unlimited alteration and variation (including . . . the introduction of a sort of flying buttress for the male lead). We end up with a set of strongly diagnostic features: a basic story line, certain key moments and dances for which the ballet is famous, a musical score of which some passages have become cynosures, and a problematic ending. But though these are severally and jointly very strongly diagnostic they are not, strictly, necessary and sufficient conditions of *Swan Lake*'s being performed. Just as important is the informed intention by those putting on the dance to do *that familiar ballet* and to orient themselves by it and not by anything alternative to it. If they do it in a new and different way, still they must be intelligently intending—that is, intending with a dance intelligence, in the light of an artistically informed understanding of what a ballet is—to do that ballet and no other. . . .

Any instance of artistic dance, like the institution of the art of dance itself, is the product of many artistic endeavors, in harmony or in tension. Even if we dismiss some of these are mere personal distortions of the work of art as such, and concentrate on the work itself as sign or as "performance" (in my artificial sense), what confronts us is ambiguous, in at least the three ways we have considered. First, it may be a true, or typical, or a malformed token of a number of types: scenario, choreographic design, danced psychodrama, danced realization of music, dancers' realization of choreographic intent. Second, it is the issue of a complex design act of creations working on each other, a single dynamic realization of all the potentialities involved. And third, it is an episode in the historic evolution of the dance it is, produced in the particular circumstances that have governed its performance and its reception. None of these three can be legitimately denied. Anyone may choose to ignore any of them, but such refusals are not binding on anyone. How could they be?

Despite all that, questions of sameness and difference can often be given quite definitive answers, provided that we spell out the interests involved. Questions of identity continue to be raised, because demands for (and promises of) continuation and change can be explained and justified. Such justifications may well conflict, and are important areas of agreement and disagreement in the fields of human cooperation and interaction. To say that something really is or is not "the same" is to downgrade or delegitimize one set of demands in favor of another, by denying its socially effective existence.

To look for a definitive answer to problems of identity, then, is futile. But to refuse to debate those problems is to deny oneself a familiar and precious tool for exploring the most vital problems in the philosophy of art. ◣

THEATER

Whereas it might have been difficult for you to name a famous and influential "artistic" dancer (that is, a dancer dancing with the intent that the dance be artwork), if you were asked to name a famous and influential playwright, you could probably do so with very little hesitation. There is, of course, Shakespeare. But other names probably come to mind immediately, such as the authors of Greek tragedies (for instance, Sophocles) or more recent playwrights such as Henrik Ibsen, Anton Chekhov, George Bernard Shaw, and even more recent people, such as Bertolt Brecht, Arthur Miller, and Eugene

O'Neill. Quite simply, theater, as an art form, has greater recognition for most of us than dance. For one thing, students are exposed to plays, at least famous scripts, in their classes from an early age. Plays can be and are treated as literary forms and so are studied and encountered independently of any performance, unlike dance. Nevertheless, theater, like dance, is a performing art. Indeed, while we might think of a play, or drama writing, as a literary form, theater is more than a play; it is more than a literary script.

What, then, is theater? It has been defined, or characterized, in various ways. It has been called "enacted literature," in which the emphasis is on the script; "performed narrative," in which the emphasis is on the acted performance; and "mimetic enactment of events within a sign system," in which the emphasis is on the stage, that is, the fact that theater is situated in a locale (usually a literal stage). As with dance and other performing arts, there are a multitude of artists (and others) involved. In theater this can include playwrights, actors, directors, stage managers, casting directors, set designers, light and sound directors, costume directors, composers and lyricists (if music is involved), even producers and theater owners. The sorts of artistic and aesthetic complexities mentioned earlier in connection with dance hold with theater as well because of the multitude of relevant artists. (For instance, there are many, sometimes conflicting, intentions or efforts at expression or representation.) Just as dance involves coordinating the interests and aims of dancers and choreographers (and others), so, too, theater has similar complexity. There are roles to fill and there are rules to follow (for example, staying true to the script), but there is no set of necessary or sufficient conditions that determine what counts as what must be done. Directors can and do drop and add lines from the playwright's script; actors can and do interpret the playwright's words and director's instructions in various ways. Besides the question of what, exactly, a play is, there are questions about what, exactly, a role is or what acting is or even what a stage is. Actors are pretending, of course, but they are not merely pretending; they are not lying to the audience by portraying a character or role!

In the following reading, David Saltz addresses theater from the perspective of what is called speech act theory. Speech act theory is a view about language that emphasizes how language is used and understood. The background is that there are various types of meaning accompanying language. There is syntactical meaning, semantic meaning, and pragmatic meaning. For example, the sentence, "It's cold in here," has syntactical (or grammatical) meaning. It has an appropriate grammatical structure in English, as opposed to the sentence, "Cold here it's in," which in English is gibberish. In addition, "It's cold in here" has semantic meaning; that is, the words themselves and the way they are combined result in a meaningful English sentence, as opposed to "Colorless green ideas sleep furiously." This last sentence is syntactically meaningful (that is, there is a subject, *ideas*, that is modified by two adjectives, and a verb, *sleep*, that is modified by an adverb; grammatically the words fit together appropriately). However, the sentence makes no sense; ideas do not have color, and if they did, they could not be both colorless and green at the same time. So syntactic meaning and semantic meaning are two different things. Furthermore, "It's cold in here" has pragmatic meaning; that is, how it is used and by whom it is used in a given context will determine a given meaning. For instance, in uttering that sentence you might be telling someone else to shut the window (without actually saying the words *Shut the window*), or you might be saying that you cannot get your work done in that room because it is too cold for you to concentrate or function. The pragmatic meaning of a sentence, then, can differ from the literal, semantic meaning. In fact, it could be the opposite of the semantic meaning, as in cases of sarcasm. (If you say, "That's a nice shirt" and intend it sarcastically, the semantic meaning of the words is that it *is* a nice shirt, but your pragmatic meaning is that it is *not* a nice shirt.)

Speech act theory focuses on the pragmatics of language, on how people use language in contexts. Of particular importance is the notion of "performatives." There are some expressions and uses of language whose uttering constitutes a performance of a speech act. That is, sometimes when we speak we perform an action above and beyond the act of speaking. For instance, if I say, "I promise to pay you back on Monday," I have done something more than merely utter some words; I have made a promise (that is, performed an action, namely, promising). By saying those words (assuming they were said sincerely and in a given context), I have made a promise; that's what it is to make a promise! Likewise, if I say, "I suggest you read Chapter 1 very closely," then I have done something (namely, performed the speech act of suggesting) beyond merely uttering words. In the context of speech acts, philosophers speak of locutionary meaning (that is, the semantic meaning of the words), illocutionary meaning (that is, the speaker's intent), and perlocutionary meaning (that is, the effect generated or the meaning received by the hearer). Sometimes the locutionary, illocutionary, and perlocutionary meanings coincide, but sometimes they do not. You can easily think of a time when you said something and you intended it one way, but the person you spoke to took it very differently. You intended to be helpful, but the person you spoke to was insulted or hurt. That is the difference between illocutionary meaning and perlocutionary meaning!

Now, how speech act theory relates to theater is that normally we take actors playing roles not to be committing speech acts. For instance, if Hamlet (the character in the play) says that he promises to do something, we do not think that the actor on stage playing Hamlet has made that promise. If, in the context of a play, a character says to another character, "I promise to pay you back on Monday," then the following Monday we do not assume that the first actor needs to pay the second actor anything. After all, the actor was only acting! However, in the reading below, Saltz argues that things are not so obvious. As he puts it: "The question is: to what extent can the actions that we attribute to a character also be actions that actors are really committing on stage?" Obviously, words are one form of a meaningful unit, but so are actions. (We can either say "hello" to people when greeting them or we can wave; both are meaningful locutions.) Saltz notes that, of course, when a character on stage stabs himself, we do not think that the actor really stabs himself; we think that it is the character who stabs himself and that the actor merely pretends to do so. But, says Saltz, things are more complex than they appear to be on the surface, especially with illocutionary actions in the context of theater. This issue is crucial, as this is a feature that is unique to theater (or fairly unique, perhaps shared with film) among the arts. Like some other arts, theater is performance, and like some other arts, theater is narrative (that is, there is a story being told), but in the case of theater, it is told via role playing by actors who are people beyond the characters in the roles. At the same time, the character acts only because the actor acts; Hamlet raises his arm only because there is an actor playing Hamlet who raises his arm. Illocutionary action, then, is a central aspect of theater, and understanding theatrical illocutionary action is crucial.

Here, then, is what Saltz says:

DAVID Z. SALTZ, "HOW TO DO THINGS ON STAGE"*

Action in the Theater

Many actors, acting instructors, and directors denounce pretense and imitation on the stage. Actors should "live" their parts, "truthfully" performing the

*Journal of Aesthetics and Art Criticism 49 (1991): 31–45.

character's actions. For example, Constantin Stanislavski asserts that to act well is "to think, strive, feel and act in unison with your role." . . .

Many other writers, and practitioners, such as Diderot and Brecht, explicitly reject this ideal, insisting that actors should maintain a cool distance from their actions in the play. I am interested here in determining the extent to which this controversy rests on a real difference. Can an actor be doing anything *but* "imitate" a character? Are the calls for actors *really* to perform their characters' actions coherent? I will try to determine how an actor might possibly realize such a goal, and at what point it becomes a logical impossibility. To do this, I need a set of criteria against which to measure actions on stage. I will employ, as a starting point, the criteria provided by the theory of speech acts developed by Austin and Searle. . . .

It is essential to make explicit the claim I am evaluating. The question is: to what extent can the actions that we attribute to a character also be actions that actors are really committing on stage? The potential to mix levels of description is great. As Searle has observed, there is no contradiction inherent in making real and true assertions about fictional events. The ability to make such assertions says nothing about the ontology of the events described. To assert that Hamlet killed Polonius in Shakespeare's play does not commit me *one way or the other* to a claim about an historical Hamlet or Polonius. Similarly, it does not commit me to a claim about the actor playing Hamlet. Such assertions are about the fictional events represented, and not the medium through which the fiction is communicated. I can make the assertion about Hamlet based on the written text, or a plot synopsis, or a stage performance. The assertion that the actor is committing the character's actions, however, is not a statement about the fiction, but about the medium. Hence, the question I am considering is not one about fictional discourse, but one specifically about theatrical performance.

Insofar as theatrical performances convey fictional stories, they allow spectators to make assertions about fiction just as printed plays do. But . . . a theatrical performance differs from a printed text in at least one concrete way. During a performance, there are living actors on stage, and we can make claims about actions they are committing in a way that we cannot about printed texts. When a book quotes a character saying the words "sit down," it does not actually say those words. But an actor does. The book cannot literally sit down when it represents a character sitting down. But an actor can. So, for a large class of actions, to say that an actor commits the character's actions makes sense, while saying the book commits those actions does not.

In some cases, however, a true description of what the actor is doing will deviate from a description of what the character is represented as doing. For example, when a character is supposed to drink wine, an actor may pick up an empty glass and drink nothing at all. An actress playing Juliet is not expected to kill herself when her character commits suicide. Even in these cases, there is no problem asserting that the actor is the agent of real actions, since it seems reasonable to consider "a man . . . the agent of an act if what he does can be described under an aspect that makes it intentional." So the actress playing Juliet is intentionally pressing a rubber dagger to her chest in order to represent the character stabbing herself with a real knife. . . .

Actors commit real actions, and often those actions can be just the actions they seem to be committing. When the character raises an arm, the actor really raises an arm; and when the character, in raising that arm, is reaching for a glass, the actor really reaches for a glass. Occasionally, an actor may really commit an action only under some of its descriptions. But only in the case of actions inappropriate or impractical on stage, such as murdering, must the actor resort to committing an action that is radically different from the character's. Does this picture represent what Stanislavski is proposing when he asks actors to act truthfully on stage? If so, what is all the fuss about? After all, an actor will "live" the part much to the extent with or without years of training in a special method. What is the difficulty, then, with the controversial project of "acting in unison" with a character?

Illocutionary Actions in the Theater

There is an enormous class of actions that this picture leaves out. If an actor in priest's robes says to a pair of actors, one in a wedding gown and the other in a tuxedo, "I hereby pronounce you man and wife," the actor commits the act of saying the words, just as a real priest would. But the priest, in committing the act of saying the words, would also be committing a speech act, an act with conventional force that would result in marrying the couple he addressed. Clearly, the actor in priest's robes would not really have committed this act, and the two actors would not be married when the play ended. To use the terminology of speech act theory, the actor's act would lack the illocutionary force of the priest's act.

Part of the reason that the actor playing a priest cannot really perform a marriage ceremony may be precisely that he is not a priest. Performing a marriage is one of those acts that can be performed successfully (or felicitously, to use Austin's phrase) only by someone with authority granted by highly formalized institutional conventions. If the actor's proclamation of marriage lacked force *only* because the actor was not a priest, marriage would simply be one of those actions, like Juliet's suicide, that actors cannot carry out in practice, but could in principle. A director might, after all, cast a priest to play a priest. But the problem here runs much deeper. Even if the actor were a real priest, the speech act would not result in a real marriage if it were performed in the course of a play.

This problem extends to all illocutionary acts, to all actions people commit in making utterances, such as ordering, swearing, complimenting, threatening. If an actor makes a promise on stage, we do not hold the actor to the promise once the play ends. If one actor insults another in the course of a play, the second actor would be unlikely to hold it against the first the next morning. As Searle has observed, within a fictional context such as a play, the performance of speech acts invokes "horizontal conventions that suspend the normal illocutionary commitments of the utterances." This suspension of normal illocutionary commitments extends to all theatrical performances, from the most alienated Brechtian performance to the most impassioned Method production. The impact of this suspension of illocutionary commitments is so complete that it prevents an actor from successfully performing even the simplest speech act on stage. If an actor states "My hair is blond," we cannot say that he has made a true assertion even if his hair is in fact blond. If later, during the curtain call, the actor removes a blond wig revealing his jet black hair, we would not accuse the actor of having lied. The point of a real assertion is to commit the speaker to the truth of a proposition, and we typically do not hold actors responsible for the truth of any assertions they make in the course of a play. The problem with illocutionary acts is not limited just to verbal utterances, but to any action with conventional force, such as when an actor nods assent, waves a greeting, or signals an invitation to sit down. In none of these cases is the actor personally committed to the action he performs as he would be offstage. The apparent inability to perform real illocutionary actions on stage affects virtually all of the actor's performance, not just special instances such as Juliet's suicide. . . .

The Representation Intention

The possibility that the actor is *always* acting as a servant of the playwright or director, even when acting "in character," might sound promising as a general principle, but it quickly falls apart under analysis. One of the principle facts that has made it difficult to ascribe illocutionary force to the actor in the first place is that we do not hold the actor responsible for illocutionary commitments, such as promises made, once the play is over. We have seen that this difficulty might be overcome if we can hold the actor responsible for those actions for the duration of the play, just as we hold employees to promises made on behalf of their company as long as they are on the job. But to suggest that the actor is acting on behalf of the director or playwright sets us back considerably, since neither of them is committed to the character's promises even for the duration of the play. Insofar as actors act from borrowed intentions that allow them sincerely to commit the illocutionary action of their characters, those intentions are *not* part of the personal motivational sets of the playwright or director. They belong to, and indeed play a key role in defining, the *character* that the actor plays. However, the actor cannot literally act on behalf of the character the way an employee can act on behalf of a boss. Since characters exist only in fiction, to take the proposal that characters authorize actors' actions literally, one would have to defend the troublesome proposition that fictional entities can take responsibility for real actions. A man would have little chance of getting off the hook for dumping toxic waste by explaining that he was acting under the directives of a fictional employer.

A closer analogy to the actor's situation is that of a player in a game. Game players, like employees, adopt a set of borrowed intentions that govern their behavior only as long as they are in a specific role. The basketball player has no need to ponder deeper motives, and the chess player need bear no particular grudge against his opponent's King. In a game, however, the motivational set adopted does not belong to another agent, even an institutional one, such as a company. Chess players do not play on behalf of anyone else, or even of the "game of chess." They simply play according to the rules; the motivation is built into the game. Hence, borrowed intentions that derive from another agent or an institution—let us call them "authorized intentions"—should be distinguished from those that derive from the rules of a game, which I will call "game intentions."

What I am proposing is that actors can perform real and sincere actions on stage by adopting game intentions that arise if they accept as part of the convention of performance a rule that actors work to achieve the conditions of satisfaction implied by the character's actions. . . . By defining the conventions of performance in this way, the actor will always have a reason to commit any action in any play, just as a basketball player has reason to get the ball into the assigned basket, or a chess player has reason to try to capture the other player's King. . . .

Belief on Stage

Game intentions might provide a way for actors to commit sincere actions when the Intentional state the action implies has what Searle calls a world-to-word direction of fit, such as promises and commands. In these cases, the condition of satisfaction implied by the action is that the world change in some way. For the actor's Intentional state to have the same conditions of satisfaction that the action has, all we need is to provide a reason for the actor to sincerely try to bring about that change. Actions with word-to-world direction of fit, such as assertions and predictions, pose a more difficult problem, since the Intentional state they imply is belief, and an actor's belief cannot be dictated by the rules of a game. The mistake here, however, may be to assume that people, on stage or off, can act felicitously and sincerely only on the basis of *their own* beliefs.

Just as agents can perform illocutionary acts with world-to-word direction of fit on the basis of borrowed intentions, perhaps they can perform illocutionary acts with word-to-world direction of fit on the basis of borrowed beliefs. Suppose I am hired to supply weather forecasts over the phone. My job is to ask callers what city they are calling from, to look up the forecast on a list in front of me, and to give the caller that forecast. The forecast I look up might even be in a highly abbreviated form, so that I do not just read it verbatim, but explain it in my own words, and answer any question the caller asks for clarification. Now, being an amateur meteorologist myself, I have my own opinions about weather which are often at odds with those of my company. Nevertheless, my job is to deliver the *company's* forecasts. The desire to express my own belief about the weather does not constitute my reasons for making the assertion; the requirements of my job supply sufficient reason. A company's public relations officer and a President's press secretary are in analogous situations; they are hired to make the best case they can for the positions held by the people or institutions they represent. No deceit is involved here, unless the *institution* is misleading the public as to *its* beliefs. The listeners are interacting with the representatives in order to ascertain the views of the institutions they represent, and not to discover the personal opinions of the press secretary or the operator who answers the phone. People in such roles who do cave in to an irrepressible desire to represent their own beliefs are dropping out of their roles. If they do not make it clear that they have stepped out of their official role, they are misrepresenting their institution. In such cases, even if they make an assertion they believe to be true, the *assertion itself* will be insincere.

An actor's personal beliefs might play a similar role in a theatrical performance. An actor, if asked, would unhesitatingly agree that most of the character's assertions are literally false. But this concession is beside the point, since actors' reasons for acting on the character's beliefs have nothing to do with the actors' belief in them in the first place. Assertions an actor makes do not refer directly to the world as the actor perceives it, but to the beliefs and desires set forth for the character. In this sense, both an actor's and a press secretary's assertions are intentional. Nevertheless, like the press secretary, actors may make real assertions about the positions they represent, and may be *committed*, while functioning within those roles, to defending those assertions. The audience does not hold actors offstage to the assertions they make on stage precisely because they understand what those assertions refer to. There is no insincerity here; the nature of the game is up front and understood by all. . . .

The Game Model of Dramatic Action

I am positing a game model of dramatic action, wherein actors do not merely imitate actions as they would be performed offstage, but really do commit illocutionary acts within the theatrical context. These acts function just like illocutionary acts in any other context, with one exception: their conditions of satisfaction are determined with respect to borrowed Intentionality, specifically game Intentionality. This Intentionality derives from the actor's acceptance of any illocutionary commitments implied by the character's actions, and, in the case of actions with world-to-word direction of fit, the actor's commitment to trying to achieve the conditions of satisfaction of the actions. Because they act from game Intentionality, actors remain committed by their stage actions—promises, commands, assertions—only while they are acting within their stage roles, just as a Monopoly player is not committed to buying Boardwalk after the game ends. . . .

Conclusion

I began by asking to what extent it is possible for actors to act "in unison" with their characters. I have suggested that actors constantly commit characters' actions at the brute force level: they stand, sit, etc. Sometimes—perhaps usually—actors commit actions *only* at this level; in other words, as Searle has proposed, they commit brute force actions, and in so doing pretend to commit illocutionary actions. I have proposed that it is in fact *possible* for actors to commit their characters' actions even at the illocutionary level by treating the conventions of the play like rules in a game. . . .

A game model of acting suggests that the audience's position within the theater event might be more akin to that of spectators at a sporting event than to
that of readers of a printed text. Spectators might not always, or even usually, try
to extract meaning from performances, or regard performances as representations
of some latent content; performances may not function as a medium through
which to convey a message, or even to tell a story. Rather, spectators might become engaged by a rich interplay of actions really taking place before them.
The "story" in this case would not be something communicated, but something
that happens; or better, it is a summary that the spectator might make of the
events on the stage once the play has ended. Hence efforts to hunt for symbols,
or to analyze narrative structure, might not get to the meat of a theatrical event:
the active, and specifically illocutionary, forces that are generated moment to
moment during the performance event. A play like Pinter's *Betrayal* is virtually
indistinguishable from an average soap opera when reduced to its plot, and yet
when performed yields a remarkable density of illocutionary significance, and
assumes entirely different force in the hand of different actors.

Theatrical texts written to be performed within game conventions such as
those described here can best be evaluated in terms of their performative potential. Some plays, like some games, have rules that are more likely to put
their players in interesting situations than others, and those are the ones worth
playing and watching. Moreover, the rules of tennis will give rise to a very different experience than those of chess. Still, good actors can be exciting to
watch for the same reasons good tennis players are: they push their game
to its limits. ◣

MUSIC

The Second Amendment of the US Constitution speaks of "the right of the
people to keep and bear arms." People have disagreed for more than two centuries over what, exactly, that phrase means. We noted earlier in this chapter
that speech act theory points out various types of meaning: locutionary (or
literal) meaning, illocutionary (or intended) meaning, and perlocutionary
(or effected) meaning. By asking what this phrase means, we are asking about
all three of these types of meaning. What, exactly, do the words literally
mean? Does the word *arms* refer to, say, anything that might be used as a
weapon (for example, a brick)? Does "keep and bear" include selling arms or
only possessing them? Perhaps more importantly, what is the intent of that

phrase? What were the writers of that phrase intending or trying to accomplish by using those words (and not other words)? Also, what does that phrase mean for us today? They were written more than 200 years ago; why would we be bound by them today? Given that today there are arms, such as nuclear weapons, that were unimaginable when those words were written, how are we to understand the phrase today? One of the basic approaches to understanding it is to ask about what is considered original intent. If there is any question about interpreting the phrase, we need to find out what the writers intended at the time. We should not, say supporters of the original intent view, interpret the phrase beyond or in any other way than whatever was the intent of those who wrote it. (According to this view, if we no longer like what was intended, then we can go through a process of changing the law; but it is inappropriate to reinterpret what was intended.)

This issue of original intent is an issue that resonates with concerns about music (and any performing art). As aesthetician Peter Kivy says, musical performers have a sort of contract with musical composers. The contract is that the performer should perform the work that was composed. In effect, the performer should go by the rule of original intent. What did the composer intend (or mean) by a certain musical phrase or melody or meter, for example? Granted, there will be some variation in exactly how different performers will interpret these, but their goal should be (that is, the perlocutionary meaning should for them be) to be as true to the original intent as is feasible. However, as Kivy points out, even if performers agree that their obligation is to perform the works that were composed, this is not necessarily the same thing as saying that their obligation is to perform the same notes (or phrases or melodies) that were composed. After all, for example, instruments might have changed since the original composition was scored, or concert halls might have changed (so the resulting sound will be different from what the composer would have imagined).

Another analogy, besides that of legal interpretation of original intent, is that of literary translation. The semiotician Umberto Eco has noted that if someone translated the English idiom, "You're pulling my leg" into Italian, it would miss the mark. One could transliterate it word for word, but the result would be strange to Italian speakers. Rather, it should be translated more closely to pulling one's nose. With respect to music (and, again, other performing arts), a similar negotiation must occur between the musical performer and the musical composition. Just as there is a difference between literal words (in a transliteration) and communicated meaning (in a translation), so there is a difference between physical sound and musical sound.

This issue of what it is for a performer to (correctly) perform a work points to a number of aesthetic and conceptual issues connected with music. One immediate issue is the question of what, exactly, a musical performance is? Is it to "make real" an instance of a musical score or composition? Certainly, in one sense it is; a musical performance is not just a musical performance; rather, it is a musical performance *of something*. It is not just sounds or notes; it is a performance of some composition. Even in cases of improvisation, for instance in jazz, it is not a simple random collection of sounds. There is still a performance (not only a performing). But asking what a musical performance is also raises the question of what music is. When a musical performer is performing a performance, what is it that is being performed? There is no single answer to this question, and, indeed, there have been numerous proposed answers. There are, of course, multiple components of music; it involves sounds but also silences, both of which are structured. There is tempo, melody, harmony, pitch, duration, and many other components of these structured sounds and silences. (Obviously, not all structured sounds are music, and some have argued that some music can omit these various components.)

With respect to aesthetics, what is it about music that is unique or particularly salient? Music shares many aspects with other arts, of course. We have already mentioned the intention of the artist. In addition, via music there is imitation or representation. For instance, part of Hendrix's performance of "The Star Spangled Banner" included using qualities of an electric guitar to imitate or represent sounds of "rockets' red glare" and "bombs bursting in air." Likewise, in Edvard Grieg's *Peer Gynt Suite*, the feel of the beginning of a new day is captured in his song "Morning." With music, unlike in any visual art, imitation and representation must be accomplished via sound. Besides issues of imitation or representation, there are the other standard issues from the perspective of the audience, such as how one ought to interpret and evaluate music. These clearly overlap with issues from the perspective of the artwork itself. For instance, how we ought to evaluate music (whether a musical composition or a musical performance) will depend in part on what we take the musical work to be. Some musical forms are highly structured, so if a given musical work fails to have that structure, it is poor as an instance of that form. Also, its evaluation will depend upon who is evaluating it. Someone who is sophisticated with respect to, say, time signatures might well appreciate (and evaluate) certain compositions (and performances) by Dave Brubeck more than would someone else who knows nothing about time signatures.

One topic that is frequently raised in connection with music especially is the expressiveness of music. How is it that "merely" through structured sounds music can either be so expressive or express so well? I say "be so expressive or express so well" because aestheticians have often distinguished these two. The difference is largely between how much feeling related to music is in the music itself and how much is in us as we encounter the music. How much of the feeling related to music do we "read out of" the music or do we "read into" the music? Sometimes this is stated as "what is expressed in or by the music" versus "the expressiveness of the music." One view is that certain structured sounds, say, make us sad; the music itself is not sad (after all, it is only a collection of sounds), but it arouses the feeling of sadness in us. Perhaps psychologists might be able to explain why this phenomenon occurs, but under this view, the feeling is not in the music itself but, rather, is aroused in us. Another view is that the feeling indeed is in the music. The reason we feel sad upon hearing it, according to this view, is because it is sad. If we heard other structured sound (that is not sad), we would not feel sad. Perhaps psychologists might be able to explain what it is about certain collections of sound that makes them sad, but nonetheless, those collections of sounds are sad.

There are, of course, many other aesthetic topics and issues related to music, some of which we have mentioned above. Others include the functions of music and the social, cultural meaning(s) attached to music. These apply, again, to music in the sense of compositions, and also to music in the sense of performances. Hendrix's performance of "The Star Spangled Banner" had particular meaning to some people because of when and where and to whom he gave the performance, as well as having significance to others in different contexts. (To a participant at Woodstock it probably meant one thing; to critics of the counterculture of the time it probably meant something very different; to a musician decades later listening to it and knowing nothing about Woodstock, it probably means yet something very different.) Here, however, we will end with Kivy's remarks about the significance of a musical performance vis-à-vis its relation to a musical composition and how to best understand that relationship.

▌ PETER KIVY, "THE OTHER AUTHENTICITY"*

The logical and ontological characteristics of music, as I see it, if it is to be construed as a performing art, are as follows:

1. There has to be some viable distinction between the performance (object) and what it is a performance of: that is to say, there must be a performance and some at least vaguely autonomous, identifiable entity that "survives" performances and endures through time—what has, since the modern era, been called the "work."
2. The performance (object) is a work of art itself, an arrangement or version of the musical work that has been performed, and, as such, a subject of the kind of evaluation and aesthetic satisfaction that artworks support and provide.
3. The performer is an artist, somewhat akin to a composer or, better, "arranger" of musical works.

Now the distinction between performance and work, item 1 on the list, is a much-disputed one, for both ontological and (more recently) historical reasons. And although I insist that it must be in place if music is properly to be thought of, as it has been, as a performing art, I want to keep that distinction informal enough so that I will not run afoul of either metaphysical or historical scruples. . . .

[There] is no need, I think, to impose upon pre-nineteenth-century music a strict concept of *the work* that is completely anachronistic. There is no doubt that we can establish *the text* of Brahms's First Symphony, for example, in a way that we cannot of even such relatively recent works as a Handel opera, let alone music from the earliest periods of musical notation. Handel was a working "theater man" and his operas in a continual state of flux. What *the* work is, as determined by establishing *the* text, might be an impossible question to answer not just in practice but in logic as well. And where a notation does not indicate determinate pitch or rhythm, the notion of work and text becomes even more obviously problematic and inappropriate. . . .

----

*In *Authenticities: Philosophical Reflections on Musical Performance*. Ithaca, NY: Cornell University Press, 1995. Pages 261–263, 270–273, 277–281.

Nevertheless, we can, I think, settle for a weak notion of text and work that possesses enough of the logic of these concepts to allow a performance/work distinction for at least as much of the music of the Western tradition as will ever be accessible to us as listeners. For we obviously cannot realize in sound any music that has not been notated at all. And where there is a notation *determinate enough* for *us* to derive therefrom a believable, viable sound experience, there is, in virtue of that, both a performance and a "what" that has been performed.

There is another way, perhaps, of making this clear. The Western musical tradition has, as far back as our performable music goes, placed a high value on "improvisation" as a musical attainment of the composer-performer. As opposed to a tradition in which there is no notation and *all* performance is "improvisation," the Western musical tradition *requires* for improvisation the standard case of performance from notation as a foil. The value of and satisfaction in musical improvisation, in the Western musical tradition, is derived in large measure from the knowledge that what is being done is being done neither from notation nor from memory of a notated, previously existing work but spontaneously. That is why the crowning glory of the improvisational art, for a long time, was the improvisation of fugue and other "strict" contrapuntal forms. For it is just those intellectually demanding forms that require the most premeditation, the most revising and reworking: they are the least spontaneous. And so to be able to produce them on the spot, on demand, spontaneously is the feat of improvisation most to be wondered at.

The point I am making is that *improvisation*, which flourished in the Western art music tradition most resplendently well *before* the development of the ironbound "work" concept in the nineteenth century, was a species of improvisation that required for its enjoyment the concept of a preplanned, preformed, and enduring kind of music as the standard against which it could be measured. (That Bach or Mozart could improvise a fugue as complicated as one that would *ordinarily* require weeks of laborious "working out" was what made the feat almost magical.) And although that concept may fall short of the ontologically firm "opus," it possesses enough of the work/performance logic to sustain my argument.

It is not, indeed, the work/performance distinction, however, that is uppermost in my mind here. Of far more importance to the argument are items 2 and 3 in the list: the performance as artwork and the performer as artist. . . .

[In] establishing certain performance practices as "historically authentic"—for example, playing the dissonant appoggiatura as half the value of the adjoining note, or playing violins without vibrato—and adopting them as, therefore, re-quired rather than optional, one is for all intents and purposes extending the concept of the musical "text" to include those things. Furthermore, I am arguing that if one were to carry this aesthetic of performance to its ultimate conclusion, performance would essentially collapse into "text"; in other words, the gap between performance and "text," in which the "art" of performance is to take place in the form of personal authenticity, is closed, and the concept of performance, at least as we know it, vanishes. Let me dilate on this.

It should be perfectly clear that in practice the gap between "text" and performance can never be completely closed. For no matter how much historical knowledge we gain of "period" sound or the performing wishes and intentions of composers, our knowledge will never be complete (which is simply a special case of the general precept that no knowledge will ever be complete). Thus the performer who adopts as his or her goal the "historically authentic performance," in either the sense of authenticity of sound or that of authenticity of intention, or both, will always have "space" in which to make performing decisions that are "free," not determined by the "text."

What I have argued [elsewhere] and want to reemphasize, is that there is a deep matter of principle here, apart from the facts of actual practice, important for us to recognize and consider. The "logic" of music as a performing art, if I may so call it, is a logic in which the gap between "text" and performance is not merely a necessary evil but at the same time a *desired*, *intended* and logically *required* ontological fact. It is in that gap that the work of art is produced that we call the "performance," and that I have likened to an "arrangement" of the work. It is in this gap that personal authenticity can either be or not be.

The quest for the historically authentic performance is a quest for closure—for absolute control of sound production, whether or not that can, in practice, ever be achieved. And the "gap" between "text" and production—I purposely refrain from calling it "performance"—under this discipline is on an entirely different "logical" or "ontological" nature from that of the gap between "text" and "performance" properly so-called. It is a gap to be closed, not to be cherished: it is a defect in the sound-production "machinery."

Imagine a print maker who has a press with mechanical troubles. Each time it makes an impression, it produces a print with a perceivable difference from its other impressions. The prints are all different from one another in some grossly perceivable respect. But the print maker does not value these differences. On the contrary, she bends every effort to make her press produce a uniform impression. Her "art" lies elsewhere. It is just such a "gap" between her plate and her prints that exists between "text" and sound production in the historically authentic performance. Only the gap is caused not by mechanical malfunction but by incompleteness of knowledge: "knowledge malfunction," if you will. The "logic" of the gap is identical. The historically authentic performer and his musicological support team have as their goal the amplification of knowledge of authorial intentions or period sound or both to the end of determining, more and more fully, the production of musical sound as a matter of "textual authority," not artistic choice. As the print maker seeks to exorcise the gremlins from her machine, so the historical performer et alii seek to exorcise the gremlins from theirs; but their machine is far more complex, and its infections more evasive, their complete elimination of course for all practical purposes impossible. But the "logic" is the same: the historically authentic performance is to its "text" as print to plate, *not* as performance to work, in the traditional sense of the performing arts. . . .

I would like to emphasize as strongly as I can that, although I *do* think it an aesthetically undesirable goal to collapse performance into text and essentially phase out performance as an independent artwork, I do *not* by any means think it is an *absurd* or *obviously* undesirable goal. Behind it is a very deep, understandable, and believable aesthetic ideology that is not just a pushover.

The ideology I have in mind might well be described as "composer worship," and it has its roots, it is obvious enough, in the nineteenth-century cult of genius. The status of the composer has risen steadily since the beginning of the eighteenth century, from artisan to artist; and the enshrinement of music by Schopenhauer and others as the romantic art above all the rest has tended to surround the composer with an aura of infallibility, symbolized in the nineteenth century by the stormy visage of "Beethoven the Creator," whose authority one questions at peril. I shall return to this point momentarily; but first let us get a general idea of what the defense of traditional performance is going to look like.

It seems clear enough that as the music of our historical past has traditionally been performed—if, that is, my analysis is right—we are in possession, always, of *two* artworks: the work of music, and, given an outstanding or high-quality performance, the performance (product) itself. Under the new dispensation, the goal, anyway, if never the fait accompli, is to have but *one* artwork, the sound production having been submerged into the text. So simple arithmetic says that the historically authentic performance has aesthetically shortchanged us by one-half. We used to have two works of art when we heard the "Goldberg" Variations, and now we have only one.

This *is*, I have no doubt, the correct way to defend personal authenticity in performance; but it is far too simplistic as it stands. For simple addition of art-works will yield the obviously absurd result that I would be aesthetically wise to trade Rembrandt's *Polish Rider* for two Utrillo watercolors. It is this vulnera-bility of the two-works defense that the historical performance advocate would undoubtedly exploit; and it is here that the ideology of the composer's hege-mony would make its influence felt.

If it is to be shown that the program of historical performance, which, I have argued, in effect eliminates performance as a separate artwork in its own right, is justified in this elimination, then its advocates must convince us that the art-work left in its place, the "text" that completely determines sound production, is a far greater aesthetic object than the two artworks together, the musical work and the performance work, of traditional practice. He must convince us that the collapsing of performance into text will produce the *Polish Rider*, and tradi-tional practice two Utrillos—that, in spirit, is the claim.

This claim has its basis, I suggest, in the ideology of the composer's infallibil-ity or, perhaps, the "cult" of the composer as "superhuman," a "supermusician." In any event, not only the writing of the composer's performing intentions into the "text" but the writing of historically authentic period sound into the "text" as well is, both directly in the former case and indirectly in the latter, an attempt to put *all* parameters of sound production under the composer's discipline (un-der the assumption that historically authentic period sound is what the com-poser literally "had in mind"). There can be only *one* artist, or the work is spoiled. Here even *two* is a crowd.

What answer might the defender of music as a performing art bring against this powerful and proliferating ideology? It would be relevant, to begin with, to point out that the charge of being overly simplistic goes both ways. It is not merely that simple "work addition" is implausible, that two paintings are not nec-essarily a greater aesthetic quantity than one. It is not the case, either, that there being *two different works* rather than one is irrelevant—not the case that "aes-thetic value" is a negotiable, uniform, common denominator. To lose the *Polish Rider* is to lose something of immeasurably greater aesthetic value than any painting by Utrillo. But to lose a painting of Utrillo's is not merely to lose some-thing of less artistic value than the *Polish Rider*; it is to lose something uniquely different from the *Polish Rider* in ways that we value for their own sake. It is to lose a style.

Thus, even if it were the case that the collapse of performance into text would produce a single work greater by far than either of the two works of traditional practice, the musical work and the performance work, and even if these two works were to the other work as Utrillos to the *Polish Rider*, we *still* would have to consider the loss of the performance work not merely as the loss of some basic "aesthetic quantity" but as the loss of a *kind* of aesthetic quantity that performance uniquely gives. Ecologists mourn the disappearance not merely of individuals but, with far greater intensity, the disappearance of *species*. To lose performance to work, no matter what measure of value of the single performanceless work might be compared with the work-performance combination of our historic tradition, is to lose a *species* of artwork, not merely a collection of individual artworks. It is to lose a whole greater than the sum of its parts.

This, by the way, is not to go to the opposite extreme and claim that the collapse of performance into text, through the archeological reconstruction of period performance, should itself be rejected outright in favor of personally authentic performance. To the contrary, what the preceding argument sanctions is the maintaining of *both*. For some of the same considerations that lead to resisting the loss of one *kind* of artwork, namely the musical performance, also lead to resisting the loss of another *kind*, namely the single artwork that is the result of collapsing performance into text in the form of historically authentic performance. This is a new kind of artwork, essentially discovered, or created, if you prefer, by historical musicology in our own times. It has turned out to be of great interest to musical listeners. And although we want to prevent, if we can, its driving into extinction the other authenticity in the interest of species variety, we likewise want it to survive itself in the interest of that selfsame variety. Wouldn't the ecologist just love to have *both* mammals and dinosaurs?

There is, incidentally, another way of looking at the historical "performance" that also imparts to it independent aesthetic value while still denying it the status of artwork. For as Bach's performance (product) of an organ fugue was a performance work of art, so a successful "reconstruction" of it, in the form of a historically accurate "performance," is a "reproduction" of a performance work of art, as my color slide is a reproduction of the *Mona Lisa*. And, it is generally agreed, reproductions possess at least some of the aesthetic values, to at least some degree, of the originals, which is why it is better to have a color slide of the *Mona Lisa* than no *Mona Lisa* at all. So again, in the interest of aesthetic variety, historically authentic performance is to be valued along with personally authentic performance: not instead of the latter, or the latter instead of the former.

But, furthermore, there is yet another answer to the argument that the one work achieved by historically authentic performance trumps the two works of traditional performance practice, with its emphasis on personal authenticity—that it is one Rembrandt to two Utrillos. For as this argument is motivated, at least so I suppose, by the "cult of the composer," its inner working must in the end be founded upon . . . the axiom that the *composer knows best* (CKB) and the related axiom of *the delicate balance* (DB). That is to say, the reason, ultimately, for collapsing performance parameters into the text is to take them out of the hands of the performer and put them under the total control of the composer. But *why* should we want total control of sound production to be in the composer's hands? Because, one must assume, of DB and CKB: because, in other words, the composer has put the work into that delicate balance that any change, no matter how apparently helpful or apparently trivial, is bound to upset, the performing parameters being part of that delicate balance, the composer knowing best how his or her work is to be realized in sound production.

But we have . . . good reason to doubt *both* these axioms. Or, rather, we have seen no good reason to accept either of them. There just is no evidence of any such delicate balance that will somehow be upset by a performance strategy departing either from the composer's wishes and intentions or from the practice and sound of his period. And, indeed, unless one simply begs the question from the start, there is good, believable evidence for the opposite—the conclusion that sometimes we have a better way than the composer's or the composer's times for performing some particular work. ◣

Questions for Discussion

1. What, if anything, makes an artistic performance aesthetically different from a nonperformed artwork?
2. Are there any art forms or artworks that could not be performances (or performing arts)? Why or why not?
3. Different performing arts blend and overlap (for instance, dance is blended with music, musical performances involve staging of performers). What, if anything, demarcates these performing arts from each other? Are there any features of one that are irrelevant to the others?
4. Because performances are so singular or unique, does it make sense to speak of formal or structural features of kinds of performances? For instance, there have been thousands of performances of *Hamlet*; is it appropriate to think of, and look for, something that makes them all performances of a (given) play as opposed to simply unique performances?
5. Why is it that music ("mere" structured sound) can be so moving to us?

CHAPTER 9

VISUAL ARTS

In Chapter 8 we focused attention on performing arts. Of course, as we noted, there are other performing arts besides dance, theater, and music. For instance, poetry readings are artworks that are intended as performances. Also, there are other kindred performance activities that are experienced in ways that we would commonly and appropriately speak of as aesthetic, such as, perhaps, some circus performances of high-wire acrobats or talented jugglers, even if we hesitate to call them art. And, of course, even those performing arts have important nonperformance aspects and features: dance notations, dramatic scripts, musical scores, and the like. Nevertheless, as performing arts, they have aesthetic features that can be highlighted.

Another broad grouping or categorizing of different art forms is visual arts. As the name implies, the core feature here is that these are art forms and artworks that are looked at. Of course, performing arts are also looked at. Theater and dance are almost always experienced by an audience watching actors or dancers. One could listen to a play, say on the radio, but that does not diminish the fact that watching a play is our common and standard experience. So, yes, performing arts are also visual in that sense. However, the term *visual arts* is usually reserved for art forms that are not performing arts and that are, at their core, ones in which the particular artworks are intended to be experienced by looking at them. This chapter will focus on three such art forms: painting, photography, and architecture. Architecture might seem to some readers as an odd choice to include; it is so different than painting and photography. Well, in some respects, yes, it is quite different. However, the aesthetic aspects of architecture—what make buildings and other architectural structures artworks that produce aesthetic experience—as opposed to the practical and purely utilitarian features of these structures, are primarily (although not completely) visual. It is the look of the Eiffel Tower or the Taj Mahal that we first notice and feel aesthetically.

Along with including architecture as a visual art, another oddity is that film is not included here. Film and video are obvious core examples of visual arts. Although film is related to photography (it used to be referred to as "moving pictures") and to theater (there is a script and, usually, a narrative story line), film has artistic features of its own (such as camera angles, camera movement, scene and image editing, among many other features). Film is excluded here only because of space restrictions, not because it is not a central form of visual art.

PAINTING

If anything is stereotypically art, it is paintings. Many colleges and universities have an art department that is separate from departments of music, theater, literature, and so on. What are included in the art department are courses on painting, jewelry design and construction, ceramics, printmaking, and the like. When people are asked to name the first artwork that pops into their head, very often the answer is some famous painting, such as the *Mona Lisa*. This is not universally true, of course, but painting is at the core of whatever art is.

When one asks what, exactly, painting is, or what paintings are, as an art form, one gets (as expected) various answers. For one thing, there are many forms of visual art that are similar to paintings in that they create a visual image on a surface: drawings, woodcuts, engravings, etchings, silk screens, stencils, collographs (that is, artworks in which objects are glued onto a surface), and many others. The mediums and techniques might be different from those of paintings, but they have in common enough aesthetic and artistic aspects and concerns that here paintings will be a stand-in for all of these forms.

Paintings are, of course, artifacts. They are created objects. We usually assume they are painted or created by humans, but as we saw with Figure 2.1, some paintings (or at least, objects that appear to be indistinguishable from paintings) are not created by humans. Because they are created, paintings have intentional features; accidentally spilling paint is not the same thing as painting. Paintings are said to be semiotic; they signify something (perhaps many things) as part of a system of signification. Sometimes the semiotic system is very structured and rule-governed; for instance, there are certain regimented styles of painting (such as some religious painting). Sometimes the semiotic system is very loose; for instance, there are other styles (such as splatter painting) that are nonregimented and even overtly in opposition to regimentation. When thinking of paintings we often think of easel paintings, that is, paintings that are done on a stretched canvas, usually of a moderate size, intended to be a stand-alone artwork. But, of course, there are many paintings that are not easel paintings, such as Michelangelo's painting of the Sistine Chapel.

When we ask about the nature of paintings and about the relevant aesthetic concerns about paintings, what we mean by the question, What is a painting? varies. We might be asking about paintings as objects or paintings as created objects or paintings as created artifacts or paintings as created visual artifacts, or paintings as something else. For instance, a painting is an object as opposed to a performance; a painting is a created object as opposed to a found object. These various characterizations of paintings speak to the various foci that might be of aesthetic concern. If we are concerned about paintings as created objects, say, and by "created" we mean intentional (and not accidentally caused), then we might not consider Figure 2.1 (the "painting" created by an elephant) to be a painting, but if we are concerned about paintings as artifacts as opposed to found objects, then we might consider Figure 2.1 as a painting.

In Chapter 8, on performing arts, we noted that different art forms have characteristic, if not actually unique and defining, features or aspects. Human bodily movement is what is essential to dance, for instance, whereas structured sound is what is essential to music. Later in this chapter we will consider functionality as a crucial aesthetic feature in architecture. What, if anything, is characteristic or unique about painting? If anything, it is color and line. If painting is the intentional putting of pigment on a surface, that pigment always has color and always has linear shape (even if that linear shape is not straight lines). There are, of course, various aesthetic features of paintings based on those aspects of color and line, such as rhythm, harmony, balance, symmetry, and texture, as well as intentional concerns, such as perspective, juxtaposition, and point(s) of focus. If we ask, for example, about *Guernica* as an artwork, we especially note color and line. Picasso purposefully used blacks and whites and grays, which—given the content and intent of the painting—is relevant to its aesthetics. (Portraying the horrors of war with light, soft pastel colors would result in a different aesthetic experience, we assume.) The lines of *Guernica* are also noteworthy and carry both a perceptual and conceptual force.

Given the centrality of color and line for paintings, and the fact that many (although not all) paintings are efforts to create a three-dimensional image on a two-dimensional surface, those features became the focus of aesthetic debate. The importance of color and line especially became of central concern in the early- and mid-twentieth century, as painters moved more and more away from the view that art was (and was supposed to be) primarily representational. In the following reading, for example, Clement Greenberg argues for the importance of what he calls "modernist painting." This is not exactly the same thing as abstract painting, but the two certainly overlap. The focus of modernist painting, he says, is to engage in self-critique. The emphasis is to look, via painting, at the very nature of painting as an art. The goal is to identify what is truly essential and defining of painting, what is unique to painting as an art, as opposed to what it shares with other arts. As he puts it, "The task of self-criticism became to eliminate from the specific effects of each art any and every effect that might conceivably be borrowed from or by the medium of any other art."

He mentions that this concern began with the philosopher Immanuel Kant, so it is worth taking a very brief look at Kant and at why Greenberg says this. According to Kant, that the mind structures experience is what makes experience possible in the first place. For example, we experience what we experience in time and space. But for Kant, space and time do not absolutely exist "out there," independent of the mind. Rather, the mind orders experience such that we always experience what we experience in space and time. Empiricists had argued that we acquire the idea of space through experience, by encountering objects outside ourselves. In contrast, Kant argued, that we encounter objects outside ourselves *presupposes* the notion of space: if we did not have the notion of space already, we would not experience objects as outside ourselves in the first place. So the idea of space is something the mind brings to experience, rather than something we encounter in experience. Similarly, the idea of time is something the mind brings to experience, rather than something we encounter in experience.

Kant claimed that what explains understanding and knowledge of such things and events is that the mind structures experience using certain concepts. These concepts are concepts the mind actively brings to experience (such as space and time); it is only because the mind organizes experience by using these concepts that we can make sense of what we experience. So, without them, knowledge is not possible. Kant called these concepts *categories*. To show that we experience objects only through the categories, Kant again considered what is necessary for experience in the first place. It seems that we cannot experience objects *as objects* unless we have the concept of object. But, according to Kant, one cannot have the concept of object unless one also has the categories. In other words, the very concept of object involves certain a priori (that is, prior to experience) concepts. For example, the concept "object" requires the concept "substance," that is, the concept of something permanent (a cup, say, is a permanent object in the sense that it does not flicker in and out of existence even when it undergoes change; even painted blue, for instance, a once-red cup is the *same* cup, just colored differently). When we make judgments about the objects we experience, Kant argued, we do so according to certain logical forms of the mind, and we always use the categories to do so.

Another underlying aspect to modernism was what was called *phenomenology*, or at least a phenomenological approach to experience. The term *phenomenology* comes from the Greek word *phaino*, meaning "to appear." So in a broad sense phenomenology is the study of how things appear to consciousness. It is the study of consciousness and the objects of consciousness—that is, consciousness and what consciousness experiences, for example, the sight of wispy clouds on a summer day, the tart taste of a raspberry, or the experience of regarding something as beautiful. Instead of studying consciousness from an outside perspective as a scientist typically does—say, by studying patterns of brain activity—phenomenology examines consciousness from the perspective of a person who is consciously experiencing, looking at what experience is like.

A fundamental claim in phenomenology about the structure of consciousness is that consciousness is intentional. In this case, the word *intentional* does not mean having a goal or purpose. Rather, it means that consciousness is *about* something, or put another way, that consciousness is always consciousness *of*. We are never simply conscious; we are conscious *of* something or another. This does not mean that whenever we have a conscious experience there is really something "out there" that actually exists in the world; phenomenologists readily agree that sometimes we hallucinate, for example. Even while hallucinating, however, a person's consciousness is directed toward *something*. Suppose, for example, a person believes she sees a red apple on a kitchen table. Whether or not the apple actually exists, the person is having an experience of seeing a red, round piece of fruit on a table, and in that sense her experience is *about* something; it has content, it is not simply empty. According to phenomenologists, all acts of consciousness, such as seeing, remembering, and wishing, are directed toward something; they are always intentional.

Edmund Husserl, the founder of modern phenomenology, wrote about phenomenology as a method. For him, the phenomenological method is a way of focusing on one's experience, without assuming that the objects one experiences are independently real. To return to the red apple on the kitchen table, the phenomenologist should not assume that the apple is actually there, existing in a physical world outside the mind. Neither should the phenomenologist assume that that apple is *not* really there. Rather, according to Husserl, the phenomenologist should suspend judgment, regarding the apple neither as real nor as unreal, "bracketing" the ordinary, everyday belief that it exists outside the mind. In general, Husserl believed that phenomenologists should suspend judgment about the reality of *all* objects of experience, because he believed that doing so helped a person to focus better on experience itself. By not assuming that the objects of experience are real, philosophers can study experience without bias, noticing features of experience they might otherwise overlook. In particular, Husserl believed that through the phenomenological method it was possible to intuit the essence of an object.

To return to painting, for Greenberg the importance of Kant's claims and of the phenomenological approach was that artists should get to the core and essence of painting by engaging in a self-critique of the experience of painting and by bracketing away those aspects of painting that are not essential and defining of painting. For Greenberg, painting, as opposed to other art forms, has essential features: the flat surface; the shape of the support; the properties of the pigment. The emphasis of painting, then, should be to highlight those features and make them the focus of attention; make them what we are overtly conscious of when we encounter paintings. Paint itself is essential to X as a painting, but not to X as a picture, since the content of a picture could be depicted by some other art form. So painters should emphasize the features of the paint itself. If the painting includes a picture, that is secondary and, for Greenberg, should not be the focus of attention or concern.

Others disagree. For instance, structured sound might be what is unique to music as an art, but what is aesthetic about music, they say, would not be captured by musicians focusing on the elements of sound. Rather, the elements of sound are used to create something beyond the sounds themselves. Or, to take another example, functionality might be what is unique about architecture as an art, but the art aspect of architectural structures lies in the use or interplay of functionality along with aesthetic nonfunctional features.

Here is what Greenberg says:

CLEMENT GREENBERG, "MODERNIST PAINTING"*

Modernism includes more than art and literature. By now it covers almost the whole of what is truly alive in our culture. It happens, however, to be very much of a historical novelty. Western civilization is not the first civilization to turn around and question its own foundations, but it is the one that has gone furthest in doing so. I identify Modernism with the intensification, almost the exacerbation, of this self-critical tendency that began with the philosopher Kant. Because he was the first to criticize the means itself of criticism, I conceive of Kant as, the first real Modernist.

The essence of Modernism lies, as I see it, in the use of characteristic methods of a discipline to criticize the discipline itself, not in order to subvert it but in order to entrench it more firmly in its area of competence. . . .

The self-criticism of Modernism grows out of, but is not the same thing as, the criticism of the Enlightenment. The Enlightenment criticized from the outside, the way criticism in its accepted sense does; Modernism criticizes from the inside, through the procedures themselves of that which is being criticized. It seems natural that this new kind of criticism should have appeared first in philosophy, which is critical by definition, but as the 18th century wore on, it entered many other fields. . . .

We know what has happened to an activity like religion, which could not avail itself of Kantian, immanent, criticism in order to justify itself. At first glance the arts might seem to have been in a situation like religion's. Having been denied by the Enlightenment all tasks they could take seriously, they looked as though they were going to be assimilated to entertainment pure and simple, and entertainment itself looked as though it were going to be assimilated, like religion, to therapy. The arts could save themselves from this leveling down only by demonstrating that the kind of experience they provided

---

Art and Literature (1965): 193–201.

was valuable in its own right and not to be obtained from any other kind of activity.

Each art, it turned out, had to perform this demonstration on its own account. What had to be exhibited was not only that which was unique and irreducible in art in general, but also that which was unique and irreducible in each particular art. Each art had to determine, through its own operations and works, the effects exclusive to itself. By doing so it would, to be sure, narrow its area of competence, but at the same time it would make its possession of that area all the more certain.

It quickly emerged that the unique and proper area of competence of each art coincided with all that was unique in the nature of its medium. The task of self-criticism became to eliminate from the specific effects of each art any and every effect that might conceivably be borrowed from or by the medium of any other art. Thus would each art be rendered "pure," and in its "purity" find the guarantee of its standards of quality as well as of its independence. "Purity" meant self-definition, and the enterprise of self-criticism in the arts became one of self-definition with a vengeance.

Realistic, naturalistic art had dissembled the medium, using art to conceal art; Modernism used art to call attention to art. The limitations that constitute the medium of painting—the flat surface, the shape of the support, the properties of the pigment—were treated by the Old Masters as negative factors that could be acknowledged only implicitly or indirectly. Under Modernism these same limitations came to be regarded as positive factors, and were acknowledged openly. Manet's became the first Modernist pictures by virtue of the frankness with which they declared the flat surfaces on which they were painted. The Impressionists, in Manet's wake, abjured underpainting and glazes, to leave the eye under no doubt as to the fact that the colors they used were made of paint that came from tubes or pots. Cézanne sacrificed verisimilitude, or correctness, in order to fit his drawing and design more explicitly to the rectangular shape of the canvas.

It was the stressing of the ineluctable flatness of the surface that remained, however, more fundamental than anything else to the processes by which pictorial art criticized and defined itself under Modernism. For flatness alone was unique and exclusive to pictorial art. The enclosing shape of the picture was a limiting condition, or norm, that was shared with the art of the theater; color was a norm and a means shared not only with the theater, but also with sculpture. Because flatness was the only condition painting shared with no other art, Modernist painting oriented itself to flatness as it did to nothing else.

The Old Masters had sensed that it was necessary to preserve what is called the integrity of the picture plane: that is, to signify the enduring presence of flatness underneath and above the most vivid illusion of three-dimensional space. The apparent contradiction involved was essential to the success of their art, as it is indeed to the success of all pictorial art. The Modernists have neither avoided nor resolved this contradiction; rather, they have reversed its terms. One is made aware of the flatness of their pictures before, instead of after, being made aware of what the flatness contains. Whereas one tends to see what is in an Old Master before one sees the picture itself, one sees a Modernist picture as a picture first. This is, of course, the best way of seeing any kind of picture, Old Master or Modernist, but Modernism imposes it as the only and necessary way, and Modernism's success in doing so is a success of self-criticism.

Modernist painting in its latest phase has not abandoned the representation of recognizable objects in principle. What it has abandoned in principle is the representation of the kind of space that recognizable objects can inhabit. Abstractness, or the non-figurative, has in itself still not proved to be an altogether necessary moment in the self-criticism of pictorial art, even though artists as eminent as Kandinsky and Mondrian have thought so. As such, representation, or illustration, does not attain the uniqueness of pictorial art; what does do so is the associations of things represented. All recognizable entities (including pictures themselves) exist in three-dimensional space, and the barest suggestion of a recognizable entity suffices to call up associations of that kind of space. The fragmentary silhouette of a human figure, or of a teacup, will do so, and by doing so alienate pictorial space from the literal two-dimensionality which is the guarantee of painting's independence as an art. For, as has already been said, three-dimensionality is the province of sculpture. To achieve autonomy, painting has had above all to divest itself of everything it might share with sculpture, and it is in its effort to do this, and not so much— I repeat—to exclude the representational or literary, that painting has made itself abstract.

At the same time, however, Modernist painting shows, precisely by its resistance to the sculptural, how firmly attached it remains to tradition beneath and beyond all appearances to the contrary. For the resistance to the sculptural dates far back before the advent of Modernism. Western painting, in so far as it is naturalistic, owes a great debt to sculpture, which taught it in the beginning how to shade and model for the illusion of relief, and even how to dispose that illusion in a complementary illusion of deep space. Yet some of the greatest feats of Western painting are due to the effort it has made over the last four centuries to rid itself of the sculptural. Starting in Venice in the 16th century and continuing in Spain, Belgium, and Holland in the 17th, that effort was carried on at first in the name of color. When David, in the 18th century, tried to revive sculptural painting, it was, in part, to save pictorial art from the decorative flattening-out that the emphasis on color seemed to induce. Yet the strength of David's own best pictures, which are predominantly his informal ones, lies as much in their color as in anything else. And Ingres, his faithful pupil, though he subordinated color far more consistently than did David, executed portraits that were among the flattest, least sculptural paintings done in the West by a sophisticated artist since the 14th century. Thus, by the middle of the 19th century, all ambitious tendencies in painting had converged amid their differences, in an anti-sculptural direction.

Modernism, as well as continuing this direction, has made it more conscious of itself. With Manet and the Impressionists the question stopped being defined as one of color versus drawing, and became one of purely optical experience against optical experience as revised or modified by tactile associations. It was in the name of the purely and literally optical, not in the name of color, that the Impressionists set themselves to undermining shading and modeling and everything else in painting that seemed to connote the sculptural. It was, once again, in the name of the sculptural, with its shading and modeling, that Cézanne, and the Cubists after him, reacted against Impressionism, as David had reacted against Fragonard. But once more, just as David's and Ingres' reaction had culminated, paradoxically, in a kind of painting even less sculptural than before, so the Cubist counter-revolution eventuated in a kind of painting flatter than anything in Western art since before Giotto and Cimabue— so flat indeed that it could hardly contain recognizable images.

In the meantime the other cardinal norms of the art of painting had begun, with the onset of Modernism, to undergo a revision that was equally thorough if not as spectacular. It would take me more time than is at my disposal to show how the norm of the picture's enclosing shape, or frame, was loosened, then tightened, then loosened once again, and isolated, and then tightened once more, by successive generations of Modernist painters. Or how the norms of finish and paint texture, and of value and color contrast, were revised and re-revised. New risks have been taken with all these norms, not only in the interests of expression but also in order to exhibit them more clearly as norms. By being exhibited, they are tested for their indispensability. That testing is by no means finished, and the fact that it becomes deeper as it proceeds accounts for the radical simplifications that are also to be seen in the very latest abstract painting, as well as for the radical complications that are also seen in it.

Neither extreme is a matter of caprice or arbitrariness. On the contrary, the more closely the norms of a discipline become defined, the less freedom they are apt to permit in many directions. The essential norms or conventions of painting are at the same time the limiting conditions with which a picture must comply in order to be experienced as a picture. Modernism has found that these limits can be pushed back indefinitely—before a picture stops being a picture and turns into an arbitrary object; but it has also found that the further back these limits are pushed the more explicitly they have to be observed and indicated. The crisscrossing black lines and colored rectangles of a Mondrian painting seem hardly enough to make a picture out of, yet they impose the picture's framing shape as a regulating norm with a new force and completeness by echoing that shape so closely. Far from incurring the danger of arbitrariness, Mondrian's art proves, as time passes, almost too disciplined, almost too tradition- and convention-bound in certain respects; once we have gotten used to its utter abstractness, we realize that it is more conservative in its color, for instance, as well as in its subservience to the frame, than the last paintings of Monet.

It is understood, I hope, that in plotting out the rationale of Modernist painting I have had to simplify and exaggerate. The flatness towards which Modernist painting orients itself can never be an absolute flatness. The heightened sensitivity of the picture plane may no longer permit sculptural illusion, or *trompe-l'oeil*, but it does and must permit optical illusion. The first mark made on a canvas destroys its literal and utter flatness, and the result of the marks made on it by an artist like Mondrian is still a kind of illusion that suggests a kind of third dimension. Only now it is a strictly pictorial, strictly optical third dimension. The Old Masters created an illusion of space in depth that one could imagine oneself walking into, but the analogous illusion created by the Modernist painter can only be seen into; can be traveled through, literally or figuratively, only with the eye.

The latest abstract painting tries to fulfill the Impressionist insistence on the optical as the only sense that a completely and quintessentially pictorial art can invoke. Realizing this, one begins also to realize that the Impressionists, or at least the Neo-Impressionists, were not altogether misguided when they flirted with science. Kantian self-criticism, as it now turns out, has found its fullest expression in science rather than in philosophy, and when it began to be applied in art, the latter was brought closer in real spirit to scientific method than ever before—closer than it had been by Alberti, Uccello, Piero della Francesca, or Leonardo in the Renaissance. That visual art should confine itself exclusively to what is given in visual experience, and make no reference to anything given in any other order of experience, is a notion whose only justification lies in scientific consistency. . . .

It should also be understood that self-criticism in Modernist art has never been carried on in any but a spontaneous and largely subliminal way. As I have already indicated, it has been altogether a question of practice, immanent to practice, and never a topic of theory. Much is heard about programs in connection with Modernist art, but there has actually been far less of the programmatic in Modernist than in Renaissance or Academic painting. With a few exceptions like Mondrian, the masters of Modernism have had no more fixed ideas about art than Corot did. Certain inclinations, certain affirmations and emphases, and certain refusals and abstinences as well, seem to become necessary simply because the way to stronger, more expressive art lies through them. The immediate aims of the Modernists were, and remain, personal before anything else, and the truth and success of their works remain personal before anything else. And it has taken the accumulation, over decades, of a good deal of personal painting to reveal the general self-critical tendency of Modernist painting. No artist was, or yet is, aware of it, nor could any artist ever work freely in awareness of it. To this extent—and it is a great extent—art gets carried on under Modernism in much the same way as before.

And I cannot insist enough that Modernism has never meant, and does not mean now, anything like a break with the past. It may mean a devolution, an unraveling, of tradition, but it also means its further evolution. Modernist art continues the past without gap or break, and wherever it may end up it will never cease being intelligible in terms of the past. The making of pictures has been controlled, since it first began, by all the norms I have mentioned. The Paleolithic painter or engraver could disregard the norm of the frame and treat the surface in a literally sculptural way only because he made images rather than pictures, and worked on a support—a rock wall, a bone, a horn, or a stone—whose limits and surface were arbitrarily given by nature. But the making of pictures means, among other things, the deliberate creating or choosing of a flat surface, and the deliberate circumscribing and limiting of it. This deliberateness is precisely what Modernist painting harps on: the fact, that is, that the limiting conditions of art are altogether human conditions.

But I want to repeat that Modernist art does not offer theoretical demonstrations. It can be said, rather, that it happens to convert theoretical possibilities into empirical ones, in doing which it tests many theories about art for their relevance to the actual practice and actual experience of art. In this respect alone can Modernism be considered subversive. Certain factors we used to think essential to the making and experiencing of art are shown not to be so by the fact that Modernist painting has been able to dispense with them and yet continue to offer the experience of art in all its essentials. The further fact that this demonstration has left most of our old value judgments intact only makes it the more conclusive. Modernism may have had something to do with the revival of the reputations of Uccello, Piero della Francesca, El Greco, Georges de la Tour, and even Vermeer; and Modernism certainly confirmed, if it did not start, the revival of Giotto's reputation; but it has not lowered thereby the standing of Leonardo, Raphael, Titian, Rubens, Rembrandt, or Watteau. What Modernism has shown is that, though the past did appreciate these masters justly, it often gave wrong or irrelevant reasons for doing so.

In some ways this situation is hardly changed today. Art criticism and art history lag behind Modernism as they lagged behind pre-Modernist art. Most of the things that get written about Modernist art still belong to journalism rather than to criticism or art history. It belongs to journalism—and to the millennial complex from which so many journalists and journalist intellectuals suffer in our day—that each new phase of Modernist art should be hailed as the start of a whole new epoch in art, marking a decisive break with all the customs and conventions of the past. Each time, a kind of art is expected so unlike all previous kinds of art, and so free from norms of practice or taste, that everybody, regardless of how informed or uninformed he happens to be, can have his say about it. And each time, this expectation has been disappointed, as the phase of Modernist art in question finally takes its place in the intelligible continuity of taste and tradition. ◢

PHOTOGRAPHY

Taking pictures is something we pretty much take for granted today; we can even do it with our phones. Most of the time we do not think of the pictures we take as artworks, nor do we intend them that way. Usually they are candid pictures of what is going on around us, or, perhaps, photos of something we find interesting that we want to be able to show to others (or even to ourselves) later on. So we take a picture; we get a photographic image of it. Just as we noted in Chapter 8 that we often distinguish between, say, social dance and artistic dance (or that we might distinguish between "merely" singing and music), so, too, we recognize that there is a difference between artistic photography—that is, photography as an art form—and simply taking snapshots. Of course, there is not a sharp line between artistic and nonartistic

9.1 Edwin Aldrin walks near the Lunar Module (July 20, 1969). Courtesy of NASA.

photography. Just as traditional folk dances and folk music can blend into artworks, so, too, photographs can be received or interpreted as artworks whether or not they were created as such. Many, probably most, of the most famous photographs of all time (which in this case means over the past century and a half) were what we would call photojournalism. That is, they were not taken in an attempt to create artworks, but were seen as meaningful (perhaps politically or socially) and had aesthetic features that captured our attention; one example is the famous photograph, taken by astronaut Neil Armstrong, of the astronaut Buzz Aldrin on the moon (Figure 9.1). Likewise, the 9/11 photograph that we mentioned in Chapter 1 was not intended as an artwork, but was "merely" a snapshot taken to record what the photographer saw as a meaningful event.

There are, of course, photographs that are intended as artworks and photographers who very consciously consider themselves to be artists, such as the well-known photographer Ansel Adams. Many of his photographs are found in art galleries. Other photographs, although not intended as artworks, have received critique and evaluation as artworks; that is, they have been assessed not only on journalistic grounds and criteria but also on aesthetic grounds and criteria.

With respect to photography as art, we have all heard the expression "A picture is worth a thousand words." Look again at the 9/11 flag photo from Chapter 1 (Figure 1.1) and think about how difficult it would be to express in words everything you see in the photograph. Just to describe the things in that picture and their relationships with each other would take quite an effort. In addition, it is even more complex to also put into words the aesthetic and artistic aspects of it, say, in terms of visual balance, texture, contrast, rhythm, and so on. Yet we see all of this, or at least much of it, instantly upon looking at the photograph. (This fullness of immediate experience is, of course, not unique to photography. Imagine the difference between hearing a musical concert and having someone describe that concert to you.)

What are the characteristic aspects of photography that make it true that a picture is worth a thousand words? For one thing, in photography there is an already-existing object in front of the camera lens. Of course, as we know, this is less true today than it used to be because of digital photography and the ability to photoshop, or digitally alter, pictures. We will return to this issue soon, but for now we can still truthfully say that for the most part photographs are photographs of something "out there." This is not at all necessarily the case for, say, painting. Photographs also have the capacity to render detail with a precision that is unique among the visual arts. Some paintings and sculptures can be remarkable in their detail, but because of the mechanics and physics of photography, its level of detail can be even greater.

What is even more characteristic of photography among the arts is its use and dependence upon light and timing. Again because of the mechanics of cameras, light is paramount and, at a very basic level, photographers are passive with respect to light. (A painter can paint a picture of a night scene, but a photographer needs a certain level of light to be able to photograph it.) Timing for photography means two things. One is timing in the sense of getting the picture when it happens. If I hope to get a photograph of a bird diving into water to catch a fish, I need to catch the bird in the act; if I am a second too late or a second too early I will not get the photograph I want. Another sense of timing in photography is shutter speed. Because of variations in light conditions, having a camera set at a particular shutter speed will affect the image that is recorded.

The reliance upon a mechanism, the camera, that is inherent in photography led many people, including aestheticians, for many years to consider photography as not a genuine art form, or at best a low-level art form. The philosopher and social critic Susan Sontag claimed that a photograph shows only how something looks (or looked), not how it functions (or functioned), so photography could give us no real understanding or appreciation of things. The aesthetician Roger Scruton wrote an influential article arguing that because photography is essentially optico-chemical (in its reliance on the mechanical and physical nature of the camera), it is not genuinely intentional or representational in the way that other art forms are. So, he argued, while there could be a beautiful painting of an ugly subject, there could not be a beautiful photograph of an ugly subject. For a photograph, he said, the beauty might be in the content or subject of the photograph, but the beauty is not in the photograph itself (that is, in the artwork itself), whereas the beauty of a painting is in the painting itself.

Others, including aestheticians but even more so photographers, have disagreed. Photography, they argue, is far from being a passive mirror of what appears in front of the camera lens. With respect to aesthetic issues, artists claim that there is artistic creativity at all levels and phases of "taking pictures." Photography starts, they say, with the whole world, not with a blank canvas. It is a matter of focus and selection; the core of photography, they claim, is "subtracting," that is, determining what not to include and by doing so determining what to include. There are, of course, mechanical and physical constraints, as have been noted. But that is true for other art forms as well. Musical instruments are also mechanically and physically constrained; a drum simply cannot produce certain sounds, nor can a flute or a piano.

In addition to considerations of focus and selection, the intentional and representational components of photography extend beyond "getting the picture." For most of the history of photography, film was the medium, and photographers remarked that much of photography took place in the darkroom where the film was processed. How much of photography took place at the shutter, meaning when and where the picture was taken, was said to be only half the picture! Photographers could manipulate and alter the final product in the darkroom, depending upon how they developed the photograph. Today, with digital technology, this is even truer. The image captured on the photoreceptor (whether film or memory cards) is only a starting point, so to speak, of a photograph. Things and events in the world are part of the creative, artistic process, but only a part. Indeed, the technology itself of a camera provides an artistic filter by allowing the photographer to focus and select and subtract in ways that are possible only because of this technology (for instance, zoom lenses).

From the perspective of the artwork itself (as opposed to the perspective of the artist), a fundamental aesthetic consideration has already been mentioned. This is the distinction between what a photograph is and what a photograph is *of*. Another way of putting this is that there is a distinction between what a photograph is *of* and what a photograph is *about*. A snapshot of my cat on a hammock might be just that, a simple photograph of a funny or pleasing event. Likewise, a photograph of three particular firefighters might be just that, a simple photograph of someone's day. However, a photograph of three particular firefighters might be a photograph about heroism or duty. Clearly, what a photograph is of is not at all necessarily what a photograph is about. Furthermore, the aesthetic and artistic aspects of a photograph do not necessarily lie with the intentions of the photographer. It could be (although this is not historically the case) that the photographer who captured the flag-raising firefighters in Figure 1.1 was an insurance claim investigator who was taking a picture of a building's structural damage but was unable to get a vantage point of it different from the one from which he took this picture. Nevertheless, others might find aesthetic and artistic (not to mention social and political) meaning and significance in the photograph. As with other art forms and artworks, the aesthetic experience does not lie only with the artist's intentions.

In the reading on the next page, Kendall Walton speaks of photographs as transparent. The literal meaning of the word *transparent* is "to show through." A transparent window lets us see things on the other side of the window because they show through it. Obviously, what Walton means here is that photographs are akin to windows in the sense that what was on the other side of the camera lens was able to show through to the photograph. However, other aestheticians have argued that transparency is not the best way to understand photographs (or, for some, not even a good way to understand them). If anything, they say, photographs are translucent, not transparent. The meaning of *translucent* is "shine through," in the sense that a translucent window allows filtered light to shine through, but one cannot see through the window. The point of this is that critics of the transparency view go back to the issue we just noted above, that there is a distinction between what a photograph is of and what a photograph is about. These critics claim that it is what the photograph is about that is central to photography as art. But what a photograph is about is not simply given in the content or subject of the photograph. What the photograph is about is a matter of interpretation and extrapolation, given certain constraints (just as *Hamlet* is subject to interpretation and extrapolation, but with constraints against interpreting it as being about, say, snowboarding or nuclear war).

Walton responds to these concerns by asking us to imagine a machine that "sees" like a camera but produces not photographs but instead verbal descriptions of what it "sees." Descriptions, he says, are different from perceptions. Descriptions depend upon criteria and standards of similarity that perceptions do not. Using the analogy above, descriptions might well be translucent (because there is no single correct description of the content or subject of a photograph), but perceptions (like a photographic image) involve a causal correspondence between what is in the world and what is in the photograph. If a photograph is of a moonrise over the Grand Canyon, then there was a moonrise over the canyon, however we might (differently) describe it. Of course, there is the capacity for altering a photograph after it has been taken, but that is secondary to the nature of photography. We cannot photograph a moonrise if the moon is not rising; we can photoshop a moon into a photograph, but that is another issue, for Walton. We can paint a nonexistent moon into a painting (and genuinely experience the painting and legitimately evaluate the painting), but we cannot photograph a nonexistent moon into a photograph. What is central to photography, then, he says, is what happens at the point of capturing the image. Others, as we have seen, disagree.

KENDALL L. WALTON, "TRANSPARENT PICTURES: ON THE NATURE OF PHOTOGRAPHIC REALISM"*

> Photography and the cinema . . . satisfy, once and for all and in its very essence, our obsession with realism. The photographic image is the object itself.
>
> —André Bazin

*Critical Inquiry 11 (1984): 246–253, 269–273.

Every photograph is a fake from start to finish.

—Edward Steichen

Photographs and pictures of other kinds have various strengths and weaknesses. But photography is commonly thought to excel in one dimension especially, that of *realism*. André Bazin and many others consider photographs to be extraordinarily realistic, realistic in a way or to an extent which is beyond the reach of paintings, drawings, and other "hand-made" pictures . . .

That photography is a supremely realistic medium may be the commonsense view, but—as Edward Steichen reminds us—it is by no means universal. Dissenters note how unlike reality a photograph is and how unlikely we are to confuse the one with the other. They point to "distortions" engendered by the photographic process and to the control which the photographer exercises over the finished product, the opportunities he enjoys for interpretation and falsification. Many emphasize the expressive nature of the medium, observing that photographs are inevitably colored by the photographer's personal interests, attitudes, and prejudices. Whether any of these various considerations really does collide with photography's claim of extraordinary realism depends, of course, on how that claim is to be understood.

Those who find photographs especially realistic sometimes think of photography as a further advance in a direction which many picture makers have taken during the last several centuries, as a continuation or culmination of the post-Renaissance quest for realism. There is some truth in this. Such earlier advances toward realism include the development of perspective and modeling techniques, the portrayal of ordinary and incidental details, attention to the effects of light, and so on. From its very beginning, photography mastered perspective (a system of perspective that works, anyway, if not the only one). Subtleties of shading, gradations of brightness nearly impossible to achieve with the brush, became commonplace. Photographs include as a matter of course the most mundane details of the scenes they portray—stray chickens, facial warts, clutters of dirty dishes. Photographic images easily can seem to be what painters striving for realism have always been after.

But "photographic realism" is not very special if this is all there is to it: photographs merely enjoy *more* of something which other pictures possess in smaller quantities. These differences of degree, moreover, are not differences between photographs *as such* and paintings and drawings *as such*. Paintings *can* be as realistic as the most realistic photographs, if realism resides in subtleties

of shading, skillful perspective, and so forth; some indeed are virtually indistinguishable from photographs. When a painter fails to achieve such realism up to
photographic standards, the difficulty is merely technological, one which, in principle, can be overcome—by more attention to details, more skill with the brush, a
better grasp of the "rules of perspective." Likewise, photographs aren't necessarily
very realistic in these sorts of ways. Some are blurred and badly exposed. Perspective "distortions" can be introduced and subtleties of shading eliminated by
choice of lens or manipulation of contrast. Photographic realism is not essentially
unavailable to the painter, it seems, nor are photographs automatically endowed
with it. It is just easier to achieve with the camera than with the brush . . .

What, then, is special about photography? There is one clear difference
between photography and painting. A photograph is always a photograph of
something which actually exists. Even when photographs portray such
nonentities as werewolves and Martians, they are nonetheless photographs of
actual things: actors, stage sets, costumes. Paintings needn't picture actual
things. A painting of Aphrodite, executed without the use of a model, depicts
nothing real. But this is by no means the whole story. Those who see a sharp
contrast between photographs and paintings clearly think that it obtains no
less when paintings depict actual things than when they do not, and even
when viewers fully realize that they do. Let's limit our examples to pictures of
this kind. The claim before us is that photographs of Abraham Lincoln, for instance, are in some fundamental manner more realistic than painted portraits
of him.

I shall argue that there is indeed a fundamental difference between photographs and painted portraits of Lincoln, that photography is indeed special, and
that it deserves to be called a supremely realistic medium.

But the kind of realism most distinctive of photography is not an ordinary
one. It has little to do either with the post-Renaissance quest for realism in
painting or with standard theoretical accounts of realism. It is enormously important, however. Without a clear understanding of it, we cannot hope to explain the power and effectiveness of photography.

Painting and drawing are techniques for producing pictures. So is photography. But the special nature of photography will remain obscure unless we think
of it in another way as well as a contribution to the enterprise of seeing. The invention of the camera gave us not just a new method of making pictures and
not just pictures of a new kind: it gave us a new way of seeing.

Amidst Bazin's assorted declarations about photography is a comparison of
the cinema to mirrors. This points in the right direction. Mirrors are aids to vi-

sion, allowing us to see things in circumstances in which we would not otherwise be able to; with their help we can see around corners. Telescopes and microscopes extend our visual powers in other ways, enabling us to see things that are too far away or too small to be seen with the naked eye. Photography is an aid to vision also, and an especially versatile one. With the assistance of the camera, we can see not only around corners and what is distant or small; we can also see into the past. We see long deceased ancestors when we look at dusty snapshots of them. To view a screening of Frederic Wiseman's *Titicut Follies* (1967) in San Francisco in 1984 is to watch events which occurred in 1967 at the Bridgewater State Hospital for the Criminally Insane. Photographs are *transparent*. We see the world *through* them.

I must warn against watering down this suggestion, against taking it to be a colorful, or exaggerated, or not quite literal way of making a relatively mundane point. I am not saying that the person looking at the dusty photographs has the *impression* of seeing his ancestors—in fact, he doesn't have the impression of seeing them "in the flesh," with the unaided eye. I am not saying that photography *supplements* vision by helping us to discover things that we can't discover by seeing. Painted portraits and linguistic reports also supplement vision in this way. Nor is my point that what we see—photographs—are *duplicates* or *doubles* or *reproductions* of objects, or *substitutes* or *surrogates* for them. My claim is that we *see*, quite literally, our dead relatives themselves when we look at photographs of them.

Does this constitute an extension of the ordinary English sense of the word "see?" I don't know; the evidence is mixed. But if it is an extension, it is a very natural one. Our theory needs, in any case, a term which applies both to my "seeing" my great-grandfather when I look at his snapshot and to my seeing my father when he is in front of me. What is important is that we recognize a fundamental commonality between the two cases, a single natural kind to which both belong. We could say that I *perceive* my great-grandfather but do not *see* him, recognizing a mode of perception ("seeing-through-photographs") distinct from vision—if the idea that I do perceive my great-grandfather is taken seriously. Or one might make the point in some other way. I prefer the bold formulation: the viewer of a photograph sees, literally, the scene that was photographed.

Slippery slope considerations give this claim an initial plausibility. No one will deny that we see through eyeglasses, mirrors, and telescopes. How, then, would one justify denying that a security guard sees via a closed circuit television monitor a burglar breaking a window or that fans watch athletic events when they watch live television broadcasts of them? And after going this far, why not speak of watching athletic events via delayed broadcasts or of seeing the Bridgewater inmates via Wiseman's film? These last examples do introduce a new element: they have us seeing past events. But its importance isn't obvious. We also find ourselves speaking of observing through a telescope the explosion of a star which occurred millions of years ago. We encounter various other differences also, of course, as we slide down the slope. The question is whether any of them is significant enough to justify digging in our heels and recognizing a basic theoretical distinction, one which we might describe as the difference between "seeing" (or "perceiving") things and not doing so.

Mechanical aids to vision don't necessarily involve *pictures* at all. Eyeglasses, mirrors, and telescopes don't give us pictures. To think of the camera as another tool of vision is to de-emphasize its role in producing pictures. Photographs are pictures, to be sure, but not ordinary ones. They are pictures through which we see the world.

To be transparent is not necessarily to be invisible. We see photographs themselves when we see through them; indeed it is by looking at *Titicut Follies* that we see the Bridgewater inmates. There is nothing strange about this: one hears both a bell and the sounds that it makes, and one hears the one by hearing the other. (Bazin's remarkable identity claim might derive from failure to recognize that we can be seeing both the photograph and the object: *what we see* are photographs, but we do see the photographed objects; so the photographs and the objects must be somehow identical.)

I don't mind allowing that we see photographed objects only *indirectly*, though one could maintain that perception is equally indirect in many other cases as well: we see objects by seeing mirror images of them, or images produced by lenses, or light reflected or emitted from them; we hear things and events by hearing the sounds that they make. One is reminded of the familiar claim that we see *directly* only our own sense-data or images on our retinas. What I would object to is the suggestion that indirect seeing, in any of these cases, is not really *seeing*, that *all* we actually see are sense-data or images or photographs.

One can see through sense-data or mirror images without specifically noticing them (even if, in the latter case, one notices the mirror); in this sense they *can* be invisible. One may pay no attention to photographic images themselves, concentrating instead on the things photographed. But even if one does attend especially to the photographic image, one may at the same time be seeing, and attending to, the objects photographed.

Seeing is often a way of finding out about the world. This is as true of seeing through photographs as it is of seeing in other ways. But sometimes we learn little if anything about what we see, and sometimes we value the seeing quite apart from what we might learn. This is so, frequently, when we see departed loved ones through photographs. We can't expect to acquire any particularly important information by looking at photographs which we have studied many times before. But we can see our loved ones again, and *that* is important to us . . .

We may be approaching a *necessary* condition for seeing through pictures and for perception in general, but we are far from having a sufficient condition. Imagine a machine that is sensitive to the light which emanates from a scene and that produces not pictures but accurate verbal descriptions of the scene. The machine's printouts are surely not transparent; in looking at them, one does not *see* the scene which the machine translated into words. Yet the printouts are made just as mechanically as any photographs are.

It is easy to say that the reason why we don't see through such mechanically generated descriptions is that we don't *see* them *as* the scene they describe; perhaps we are incapable of seeing them this way. If one fails to see a photograph as Dwight Eisenhower, or as a person, or as anything but a collection of blotches on a flat surface, we might deny that one sees Eisenhower through the photograph. One doesn't see Eisenhower, perhaps, unless one *notices* him, in some appropriate sense (although it isn't necessary to recognize him as Eisenhower or even as a person). But this doesn't help without an account of *seeing-as* and an explanation of why our not seeing the descriptions as the scene should make a difference. Nor will it help to declare that only *pictures*, not representations of other kinds, can be transparent. We need to know why the machine's printouts don't qualify as pictures and why nonpictures can't be transparent.

Investigating things by examining pictures of them (either photographs or drawings) is strikingly analogous to investigating them by looking at them directly and disanalogous to investigating them by examining descriptions of them. One such analogy concerns what is easy and what is difficult to ascertain and what mistakes the investigator is susceptible to. The numerals "3"and "8" are sometimes easily mistaken for each other. So when reading about a tree which is actually 85 feet high, one might easily take it to be 35 feet high. This mistake is much more likely than that of thinking it is 85.00001 rather than 85 feet high. The reverse is true when we look at the tree directly or examine a picture of it. A *house* is easily confused with a *horse* or a *hearse*, when our information comes from a verbal description, as is a *cat* with a *cot*, a *madam* with a *madman*, *intellectuality* with *ineffectuality* and so on. When we confront things directly or via pictures, houses are more apt to be confused with barns or woodsheds, cats with puppies, and so forth . . .

We are not similarly intimate with the world when we investigate it through descriptions, even mechanically generated ones. Descriptions scramble the real similarity relations. Houses are not much like horses or hearses. The difficulty of distinguishing a house from a hearse when we are reading about it is due not to the nature of the house and hearses but to facts about the words used to describe them. So we think of the words as getting between us and what we are reading about, as blocking our view of it, in a way that photographs and sense-data do not block our view of what they are photographs or sense-data of. The structure of discrimination by means of mechanically generated descriptions does not correspond to the structure of the world and, so, does not qualify as perception . . .

It now looks as though mechanically generated descriptions could, in the right circumstances, be transparent. Suppose that we used description-generating devices regularly to investigate the world. Perhaps this would affect what we think of as similarities, thereby changing our conceptual scheme. We might recognize such properties as *apparent-via-description-generating-devices houseness* and *apparent-via-description-generating-devices hearseness* and regard these properties as analogous to visible colors, as characteristics of things themselves in virtue of which they can be alike, not just as capacities to affect us through the devices. In that case difficulty of discrimination by means of description-generating devices would be correlated with what we think of as similarities. So we might well think of ourselves as seeing through the descriptions, and—especially if there is nothing to "real" similarity among things except being thought of as similar—we might really be seeing through them. Perhaps the mechanically generated descriptions would then be transparent . . .

We have learned that perceptual contact with the world is to be distinguished from two different sorts of nonperceptual access to it: access mediated by intervening descriptions as well as access via another person. The common contrast between seeing something and being told about it conflates the two. When someone describes a scene to us, we are doubly removed from it; contact is broken both by the intervention of the person, the teller, and by the verbal form of the telling. Perceptual contact can itself be mediated—by mirrors or television circuits or photographs. But *this* mediation is a means of *maintaining* contact. Viewers of photographs are in perceptual contact with the world. ◣

ARCHITECTURE

It is very likely that as you are reading these words you are inside a building. That building did not simply pop into existence; it was designed and constructed. An architect (or probably a group) designed it. At first glance, it might seem somewhat odd that in a chapter on visual art, architecture would be one of the topics of discussion. But one of the main aspects of architecture is that architectural objects, especially in the sense that they are experienced as artworks, are looked at; the way they appear to us is crucial and our aesthetic experience of them is largely, although not completely, a matter of their visual appearance.

Aestheticians, and for that matter architects, sometimes distinguish architecture from "mere" buildings. Just as painting a wall does not in itself make the wall a painting (an artwork), and just as structuring sound does not in itself make something music, so, too, designing a building does not in itself make it a work of architecture (an artwork). To be a work of architecture, they say, there must be something more than simply having been designed. As well as being a building, a work of architecture is intended as or received as an artwork.

What, then, is architecture? As with every other art form, there is no universally accepted answer to this question. It has been called "frozen music," because its structured nature can also be eloquent. (Perhaps this means that music is really "melted architecture"?) For one thing, although so far we have used the word *building*, works of architecture are quite varied. There are, for lack of a better term, housings. These can include typical residences (such as a family's house), offices, schools, churches, factories, and others. The term *housings* is meant to refer to buildings in which people are lodged or housed. This includes residences—houses and homes where people live—but also other buildings in which they at least temporarily reside, such as an office. This notion of housings, then, could actually be expanded to structures such as garages or stadiums, since they are designed and constructed with the intention that people will be "in" them at least for some length of time. Besides housings, there are other architectural structures, for instance, dams or bridges. People, of course, use bridges, but the assumption is that they do not reside there; they are not housed there even temporarily. Some monuments are also works of architecture, for instance, the Washington Monument in Washington, DC, or the Eiffel Tower in Paris: whether they are thought of as monuments or not, they are not housings. In addition, plazas are works of architecture. Here the focus is on open, yet bordered, space. Whole neighborhoods and even cities themselves (in the sense of city designs) are within the purview of architecture. We also speak of landscape architecture, including, at a smaller scale, some cases of gardening as works of architecture. So when we speak of buildings as the focus of architecture, this really is shorthand for a wide variety of designed structures. (For this reason, some people claim that there is no sharp line between architecture and sculpture. For example, are the Washington Monument or the Gateway Arch in St. Louis architectural structures or elaborate and very large sculptures?)

However we might characterize architecture, it has some basic features. As we have already noted, whatever is architecture (that is, a work of architecture) is designed and constructed. It does not "just happen," and it must be embodied. A disembodied architectural work is, perhaps, a blueprint, at best. For it to be a work of architecture, it must be built. Perhaps most important, a work of architecture must be functional. (This is not universal—for example, the Eiffel Tower does not have a function, at least not as a primary aspect—but it is characteristic of architecture.) Insofar as architecture requires functionality, it is unique among the arts. It might be that other art forms and other artworks have some function(s) and were even created with those functions in mind, but being functional is not fundamental to painting or music or poetry. With architecture, function is fundamental. Most architectural structures are created not only to be artworks but also (perhaps even more so) to be functioning structures for nonartistic purposes.

Another crucial feature of architecture is that architectural structures are situated in specific locales. As Roger Scruton points out in the reading on page 299, this is a basic, perhaps a defining, aspect of architecture. Some other art forms and artworks are not, and cannot be, so situated. A musical composition, for example, is an abstract thing. A poem might be created without even the intention that it ever be seen or read by anyone other than the poet. A painting might hang on any number of walls. An architectural work, however, is (usually) intended and created for a specific place. At the same time, works of architecture are inherently public. Although some artworks can be private (for instance, a poem or painting can be created and then put away), architectural works cannot. In this sense, they are more akin to performing arts than to plastic arts. Finally, the nature of architectural works is that they last; they are intended to be durable. This is largely because they are intended to be functional. Whereas we might be content with a play to be performed

9.2 *Fallingwater* by Frank Lloyd Wright. Robert P. Ruschak/Courtesy of the Western Pennsylvania Conservancy.

in, say, two hours or to have an exhibit of some paintings available for, say, two months in a gallery, we want and expect that architectural works will last for a long time (however vague "long time" is). These many features of architecture have been recognized for a long time; the Roman architect Marcus Vitruvius wrote more than 2,000 years ago of durability, utility, and beauty as the basic features of architecture, each of them necessary.

What are the aesthetic elements of architecture? There are many. Because a work of architecture is a physical structure, various aspects of that physicality are important. For example, the materials that constitute the actual structure obviously matter. Given the nature of different materials, different aesthetic features are possible. For instance, steel has features that wood does not (and vice versa), and concrete has yet other features. Because of physical possibilities and limits, certain architectural forms are possible for steel that are not possible for wood. As one example, because of the strength of reinforced concrete, it can be used for a cantilever, which is a horizontal overhang. A famous illustration of cantilevers is the house called Fallingwater, designed by the famous architect Frank Lloyd Wright (Figure 9.2).

Architectural works involve not just physical structures but also space. Just as music involves both sounds and silences, architecture necessarily involves spaces, not just physical things. When architects think of space, or spaces, they think of a variety of spaces. There is physical space, of course. That is, a building takes up so much physical space. But there is also perceptual space. How that physical space is designed and "carved up" is related to how we perceptually—and aesthetically—experience it. A room that is twenty feet wide and forty feet long with only four walls can look and feel like a huge cavern, but depending upon how it is designed (say, with nooks or different vertical levels), it can take on a number of appearances. This is also related to the notion of behavioral space. Spaces with the same physical dimensions can be designed so that one moves through them in straight lines or not in straight lines. Because works of architecture are functional structures (such as housings), the behavioral space is crucial.

Furthermore, all these sorts of spaces are both internal to the physical structure and external. That is, there is physical and perceptual and behavioral space within a building, but also outside the building. Because buildings are situated in specific locales, what is relevant about spaces goes beyond the building itself. How does the structure fit in with any other structures around it? Fallingwater is a perfect example. Because the house is located where it is, in a spot with trees and a small stream and waterfall, the building was designed with those elements in mind. The environment and the external spaces were relevant to the design of the building and its internal spaces. That same structure in the middle of a busy New York City street would have been odd, perhaps unthinkable, just as designing a tall skyscraper where *Fallingwater* is would have been odd, perhaps unthinkable. (This point about external spaces, of course, points to the aesthetics of landscape architecture, which has additional aesthetic and artistic aspects of its own.) Unlike many other art forms, architecture must consider how a particular architectural work coheres with its various environments, not only natural environment, but also the social, cultural, historical, and aesthetic environments. Although a dance can exist on its own, so to speak, a building cannot, or at least, its status as art depends on its environmental fit far more than is true for other art forms. One way that architects speak of this is to say that with architecture, there is not only a sense of space, but also a sense of place.

When architects, then, focus on aesthetic aspects of structures, along with their sense of space and place, they consider issues of visual texture and rhythm and contrast, much as painters do. In addition, architects must consider aspects such as sound (which painters do not), at least for housings. Architects must be aware of proportion and scale. Designing an office building with ceilings that are forty feet high or only five feet high would be odd, at best.

Of course, many of the issues and questions related to the arts generally apply to architecture. With respect to concerns from the perspective of the artist, can architecture express, communicate, or evoke feelings? And, if so, how? If we assume that some form of expression or communication is fundamental to what artists are doing via creating art, how, if at all, does that apply to architects (and architecture)? Or, with respect to the perspective of the audience, how are buildings to be interpreted? (There is a famous essay by Nelson Goodman entitled "How Buildings Mean.") Is there an architectural "sense" or an architectural "attitude?" Can we (and if so how) learn from buildings, as many people claim that we can learn from art? Are there correct or incorrect ways of interpreting and appreciating architectural structures? What would it mean to misunderstand a building? Are there moral or social conflicts about buildings *as art* (as opposed to, say, economic costs or political associations related to architecture)?

In the following reading, Scruton reiterates some of the points made above about the nature of architecture as an art; works of architecture are fundamentally functional (as he says, buildings are means, not ends in themselves); also, place, being situated, is basic to architecture. In addition, he notes that architecture, because it is inherently technical, is something of a blend or synthesis between arts and crafts and that, while there might be aspects of expression connected with architecture, expression is not basic. Although it is not explicit here, Scruton notes that there is continuity between architecture and what he calls the decorative arts (for instance, jewelry making), because architecture is a means toward other ends and often involves ornamentation and adornment as important features.

ROGER SCRUTON, "THE PROBLEM OF ARCHITECTURE"*

Now as a matter of fact architecture presents an immediate problem for any general philosophical theory of aesthetic interest. Through its impersonal and at

---

*In *The Aesthetics of Architecture*. Princeton: Princeton University Press, 1979. Pages 5–8, 9–13.

the same time functional qualities architecture stands apart from the other arts, seeming to require quite peculiar attitudes, not only for its creation, but also for its enjoyment. . . .

[It is] natural to suppose that music has expressive, sensuous and dramatic powers in common with the representative arts. Only architecture seems to stand wholly apart from them, being distinguished from the other arts by certain features that cannot fail to determine our attitude towards it.

First among these distinguishing features is utility or function. Buildings are places where human beings live, work and worship, and a certain form is imposed from the outset by the needs and desires that a building is designed to fulfill. While it is not possible to compose a piece of music without intending that it should be listened to and hence appreciated, it is certainly possible to design a building without intending that it should be looked at—without intending, that is, to create an object of aesthetic interest. Even when there is an attempt to apply "aesthetic" standards in architecture, we still find a strong asymmetry with other forms of art. For no work of music or literature can have features of which we may say that, because of the function of music, or because of the function of literature, such features are unavoidable. Of course a work of music or literature may *have* a function, as do waltzes, marches and Pindaric odes. But these functions do not stem from the essence of literary or musical art. A Pindaric ode is poetry *put* to a use; and poetry in itself is connected only accidentally with such uses.

"Functionalism" has many forms. Its most popular form is the aesthetic theory, that true beauty in architecture consists in the adapting of form to function. For the sake of argument, however, we might envisage a functionalist theory of exemplary crudeness, which argues that, since architecture is essentially a means to an end, we appreciated buildings as *means*. Hence the value of a building is determined by the extent to which it fulfills its function and not by any purely "aesthetic" considerations. This theory might naturally seem to have the consequences that the appreciation of architecture is wholly unlike the appreciation of other forms of art, these being valued not as means, but for their own sakes, as ends. However, to put the point in that way is to risk obscurity—for what is the distinction between valuing something as a means and as an end? Even if we feel confident about one term of that distinction (about what it is to value something as a means), we must surely feel considerable doubt about the term with which it is contrasted. What is it to value something as an end? Consider one celebrated attempt to clarify the concept—that of the English philosopher R. G. Collingwood. Collingwood began his exploration of art and the aesthetic from a distinction between art and craft. Initially it seems quite reasonable to distinguish the attitude of the craftsman—who aims at a certain result and does what he can to achieve it—from that of the artist, who knows what he is doing, as it were, only when it is done. But it is precisely the case of architecture which casts doubt on that distinction. For whatever else it is, architecture is certainly, in Collingwood's sense, a craft. The utility of a building is not an accidental property; it defines the architect's endeavor. To maintain this sharp distinction between art and craft is simply to ignore the reality of architecture—not because architecture is a *mixture* of art and craft (for, as Collingwood recognized, that is true of all aesthetic activity) but because architecture represents an almost indescribable *synthesis* of the two. The functional qualities of a building are of its essence, and qualify every task to which the architect addresses himself. It is impossible to understand the element of art and the element of craft independently, and in the light of this difficulty the two concepts seem suddenly to possess a formlessness that their application to the "fine" arts serves generally to obscure.

Moreover, the attempt to treat architecture as a form of "art" in Collingwood's sense involves taking a step towards expressionism, towards seeing architecture in a way that one might see sculpture or painting, as an expressive activity, deriving its nature and value from a peculiarly artistic aim. For Collingwood "expression" was the primary aim of art precisely because there could be no *craft* of expression. In the case of expression, there can be no rule or procedure, such as might be followed by a craftsman, with a clear end in view and a clear means to its fulfillment; it was therefore through the concept of "expression" that he tried to clarify the distinction between art and craft. . . .

[Clearly], it would be a gross distortion to assume that architecture is an "expressive" medium in just the way that sculpture might be, or that the distinction between art and craft applies to architecture with a neatness which such a view supposes. Despite the absurdities of our crude functionalism (a theory which, as Théophile Gautier once pointed out, has the consequence that the perfection of the water closet is the perfection to which all architecture aspires) it is wrong to see architecture in such a way. The value of a building simply cannot be understood independently of its utility. It is of course *possible* to take a merely "sculptural" view of architecture; but that is to treat buildings as forms whose aesthetic nature is conjoined only accidentally to a certain function. Texture, surface, form, representation and expression now begin to take precedence over those aesthetic aims which we would normally consider to be specifically architectural. The "decorative" aspect of architecture assumes an unwonted autonomy, and at the same time becomes something more personal than any act of mere decoration would be. Consider, for example, the Chapel of the Colonia Guëll, Santa Coloma de Cervelló, by Gaudi. Such a building tries to represent itself as something other than architecture, as a form of tree-like growth rather than balanced engineering. The strangeness here comes from the attempt to translate a decorative tradition into a structural principle. In the sixteenth-century Portuguese window by J. de Castillo the nature of that tradition is apparent. Structurally and architecturally the window is *not* an organic growth; its charm lies in its being decked out like that. In Gaudi, however, the accidental has become the essential, and what purports to be architecture can no longer be understood as such, but only as a piece of elaborate expressionist sculpture seen from within. It is perhaps the same sculptural view of architecture which finds an architectural significance in the polished geometry of an Egyptian pyramid. . . .

The sculptural view of architecture involves the mistaken idea that one can somehow judge the beauty of a thing *in abstracto*, without knowing what *kind* of thing it is; as though I could present you with an object that might be a stone, a sculpture, a box, a fruit or even an animal, and expect you to tell me whether it is beautiful before knowing what it is. In general we might say—in partial opposition to a certain tradition in aesthetics (the tradition that finds expression in eighteenth-century empiricism, and more emphatically in Kant)—that our sense of the beauty of an object is always dependent on a conception of that object, just as our sense of the beauty of a human figure is dependent on a conception of that figure. Features that we would regard as beautiful in a horse—developed haunches, a curved back, and so on—we would regard as ugly in a man, and this aesthetic judgment would be determined by our conception of what men are, how they move, and what they achieve through their movements. In a similar way, our sense of the beauty in architectural forms cannot be divorced from our conception of buildings and of the functions that they fulfill.

Functionalism can be seen, then, as part of an attempt to reassert architectural against sculptural values. As such it has sought to extend its explanatory powers through more subtle, and more vague, presuppositions. We are told that in architecture form "follows," "expresses, " or "embodies" function, ideas associated with [Eugène] Viollet-le-Duc, with the American pragmatism of [Louis] Sullivan, and with certain aspects of the modern movement. There is also the more subtle functionalism of [Augustus] Pugin and the medievalists; according to this view the reference to function is necessary as a standard of taste, a means of distinguishing genuine ornament from idle excrescence. In such diluted forms, functionalism no longer has the ring of necessary truth. Indeed, until we know a little more about the essential features of architectural appreciation we will not even know how the theory of functionalism should be formulated, let alone how it might be proved.

A further distinguishing feature of architecture is its highly localized quality. Works of literature, music and pictorial art can be realized in an infinite number of locations, either through being performed or moved, or even, in the limiting case, reproduced. With certain rare exceptions—frescoes, for example, and monumental sculpture—this change of place need involve no change in aesthetic character. The same cannot be true of architecture. Buildings constitute important features of their own environment, as their environment is an important feature of them; they cannot be reproduced at will without absurd and disastrous consequences. Buildings are also affected to an incalculable extent by changes in their surroundings. Thus the architectural *coup de théâtre* planned by Bernini for the piazza of St. Peter's has been partially destroyed by the opening up of the Via Della Conciliazione, as the effect of the spire of St. Bride's from the Thames bridges has been destroyed by the saw-like edges of the Barbican. We know of buildings whose effect depends in part on their location, either because they are ingenious solutions to problems of space—such as [Francesco] Borromini's church of S. Carlo alle Quattro Fontane—or because they are built in some striking or commanding position that is essential to their impact—such as the temple at Agrigento in Sicily—or because they involve a grandeur of conception that embraces a whole environment, in the manner of Versailles, where the architectural influence of [André] Le Nôtre's garden is infinite in ambition. This is not to say that buildings cannot be reproduced—there are several neo-classical examples to the contrary, such as the composite souvenir of Athens knows as St. Pancras' church. However, it must be acknowledged that the point of reproducing buildings is not generally comparable to the point of reproducing or copying paintings, and is certainly unlike the point of performing the same piece of music again. It is a scholarly exercise, playing no part in the natural distribution and enjoyment of a work of art. Indeed, we often feel a certain hostility towards the attempt to translate buildings, in this way, from one part of the world to another. We expect an architect to build in accordance with a sense of place, and not to design his building—as many a modern building is designed—so that it could be placed just anywhere. It is true that the architectural instinct can show itself even in the dwellings of nomadic tribes, but the impulse to which we owe most of the fine architecture that we have inherited is an impulse founded in the sense of place—the desire to mark a sacred spot or place of martyrdom, to build a monument, church or landmark, to claim possession and dominion of the land. This impulse is to be found in all serious architecture, from the antique temple and the martyrium, to the Chapel at Ronchamp and the Sydney Opera House, and it is an impulse which leads us to separate architecture from nature only with a certain considered reluctance.

This sense of place, and the consequent impression of the immovability of architecture, constrains the work of the builder in innumerable ways. Architecture becomes an art of the ensemble. It is intrinsic to architecture that it should be infinitely vulnerable to changes in its surroundings. This is a feature that architecture shares with such pursuits as interior decoration, dress, and the many quasi-moral, quasi-aesthetic activities that fall under the notion of taste. The interest in *ensembles* is partly responsible for the attention paid in architectural theory to style, and to repeatable form. . . .

A further feature of architecture should here be mentioned—the feature of technique. What is possible in architecture is determined by the extent of human competence. In architecture there are changes initiated quite independently of any change in artistic consciousness; the natural evolution of styles is cast aside, interrupted or sent off at a tangent by discoveries that have no aesthetic origin and no aesthetic aim. Consider, for example, the discovery of reinforced concrete, and [Robert] Maillart's use of it in his well-known bridges, which curve through the air across ravines where no straight path would be apt or possible. The aesthetic consequences of that technical discovery have been enormous, and nobody could have envisaged them, still less intended them, in advance. In music, literature and painting evolution has followed more nearly a changing *attitude* to art, and hence a shifting spirit of artistic creation. And while it is true that here, too, there can be technical discoveries, such as that of the piano, which actually interrupt the flow of aesthetic consciousness (as well as others, such as those of the violin, the clarinet, the saxophone and the Wagner tuba, which are more naturally seen as *consequences* of a change in taste); and while there are also engineering achievements (like that of Brunelleschi's dome), which result from aesthetic aspiration, these passing similarities only serve to underline the real distinction between architecture and the other arts. One must greet with a certain skepticism, therefore, those critics who hail the modern movement as a creation of architectural forms more in keeping with the "spirit of the age," as though the change in these forms were a product only of artistic enterprise, and not of engineering skill.

A more important distinguishing feature of architecture is provided by its character as a public object. A work of architecture imposes itself come what may, and removes from every member of the public the free choice as to whether he is to observe or ignore it. Hence there is no real sense in which an architect creates his public; the case is wholly unlike those of music, literature and painting, which are, or have become, objects of free critical choice. Poetry and music, for example, have become self-consciously "modern" precisely because they have been able to create for themselves audiences attuned to novelty and active in the pursuit of it. Clearly, the architect may change public taste, but he can do so only by addressing himself to the whole public and not merely to some educated or half-educated part of it. "Modernism" in architecture therefore raises a special problem which is not raised by modernism in the other forms of art. . . .

The artist's ability to create his audience, to demand of them a permanent sense of their own modernity, is a necessary precondition not only of the success of such an enterprise but also of its attempt. It is in this way that music, painting and literature continue to survive, even in a state of cultural chaos, through the invention of what are at first (before the successful adoption of a style) arbitrary choices and arbitrary constraints.

Now I doubt that we could freely take up such an attitude to architecture as the one I have sketched. For I doubt that we could consistently view architecture either as a form of personal expression, or as a self-conscious gesture designed for the "modern consciousness" alone. Architecture is public; it imposes itself whatever our desires and whatever our self-image. Moreover, it takes up space: Either it crushes out of existence what has gone before, or else it attempts to blend and harmonize. . . .

But perhaps the most important feature of architecture, the feature which serves most of all to give it a peculiar status and significance in our lives, is its continuity with the decorative arts, and the corresponding multiplicity of its aims. Even when architects have a definite "aesthetic" purpose, it may not be more than a desire that their work should "look right" in just the way that tables and chairs, the lay of places at a table, the folds in a napkin, an arrangement of books, may "look right" to the casual observer. Architecture is primarily a vernacular art: It exists first and foremost as a process of arrangement in which every normal man may participate, and indeed does participate, to the extent that he builds, decorates or arranges his rooms. . . .

One might say that in proposing an aesthetics of architecture, the least one must be proposing is an aesthetics of everyday life. One has moved away from the realm of high art towards that of common practical wisdom. And here one might begin to see just how inappropriate is our post-romantic conception of art to the description of the normal aesthetic judgments of the normal man, and how obscure are all the concepts, such as the concept of expression, which have been used to elucidate it.

Against the background of these difficulties, we must recognize the immense difficulty that exists in giving any articulate criticism of architecture. ◣

Questions for Discussion

1. We hear the expression that beauty is in the eye of the beholder. With respect especially to visual arts, is this true? Are there features of visual arts that are not subjective? If the aesthetics of visual arts are relative (as opposed to subjective), what standards or criteria are they relative to?

2. Are there features of paintings other than color and line that are central or essential to painting as an art form? Do the same aesthetic aspects apply to easel paintings as to other types of paintings?

3. Would your aesthetic experience of the photograph of the astronaut on the moon be different if you knew that it was a staged photograph rather than a picture of the actual original event?

4. Functionality, durability, and "beauty" were each said to be important for architecture. Are these three aspects truly independent of each other? Why or why not?

5. In what senses are the visual art forms discussed in this chapter also performing arts and in what sense are the performing art forms discussed in Chapter 8 visual arts? How useful is the distinction between performing and visual arts (or in what ways, if any, is that distinction useful)?

CHAPTER 10

LITERARY ARTS

At this very moment you are reading. You are reading about the philosophy of art. Whatever you might be thinking about what you are reading, it is a safe bet that you are not thinking this is literature. But why isn't it? Well, for one thing, you might say that it is nonfiction. But that won't do, since there is a vast body of literature that is nonfiction. Indeed, toward the end of this chapter we will consider some of that nonfiction literature. Perhaps this is not literature because it does not tell a story. That's true, depending upon what you mean by "a story." There have certainly been books written about, say, the story of human history or the story of the invention of the television or the story of Magellan's voyage around the world. If by "a story" you mean a coherent narrative of events, then these are certainly stories (or can be). Even a lawyer in a courtroom can tell a story about events and situations leading up to some arrest and trial, but we would not consider that literature. It might be the case that all literature involves telling a story, but it is definitely not the case that all storytelling is literature. In fact, if we turn to poetry as a form of literature, then it is also not the case that all literature involves telling a story. Many poems do not tell a story.

Perhaps this particular book is not literature because it is not very interesting or imaginative. That is, conditions such as being fictional or being a story are more descriptive notions, but really to be literature is about a certain quality of writing. In a way, "literature" is an honorific term, reserved for writing that has a certain style or feel or aesthetic quality. Maybe. It really is not very clear, is it? I won't say that this writing is interesting or imaginative, but there are lots of cases of interesting or imaginative or moving writing that is not obviously literature. For instance, there are some political speeches that are quite stirring, but it is not obvious that we would want to call them literature. (Of course, we might, but then we would need to have some criterion for why they are, and then we are right back where we started, asking just what that criterion is.)

Whatever literature is, it seems safe to say that it must involve language. The core of some arts, as we have seen in previous chapters, is that they are performed or that they are looked at. Literary arts, however, are literary! They are arts involving language. What will be the focus here is what sorts of language are literary, how they are used, and why. So there are—yes, you guessed it!—metaphysical, epistemological, and axiological aspects of literature. In this chapter, we will look at three broad types, or genres, of literature: fiction, poetry, and creative nonfiction. (Drama is another broad genre of literature, but because we have already touched on theater in Chapter 8, we will focus here on the other three literary arts.)

FICTION

Everyone would agree that Herman Melville's famous book *Moby Dick* is a work of fiction. Likewise, everyone would agree that D. Graham Burnett's lesser-known book *Trying Leviathan: The Nineteenth-Century New York Court Case That Put the Whale on Trial and Challenged the Order of Nature* is not a work of fiction (whether or not they would consider it a work of creative nonfiction). What is the difference? As with the broader term "literature," the term "fiction" is somewhat loose. In the reading on page 312, Christopher New offers, though not a definition of fiction, then at least a characterization. He suggests that fiction is invented narrative. He also includes a further feature that it is not formed by direct unconscious recall. We will get to that last feature soon, but first we will look at the notion that fiction is invented narrative.

To say that fiction is invented means that the content of fiction is not merely a description of things or events in the world. It certainly does not exclude describing things or events in the world as part of an invented narrative. For example, *Moby Dick* includes lots (and lots and lots!) of descriptions of whales and whaling practices and whaling paraphernalia. Charles Dickens's *David Copperfield* has descriptions of 19th century England that are true descriptions. But for something to be fiction it must be largely and primarily invented. To say that the content of the work is invented (or created) means that some of the sentences are false; they do not describe things or events in the world. The whale Moby Dick was fictional and the person David Copperfield was fictional. Neither actually existed, so the stories about them are literally false in the sense that they do not correspond to historical facts. This raises an issue about the relationship of truth and fiction that we will turn to soon. First, however, there are some preliminary points to raise and settle.

In the reading, New mentions the philosopher John Searle, who characterized fictional discourse as "nondeceptive intended illocutionary acts." Back in Chapter 8 we noted various types of meaning: locutionary (that is, literal, semantic) meaning; illocutionary (that is, intended meaning); and perlocutionary (that is, effected) meaning. Searle claimed that fictional statements are illocutionary speech acts; that is, authors intend to communicate something or other by what they write, even though what they write—as fiction—is false. (Melville knew that there was no actual whale Moby Dick.) However, lying is also an intended illocutionary act, in which a person intends something that is false. But, in the case of fiction, as opposed to the case of lying, the intent is nondeceptive. Melville was not lying to anyone by writing *Moby Dick*; he was not trying to deceive anyone into believing that that whale really was out there somewhere. Now, New agrees with Searle that fiction is a speech act (if we include writing as a form of speech) that is intentional but not intended to be deceptive. However, he says that this in itself does not capture fictional sentences. That is because there are other forms of nondeceptively intended illocutionary acts that are not fiction. In particular, he identifies irony and metaphor. (In the reading he does not discuss metaphor. Another example is parody or written caricature, in which literally false claims are made but with the intention not to deceive but to exaggerate or emphasize something or other.) In the case of irony, someone says one thing, but means something else. But that is not what is happening with fiction. Irony and fiction, New says, have different aims. With irony, one says the opposite of what one means, as with sarcasm. Fiction is not really trying to say the opposite of what the words themselves mean; the illocutionary meaning is not intended to contradict the locutionary meaning, as it is with irony. With fiction, says New, the writer is not intending to assert facts about things and events in the world, at least not directly, with the content of the specific fictional sentences. Rather, with fiction one is inventing or creating "facts."

A second point for New is that fiction is not merely a collection of fictional sentences but is a narrative; it involves a story or a coherent account with meaning. Sentences themselves are not narratives, but works are. In addition, New claims that for a work to be fiction, it must not be formed by direct unconscious recall. He gives an example of someone believing she is inventing a narrative, but by sheer coincidence it turns out that the narrative (or enough of it) is actually true of the world. It might even be that it is true because of an unconscious recall. Nevertheless, says New, it is a work of fiction because of the nature of the intention.

These comments point to a topic that aestheticians have wrestled with for quite a while, namely, what is the relation between truth and fiction. By its very nature, fiction is invented or created. It is nonfactual. The events of *Moby Dick* did not happen. Does that mean that whatever is contained in a work of fiction is false? Hardly! Just because *Moby Dick* is fiction does not mean that the town of Nantucket, Massachusetts, did not exist. It did and it still does. On the other hand, if something is fiction, then there must be falseness about it; a true narrative is simply not fiction. This seems to be a paradox. Aestheticians have suggested that one solution is to distinguish between something being fiction and something being false (which is a large part of what Searle and New were talking about). Another solution is to look more closely at the notion of truth and the different sorts of relations there are between truth and fiction. One sort of relation is to focus on truth *in* fiction. Within an invented narrative, there can be true sentences (such as sentences describing certain whaling practices). For New, the fiction is the work as a whole, not the particular sentences in it. So there can be true sentences contained in a fictional work.

Presumed here is that "truth" means correspondence to things and events in the world. But, as we noted in Chapter 1, there are other conceptions of truth, including a coherence notion of truth and a pragmatist notion of truth. These notions point to other relations between truth and fiction. For example, besides the topic of truth in fiction, there is also the topic of the truth *of* fiction. Is the work of fiction as a whole one that we would call true? Regardless of the specific sentences making up *David Copperfield*, was the work as a whole true; did it portray or depict correctly (or correctly enough) nineteenth-century England? For many, it did and this why it was important. Because of its artistic and aesthetic qualities and power, it made people see and feel the unpleasant truth about its contemporary social conditions. Likewise, for many people, *Moby Dick* truly portrays or depicts the nature and consequences of obsession or hubris.

In this context people sometimes speak of literary truth, or empathic truth, by which they mean coming to know what something is like because of its portrayal or depiction in literature. Indeed, this is exactly what many people say is truth *through* fiction, and also what they say is the value and purpose of fiction. The goal of a writer might be to represent things and events in the world or to express beliefs or feelings or values or to communicate or even to evoke or provoke others. The impact of fiction might be any of these things. But the value of fiction, say many, is that it does something to us and does it in a way that is not done (and perhaps cannot be done) nonaesthetically. The politician Robert F. Kennedy famously remarked, "There are those who look at things the way they are and ask why; I dream of things that never were and ask why not?" Both aspects (why things are the way they are and why they cannot be another way) are the value and hoped-for impact of fiction, as least of some fiction.

A few final remarks before we turn to New's comments. We just suggested a value about fiction, namely, that it can provide a lens toward seeing truth and a prod toward creating change and making something come true. There are also values within fiction. These are the aesthetic features of fiction. For example, whereas visual balance or harmony might be a value for painting, in fiction harmony would need to be connected to, say, the actions of characters. For fictional characters to be believable (within the work itself), their actions would need to be "genuine," which is a way of having internal harmony in that character. If disharmony is sought, that could be achieved via characters' inconsistent actions. Or, to give another example, pacing of events is an aesthetic value in fiction that would not apply to some other arts (such as painting).

Pacing is one of a sort of aesthetic features that are central to fiction and to literary arts generally. They are features that have to do with the linguistic nature of fiction. Besides pacing, there are features about the language itself, such as imagery, which can be achieved by metaphor or simile. There are also clarity of language and vividness of language. A passage can portray or depict some setting or situation in ways that are more or less immediate and forceful. The fecundity, or fruitfulness, of expressions or phrases can help (or not) carry an image further along in a story, which points to the notion of the linguistic flow of a work of fiction. The point here is that it is the features of language itself that are of central aesthetic concern for fiction, whereas they are inessential, and even nonexistent, for some other art forms.

Related to the immediate features of language are aesthetic aspects of language in terms of the use of language. For example, fiction (and all literary arts) makes use of symbolism, having something stand in for or represent something else. Pacing was already mentioned; it, too, is an aesthetic feature connected to the use of language, particularly in the storytelling aspect of fiction. Other components of storytelling include the construction and resolution of conflict. These might relate to the plot(s) of the work or to the characters within the work. The point is that all these various processes in fiction must be carried out via the use of language. (One might wonder about graphic novels. They are fictional literature, but their graphic nature and quality is paramount. To the extent that they are literature and fiction, however, they must rely importantly on language to avoid being "merely" a collection of pictures. A graphic novel, to be a novel, must have language as a central component.)

So, as noted above, fiction, like any art form, has fundamental metaphysical features (for example, what a story or a character or a setting is), epistemological features (for example, how a story is to be interpreted or what the relation between fiction and truth is), and axiological features (for example, what makes a good or bad story; what the aim or purpose of the work itself is, or what the aim or purpose is of some specific detail within the work to enhance the aesthetics of the work). Below, Christopher New focuses on the broad, basic question of what makes something fiction.

CHRISTOPHER NEW, "FICTION"*

Some literature is fiction, but not all fiction is literature. A wordless strip cartoon and a mime play, if they show us imaginary characters acting in imaginary scenes and situations, are works of fiction, but they are not linguistic productions, and are not literature. How much does fiction cover, then? Kendall Walton has suggested that representational paintings are as much works of fiction as are novels, plays, films, and the like. Walton says Seurat's painting *Sunday on the Island of La Grande Jatte*, for instance, is a work of fiction. It is not at all clear that this is so according to the ordinary meaning of (the relevant sense of) "fiction," which the dictionary defines broadly as "a thing feigned or imagined," or, more narrowly, as "an invented statement or narrative." If *La Grande Jatte* is a representation of an actual scene, it is neither feigned nor imagined (though

*In *Philosophy of Literature: An Introduction*. New York: Routledge, 1999. Pages 39–40, 41–43, 46–50.

imagining may be involved in our apprehension of it), nor an invented statement or narrative. Representational paintings (and other visual works) can only properly be called works of fiction, if at all, when they represent imaginary scenes. Works of fiction may, indeed, be representations, but not all representations are works of fiction. A photograph of Buckingham Palace is a representation of it, but it is not a work of fiction. Walton, however, revises both these terms, and advocates using "fiction" and "representation" interchangeably. I believe this is confusing and perhaps confused . . . and I shall use "fiction" in its ordinary sense here. . . . To the extent that *La Grande Jatte* represents an actual scene, it is not a work of fiction. To the extent that a cartoon strip, a mime play and *Anna Karenina* represent imaginary persons and actions, they are works of fiction. Moreover, I am going to suggest in the following discussion that the central idea involved in the term "work of fiction" is that of an invented *narrative*; and that it is this idea that we need principally to understand.

The question I want to answer [here] is this: What makes a discourse a work of fiction? We sometimes call lies and prevarications fictions; and, while works of fiction do not consist of lies, there is a connection between these two uses of the term. For neither lies nor works of fiction (nor sole fictional sentences) are intended to be true (though fictional works may, nevertheless, be intended to *suggest* or *imply* highly important truths). This provides us with a startline for the analysis of fiction. . . .

To utter a fiction sentence, according to [John] Searle, is to perform a nondeceptive pretended illocutionary act, but he does not say whether he thinks the converse is true, that is, whether to perform a nondeceptive pretended illocutionary act is to utter a fictional sentence. If what he is offering us is a traditional definition, the converse would have to be true; for such a definition states an equivalence—if the definition of "man" is "rational animal," then all men are rational animals and all rational animals are men. But it seems that either Searle is not offering such a definition, or else it must be flawed. For the case of irony (and metaphor—but we will not discuss that here) suggests that in fact the converse is not true. Let us look briefly at irony, then.

Irony and Fiction

It is common to define irony as saying one thing and meaning another, or saying something in order to convey the opposite. Thus when, in Shakespeare's *Julius Caesar*, Antony says, ironically, "And Brutus is an honorable man," it is claimed he means, or contrives to convey, that Brutus is not an honorable man at all. But there is something unsatisfactory about this account. In the first place, it does not explain what the point of such a procedure could possibly be. If Antony wants his audience to believe that Brutus is not an honorable man, why does he not just say so, instead of apparently saying that he is? In the second place, what sense of "saying" is operative here: merely uttering the sentence "Brutus is an honorable man," or also thereby making the *statement* that he is? Whichever is meant, the account is obscure. For how can we, either by uttering a sentence with the meaning that Brutus is an honorable man, or by actually asserting the sentence (and thereby making a statement to the effect that he is) manage to convey in some conventional way that he is not? If it does not tell us that, the theory does not so much solve a problem as enlarge it. . . .

[The] ironical speaker is speaking in order to achieve a certain effect which contrasts with the effect that would standardly be intended by uttering a sentence, i.e. when speaking seriously in order to make a statement. The ironist is not quoting a sentence but uttering it nonseriously. (Perhaps I should assure some readers here that, just as "nonstandard" was not derogatory earlier, so "nonserious" is not now; irony is an accomplishment, not a defect.) What exactly is this effect which the ironist seeks to achieve?

Consider this example. Someone arrives an hour late for a dinner party, wearing jeans and a sweater although the invitation specified formal dress. The hostess rises from the dinner table, where the guests are already half-way through the main course, and says, in a tone that betokens her ironical intention, "So glad you could get here on time. And perfectly dressed, as well!"

What is going on here? I suggest it is that the hostess is seeking to embarrass or make fun of the tardy and unsuitably attired guest by drawing attention to his late arrival and casual dress in terms (to put it generally, for the moment) which exploit the incongruity between the circumstances actually prevailing and those which would normally be appropriate for uttering the words seriously, i.e., nonironically—circumstances, in other words, which would render a serious utterance of her words true.

. . . The hostess does not *quote* a sentence; she *pretends to perform a certain illocutionary act* by uttering it. She pretends, that is, to compliment the late-arriver, while all the time intending that the audience should understand that she is only pretending, and that really she is rebuking or ridiculing him by drawing attention to the gap between the actual circumstances (the guest's being late and improperly dressed) and the circumstances that would render her remark appropriate (the guest's being punctual and properly dressed). For the irony to be effective, the audience, including the person addressed, must, of course, understand her intention. In the same way, the teacher who quotes her delinquent pupil's excuse is pretending to repeat it neutrally while all along intending the audience to understand that she is not neutral at all—on the contrary, she disbelieves it—and is really mocking or reproving him. Antony, in *Julius Caesar*, pretends to be stating that Brutus is an honorable man while really drawing attention to the gap between the actual circumstances, as described in his speech, and the circumstances that would make the statement appropriate. Ironical utterances are, thus, nondeceptive pretended illocutionary acts.

So the converse does not hold. Even if all fictional utterances did turn out to be nondeceptive illocutionary acts, not all nondeceptive illocutionary acts would be fictional utterances. . . . Fiction and irony are different. . . .

We need a perspicuous term here, to capture the distinction between what I have been calling nonstandard or nonserious utterances, which are not illocutionary acts, and those which are. Ironical and fictional utterances, we have seen, are characteristically utterances of sentences by means of which the author uses a sentence apt for performing an illocutionary act in order to perform an act of another and more sophisticated kind. Let us call such acts *para-illocutionary* acts. The ironist and the fiction-maker perform para-illocutionary acts. But there are other types of para-illocutionary acts apart from these. Lies are one type: liars typically utter a sentence in order to appear (i.e., they pretend) to be making an assertion expressing their belief, whereas in fact they are only trying to get their audience to believe to be true something which (*they* believe) is false. Metaphors are another type: someone who issues the metaphor "Life is not a bed of roses" does not assert a glaring literal truism that life is not a bed of roses, but uses a sentence apt for making that superfluous assertion in order to perform a different and more sophisticated kind of act altogether. . . .

Invented Narratives

This is, however, to speak of fictional sentences only; and what we want to get at is fictional *discourses*, or *works* of fiction. Here another important feature of fiction (which, incidentally, also distinguishes it from irony) should come to our notice: *works* of fiction are all narratives. A necessary feature of a work of fiction is that it tells, or in the case of drama, presents, a story. This is the sense noted by the dictionary, that fiction is an "invented narrative."

What is it, though, for a discourse to tell a story, to be an invented narrative? There is no clearcut answer to this question. "Story" and "narrative" are words whose edges are blurred. This does not limit their usefulness, but it does frustrate misguided attempts to draw sharp boundaries round them. A narrative or story, not only in fiction, but also in such uses as "the story of my early life," "the story of the universe," "the story of our nation," etc. are accounts (or dramatic presentations—I shall ignore this tiresome qualification from now on) of a sequence of (however loosely) connected events, characteristically involving persons, objects and institutions. Because of the blurry edges, it is impossible to say just how extensive a sequence must be in order to qualify as a story, though the longer and more connected it is, the more sure we may be that it is one. Nor is it possible to say what the subjects of stories must be. In fictional works, the stories usually concern persons (whether they themselves are fictional or not—Anna Karenina or the emperor Hadrian), or quasi-persons (the Tin Man, the little blue engine). This feature, however, reflects the kinds of fictional stories or narratives we are most interested in, rather than the limits of possible story-telling or narratives. A story can be told about a fictional kettle or a blade of grass, where these are not treated as quasi-persons; but it would be unlikely to hold our interest long, and certainly not in the way a story or narrative about a fictional person or quasi-person might. This fact, incidentally, suggests one reason why fiction is important to us. As the Roman playwright Terence put it in 163 BC: "I am a man; I hold nothing human foreign to me." Fiction standardly deals with human life under one aspect or another, and there are few of us who are not interested in that.

Fictional discourses and irony both involve make-believe or nondeceptive pretence. But the way in which pretence enters into each of them is different. The difference arises from the different aims which each has: irony to contrast how things are with how they should have been, or might have been expected to be; fiction to engage the audience in make-believe, in a nondeceptive pretending to themselves, to tell a tale, a story, to provide a narrative. This is not to deny, of course, that there may be ironical stories or narratives; it is only to say that ironical utterances are not *ipso facto* fictional; they need not constitute a story. . . .

Invention and Reality

A work of literary fiction is an invented narrative, consisting of sentences which the author invites the audience to make-believe are true, or to make-believe are authentic utterances of a real or imaginary utterer. We must say something more about the notion of invention that we have invoked here. I will speak only of fictional sentences now, but what I say about them will be true, *mutatis mutandis*, of narratives as well, and also of nonlinguistic forms of fiction-making. I shall speak, for the sake of simplicity, only of fictional sentences that the author invites the audience to make-believe are *true* (again, my remarks can be adapted easily enough to other kinds of fictional sentences).

A fictional sentence of this type is one which the author invites the audience to make-believe is true. But this is not enough; we need to add two other conditions. The first is that the sentence is one that he himself does not believe to be true. We need this condition to capture the notion of invention which is part of the notion of fiction. For the idea of invention employed here is that of *making something up*—authors of fictional sentences must have made up or invented their contents, the scenes and events they describe. They cannot, in the relevant sense, have made up the contents of a sentence if they simultaneously believe it is true. . . .

Here is an illustration of this point. Suppose a nineteenth-century Russian mother uttered a sentence with the implied invitation to her children that they should make-believe it was true, and suppose it was a sentence which, though she did not assert it, she herself believed was true (or believed expressed a true proposition). She might have announced, for instance, that she was going to tell the children a story, and gone on to utter the sentence "Napoleon rode through the streets of Moscow bare-headed on the day he ordered his troops to withdraw." She would not have *asserted* that Napoleon did that, she would have invited her audience to *make-believe* it. But she herself might have believed that Napoleon rode through the streets of Moscow bare-headed on that inauspicious day. Then she would not have uttered a fictional sentence, although she would have fulfilled the first condition of doing so, and although her audience might well have believed she had done so; for, since she believed that what she was saying was true, it would not be something that she had made up or invented. That would be so even if in fact her belief was false and Napoleon did not ride bare-headed through the streets of Moscow on that day; people who have a false belief do not make it up—they are simply mistaken.

What we have just said should not be confused with the view that a fictional sentence cannot turn out to be true. For there is no incompatibility between a sentence's being "made up" in the way we have explained and its being in fact true. Suppose, for example, that the author of the story beginning with the sentence mentioned above did not in fact believe that Napoleon rode bare-headed through the streets of Moscow on the day he ordered his troops to withdraw—suppose, in other words, that the sentence was a fictional one. Yet it might still turn out to be a true one as well. Subsequently discovered documents might show that is exactly what Napoleon did. That would not, however, show that the author had not, after all, produced a fictional sentence. Some fictional sentences might turn out to be coincidentally true in this way, and it is even conceivable that a whole fictional narrative might, too.

A possible case of a narrative's turning out to be true shows the need for the third condition which a sentence must satisfy in order to be a fictional sentence. The case is that of "unconscious memory." Suppose Virginia Woolf had produced a narrative which she believed herself to have invented, but which, it turned out later, was true of some of her own childhood experiences, although at the time of writing the narrative she had no conscious memory of them. Suppose, further, that it was those experiences that determined the content of the sentences in which she formulated her narrative. To give this bare suggestion some color, we can suppose that the narrative was a short one about nineteenth-century London and that it began with a sentence describing Queen Victoria riding through the gates of Buckingham Palace in a black carriage accompanied by two of her ladies in waiting. We will suppose now that in fact, as a child, Woolf actually saw Queen Victoria exactly as the narrative's opening scene described her, but that she had since completely forgotten it—as far, at least, as her conscious memory went. Although she had no conscious memory of what she saw, however, it was the experience of seeing the old Queen that caused the thoughts and images which she expressed in the opening sentence of her narrative, and which she believed herself to have invented.

This imaginary case of unconscious recall suggests that, although she would not have believed her sentence to be true, Woolf would not have been inventing, or making up, its content in the way that fiction requires. Hence it seems we need to add a third condition to those we have already stated for a sentence to be fictional. It is not easy to formulate this condition precisely without either letting in or keeping out too much. A faint echo of a past experience would surely not disqualify an author's sentences from being fictional; but requiring an exact match of detail before we disqualified them, supposing we could make sense of that idea, might exclude too much. Perhaps we should say that the contents of the author's sentence should not be preponderantly determined by unconscious recall, and acknowledge that there will be a blurry area where it will be uncertain whether this condition has been satisfied or not. Alternatively, we might say that if the fiction is true, it must be so only coincidentally; an unconscious memory will not be true coincidentally, but by virtue of a causal connection through memory to the events which produced the memory. . . .

Fictional sentences of the type we have discussed, then, are sentences which the author invites the audience to make-believe are true, which the author himself does not believe are true, and the contents of which are not formed by direct unconscious recall. This account can be adapted quite easily to accommodate the other types of fictional sentences that it does not fit as it stands. ◣

POETRY

The following lines are part of a literary work:

There was a merry passenger,
A messenger, a mariner:
he built a gilded gondola
to wander in, and had in her
a load of yellow oranges
and porridge for his provender;
he perfumed her with marjoram
and cardamom and lavender.

This is the first stanza of a poem entitled "Errantry," written by J. R. R. Tolkien (yes, the author of *The Lord of the Rings*). You, no doubt, identify it as poetry rather than prose, a form of writing that corresponds much more to everyday speech (as is found in fiction). Why? Why is this so readily recognizable as poetry? Just as with every other art form, there is great variability within what is considered poetry. In Chapter 5 we looked at two poems. The one written by William Carlos Williams was in free verse, that is, there was no regimented or set pattern of line structure or intonation. Another was written by Robert W. Service; it was structured to the point of being "sing-songy" and there was a definite stress on having words rhyme at the end of lines, unlike in Williams's poem. Poetic variability goes far beyond this, however; for example, both Homer's *Iliad* (which is thousands of lines long) and Matsuo Basho's haikus (which are only three lines long) are both considered to be poems. Also, just as with every other art form, poems are stand-alone artworks as well as components used for other purposes or as means toward other ends. In some cases poems—or, at least, poetic forms—are components of other artworks. For instance, lyrics to songs are often written in poetic style and are even intended by their authors as poems put to music. In other cases, the purposes for which poems are used is not connected to art, as in the case of written messages contained in greeting cards.

Given this variability and multiplicity, poetry is (like other art forms) more easily recognized and characterized than defined. There are several

features of poetry that, although perhaps not definitive, are much more characteristic of poetry as a literary art form. One of those features is the use of line as
opposed to sentence. The writing contained in many poems is technically un-
grammatical; it often is comprised of incomplete sentences. Often, too, poetic
lines are written in styles that vary from normal grammar. For instance, in the
following line from Shakespeare—"In ourselves do lie our remedies"—the subject of the sentence is at the end of the sentence, which is unusual for common
English practice. Likewise, a line from Wordsworth—"Strange fits of passion
have I known"—has the verb at the end of the sentence, also unusual for common English practice. Of course, the ungrammaticality, when it occurs in poems, is not the central aspect of poetic lines. The point is that poetic writing
emphasizes lines over sentences. The reason is that poetic writing is guided
largely by association, image, and feel rather than by descriptive assertion. It is
worth noting that another feature of at least some poetry is the visual aspect of
the writing. Because it is lines and not sentences that are important, some poems stress their physical, visual appearance on the page.

This points to other characteristic features of poetry and poetic writing.
One of those features is the emphasis on sound. How a poetic line sounds,
the combination and arrangement of specific sounds within and between
lines is a fundamental aspect of poetry. This is evident in the stanza above
from "Errantry." Poets often speak of various "devices" of sound combinations that are used in poetry. There is alliteration (similar initial sounds of
different words). The teaching phrase, "A little alliteration lets the learning
last longer" points to and uses this very device! There is also assonance (similar vowel sounds) and consonance (similar consonant sounds). In "Errantry"
both assonance and consonance are abundant. It is in this connection, that
is, the focus on sound, that rhyme is so closely associated with poetry, even
though it is rarely seen as being important to most poets today. (There is also
onomatopoeia, or similarity between the sound of a word and the meaning
of the word, as in *woof* and *meow*.)

Along with the focus on sound, poetry also emphasizes rhythm or meter,
that is, the flow of sounds in and between the lines. In the reading on page
322, Harvey Gross argues that rhythmic structure is the core of poetry; as he
puts it, meter is meaning. We will see soon what, exactly, he means by that.
For now, the point is that rhythmic structure is a central aspect of poetry,
and one that distinguishes it from other literary forms.

Another characteristic feature of poetry has more to do with phonetic
(or sound) aspects and less to do with the semantic (or meaning) aspects of

language. This feature is the density of poetic language. "Density" here does not mean thick or difficult to understand; rather, it means focusing on connotative meaning or symbolic meaning (as opposed to denotative or literal meaning). Just as a great deal of meaning can be packed into (or extracted out of) a picture, a visual image, so, too, a great deal of meaning can be packed into (or extracted out of) a well-chosen phrase or line, a linguistic image. When T. S. Eliot wrote in *The Waste Land*, "April is the cruelest month," he produced a phrase that is literally nonsense. Months are not the sort of thing than can be cruel (or, for that matter, nice). Months are abstractions, time intervals that we have decided are important enough to treat as "things." The word *April* denotes just this abstraction, and the denotative meaning of Eliot's phrase is false, if not simply nonsensical. However, its connotative meaning, what we associate with it, is far from false or nonsensical. A poetic turn of phrase, just like a picture, can be poignant and convey meaning. Again, the density of poetic writing has to do with "dense" meaning, that is, with a great deal of symbolism and imagery that is associated with the often-sparse language of the poem.

It is important to note that there are, of course, aspects of poetry that are shared with, or similar to, aspects of other literary arts. Many poems, especially epic poems such as Homer's *Iliad* or Dante's *Divine Comedy*, contain a narrative and themes. They are intended to do something (represent, express, communicate, evoke, provoke, and so on), and the linguistic content of the poem is the means by which this intention is carried out. It is also worth noting that not all poets or aestheticians see this aspect of poetry as crucial. The poet Archibald MacLeish, for instance, in his work "Ars Poetica," remarked, "A poem should not mean / But be." This is his way of emphasizing what was mentioned above: that the connotative aspects of poetry are what are important, along with the feel and imagery that is evoked. Gross expresses the same sentiment when he remarks that "paraphrase is heresy," by which he means that trying to restate a poetic line or image with "mere" factual, descriptive denotations is simply wrong-headed. It misses the nature, power, and value of poetry.

This issue of the nature and relation of connotative meaning in and for poetry has probably received the most attention from aestheticians about poetry. Some have claimed that if poetry has any force, it must be because of its content, what it says. So if a poem is profound in terms, say, of pointing out human foibles or growth or understanding, it is because the language that comprises the poem says something profound. Likewise, if a poem is whimsical, it is because of the meaning and tone of the language used. For many of these aestheticians, then, denotation is important in and for poetry. Other aestheticians, however, disagree, for reasons already alluded to above. They claim that it is the symbolism and imagery and phonetic features of poetry that matter. The philosopher Hans-Georg Gadamer, for instance, claims that poetry is a self-contained, autonomous, complete text; it does not refer beyond itself. Much as the philosopher Ludwig Wittgenstein argued that language is used for many purposes, and especially many nondenotative purposes, Gadamer insists that poetic language is akin to a performative utterance in a speech act; a poetic "utterance" does not describe the world, it engages and interacts with the world.

In the reading below, Harvey Gross also takes the view that poetry is not denotative. Even more, Gross argues that the prosodic aspects of poetry, that is, the sound and rhythmic structures, are the core components of poetry. Above, we noted that he remarked, "meter is meaning." What he means by this is that rhythmic structures are actually cognitive. It is through rhythm that meaning is conveyed. He argues that rhythmic forms actually transmit information and states that this is true of nature itself as well as of human life and experience. Even scientists today recognize that a great amount of information is conveyed and learned by us outside of formal language. This is obvious in cases of gestures or cases of "body language." Much of what we know about ourselves and about others is not explicitly cognitive, and indeed the notion of a "gut feeling" is taken very seriously today by cognitive scientists as a means of knowing how to function well. For Gross, basic among these sorts of noncognitive (or, at least, nonexplicit) forms of knowledge are rhythmic structures. It is for this reason that poetry can "speak" to us and can convey feelings and knowledge through associations and images and symbols.

▌ HARVEY GROSS, "PROSODY AS RHYTHMIC COGNITION" *

1. Our understanding of prosody's function is based on what a poem is and how we conceive the nature of rhythm. Without launching into extended aesthetic theory, let us scrutinize briefly the ontological terrain. A poem is not an "idea" or "experience" rendered into metrical language; still less is it an attitude

---

*In *Sound and Form of Modern Poetry*. Ann Arbor: University of Michigan Press, 1964. Pages 10–12, 14–17, 20–23.

toward an experience. A poem is a symbol in which idea, experience, and attitude are transmuted into feelings; these feelings move in significant arrangements: rhythmically. It is prosody and its structures which articulate the movement of feeling in a poem, and render to our understanding meanings which are not paraphrasable. Prosody enables the poet to communicate states of awareness, tensions, emotions, all of man's inner life which the helter-skelter of ordinary propositional language cannot express.

Rhythmic structure, like all aesthetic structure, is a symbolic form, signifying the ways we experience organic processes and the phenomena of nature. We speak of the rhythm of life: the curve of human development up from birth, through growth, and down to decay and death. These are not elements in a pattern of simple recurrence. They form patterns of expectation and fulfillment; birth prepares us for each succeeding stage of human development, but no stage merely repeats the stage which precedes it. All process, human or natural, thus has characteristic rhythm. We experience life not only by clock and calendar; we live by another kind of awareness. We shall, let us say, be taking a trip in a few months. We chafe with expectation; the day comes to leave and the tensions of expectation disappear. Our calendar has told us a certain period in time has been traversed; our "other awareness" has told us a certain passage of time has been experienced. The period is a series of separate events, which we can measure and date; the passage of time itself is experienced as a continuum; a mounting tension and its resolution, a rhythm.

It is rhythm that gives time a meaningful definition, a "form." "[If] the feeling of rhythm must be granted the status of a genuine experience, perhaps even of a cognition, then what is experienced in rhythm can only be time itself," [says Victor Zuckerkandl]. In the arts of time, music, and literature, rhythmic forms transmit certain kinds of information about the nature of our inner life. This is the life of feeling which includes physiological response as well as what psychologists term affect. There is often difficulty in distinguishing between affect, or emotion, and certain kinds of physical sensation. Those who attempt the neurological explanation of human experience see the difference between physiological and emotive behavior as one of degree and not one of kind. Wild anger or mild irritation depends on how much current flows along the nerves and across the synapses.

Rhythmic sound has the ability to imitate the forms of physical behavior as well as express the highly complex, continually shifting nature of human emotion. . . . Prosody does not imitate the noise of the wind, but gives a curve of feeling, the shape of an emotion. Prosodic elements include the formal patterning of syntax and stress, the quantities of the vowels, and the alliteration of consonants.

As I see it, then, prosody—rhythmic form in poetry—has a more crucial role to play than most theoreticians have previously discerned. The function of rhythmic form in poetry has been treated almost exclusively as a matter of meter and meaning. . . .

The view I take is that meter, and prosody in general, is itself meaning. Rhythm is neither outside of a poem's meaning nor an ornament to it. Rhythmic structures are expressive forms, cognitive elements, communicating those experiences which rhythmic consciousness can alone communicate: empathic human responses to time in its passage. . . .

All expressive rhythms are variations upon a pattern of expectation. The "prosody of prose" functions first as those departures from the normal grammatical structures of the language which set up lesser or greater impulses of meaning. When phonetic patterning increases . . . prose is shocked into verse. We usually think of the difference between prose and verse as a matter of meter; this is partially true. But the difference lies in the ability of poetry, through *all* the organizing devices of prosody, to achieve a higher expressiveness. The overlappings and concurrences of meter, quantity, and syntax can symbolize the movement of many simultaneous physical or physiological tensions. The tensions of life are never felt singly, in a straight line, as it were; they cross and overlap each other. They exist in depth and are felt in many dimensions. As one tension resolves a second begins, and a third or fourth may be in yet another stage of development. Prosody transmits the intricacy of the life of feeling—an organism where systems of bone, blood, muscle, and nerve often work on different frequencies, cross rhythmically.

2. The function of prosody is to image, in a rich and complex way, human process as it moves in time. On the lower level, prosody can be a direct representation of physical activity. Numerous theorists have pointed out that iambic pentameter resembles simple human physiology: the systole and the diastole of the heartbeat or the inhalation and exhalation of breathing. But human process, even in its more basic physiological aspects, is enormously complicated. Growth, fruition, decay, stasis; the process of maturation and decay: all have rhythms which prosody can image. Prosody can also trace the curves of psychological process: perception, sensation, and affect move in time and have their characteristic rhythms. The rhythmic structures of prosody reveal the mind and nerves as they grow tense in expectation and stimulation and relax in fulfillment and quiet.

A short poem of Emily Dickenson shows, in a highly dramatic way, prosody's functions; the poem's subject is the very nature of the inner life of feeling:

1 After great pain, a formal feeling comes—
2 The Nerves sit ceremonious, like Tombs—
3 The stiff Heart questions was it He, that bore,
4 And Yesterday, or Centuries before?
5 The Feet, mechanical, go round—
6 Of Ground, or Air, or Ought—
7 A Wooden way
8 Regardless grown,
9 A Quartz contentment, like a stone—
10 This is the Hour of Lead—
11 Remembered, if outlived,
12 As Freezing persons, recollect the Snow—
13 First—Chill—the Stupor—then letting go—

A prose paraphrase (a deliberate heresy) tells us that profound physical suffering leaves mind and body in a curious state of detachment. The mind sees the
body from a great distance; feelings of depression, inadequacy, indifference af-
flict consciousness but cause no tremor of emotion. Life has been arrested; the
soul has crossed over to the country beyond despair.

Our paraphrase is inadequate, of course. The experience is rendered in the
movement of the lines, and part of what the poem "means" is the movement itself. Syntax, meter, quantity, and pause articulate feelings of formal detachment,
stupefied indifference, and ceremonious numbness. Rhythmic structure conveys
those "ideas"; the rhythms or conveyers are forms for the feelings they convey.

The poem opens with an abstract statement of feeling in a syntactically complete proposition. At the fourth line the syntax becomes fragmentary, and the
soundless rhythm of meaning falters on an unresolved grammatical ambiguity.
A similar ambiguity arrests the meaning of line eight. Metrically, the lines are of
uneven length, although iambic movement dominates. In the second stanza the
meter beats metronomically:

Of Ground, | or Air, | or Ought—

The quantities of the vowels are nearly equal. The poem ends with a slowing
down of rhythmic energy as consciousness dwindles into coma: the stupefac-
tion after terrible suffering. . . .

We approach the crux of the problem, and we can formulate a working definition of what prosody is and how it functions in poetic structure. It comprises

those elements in a poem which abstract for perception the flow of time. This time, experienced in a passage of verse, is not chronological time, measured by metronomic pulse, but *felt* time, musical "duration." If we understand this, the widely used term "the music of poetry" becomes more than an empty honorific—a facile way of complimenting a poet for smoothness of texture or skillful use of verbal color. Prosody is the musical element in poetry because it reveals time in its passage and the life of feeling that moves between points *then* and *then*. Prosodic structures are akin to musical structures because phonetic patterning and syntactical expectation constitute a semantic system, a language, as it were. Like music, the language of prosody is abstract: it represents nothing and may suggest everything. But "nonverbal" languages are meaningful; few modern aestheticians are prepared to assert that the abstract art of music is purely formal, devoid of human qualities and human import.

To insist on "prosody as music" neither denies that prosody develops out of, or emphasizes, conceptual meaning nor asserts that rhythmic and phonetic elements are autonomous structures. A poem's prosody cannot exist apart from its propositional sense. Prosodic rhythm and propositional sense work as identities in poetic language. Phonetic patterning creates meaning in language; rhythm in linguistic structure is itself *sense*. . . .

3. The analysis of poetic structure must show the identity of content or "idea" and the rhythmic conveyers of feeling. But the poet's private experience of the rhythms of nature and human process must be accessible, through the senses, to the reader. The poet makes them accessible by providing a primary "aesthetic surface": an unbroken texture of phonetic values and patterns. Poetry exists in a sensuous realm of sound; we cannot feel a poem's rhythms until our ears have engaged its "aesthetic surface." In most poems this surface is its meter—heard in spoken performance or imagined in silent reading.

Some poems present this surface so obviously that we are aware of little else:

> Before the beginning of years
> There came to the making of man
> Time with a gift of tears;
> Grief with a glass that ran.

Prosody, if it is a valuable part of poetic structure, must create the illusion of experienced or durational time and what we experience in those fictitious intervals—the movement, stress, and tensions of our emotional life. Swinburne's verse [above] creates little more than an illusion of automatic physical activity; we hear marching men or galloping horses. The higher purpose of prosody is not imitation of physical process, though we can, if we like, do sitting-up exercises to:

> Strong gongs groaning as the guns boom far,
> Don John of Austria is going to the war. . . . [Gross's ellipsis.]

These examples return us to an earlier question: what is the relation of a poem's prosody to its referential meaning, its paraphrasable content? Certainly prosody has, or should have, mimetic value; there should be some correlation of idea and rhythm. If we sense a disparity between thought and movement—if the meter sounds incongruous to the idea—we have valid grounds for making negative judgments about the poem's value. Swinburne's rhythm, with its catch swing, seems inappropriate to man's making and the tears of time. We should have rhythms expressive of mystery and grief; not a quick march tempo. We feel muscular exhilaration: scarcely what the subject requires.

I do not believe that every emotion has a precise symbolic form, and in the case of poetry, an exact rhythmical equivalent. The rhythms of poetry belong to the "non-discursive" forms of human symbolism. Rhythms are highly connotative structures, and we cannot say the meter of Swinburne's poem denotes anything more than its patterns of stress:

$$\breve{\ }\ \acute{\ } \mid \breve{\ }\ \breve{\ }\ \acute{\ } \mid \breve{\ }\ \breve{\ }\ \acute{\ }$$
$$\breve{\ }\ \acute{\ } \mid \breve{\ }\ \breve{\ }\ \acute{\ } \mid \breve{\ }\ \acute{\ }$$
$$\acute{\ } \mid \breve{\ }\ \breve{\ }\ \acute{\ } \mid \breve{\ }\ \acute{\ }$$
$$\acute{\ } \mid \breve{\ }\ \breve{\ }\ \acute{\ } \mid \breve{\ }\ \acute{\ }$$

Swinburne's meter does not fulfill his denotational content. It is as if a composer were to write a funeral march *presto giocoso* [that is, playful] in one of the more brilliant major keys. There is no absolute aesthetic demand that funeral marches be written in minor keys or in tempi suited to an actual procession of mourners. We feel, however, that speed and brilliance do not connote dignity and grief; they are not the proper forms for emotions we normally associate with funerals. Swinburne's galloping meter is not an emotional form suitable to his subject.

If prosody is itself meaning, meaning also forms prosody. Rhythmic structures grow out of patterns of rhetorical emphasis: patterns that sometimes move against or across the meter. We find in Donne's poetry many startling instances of expressive rhythms emerging out of ambiguities of emphasis: where meter pulls the propositional sense in one direction, rhetorical emphasis in the other. In *A Valediction: of my name, in the window*, the poet imagines that his mistress might take another lover; he hopes that his name, scratched in the window-glass, will blot out the name of his successor:

> And when thy melted maid,
> Corrupted by thy Lover's gold, and page,
> His letter at thy pillow 'hath laid,
> Disputed it, and tam'd thy rage,
> And thou begin'st to thaw towards him, for this,
> May my name step in, and hide his.

The last line presents a metrical crux. If we follow the meter closely, we scan and read:

> May mý | name stép | ín and | hide hís . . . [Gross's ellipsis]

My and *his* are thrown into rhetorical balance; the parallel is between *my name* and *his* [*name*] [Gross's brackets]. The poet feels reasonably secure that his name will cover the name of her new lover. But if we follow the "prose" stress of the words, we scan:

> Máy my | náme step | ín and | híde his . . . [Gross's ellipsis]

The meter breaks down and we do not even have a regular final foot. *May* is stressed; it now seems highly conditional that the image of the poet's name can keep his mistress faithful. The stressed *hide* tinges the whole line with interrogation—and the poet dissolves in doubts. Although the poet never says he is anxious, his rhythm gives him away.

Whether the patterns of rhythm and meter genetically precede conceptualization; whether they are formed after the idea has been formulated; or whether rhythmic form and conceptual meaning are conceived simultaneously seems matters of individual poetic genius. It is reported that Yeats first wrote his lines out as prose and counted the meters off on his fingers; it is also reported that he always had a "tune in his head" when he composed. Eliot remarks, "I know that a poem, or a passage of a poem, may tend to realize itself first as a particular rhythm before it reaches expression in words, and that this rhythm may bring to birth the idea and the image . . ." [Gross's ellipsis]. However the poet works, the meaningful structures of language can form rhythms and meters. The grammatical function of a word can determine whether it is metrically stressed or unstressed:

This is | the end | of the whale road | and the whale . . .
Time that | with *this* | strange ex | cuse . . . [Gross's ellipses]

The individual word also has characteristic rhythm, depending on its pattern of stress, and isolated words may form cross-rhythms with basic metrical structure. The opening of *The Waste Land* is written in four-beat strong-stress meter:

> April is the cruellest month, breeding
> Lilacs out of the dead land, mixing
> Memory and desire, stirring
> Dull roots with spring rain.

Words in trochaic form (*April, cruellest, breeding, Lilacs, mixing, stirring*) predominate, and the falling rhythm they create weaves itself about the underlying four-stress beat.

The manifold ways in which sound and meaning coalesce in poetry are, of course, the subjects of our inquiry. It is perhaps sufficient, at this point, to say neither meaning nor sound can operate independently. It is also important to distinguish between what we term the primary and secondary devices of prosody. The articulations of sound in temporal sequences, rhythms and meters, present us with "aesthetic surface"; it is this surface which our perception immediately engages. Prosody is an aural symbolism, a significant arrangement of acoustical phenomena. But since poetry has been written, and more importantly, *printed*, visual qualities have contributed to prosodical arrangement. Line endings, stanzaic shape, the general appearance of the poem on the page—all contribute to rhythmic effect. These visual elements, however, are, and *should be* secondary—in the way that written directions in a musical score are in no sense the music but only useful guides to realizing a correct performance. Visual elements are aids to performance—remembering that "performance" includes the mind's silent re-creation of a poem as we read to ourselves.

To multiply the visual elements in a poem reduces for perception the available "aesthetic surface." Through the agency of sound, poetry makes imaginative facts out of the deepest, most elusive feeling. The poet who substitutes visual tricks for a surface of articulated sound limits his range of feeling; he gives up the primary means by which feelings can be symbolized and apprehended. A poem must sound; it is sound that we first experience as pleasure in the reading of poetry. Nursery rhymes, children's game verses, primitive charms: all appeal through the movement of sound. Prosody offers in the basic forms of metrical structure a continuous articulating surface which makes rhythmic cognition possible. ◣

CREATIVE NONFICTION

Consider the following two literary passages. One of them is from a work of fiction and one of them is from a work of nonfiction. Which is which?

The Feast of the New Yam was held every year before the harvest began, to honor the earth goddess and the ancestral spirits of the clan. New yams could not be eaten until some had first been offered to these powers. Men and women, young and old, looked forward to the New Yam Festival because it began the season of plenty—the new year. . . .

The New Yam Festival was thus an occasion for joy throughout Umuofia. And every man whose arm was strong, as the Ibo people say, was expected to invite large numbers of guests from far and wide. Okonkwo always asked his wives' relations, and since he now had three wives his guests would make a fairly big crowd.

But somehow Okonkwo could never become as enthusiastic over feasts as most people. He was a good eater and he could drink one or two fairly big gourds of palm-wine. But he was always uncomfortable sitting around for days waiting for a feast or getting over it. He would be very much happier working on his farm.

The agreement came to this that Jogona should take over his dying friend's wife and child, and pay to her father the two goats that were still due to him from the sum of her purchase price. From now the report became a list of expenses, which Jogona had brought upon himself through the adoption of the child Wamai. He had, he stated, purchased an extraordinary good medicine for Wamai just after he had taken him over, when he was sick. At some time he had bought rice from the Indian duca for him, as he did not thrive on maize. Upon one occasion he had had to pay five Rupees to a white farmer of the neighborhood, who said that Wamai had chased one of his turkeys into a pond. This last amount of hard cash, which he had probably had difficult in raising, had stamped itself upon the mind of Jogona; he came back to it more than once. From Jogona's manner it appeared that he had, by this time, forgotten that the child whom he had now lost had not been his own.

The first passage is from *Things Fall Apart*, written by Chinua Achebe and the second passage is from *Out of Africa*, written by Isak Dinesen. *Things Fall Apart* is fiction; *Out of Africa* is nonfiction. Is there any obvious, telling difference? Both narrate events, or at least settings with characters. Of course, both passages are excerpted from much longer works, and there are other passages from those works that might be easier to identify as being fictional or nonfictional. However, they do point to the fact that the distinction between fiction and nonfiction is not a sharp one.

As Robert Root and Michael Steinberg note in the reading on page 334, literature has long been presented and analyzed as consisting of three broad categories, or genres: fiction, poetry, and drama. At the same time, other forms of writing have existed alongside these three genres for as long as we have written records. Some of those other forms of writing we would not typically identify as being literature (or even literary): court records, historical descriptions, legal documents, at least some academic works, and others. However, there are many forms of writing that are literary, or at least have been treated as such, but do not quite fit into the genres of fiction, poetry, or drama. For instance, there is a long history of memoirs, biographies, critiques, literary journalism, and essays of various types (including nature essays, personal essays, political satire, and parody). Many quite famous works fit into these categories of writing, such as Jonathan Swift's "A Modest Proposal," Michel de Montaigne's "An Apology for Raymond Sebond," Desiderius Erasmus's *In Praise of Folly*, Izaak Walton's *The Compleat Angler*, Galileo Galilei's *Dialogues Concerning the Two Chief World Systems*, Virginia Woolf's *A Room of One's Own*, Truman Capote's *In Cold Blood*, and *The Diary of Anne Frank*, among countless others.

Root and Steinberg remark that these forms of literary writing that do not fit into the categories of fiction, poetry, or drama have come to be labeled as *literary nonfiction* or *creative nonfiction*. These terms are intended to distinguish these forms and examples of writing not only from the sorts of nonliterary writing mentioned above, but also from the typical three literary genres. They could just as well be labeled as creative nonpoetry or creative nondrama; however, the writing styles and forms are quite recognizably not poetry or drama, whereas (as the two passages above indicate) they can be quite like some styles or forms of fiction, so they are labeled as nonfiction to emphasize their distinction from fiction. So, creative nonfiction is distinguished from other literary arts as well as from noncreative nonfiction.

As with every other art form that has been considered in this book, there is no defining set of characteristics of creative nonfiction. A necessary condition is that the content be nonfiction, of course. Nevertheless, it is literary because it is creative. It is a narrative that is intended to be an artwork, with aesthetic features (as opposed to, say, a work of "straight" journalism). Besides the fact that creative nonfiction is (intended to be) creative and a true or factual narrative, does it have any distinguishing features? One feature that is often emphasized is the personal presence of the author. This is especially the case for memoirs, but it is not unique to that style. The point is that for creative nonfiction, the content of the writing is clearly (intended as) the author's own story; it is representational of events in the author's life or of beliefs and values held by the author. In fiction, an author can present or depict events, attitudes, beliefs, feelings, values, and so on that are not his or her own and, indeed, the literary work itself can be approached and experienced independently of the author. With creative nonfiction (at least most forms of it), the author is always in the foreground. Who is telling the story is foremost. The nature of creative nonfiction as nonfiction also emphasizes the notion of veracity, or truthfulness. Even if a story is being told, and being told creatively, the content must be true for it to be nonfiction. This has led some aestheticians to speak of creative nonfiction as a factual rendering through features associated with fiction.

What aesthetic aspects are involved with creative nonfiction? First, from the perspective of the literary work itself, the same features that are present and important for fiction apply here as well. The overwhelming feature is language, including those issues of linguistic imagery, flow, clarity, vivacity, fecundity, and so on. Closely related are issues involving the use of the language, such as pacing and narrative structure. Of course, these last issues will vary in tone and significance depending upon the type of creative nonfiction. Pacing of events will probably be more important in a memoir than in a satirical essay. Although plot is fundamental to fiction, it is not quite the same concern in creative nonfiction. However, plot in the sense of a constructed narrative that flows, perhaps even with conflict and resolution, can be central to some creative nonfiction.

From the perspective of the artist-author, the same issues that arise for fiction arise also for creative nonfiction. The author obviously has intentions and these are basic for creative nonfiction. Why is that person writing this essay or biography or critique? Because personal presence is so prevalent in creative nonfiction, author intention is even more central here than in fiction.

Although many aestheticians have criticized the view that the author's intention is ineliminable for an artwork—this is the "intentional fallacy" that was mentioned in Chapter 4—such criticism is less well founded in the case of creative nonfiction. Here author intention (personal presence) is fundamental to the nature of the work. Of course, the impact and meaning, even of a memoir, on the reader can transcend the author's intentions, but this does not negate the claim that intention for this genre is crucial.

Issues of representation, expression, communication, and change apply to creative nonfiction, as well. Creative nonfiction writers tell stories, but because veracity (truth) is central to this genre, representation is also central. By relating the poignancy of events from one's life to the development of the author (or others in the story) based on actual events and episodes, the creative nonfiction writer must be more attentive to representation than other artists. At the same time, that author is communicating the significance of these events to an audience. The diary of Anne Frank is as moving as it is because it details real events that transcend that girl and that time. It communicates to others and evokes a response. Of course, this is independent of the intentions of the author (in this case Anne Frank), so this has led some aestheticians to question the claim that the centrality of personal presence in creative nonfiction makes author intention so central.

On the other hand, evocation or provocation are unquestionably the central focus of some forms of creative nonfiction, especially some essays, satire, and parody. The primary aspect of much literary satire and parody, as well as less comedic essay writing, is the desire to bring about change. Such literature is social, political, or moral critique with a smile. As noted earlier in this book, many artworks are intended by artists to be agents of social and political change, and literary satire–parody is a major artistic form in this tradition. This obviously relates aesthetic concerns from the perspective of the artist (intention) with concerns about art and society (as noted in Chapter 6).

What about aesthetic issues from the perspective of the audience? What is it to have an aesthetic experience of a work of creative nonfiction? There is no single answer to this question. The aesthetic experience that results from reading, say, a social satire would be, one hopes, amusement along with a sense of enlightenment and urgency to change those things or conditions that were parodied. Many other forms of creative nonfiction would, one hopes, generate not amusement but, instead, thoughtful reflection or perhaps a sense of connectedness to the lives of others.

Given that creative nonfiction is closely aligned as an art form with fiction—as was noted above, it is said to be a factual rendering through features associated with fiction—is there anything aesthetically unique about creative nonfiction? Its unique feature, as an art form, might well be the necessity of truthfulness. No one would criticize *Moby Dick* if it were discovered that Herman Melville had simply made up many of the whaling details in the book. (They might remark that he did not do his research very well to tell a good whaling story, but the factual details are not really the important component of the story.) However, the reception, interpretation, and evaluation of creative nonfiction depend much more on truthfulness. For instance, in 2003 the book *A Million Little Pieces*, written by James Frey, was published. It was said to be an account of his life as a young man involved with a life of drugs, alcohol, and substance abuse, followed by his treatment in trying to recover. Three years later, it was revealed that he had fabricated much of the story, with the result that the author was roundly criticized, and many who had originally spoken of the positive aesthetic qualities of the work retracted those evaluations. (The book was then republicized as not nonfiction but "semi-fiction.") Veracity, then, is certainly a central feature of creative nonfiction, and it points to other features of creative nonfiction that are, if perhaps not unique, at least aesthetically singular. It also points to the fact that creative nonfiction stands apart, at least in some ways, from other literary arts.

This being said, creative nonfiction has received far less attention from aestheticians than any of the other literary arts. In the following reading, Robert L. Root Jr. and Michael Steinberg give an overview of the landscape of creative nonfiction as one small step toward rectifying this inattention.

▌ ROBERT L. ROOT JR. AND MICHAEL STEINBERG, "CREATIVE NONFICTION, THE FOURTH GENRE"*

Creative nonfiction is the fourth genre. This assumption . . . needs a little explaining. Usually literature has been divided into three major genres or types: poetry, drama, and fiction. Poets, dramatists, and novelists might arrange this trio in a different order, but the idea of three literary genres has, until very re-

*In *The Fourth Genre: Contemporary Writers of/on Creative Nonfiction*. 3rd ed. New York: Pearson Longman, 2005. Pages xxiii–xxx.

cently, dominated introductory courses in literature, generic divisions in literature textbooks, and categories of literature in bookstores. Everything that couldn't be classified in one of these three genres or some subgenre belonging to them (epic poetry, horror novels) was classified as "nonfiction," even though . . . they could be classified as "nonpoetry" as well. Unfortunately, this classification system suggests that everything that is nonfiction should also be considered nonliterature, a suggestion that is, well, nonsense.

We refer to creative or literary nonfiction as the fourth genre as a way of reminding readers that literary genres are not limited to three; we certainly do not intend the term to indicate a ranking of the genres but rather to indicate their equality. It would be better to have a more succinct, exclusive term for the genre. Writers have been composing literary forms of nonfiction for centuries, even if only recently they have begun to use the terms *creative nonfiction* or *literary nonfiction* to separate it from the nonliterary forms of nonfiction. And, after all, although it is creative or imaginative or literary, its being nonfiction is still what distinguishes it from the other literary genres.

The shape of creative nonfiction is, in Robert Atwan's phrase, "malleable" and, in O. B. Hardison's, "Protean." Perhaps we can picture its throbbing, pulsating, mercurial existence as locations on a series of intersecting lines connecting the poles of the personal and the public, the diary and the report, the informal and the formal, the marginalia and the academic article, the imaginative and the expository. Creative nonfiction essays would be located on these lines somewhere within the boundaries set by neighboring genres, not only "the three creative genres" of fiction, poetry, and drama but also the "expressive" genres of diary, journal, and autobiography and the "objective" genres of traditional (as opposed to literary) journalism, criticism, and polemic and technical writing. It may be fair to say that creative nonfiction centers in the essay but continually strains against the boundaries of other genres, endeavoring to push them back and to expand its own space without altering its own identity.

The Elements of Creative Nonfiction

Yet despite all the elusiveness and malleability of the genre and the variety of its shapes, structures, and attitudes, works of creative nonfiction share a number of common elements, although they may not all be present all the time in uniform proportions. The most pronounced common elements of creative fiction are *personal presence, self-discovery and self-exploration, veracity, flexibility of form,* and *literary approaches to nonfiction.*

Personal Presence

Writers of creative nonfiction tend to make their personal presences felt in the writing. Whatever the subject matter may be—and it can be almost anything— most creative nonfiction writing, as Rosellen Brown says of the essay, "presents itself, if not as precisely true, then as an emanation of an identifiable speaking voice making statements for which it takes responsibility." In such writing the reader encounters "a persona through whose unique vision experience or information will be filtered, perhaps distorted, perhaps questioned"; the writer's voice creates an identity that "will cast a shadow as dense and ambiguous as that of an imaginary protagonist. The self is surely a created character."

Throughout the various forms of creative nonfiction, whether the subject is the writer's self (as perhaps in personal essays and memoirs) or an objective, observed reality outside the self (as perhaps in nature essays and personal cultural criticism), the reader is taken on a journey into the mind and personality of the writer. Some writers directly engage in interrogations of the self by unequivocally examining and confronting their own memories, prejudices, fears, even weaknesses. Others are more meditative and speculative, using the occasion of remembered or observed experience to connect to issues that extend beyond the self and to celebrate or question those connections. Still others establish greater distance from their subjects, taking more of an observer's role than a participant's role. Yet even as they stand along the sidelines we are aware of their presence, because their voice is personal, individual, not omniscient.

The sense of the author's presence is a familiar element of essays and memoirs, of course. These center on the author's private reflections and experiences. . . . But personal presence can also pull subject-oriented writing (principally journalistic and academic writing) into the realm of creative nonfiction. Arguing a need for "writerly models for writing about culture," Marianna Torgovnick insists, "Writing about culture is personal. Writers find their material in experience as well as books, and they leave a personal imprint on their subjects. They must feel free to explore the autobiographical motivations for their work, for often this motivation is precisely what generates writers' interests in their topics. Including this personal voice in cultural criticism surrenders some of the authority—or the pretense of authority—generally found in academic writing, but substitutes for it the authority of apparent candor or personal honesty. What Rosellen Brown writes of the personal essayist is applicable to all creative nonfiction writers: 'the complex delight of the essayist's voice is that it can admit to bewilderment without losing its authority.'" This sense of personal presence is one of the most forceful elements of creative nonfiction.

Self-Discovery and Self-Exploration

[This] genre encourages self-discovery, self-exploration, and surprise. Often, the writer "is on a journey of discovery, often unasked for and unplanned," Rosellen Brown writes. "The essayist is an explorer, whereas the fiction writer is a landed inhabitant." Phillip Lapate speaks of self-discovery that takes place in essays as writing that "not only monitors the self but helps it gel. The essay is an enactment of the creation of the self." This genre grants writers permission to explore without knowing where they will end up, to be tentative, speculative, reflective. Because writing creative nonfiction so often reveals and expresses the writer's mind at work and play, the genre permits us to chart the more whimsical, nonrational twists and turns of our own imaginations and psyches. More frequently than not, the subject matter becomes the catalyst or trigger for some personal journey or inquiry or self-interrogation. Writers who seem most at home with this genre are those who like to delve and to inquire, to question, to explore, probe, meditate, analyze, turn things over, brood, worry—all of which creative nonfiction allows, even encourages.

Such interests may seem at first glance appropriate only to a narrow range of "confessional writing," but in much of the best creative nonfiction, writers use self-disclosure as a way of opening their writing to a more expansive exploration. This genre, then, is a good choice for writers who like to reach for connections that extend beyond the purely personal. As W. Scott Olson writes, "As the world becomes more problematic, it is in the little excursions and small observations that we can discover ourselves, that we can make an honest connection with others, that we can remind each other of what it means to belong to one another."

Flexibility of Form

One of the most exciting elements of creative nonfiction is the way in which contemporary writers "stretch the limits of the form" and "are developing a [nonfiction] prose that lives along the borders of fiction and poetry," [writes Robert Atwan]. Contemporary creative nonfiction uses the full range of style and structure available to other literary and nonliterary forms. Most often, readers have noticed the use of fictional devices in creative nonfiction, particularly in what is termed *the nonfiction novel* or in certain examples of literary journalism, which Mark Kramer has defined as "extended digressive narrative nonfiction." Rosellen Brown, who refers to the personal essay as a "nonfiction narrative," believes it is "every bit as much an imaginative construction as a short story" and that "it must use some, if not all, of the techniques of fiction: plot, characterization, physical atmosphere, thematic complexity, stylistic appropriateness, psychological open-endedness."

And yet, while narrative elements may frequently play a part in creative nonfiction, the genre often works with lyrical, dramatic, meditative, expository, and argumentative elements as well. As Annie Dillard says, "The essays can do everything a poem can do, and everything a short story can do—everything but fake it." It can also do everything a diary, a journal, a critical article, an editorial, a feature, and a report can do.

Moreover, perhaps more frequently than in other genres, creative nonfiction writers are likely to innovate and experiment with structure. They draw not only on narrative chronology and linear presentation but also on nonlinear, "disjunctive," or associative strategies. They use different angles and perspectives to illuminate a point or explore an idea, drawing on visual and cinematic techniques such as collages, mosaics, montages, and jump cuts. They can leap backward and forward in time, ignoring chronology of event to emphasize nonsequential connections and parallels; they can structure the essay around rooms in a house or cards in a tarot deck; they can interrupt exposition or narrative with passages from journals and letters or scenes from home movies. Part of the excitement of the genre is its openness to creative forms as well as to creative contents, its invitation to experiment and push at boundaries between genres, and its ability to draw on an unlimited range of literary techniques.

Veracity

Because it sometimes draws on the material of autobiography, history, journalism, biology, ecology, travel writing, medicine, and any number of other subjects, creative nonfiction is reliably factual, firmly anchored in real experience, whether the author has lived it or observed and recorded it. As essayist and memoirist Annie Dillard writes, "The elements in any nonfiction should be true not only artistically—the connects must hold at base and must be veracious, for that is the convention and the covenant between the nonfiction writer and his reader." Like the rest of us, the nonfiction writer, she says, "thinks about actual things. He can make sense of them analytically or artistically. In either case he renders the real world coherent and meaningful, even if only bits of it, and even if that coherence and meaning reside only inside small texts." For critic Barbara

Lounsberry, who is principally speaking of literary journalism, factuality is central, by which she means: "Documentable subject matter chosen from the real world as opposed to 'invented' from the writer's mind"; she adds that "anything in the natural world is game for the nonfiction artist's attention." . . .

Artistry needs some latitude; self-disclosure may be too risky to be total, particularly when it involves disclosure of others. Just as Thoreau compressed two years at Walden Pond into one to get the focus he needed for his great book, creative nonfiction writers sometimes alter the accuracy of events in order to achieve the accuracy of interpretation. Some of this is inadvertent—the great challenge of memoir writing is knowing how much we remember is reliable and accepting the likelihood that we are "inventing the truth." "You can't put together a memoir without cannibalizing your own life for parts," Annie Dillard writes in "To Fashion a Text." "The work battens on your memories. And it replaces them." Memories blur over time and edit themselves into different forms that others who had the same experience might not recognize. Finding the language to describe experience sometimes alters it, and your description of the experience becomes the memory, the way a photograph does. At the least we may feel a need to omit the relevant detail or protect the privacy of others not as committed to our self-disclosure as we are. The truth may not necessarily be veracious enough to take into court or a laboratory; it need only be veracious enough to satisfy the writer's purpose and the art of the writing.

Literary Approaches to Nonfiction

The language of creative nonfiction is as literary, as imaginative, as that of other literary genres and is similarly used for lyrical, narrative, and dramatic effects. What separates creative nonfiction from "noncreative nonfiction" (if we can be forgiven the use of that term for a moment to categorize all nonfiction outside this genre) is not only "the unique and subjective focus, concept, context and point of view in which the information is presented and defined" [according to Lee Gutkind] but also the ways in which language serves the subject. This is partly what Chris Anderson is alluding to when he writes that certain essays and journalism are not literary, and what Barbara Lounsberry means by claiming that, no matter how well the other elements of a nonfiction work are achieved, "it may still fail the standards of literary nonfiction if its language is dull or diffuse." . . . When writers of poetry or fiction turn to creative nonfiction, as poet Mary Karr does in her memoir, *The Liars' Club*, or poet Garrett Hongo does in his memoir, *Volcano*, they bring with them the literary language possible in those other genres and are able to use it. . . .

The writer in creative nonfiction is often the reader's guide, pointing out the sights along the way, the places of interest where special attention is required. In such writing the reader is treated like a spectator or an audience. But often the writer is the reader's surrogate, inviting her to share the author's space in imagination and to respond to the experience as if she is living it. In such writing the reader is treated like a participant. In creative nonfiction, then, in addition to exploring the information being presented—the ways in which various ideas, events, or scenes connect to one another and relate to some overarching theme or concept or premise—the reader also has to examine the role the writer takes in the work. The writer's role and the structure of the writing are not as predictable in creative nonfiction as they are in other forms, such as the news article or the academic research paper, the sermon or the lecture. The structure of the essay or article may be experimental or unexpected, an attempt to generate literary form out of subject matter instead of trying to wedge subject matter into an all-purpose literary form. When it departs from linear, tightly unified forms to achieve its purpose, contemporary creative nonfiction does not simply meander or ramble like the traditional essay; instead it moves in jump cuts, flashbacks, flash-forwards, concentric or parallel or tangential strands. Readers sometimes have to let the works themselves tell them how they should be read.

Writers, Readers, and the Fourth Genre

The interaction between the writer and the genre in which the writer works influences the outcome of the work. Writers of other nonfiction forms such as criticism, journalism, scholarship, or technical and professional writing tend to leave themselves out of the work and to view the works as a means to an end; they want to explain, report, inform, or propose. For them the text they produce is a vehicle, a container or package, to transport information and ideas to someone else, the intended readers. Some people have referred to these forms as *transactional writing*. Writers of other literary forms such as poetry, fiction, and drama tend to put themselves in the work and to view the work as an end in itself; they want to reflect, explore, speculate, imagine, and discover, and the text they create is a structure, an anchored shape like a sculpture or a monument or a building, to which interested readers are drawn. The result is often called *poetic* or *creative writing*. Writers of creative nonfiction by definition share the qualities of both groups of writers, and the work they create reflects varying measures of both kinds of writing. . . .

Readers come to creative nonfiction with different expectations from those they bring to the other genres. At the core of those expectations may be, in a sense, the hope of becoming engaged in a conversation. Much fiction, drama, poetry, and film is presented as performance, as entertainment essentially enclosed within itself—we are usually expected to appreciate or admire its creators' artistry whether we are encouraged to acknowledge their intensity or insight. Much nonliterary nonfiction (various forms of journalism and academic writing, for example) is presented as a transaction delivering information, sometimes objective, sometimes argumentative—we are usually expected to receive or accept their creators' knowledge or data the way we would a lecture or a news broadcast. Creative nonfiction, which is simultaneously literary and transactional, integrates these discourse aims: it brings artistry to information and actuality to imagination, and it draws on the expressive aim that lies below the surface in all writing. Expressive writing breaks the surface most notably in personal writing such as journals, diaries, and letters, but it has connected with the reader most prominently in the personal or familiar essay. Other forms of writing have at center the personal impulse, the need for expression, but the essay has traditionally been the outlet by which that impulse finds public voice.

Readers turn to creative nonfiction to find a place to connect to the personal voice, to connect not to art or knowledge alone but to another mind. This means that writers too have a place to connect, a genre that gives them permission to speak in the first person singular, not only about their knowledge and their beliefs but also about their uncertainties and their passions, not only about where they stand but also about the ways they arrived there, not only about the worlds they have either imagined or documented but also about the worlds they have experienced or inhabit now. Creative nonfiction may be the genre in which both reader and writer feel most connected to each other. ◣

Questions for Discussion

1. Drama is one of the literary arts and is also, in the guise of theater, a performing art. Can the other literary genres also appropriately be considered performing arts? Why or why not?

2. Are there different aims or goals or purposes for the different forms of literary arts? Does poetry have a purpose (or set of purposes) that differs from the purpose (or purposes) of fiction? Who determines those aims, goals, or purposes?

3. Why is poetry not also creative nonfiction? Or is it? What aspects of creative nonfiction are also significant for poetry?

4. Are there fictional or poetic truths? What would this mean? Truth is a relation between things (such as a belief and some state of affairs in the world). What would a fictional or poetic truth be other than a "normal" truth?

5. Epistemological issues seem to emerge for all of the literary arts. Because these arts necessarily involve language, they seem to have necessary connections to the world (since language relates thoughts and beliefs to the things and events in the world). What is the importance or relation of knowledge to literature? How can we acquire knowledge from literature? Knowledge about what? Could that knowledge turn out to be false?

Further Reading

There are a great number of books available on the philosophy of art and aesthetics. Below is a small selection of titles that would be fruitful for further study of these topics.

General Reference Works

Cooper, David, ed. *A Companion to Aesthetics*. Malden, MA: Blackwell, 1992.

Gaut, Berys, and Dominic McIver Lopes, eds. *The Routledge Companion to Aesthetics*. New York: Routledge, 2005.

Kelly, Michael, ed. *Encyclopedia of Aesthetics*. Oxford: Oxford University Press, 1998.

Kivy, Peter, ed. *The Blackwell Guide to Aesthetics*. Malden, MA: Blackwell, 2004.

Levinson, Jerrold, ed. *Oxford Handbook of Aesthetics*. Oxford: Oxford University Press, 2003.

Anthologies of Primary Readings

Cahn, Steven, and Aaron Meskin, eds. *Aesthetics: A Comprehensive Anthology*. New York: Blackwell, 2007.

Cazeaux, Clive, ed. *The Continental Aesthetics Reader*. 2nd ed. New York: Routledge, 2012.

Goldblatt, David, and Lee B. Brown, eds. *Aesthetics: A Reader in Philosophy of the Arts*. 2nd ed. Upper Saddle River, NJ: Prentice Hall, 2005.

Lamarque, Peter, and Stein Haugom Olsen, eds. *Aesthetics and the Philosophy of Art: The Analytic Tradition*. New York: Blackwell, 2004.

Neill, Alex, and Aaron Ridley, eds. *The Philosophy of Art: Readings Ancient and Modern*. New York: McGraw Hill, 1995.

Richter, Peyton E., ed. *Perspectives in Aesthetics: Plato to Camus*. Indianapolis: Bobbs-Merrill, 1967.

Wartenberg, Thomas E., ed. *The Nature of Art: An Anthology*. 3rd ed. Boston: Wadsworth, 2012.

General Introductions and Overviews

Eaton, Marcia Muelder. *Basic Issues in Aesthetics*. Prospect Heights, IL: Waveland Press, 1988.

Freeland, Cynthia. *But Is It Art? An Introduction to Art Theory*. Oxford: Oxford University Press, 2002.

Graham, Gordan. *Philosophy of the Arts: An Introduction to Aesthetics*. 3rd ed. New York: Routledge, 2005.

Passmore, John. *Serious Art*. Chicago: Open Court, 1991.

Rader, Melvin, and Bertram Jessup. *Art and Human Values*. Englewood Cliffs, NJ: Prentice Hall, 1976.

Sheppard, Anne. *Aesthetics: An Introduction to the Philosophy of Art*. Oxford: Oxford University Press, 1987.

Specific Arts

Alperson, Philip, ed. *The Philosophy of the Visual Arts*. Oxford: Oxford University Press, 1992.

———, ed. *What Is Music? An Introduction to the Philosophy of Music*. University Park: Pennsylvania State University Press, 1994.

Carroll, Noël, and Jinhee Choi, eds. *Philosophy of Film and Motion Pictures*. New York: Blackwell, 2005.

Krasner, David, and David Z. Saltz, eds. *Staging Philosophy: Intersections of Theater, Performance, and Philosophy*. Ann Arbor: University of Michigan Press, 2006.

Lopes, Dominic McIver. *Understanding Pictures*. Oxford: Clarendon Press, 1996.

New, Christopher. *Philosophy of Literature: An Introduction*. New York: Routledge, 1999.

Scruton, Roger. *The Aesthetics of Architecture*. Princeton: Princeton University Press, 1979.

Sparshott, Francis. *In a Measured Pace: Toward a Philosophical Understanding of the Arts of Dance*. Toronto: University of Toronto Press, 1995.

Thom, Paul. *For an Audience: A Philosophy of the Performing Arts*. Philadelphia: Temple University Press, 1993.

Credits

The following gives the original publication information for the boxed readings and short quotations included in the text. All excerpts are reprinted by permission.

Chapter Two

Quote about Warhol from the National Gallery of Canada (URL: *http://www .gallery.ca/en/see/collections/artwork.php?mkey=7249)*. Courtesy of the National Gallery of Canada.

Morris Weitz. "The Role of Theory in Aesthetics." *Journal of Aesthetics and Art Criticism* 15 (1956): 27–35. Reproduced with permission of Blackwell Publishing Ltd.

Jerrold Levinson. "Defining Art Historically." *British Journal of Aesthetics*. Copyright © 1979 Oxford University Press. Reproduced with permission of Oxford University Press in the format Textbook via Copyright Clearance Center.

From *Art as Experience* by John Dewey, copyright © 1934 by John Dewey, renewed © 1973 by The John Dewey Foundation. Used by permission of G. P. Putnam's Sons, a division of Penguin Group (USA) Inc.

Chapter Three

Joseph Margolis. "The Ontological Peculiarity of Works of Art." *The Journal of Aesthetics and Art Criticism* 36 (1977): 45–50. Reproduced with permission of Blackwell Publishing Ltd.

Frank Sibley. "Aesthetic Concepts." *Philosophical Review* 68 (1959): 421–426, 437–439, 442–445.

Clive Bell. "Art and Significant Form." In *Art*. London: Chatto & Windus, 1914. Reprinted by permission of the Society of Authors.

Chapter Four

Ayn Rand, *Atlas Shrugged;* New York: New American Library, 1957. Pages 591–592.

Nathaniel Brandon, *Who Is Ayn Rand?* New York: Paperback Library, 1962. Pages 111–112, 114.

Gombrich, E. H. *Art and Illusion*. Copyright © 1960 Princeton University Press. 1988 renewed PUP, 2000 paperback edition. Reprinted by permission of Princeton University Press.

Principles of Art by R.G. Collingwood (1938), pp. 109–117, 121–123. By permission of Oxford University Press.

George Orwell, "Why I Write?" In *Essays*. New York: Everyman's Library, Alfred A. Knopf, 1968. Pages 1082–1083, 1084. (Originally published in *Gangrel* #4 Summer, 1946.)

Anne Bogart, *A Director Prepares: Seven Essays on Art and Theatre*. New York: Routledge, 2001. Pages 2–3.

Anne Lipton. *Ecovention*. http://greenmuseum.org/c/ecovention/sect11.html.

From *And Then, You Act: Making Art in an Unpredictable World*, by Anne Bogart, copyright © 2007 Routledge. Reproduced by permission of Taylor & Francis Books UK.

Chapter Five

Quote from *Hamlet*, http://shakespeare.mit.edu/hamlet/full.html.

David E. W. Fenner. From *Journal of Aesthetic Education*. Copyright © 2003 by the Board of Trustees of the University of Illinois. Used with permission of the author and the University of Illinois Press.

William Carlos Williams, from *The Collected Poems: Volume I, 1909–1939*, copyright © 1938 by New Directions Publishing Corp. Reprinted by permission of New Directions Publishing Corp.

Richard Wollheim. "Criticism as Retrieval." In *Art and Its Objects, Second Edition with Six Supplementary Essays*. Copyright © 1980 Cambridge University Press. Reprinted with the permission of Cambridge University Press.

Robert W. Service, "The Telegraph Operator," in *Ballads of a Cheechako* (New York: Barse and Hopkins, 1909).

Monroe C. Beardsley. From *Journal of Aesthetic Education*. Copyright © 1968 by the Board of Trustees of the University of Illinois. Used with permission of the author and the University of Illinois Press.

Chapter Six

Berys Gaut. "The Ethical Criticism of Art." In *Aesthetics and Ethics: Essays at the Intersection*. Edited by Jerrold Levinson. Copyright © 1998 Cambridge University Press. Reprinted with the permission of Cambridge University Press.

Maxine Greene. "The Artistic-Aesthetic Curriculum: Leaving Imprints on the Changing Face of the World." In *Variations on a Blue Guitar*. Copyright © 2001 Teachers College Press. Reproduced with permission of Teachers College Press in the format Textbook via Copyright Clearance Center.

Geertz, Clifford. *Art as a Cultural System*. MLN 91:6 (1976), 1473–1476, 1488–1494, 1497–1499. Copyright © The Johns Hopkins University Press. Reprinted with permission of The Johns Hopkins University Press.

Chapter Seven

C. P. Snow, *The Two Cultures and A Second Look;* Cambridge: Cambridge University Press, 1963. Pages 20–21.

Howard Gardner, *The Arts and Human Development: A Psychological Study of the Artistic Process*. Copyright © 1994 Basic Books. Reproduced with permission of Perseus Books Group in the format Textbook via Copyright Clearance Center.

Nelson Goodman. "Art and the Understanding." in *Languages of Art*, 2nd ed. Copyright © 1976 Nelson Goodman. Reprinted by permission of Hackett Publishing Company, Inc. All rights reserved.

Bender, John W.; Blocker, H. Gene, *Contemporary Philosophy of Art*, 1st edition, © 1993. Reprinted by permission of Pearson Education, Inc., Upper Saddle River, NJ.

Chapter Eight

Francis Sparshott, "The Identity of a Dance." *In A Measured Pace: Toward a Philosophical Understanding of the Arts of Dance*. Copyright © 1995 University of Toronto Press. Reprinted with permission of the publisher.

David Z. Saltz. "How to Do Things on Stage." *Journal of Aesthetics and Art Criticism* 49 (1991): 31–45. Reproduced with permission of Blackwell Publishing Ltd.

Reprinted material from *Authenticities: Philosophical Reflections on Musical Performance,* by Peter Kivy. Copyright © 1995 Cornell University Press. Used by permission of the publisher, Cornell University Press.

Chapter Nine

Clement Greenberg. "Modernist Painting." Art and Literature (1965): 193–201.

Kendall L. Walton, "Transparent Pictures: On The Nature of Photographic Realism." *Critical Inquiry* 11, 2 (1984). Reprinted by permission of the University of Chicago Press.

Scruton, Roger. *The Aesthetics of Architecture.* Copyright © 1980 Princeton University Press. Reprinted by permission of Princeton University Press.

Chapter Ten

From "Fiction." In *Philosophy of Literature: An Introduction* by Christopher New. Copyright © 1999 Routledge. Reproduced by permission of Taylor and Francis Books UK.

J.R.R. Tolkien poem "Errantry" from "The Adventures of Tom Bombadil" in *The Tolkien Reader*; New York: Ballantine Books, 1966.

Harvey Gross. "Prosody as Rhythmic Cognition." In *Sound and Form in Modern Poetry.* Copyright © 1964 University of Michigan Press. Reprinted by permission of the publisher.

Root, Robert L.; Steinberg, Michael J., *The Fourth Genre: Contemporary Writers of/on Creative Non-Fiction*, 3rd ed. © 2005. Reprinted by permission of Pearson Education, Inc., Upper Saddle River, NJ.

Index

Achebe, Chinua, 331
Acting. *See* Theater
Adams, Ansel, 284–285
Adorno, Theodor, 166
Aesthetic criticism. *See* Evaluating art
Aesthetic experience
  catharsis and, 130–131
  description, 18–20, 21, 129–130
  Fenner on, 133–141
  focus and, 133
  sensitivity and, 133
  taste and, 132, 136, 139–140
  See also Fenner, David E.W. on
    aesthetic experience;
    Interpretation of art
Aesthetic interpretation. *See*
  Interpretation of art
Aesthetic objects, 17–18
Aesthetic properties, 18
Aestheticism, 132, 168
Aesthetics
  beauty and, 17–18
  of nature, 75
  "philosophy of art" and, 16
  value(s) and, 12–13
  Weitz on, 29–35

word derivation, 16–17
  See also Beauty
Aesthetics of artworks
  emergent features and, 70–71,
    73–74
  Guernica example, 71–72
  harmony and, 73–74
  intention and, 72–73
  intrinsic features and, 74
  nonaesthetic features and, 71–72,
    77–79, 80, 81
  Sibley on, 71, 73, 76–82
Aldrin, Edwin walking on moon, 284,
  284 (fig.)
Alison, Archibald, 135–136
Alliteration, 320
American Idol, 166
Analyzing in philosophy, 6–7
Anderson, Chris, 339
Animal Farm (Orwell), 117
Antiessentialism
  Weitz and, 28, 29–36, 37
  Wittgenstein and, 7, 28–29, 30, 31
Architecture
  function and, 296, 298, 299–301,
    302–303